The Return of Jazz

THE RETURN OF JAZZ
Joachim-Ernst Berendt and West German Cultural Change

Andrew Wright Hurley

Berghahn Books
New York • Oxford

First published in 2009 by
Berghahn Books
www.berghahnbooks.com

©2009 Andrew Wright Hurley

All rights reserved. Except for the quotation of short passages for the purposes of criticism and review, no part of this book may be reproduced in any form or by any means, electronic or mechanical, including photocopying, recording, or any information storage and retrieval system now known or to be invented, without written permission of the publisher.

Library of Congress Cataloging-in-Publication Data

Hurley, Andrew Wright.
  The return of jazz : Joachim-Ernst Berendt and West German cultural change / Andrew Wright Hurley.
    p. cm.
  Includes bibliographical references and index.
  1. Jazz—Social aspects—Germany—History. 2. Jazz—Germany—History and criticism. 3. Berendt, Joachim-Ernst, 1922–2000. I. Title.

ML3917.G3H87 2009
781.650943—dc22

2008052536

British Library Cataloguing in Publication Data
A catalogue record for this book is available from the British Library

Printed in the United States on acid-free paper.

ISBN: 978-1-84545-566-8 Hardback

For Meredith

Contents

List of Figures	ix
Foreword by Dan Morgenstern	xi
Preface	xiii
Acknowledgments	xv
Terms and Abbreviations	xvii
Introduction: In Search of the Jazz Pope	1

Part I:
Joachim-Ernst Berendt and the Postwar Legitimation of Jazz

1	Jazz and the Divide between Serious and Entertainment Music	15
2	Dance as Escape?	35
3	Jazz Greetings to and from the East?	45
4	Jazz, Race, and Colorblindness	60

Part II:
Europeanizing Jazz

5	The Blues of German Jazz	73
6	Emancipation and the Dilemma of *Volk*-Jazz	88
7	*Globe Unity:* Free Jazz Meets European New Music	105
8	Emancipation from the Jazz Pope	116
9	On the Uses of European Jazz	136

Part III:
Jazz Meets the Other

10	The Marco Polo of Jazz	147
11	The Goethe Institut's Jazz Ambassadors Strike Up	158
12	Japanesing Jazz, or, Kimono Today, Swing Tomorrow	168
13	Doing the Bossa in Berlin	177
14	The 1967 World-Jazz Encounters: An East-West Jazz-Divan?	186
15	Finding the *Blut und Boden* in African Roots	206

Conclusion: Berendt and the Utopia of *Weltmusik*	218
Epilogue: *Joachim-Ernst Berendt: A Personal Reflection upon His Importance to Jazz in Germany* by Wolfram Knauer	233
Chronology	238
Discography	244
Works Cited	259
Index	286

Figures

Figure 1. Berendt (left) with Chick Corea at the Jazz Now festival, Munich Olympics, 1972. © Paul G. Deker. Used with permission. — 4

Figure 2. Berendt at the typewriter. From the Jazzinstitut Darmstadt. Used with permission. — 12

Figure 3. Berendt and the Modern Jazz Quartet's John Lewis enjoy a meal. Courtesy of the Jazzinstitut Darmstadt. Used with permission. — 23

Figure 4. "Café au lait beauty" Lena Horne graces the cover of *Der Spiegel* in 1952. © *Der Spiegel*. Used with permission. — 62

Figure 5. Günther Kieser's poster for the 1968 Berlin Jazz Days. © Günther Kieser. Used with permission. — 81

Figure 6. Albert Mangelsdorff in the SWF studio, Baden-Baden, 1966. © Paul G. Deker. Used with permission. — 90

Figure 7. Günther Kieser's poster design for the first American Folk Blues Festival, 1962. © Günther Kieser. Used with permission. — 96

Figure 8. The 1966 Baden-Baden Free Jazz Meeting. *From left to right:* Albert Mangelsdorff, Manfred Schoof, Alexander von Schlippenbach, Buschi Niebergall, Berendt. © Paul G. Deker. Used with permission. — 108

Figure 9. Peter Brötzmann, Baden-Baden, 1967. © Paul G. Deker. Used with permission. — 119

Figure 10. The European avant-garde and select American guests at the 1968 Anti-Festival/TMM. *From left to right:* Sonny Sharrock, Pharoah Sanders, Gunter Hampel, Evan Parker and Han Bennink. © Paul G. Deker. Used with permission. — 123

Figure 11. European and free: Fred van Hove, Han Bennink, Albert Mangelsdorff and Peter Brötzmann perform at the 1975 Total Music Meeting, Berlin. © Paul G. Deker. Used with permission. 143

Figure 12. John Coltrane on the set of *Jazz - Heard and Seen*, Baden-Baden, 1961. Hanns E. Haehl; courtesy of the Jazzinstitut Darmstadt. Used with permission. 148

Figure 13. Berendt in Indonesia, 1967. Pabel Stern, Hamburg; courtesy of the Jazzinstitut Darmstadt. Used with permission. 151

Figure 14. Klaus Doldinger and his Quartet take time out during their 1969 Asian tour for the Goethe Institut. Courtesy of the Jazzinstitut Darmstadt. Used with permission. 161

Figure 15. Manufactured biculturalism? The front and back covers of the 1965 *Sakura Sakura* recording. Design: Hans Pfitzer; photos: Berendt and K. Hucke; courtesy of Universal Music. Used with permission. 173

Figure 16. Brazilian dancer Marly Tavares gazes at the record buyer from the cover of *Folklore e Bossa Nova do Brasil*. Design: Marhold Eigen; courtesy of Universal Music. Used with permission. 183

Figure 17. *Noon in Tunisia*, 1969. *From left to right:* Don Cherry, Hattab Jouini, Sahib Shihab, Jelloul Osman, Moktar Slama, unknown, Henri Texier. © Pete Ariel; courtesy of the Jazzinstitut Darmstadt. Used with permission. 191

Figure 18. The Indonesian All-Stars perform in Germany, 1967. *From left to right:* Benny Mustafa, Yopi Chen, Jack Lesmana, Bubi Chen, Marjono. © Paul G. Deker. Used with permission. 202

Figure 19. Don Cherry performing *Eternal Rhythm* in Berlin, 1968. © Paul G. Decker. Used with permission. 213

Figure 20. Tabla player Pandit Prakash Maharaj performs as part of the *Weltmusik* Summit at the Donaueschingen Music Days, 1985. In the background, Luis di Matteo (*bandoneon*), Bernd Konrad, and Lennart Aberg (saxophones). © Hans Kumpf. Used with permission. 220

Foreword

If anyone had suggested that at the end of the Second World War the most successful book about jazz would be written by a German, published in his language, would sell hundreds of thousands of copies, and be translated into nine other languages, he or she would surely have been considered somewhat daft. After all, jazz had been banned (quite effectively) by the Nazis, and by 1953 when Joachim "Call me, Jo" Berendt's *Das Jazzbuch* was published, Germany was hardly a jazz cynosure.

It wasn't even Jo's (forgive the familiar, but we were well acquainted) first book on the subject, having been preceded by the perhaps more ambitious *Jazz: Eine zeitkritische Studie* (ah, those weighty German titles), a noble attempt to bring the music into the purview of intellectuals, whereas *Das Jazzbuch* book was aimed at a wide audience. Such varied efforts on behalf of the music he had first encountered on the radio as a teenager and then came to love, fiercely and possessively, would become characteristic of this tirelessly energetic (and not unambitious) lifelong jazz proselytizer. As you will learn from Andrew Hurley's fascinating book—certainly more than just a biography—Jo's career blossomed as he became a man of many parts. Having gotten in on the ground floor of what would grow into a major radio and television network, and becoming involved in record production as well, he soon had made himself into to the European counterpart of Leonard Feather—the only other jazz critic also active on such a broad media front, and comparably influential.

I came to know Jo when, having discovered my Austrian roots, he approached me about translating what by then was *Das Neue Jazzbuch*, an expanded and updated edition, which had, finally, found a publisher for an English-language version. We spoke on the telephone, my first encounter with Jo's fluent, jazz-idiomatic and heavily accented English; the offer was a welcome one since *Metronome*, the magazine I had been editing, collapsed at the end of 1961.

So I was at liberty, and had no trouble with Jo's prose, less convoluted in syntax than German can be—and too often is. I found him very open to the occasional suggestion, and almost embarrassingly appreciative of my work. As you will learn, the book went through several expanded American editions, eventually adding "rock" to the title (Jo never shied away from trends), but I had less and less to do with these.

The Return of Jazz illuminates much about the German (and in context, European) jazz scene over Jo's five decades of activity. Not surprisingly, he was often a target of critical barbs, not all of them exactly free from envy, though serious scholars justly took exception to his sometimes glib journalistic generalizations. These can be more intellectually irritating in German, a language that has many wonderful qualities but can also make simplistic thoughts appear profound. And Jo was a fast talker and facile writer; I don't think he ever missed a deadline (neither did Feather).

The bottom line is that Jo Berendt did a huge amount of good on behalf of jazz, a music he perceived as being without borders—among other things, he was one of the pioneers of jazz's globalization. His legacy lives on at the wonderful Darmstadt Jazz Institute, based on his rich collection of all kinds of materials, as well as in the many great records he produced, in what he documented on film, and in much of his prolific writings, which often did capture the *Zeitgeist*.

I miss our conversations. Jo had his own sound, which is what matters most in jazz matters. And he would surely have appreciated the research, scholarship, and objectivity that distinguish this important book.

—Dan Morgenstern

Preface

The writer, broadcaster, and record producer Joachim-Ernst Berendt (1922–2000) is not all that well known in the English-speaking world. And yet his *Jazzbook*, first published in 1953 and currently in its seventh edition, is thought to be the best-selling jazz book in the world. At last count, it had sold over 1.5 million copies worldwide in at least twelve different languages. Berendt also holds the credit for being the author of perhaps the most expensive jazz book; *Jazz Life*, his 1960–61 collaboration with the American photographer William Claxton was recently published in an expanded second edition and is also the finest book of jazz photography yet. The way Berendt himself might have preferred to be remembered, however, could well have been as the author of *Nada Brahma* (1983), his speculative book on the nature of hearing.

Berendt looms particularly large in the German jazz scene in the second half of the twentieth century. In the wake of jazz's renunciation during the Nazi era, he tirelessly sought to re-legitimate it in West Germany. In the process he also established himself as West Germany's "Jazz Pope," with considerable power to consecrate—and excommunicate—musicians and other critics, as well as to promote his own activities; a position of authority that ultimately gave rise to a groundswell of criticism in the wake of 1968. This book draws on written and oral sources to explain Berendt's significance as the preeminent mediator of jazz to postwar Germany, how and why his theories differed from those being expounded elsewhere in the jazz world, and the reasons why he came to be criticized at home.

Berendt was not just a writer; he was also very active as a producer of jazz concerts, particularly at the Berlin Jazz Days, which during their heyday in the 1960s and 1970s were probably the most significant jazz festival in Europe. His record productions—estimated at over four hundred albums for European, American and Japanese labels—likewise fostered many innovative musical activities, not just in Germany and other fascinating "jazz-peripheries," including Europe (East and West), Japan, and Indonesia; but also in the United States itself. From the 1960s, he especially promoted the activities of European musicians, as they began to question their erstwhile all-too-eager adoption of American jazz and strove to make valid artistic statements reflecting their identity *as Europeans*. Himself an enthusiastic traveler, he also encouraged an engagement with "world musics." In these ways, he was at the forefront of activities in which non-American musicians made jazz their own.

Berendt's writings and his work as a producer—including of the landmark *Jazz Meets the World* series—throw light on how a cosmopolitan West German identity could be constructed after the "Third Reich." The invitations to perform, which he extended to musicians from as far afield as Brazil, Tunisia, Japan, and Indonesia also indicate how Others were both the subject of German discourse *and* enabled to represent their own Selves.

Acknowledgments

The research for this book was undertaken with the assistance of Australian government research funds. The Australian German Association was also kind enough to support preliminary research, and I thank Andrew Grummet and the AGA for its assistance. I also wish to express my sincere gratitude to Alison Lewis and Colin Nettelbeck for reading a draft and giving me their feedback. My research also could not have been undertaken without the guidance and assistance, over many years, of Wolfram Knauer and his team at the Jazzinstitut Darmstadt—Arndt Weidler and Doris Schröder. I thank the Jazzinstitut and the City of Darmstadt, which had the wisdom to purchase J-E Berendt's archive in 1983, and to finance the ongoing work of the Jazzinstitut; it also kindly invited me to present papers at the Jazzforum in 2005 and 2007. Wolfram Knauer was also kind enough to write an epilogue for this book. Valuable advice was also given by Wolfgang Martin Stroh of the University of Oldenburg. In addition, I would like to the thank the following people who were generous to me with their time: Jadranka M. Berendt; Karl Berger; Peter Brötzmann; Hans-Georg Brunner-Schwer; Bubi Chen; William Claxton; Salah El Mahdi; Michael Frohne; Willi Fruth; George Gruntz; Mike Hennessey; Bernd Hoffmann; Terumasa and Susan Hino; Ekkehard Jost; Reinhard Kager; Hans Kumpf; Gunter Lebbe; Albert Mangelsdorff; Belinda Moody; Mani Neumeier; Mike Nock; Uli Olshausen; Martin Pfleiderer; Fred Ritzel; Michael Rüsenberg; Keshav Sathe; Siegfried Schmidt-Joos; Manfred Schoof; Claus Schreiner; Ralf Schulte-Bahrenberg; Peter Schulze; Irene Schweizer; Pr. Sudibyo; Alfred D. Ticoalu; Ihno von Hasselt; Alexander von Schlippenbach; Kris Wanders; Karl-Ernst Went; Colin Wilkie and Shirley Hart; and H. Werner Wunderlich.

Thanks to Dan Morgenstern for kindly offering to write a foreword, to the photographers Paul G. Deker, Josef Werkmeister, Pete Ariel, Hans Kumpf, and German Hasenfratz, as well as to the Jazzinstitut Darmstadt and Doris Schröder, and to the Brunner-Schwer family for supplying photographs; to Günther Kieser for his poster images; to Christian Kellersmann of Universal Music for allowing me to reproduce the Saba/MPS album covers; to TASCHEN and William Claxton for supplying images from *Jazz Life;* to *Der Spiegel* for permission to print the magazine cover, to Toni Schifer of Monitorpop for permission to reproduce the Saba/MPS discographical information, to Warren Taylor for his design assistance, to Katie Sutton for assistance with the index and to Julia B. Hurley for her editing. Finally, I wish to thank Ann Przyzycki at Berghahn Books and my anonymous reader for his/her suggestions.

Early versions of some parts of this study have appeared in the *Darmstädter Beiträge zur Jazzforschung, Perfect Beat: The Pacific Journal of Research into Contemporary Music and Popular Culture,* and the *University of Melbourne School of Languages Research Papers on Language and Literature.*

Terms and Abbreviations

AACM: Association for the Advancement of Creative Musicians. Chicago-based free jazz musicians' collective, many members of which moved to Europe in the late 1960s.

AFN/BFN: American Forces Network/British Forces Network. Broadcasters set up in West Germany by the American and British Administrations after WWII.

Anti-Festival/Total Music Meeting: A festival devoted to more avant-garde forms of jazz and free music, timed to coincide with the official Berlin Jazz Days. First held as an Anti-Festival in 1968. Soon after retitled as the Total Music Meeting.

ARD: Arbeitsgemeinschaft der Rundfunkanstalten Deutschlands. Association of (West) German public radio broadcasters, founded in 1950.

bandoneon: A small Argentinian button accordion.

barong: A Balinese dance that culminates in the head of live chicken being bitten off.

Berliner Festwochen: Annual Berlin cultural festival established by the Western Allies in 1951 and now run by the Berliner Festspiele GmbH.

Berlin Jazz Days: Annual jazz festival (since 1964). Since 1981 has been called JazzFest Berlin.

bossa nova: A Brazilian form of popular music developed in the late 1950s. Quickly exported to the United States and beyond.

Burg Waldeck folk festival: A (West) German folk festival held in the Hunsrück (for the first time in 1964).

CDU/CSU: Christlich Demokratische Union Deutschlands/Christlich-Soziale Union in Bayern. The (West) German conservative party.

djanger: A Balinese sitting dance.

DJF: Deutsche Jazz Föderation. The German Jazz Federation, an umbrella organization of West German jazz clubs formed in 1950–51. Launched the *Jazz Podium* as its press organ in 1952. Organized the first German Jazz Festival in 1953.

Die Gondel/Jazz Echo: A Hamburg-based magazine which, from 1950, contained a jazz supplement. From mid-1954, this supplement was called the *Jazz Echo*. During the 1950s, the jazz section was edited by Berendt under the pseudonym "Joe Brown."

Donaueschingen Music Days: An avant-garde music festival held annually in Donaueschingen. First held in 1922. After its demise under National Socialism, was resuscitated by Heinrich Strobel and the SWF in 1950. Jazz concerts held as part of the festival in 1954, 1957, 1967, and then annually from 1970.

ECM: Edition of Contemporary Music. A Munich-based independent record label founded by Manfred Eicher in 1969. Initially concentrated on jazz, but since 1984 has also released a classical music series.

electro-acoustics: The musical combination of treated electronic sounds and standard acoustic instrumentation. Electro-acoustic jazz can be traced back at least to the American jazz pianist Bob James' 1965 recording *Explosions*. The concept of performing in conjunction with tape recordings was used within the New Music tradition by the German composer Karlheinz Stockhausen as early as 1959–60 for his composition *Kontakte*.

E-Musik: Ernste-Musik. Serious music, the traditional German designation for high art classical music.

Flamenco: Rhythmic Spanish (Andalusian) dance and musical style.

FMP: Free Music Production. Founded in 1969 as a Berlin-based musicians' collective responsible for the organization of concerts (including the annual Total Music Meeting) and the recording, manufacture and distribution of free music, a term used in preference to the more Americo-centric "free jazz."

Free Jazz Meeting Baden-Baden: An annual meeting organized at the SWF since 1966. Avant-garde jazz musicians are invited and are given the opportunity to rehearse for several days and then to perform a concert that is broadcast. After a hiatus in 1972, was renamed the New Jazz Meeting.

gamelan: A collective term used to refer to orchestras from the Indonesian islands of Bali, Java and Madura. Typically consist of gongs, metallophones, drums, flutes, and strings.

German Jazz Festival: Annual jazz festival held in Frankfurt am Main since 1953.

Goethe Institut: A (West) German government-funded body founded in 1952 and initially charged with the teaching of German to foreigners. Since 1960, has also been responsible for carrying on cultural institutes around the world and generally with representing (West) Germany to the world. Since 1964, has sent jazz musicians on tour.

GUO: The Globe Unity Orchestra, a predominantly European avant-garde big band, formed by the German pianist Alexander von Schlippenbach in 1966.

Halbstarke: Literally, "half-strong." Term of derision for a member of the "rocker" youth subculture of the 1950s.

harmonium: Small, portable reed organ. Often used in South-Indian Carnatic music.

HR: Hessischer Rundfunk. The Hessian public broadcaster.

Jazz Ambassadors: Jazz musicians sent abroad by the U.S. State Department from 1956 until the 1970s.

JMTW: *Jazz Meets the World.* The series of concerts and recordings produced by J-E Berendt between 1965 and 1971. At one time or another, it included *Sakura Sakura* (1965), *Folklore e Bossa Nova do Brasil* (1966), *Globe Unity* (1966), *Tristeza on Guitar* (1966), *Djanger Bali* (1967), *Flamenco Jazz* (1967), *Jazz Meets India* (1967), *Noon in Tunisia* (1967), *Auto Jazz* (1968), *Eternal Rhythm* (1968), *Wild Goose* (1969), and *El Babaku* (1971).

Jazz Podium: The jazz periodical first set up in 1952 by the DJF as its press organ. Initially associated with the Viennese magazine the *Podium*, it quickly took on a life of its own. Edited for many years by Dieter Zimmerle.

Kaputtspielphase: Literally, the "phase of playing things to pieces." A term coined by the German bassist Peter Kowald—although he later distanced himself from it—for the period during the late 1960s when German and European free jazz musicians called into question traditional jazz norms.

ketjapi: Indonesian zither.

koto: Thirteen-stringed Japanese psaltery. Since the seventeenth century has been regarded as the Japanese national instrument.

L+R: Lippmann und Rau. West German concert agents and jazz lobbyists Horst Lippmann and Fritz Rau. Organizers of a range of "authentic documentations" during the 1960s, including annual *American Folk Blues Festivals* (from 1962), *Spiritual and Gospel Festivals* (1965 and subsequently), *Flamenco Gitano Festivals* (annually from 1965 until 1970), a *Festival Folklore e Bossa Nova do Brasil* (1966), and a *Festival Musica Folklorica Argentina* (1967).

MJQ: Modern Jazz Quartet, the U.S. group founded in 1952 and led by the pianist John Lewis.

MPS: Musik Produktion Schwarzwald. *See* SABA.

Musica mundana: According to the tripartite scheme of the sixth-century philosopher Boethius, "music" corresponding to cosmic harmonic proportions (the "harmony of the spheres").

Musique concrète: The term coined by the French avant-garde composer Pierre Schaeffer in 1948 to designate music which he painstakingly assembled from recorded "concrete" sound objects (for example snippets of taped bird-song or traffic).

NAACP: National Association for the Advancement of Colored People. One of the oldest and most influential American civil rights organizations. Founded in 1909.

Nada Brahma: A Hindi expression literally meaning "God is Sound." The title of a series of radio programs made by Berendt during the early 1980s, which were then released in book format in 1983. Berendt used the term to signify that "the world is sound."

NDR: Norddeutscher Rundfunk. North German public broadcasting station.

Négritude: An Afrocentric concept celebrating a positively weighted African core identity. First advanced by francophone intellectuals such as Léopold Senghor (later President of Senegal) and Aimé Césaire during the 1930s in the context of the de-colonialization movement.

New Age: An alternative movement beginning in the late 1970s and stretching through the 1980s, which eclectically combined spiritual, esoteric, and popular philosophical elements. Its proponents advanced a "holistic" model. As an antirational theory appealed to those disenchanted with rationalized, (post)modern Western society and searching for a more spiritual existence.

Nihonteki jazu: "Japanese Jazz." A notion advanced by various Japanese musicians and critics particularly during the 1960s and 1970s. Held that there was a peculiarly Japanese form of jazz expression. Retained the notion of jazz as a universal language, but was also committed to the idea of a core Japanese cultural identity.

Pantja Sila: An Indonesian term meaning, literally, "five fundamental principles." The guiding principles formulated by President Sukarno in 1945 as guiding the newly established Indonesian Republic.

PKI: Indonesian Communist Party.

prepared instruments: The term used for a technique developed in the 1930s by the American avant-garde composer John Cage (whose ideas were influential upon many jazz musicians of the 1960s and 1970s). "Preparing" a piano involves changing the notes and timbres produced by inserting objects into the strings.

raga: In Indian classical music, a melodic type based on an unchanging series of notes, presented as an ascending and descending scale. Individual ragas are associated with different moods, times of the day or year and particular ceremonial occasions. They are drawn upon when improvising.

ramwong: A Southeast Asian form of dance.

RIAS: Radio in the American Sector. U.S. Information Service station in (West) Berlin, broadcasting in German, affiliated with the ARD.

Saba: Privately owned record label founded by Hans-Georg Brunner-Schwer in the late 1950s. Launched its jazz series in the early 1960s. Renamed MPS (Musik Produktion Schwarzwald) in 1968, after the record label's parent business was sold. Continued to produce jazz records until 1983.

samba: A Brazilian type of dance music.

samba-canção: A variant of the samba with songlike lyrical character.

sarod: A North Indian lute with played and resonance strings.

Schlager: German pop song.

SED: Sozialistische Einheitspartei Deutschlands. The East German communist party.

serial music: Music in which a structural "series" of notes determines the development of a composition. This technique, which replaced traditional melodic, harmonic, rhythmic, and tonal rules and conventions, is primarily associated with Schoenberg, who in 1923 developed a system of composing by using twelve tones. Later used and developed by Webern, Berg and others.

SDS: Sozialistischer Deutscher Studentenbund. German socialist students' association; the leftist student body that was instrumental in forming the so-called "extra-parliamentary opposition" during the era of the Great Coalition between the CDU/CSU and the SPD, (1966–9).

SFB: Sender Freies Berlin. West Berlin public broadcasting station.

sitar: Indian lute with played, drone and resonance strings.

Sounds: A West German music magazine founded by Rainer Blome in 1967 and initially devoted to free jazz. Soon transferred its attention to rock music.

SPD: Sozialdemokratische Partei Deutschlands. The (West) German social democrat political party.

steel drum: A Caribbean tuned drum made from a beaten-out 44-gallon drum.

sura: A verse from the Koran.

SWF: Südwestfunk. South-West German public broadcasting station. Now the SWR (Südwestrundfunk). Berendt's employer until his retirement in 1987.

Swingheini: Literally, "Swing-Harry." Term of derision for an enthusiast of swing music. First used during the 1930s. Also used during the 1940s and 1950s to denote overenthusiastic fans. *See also* HALBSTARKE.

tabla: Pair of small North Indian hand drums.

Third Stream: A term advanced by U.S. composer and musicologist Gunther Schuller in the mid- to late 1950s to signify a "third stream" of music independent from but drawing on both jazz and the classical tradition.

TMM: Total Music Meeting. *See* ANTI-FESTIVAL.

Twen: A West German magazine launched in 1959 and pitched at well-to-do twenty-somethings. Also distributed a record series.

U-Musik: Unterhaltungsmusik. Literally, "entertainment music." The traditional German designation (and denigration) for popular music.

universals: Qualities common to the world's musical cultures. Was historically of interest to comparative musicologists; however, over time, the academic focus shifted to questions of difference. In *Weltmusik* discourses, designates the idea that there is common ground between musicians from widely different backgrounds such that they are able to communicate intuitively.

USIS: United States Information Service.

VOA: Voice of America. Radio broadcasts run by the USIS since the 1940s.

Wandervogel: A bourgeois youth movement founded at the turn of last century which, inspired by Romantic ideals, sought to avoid the pressures of authoritarian society by escaping into nature.

WDR: Westdeutscher Rundfunk. (West) German public broadcasting station.

Weltmusik: Literally, "world music." Here, a form of music in which elements from a wide range of the world's musical cultures are sought to be integrated into a new whole.

ZDF: Zweites Deutsches Fernsehen. (West) German public television station, founded in 1961.

INTRODUCTION

In Search of the Jazz Pope

> I learned how to talk about jazz from ... [Berendt].
> —Fritz Rau, impresario, quoted in *Fritz Rau: Buchhalter der Träume*[1]

> Someone, like Berendt, who sets as much in motion, organizes, produces and criticizes, someone who is as hardworking and successful in the jazz scene, he obviously all-too-readily runs the risk of considering his own role as general representative in all matters jazz to be more important than the music itself.
> —Volker Kriegel, guitarist, *Manchmal ist es besser, man sagt gar nix*

If jazz is, in Whitney Balliet's memorable *mot*, "the sound of surprise," then that is just what Joachim-Ernst Berendt's *Jazz Meets The World* (*JMTW*) series was for me. When I heard *"Djanger Bali"* on the radio ten years ago, my interest was piqued. Was this modal jazz or Indonesian gamelan music? Who were Tony Scott and the Indonesian All-Stars? Why had they released an album in the late 1960s on an obscure German label? But *"Djanger Bali"* was no flash in the pan. There were other *JMTW* records, released between 1965 and 1971, which were now being reissued. The titles alone were curious—*Djanger Bali, Jazz Meets India, Sakura Sakura, Folklore e Bossa Nova do Brasil, Flamenco Jazz, Noon in Tunisia, El Babaku, Tristeza on Guitar*. A 1999 discography of the Saba/MPS label indicated that the series included more recordings yet—*Globe*

---

1. Translations are mine unless otherwise noted in the list of works cited.

Unity, Eternal Rhythm, Auto Jazz, and *Wild Goose*—which variously combined jazz with European New Music, brought together expatriate American and European jazzmen, and presented English folk singers in a contemporary jazz setting! What's more, these records were often made in tandem with live appearances at the famed Berlin Jazz Days.

Here was something that was an ancestor of the "world music" that had been popular yet controversial during the 1980s and 1990s and was an early milestone in what is now referred to as ethno- or world jazz. It was also peculiarly German. Convinced that there was an important story here, which might offer a perspective on recent German cultural history, I conducted some preliminary research about the *JMTW* series producer, Berendt.

This revealed a recently deceased broadcaster, author, and producer who for over thirty years had devoted himself with great verve to promoting jazz, only to give it all away (or, rather, sell it off[2]) during the early 1980s and pursue a career as a New Age writer. Here was a man who had written *The Jazzbook*, which had been translated into countless languages and was rumored to be the best-selling jazz book in the world,[3] a man who had had a large hand in legitimating jazz in postwar West Germany, within a context in which it had been scorned by Nazis, cultural conservatives, and critical theorists alike and in which, curiously, it was also used as a "Cold War secret weapon." Yet here was also a figure who was highly controversial, particularly with members of the 1968 generation. A man, who despite his importance within the West German jazz scene[4]—he was mockingly dubbed the "Jazz Pope"—was nowadays often only unwillingly called to mind (Broecking 2002: 49).

---

2. The city of Darmstadt purchased his records and library in 1983, and this became the basis for its Jazzinstitut.

3. The book sold 41,000 copies in the first six weeks ("Jazz News" 1954a). By October 1955, it had sold 100,000 copies. It was also being promoted as best-selling jazz book in the world ("Jazz News" 1955e). By 1959, it had sold 250,000 copies (Schmidt-Joos 1959a). New editions followed in 1959 (*Das neue Jazzbuch*), 1968 (*Das Jazzbuch. Von New Orleans bis Free Jazz*), 1973 (*Das Jazzbuch. Von Rag bis Rock*), 1981 (*Das große Jazzbuch. Von New Orleans bis Jazz-Rock*), 1989 (*Das Jazzbuch. Von New Orleans bis in die achtziger Jahre*), and 2005 (*Das Jazzbuch. Von New Orleans bis ins 21. Jahrhundert*). It was translated into: Dutch (1953), Italian (1960, 1973, 1979), Spanish (1962, 1976, 1993), English (1962, 1965, 1975/6, 1982/3, 1992), French (1963), Czech (1968), Polish (1969, 1979, 1991), Japanese (1972, 1975), Portuguese (1975), Finnish (1999), and Greek. By repute, it also circulated as a "*samizdat*" in the USSR. By Berendt's death in 2000, the book had sold 1.3 million copies worldwide ("'Jazzpapst' Joachim Ernst Berendt ist tot." 2000). By 2005, its sales were estimated at 1.5 million (Knauer 2005).

4. The term *jazz scene* has been in currency at least since Francis Newton's (a.k.a Eric Hobsbawm's) 1959 book of the same name. Following Jost, I use this term to denote the combination of organizational forms related to jazz production, distribution, and recep-

This book is, in part, a *critical biography* of Berendt, the Jazz Pope and "thwarted theologian" (Stroh 1994: 352). In many ways, his was a remarkable twentieth-century German life, colored both by victimhood and having been a perpetrator. The son of Ernst Berendt Jr, a Protestant minister and member of the Confessing Church who died in Dachau in 1942, Berendt was conscripted into the *Wehrmacht* and fought on the Eastern front (including in the siege of Leningrad). After 1945, he became one of the first (and longest serving) employees of the Südwestfunk (SWF) public broadcaster, yet still found the time to write countless books and articles and to produce concerts and recordings and to spark debate both within the jazz scene and beyond it. By the early 1960s, he was also exercising a sustained passion for international travel that began to influence his writings and burgeoning production activities.[5]

Following an approach similar to John Gennari in his "secret history of jazz," *Blowin' Hot and Cool: Jazz and its Critics* (2006), this book uses the central figure of Berendt as a new prism through which to take a view of the West German jazz scene. After jazz gained acceptance (if not universal approval) in West Germany toward the end of the 1950s, Berendt's role as Germany's most influential jazz broadcaster, critic, and writer began to change—as increasingly he became an important producer and festival director as well. By focusing on Berendt's crucial role in the jazz scene, this study contributes to deepening our understanding of the *social history of jazz* in West Germany since World War II, the more general outline and earlier part of which has been sketched by the historian Uta Poiger in her excellent study *Jazz, Rock and Rebels: Cold War Politics and American Culture in a Divided Germany* (2000). However, this book also contains more general reflections on the role of the critic and producer within the field of cultural production, reflections thrown up by the debates in which Berendt became embroiled.

Using the *JMTW* series, which gives a snapshot both of some of Berendt's own productions and some of the important happenings on the broader West German and international jazz scenes, I examine key developments with which he was intimately involved. In this context, I explore how, by the early 1960s, a raft of issues weighed upon West German musicians and critics. Some of these were "intramusical." Others were economic. Still others were ideological and related—not atypically for postwar West Germany—to questions of personal and/or national

---

tion and the social groups associated therewith (i.e., performers, critics, and audiences) (1982: 9).

5. This outline of Berendt's biography is drawn from his memoir, the Berendt papers at the Jazzinstitut Darmstadt and other sources (Berendt 1996a; Rüsenberg 2002; "Die Stephanus-Stiftung: Aus der Geschichte" 2003).

Figure 1 | Berendt (left) with Chick Corea at the Jazz Now festival, Munich Olympics, 1972. © Paul G. Deker. Used with permission.

identity. If jazz was eagerly "imported" from the United States at a time when much indigenous culture was retroactively haunted by Hitler, how could a West German musician "find a voice," not totally dependent on U.S. models?

Whereas the first part of this book focuses on Berendt's activities seeking to legitimate jazz in West Germany during the 1950s, the focus of the second and third parts is the *JMTW* series itself. However, mine is not primarily a musical analysis, such as the German musicologist Ekkehard Jost's study *Europas Jazz* (1987) or Mike Heffley's *Northern Sun, Southern Moon: Europe's Reinvention of Jazz* (2005): it is an historical, contextual study of the series and its diverse "web of significations" for its makers and critical recipients.[6] This is because jazz, the *JMTW* series, and its "*Weltmusik*" successors in the 1980s[7] were—for Berendt and oth-

---

6. I take the concept of "web of significations" from the cultural historian William Washabaugh's study of flamenco (1996: x–xiii). Washabaugh's approach is informed by the insights of poststructuralism and the notion that the meaning of music is constantly being remade by artists, impresarios, and writers. As Stephan Richter has observed, each individual's interpretation of a piece of music occurs in the complex play with intra- and extramusical forms (1998: 28). An approach attending to these diverse constructions of meaning is now called for by some jazz scholars (see, e.g., Knauer 1999: 37–8).

7. I make a somewhat arbitrary distinction between the *JMTW* series (1965–71) and the more spiritually inflected notion of *Weltmusik* which Berendt advanced in the 1970s and 1980s. I deliberately use the label *Weltmusik* rather than the direct English translation

ers—not just about music per se. Among other things, discourse about these musics also threw into relief peculiarly West German anxieties about culture and national identity. It tells us about the complex ways in which identities—including those of the Other musicians who were invited to perform in Berlin—were negotiated and constructed during this era. It also tells us a little about the complicated ways in which ethnic Others (and their culture and nationalisms) were the subject of discourse in post-Nazi West Germany. By analyzing this German discourse, this book contributes a new perspective to the pioneering work done by Martin Pfleiderer in *Zwischen Weltmusik und Exotismus: Zur Rezeption asiatischer und afrikanischer Musik im Jazz der 60er und 70er Jahre* (1998), his study of African and Asian influences in the international jazz scene more broadly. Beyond the German historical frame, however, my analysis of the *JMTW* series and Berendt's *Weltmusik* activities also casts light on some of the issues involved with intercultural appropriation and collaboration in a globalizing world.

Approach

Insofar as this is a social history of jazz in postwar West Germany, it is significantly informed by the methodology first outlined by Ekkehard Jost in his 1982 social history of jazz in the United States. Jost is interested in the connections between modes of expression, the social situation of musicians, and economic history. He thereby integrates three perspectives—the historical, sociological, and musical/aesthetic. Jost posits a complex network of interactions between society and art, and advances three inquiries capable of throwing light on this interrelation, namely: how do social factors impinge on jazz production; what does musical form tell us about social tendencies; and what purpose and functions does jazz fulfill within a particular social constellation (i.e., how is it received)? (1982: 9–11)

By focusing on the extramusical discourse surrounding the music (including the links made to different political, cultural, and spiritual currents in circulation in an era where the anxious memory of the Nazi past was still present), I explore, from a sociopsychological point of view, why Berendt's theories were popular (or unpopular) with various segments of West German society at different times. However, this is not an

---

"world music," which has tended to signify "authentic" musics from the periphery (albeit those marketed in the West). By contrast, *Weltmusik*, as it will be used here, tends to signify utopian (Western) musics that, in some way, seek to synthetically integrate world musics.

empirical sociological study of the West German jazz scene, in the sense of that undertaken by Dollase, Rüsenberg, and Stollenwerk in 1978. My sources are primarily the musicians' testimony and Berendt's writings as well as critical reviews from the print media.

In reflecting on the "web of significations," particular attention has been paid to the ways in which two schools of theory were employed historically within West German jazz discourse. Firstly, I examine how critical theory was applied during the 1950s to mount a highly critical interpretation of jazz as an emblem of the Culture Industry and stupefying mass entertainment. I also consider how, in the context of the 1968 generation, critical theory was reemployed by a new generation of leftists in order to establish free jazz as an "immanently critical" art form and to attack Berendt's interpretation of an organically evolving jazz history. Finally, I analyze the ways in which a West German variant of postcolonial theory was called on in order to critique Berendt's 1980s conception of *Weltmusik* as a utopian domain in which difference was transcended. The postcolonial perspective has also inspired my analysis of the complex ways in which race figured in West German jazz discourse during the 1950s, in Berendt's reflections upon the intercultural encounter, and in the ways in which cultural identity and alterity were imaginatively constructed by the protagonists and critical recipients of the *JMTW* series and *Weltmusik*.

When it comes to analyzing the role of the "Jazz Pope" and the controversies in which he became embroiled, John Gennari's critics-based focus—which looks at the critic as the site where complex "negotiations and interactions … take place between musicians and superstructure as jazz is delivered to the audience"—is instructive (2006: 4). Pierre Bourdieu's theories relating to the notions of cultural capital, the field of cultural production, and the agent are also particularly useful. In the Federal Republic's first decade, jazz was an art form in the process of becoming legitimated and accumulating symbolic capital. The jazz scene thereby became part of the subfield of restricted cultural production—where production is not aimed at a large-scale market—and Berendt increasingly operated as an agent of legitimation within it, with considerable authority to recognize, consecrate, and confer prestige on musicians and other critics (cf. Bourdieu 1993: 42). Berendt's unique post justifies paying attention to him, given that Bourdieu's call for a sociology of art directs attention

> not only [to] the material production but also the symbolic production of the work, i.e. the production of the value of the work or, which

amounts to the same thing, of belief in the value of the work. It therefore has to consider as contributing to production not only the direct producers of the work in its materiality (artist, writer, etc.) but also the producers of the meaning and value of the work—critics, publishers, gallery directors and the whole set of agents whose combined efforts produce consumers capable of knowing and recognizing the work of art as such (1993: 37).

In conferring meaning and value to jazz and other musical works, Berendt—like any critic—was never entirely free. His strategies were, of course, guided by his individual and class habitus, that is, by his "durable, transposable dispositions" inculcated over the course of his singular life, including during the "Third Reich" and the battles to legitimate jazz in the 1950s, as well as by the rules of the field of cultural production and by the post he occupied within that field (Bourdieu qtd. in Johnson 1993: 5). The rules of the field also guided, to some extent, the struggles with and polemics against Berendt by a younger generation of critics holding a divergent 1968 habitus. The focus on Berendt therefore offers a case study of the ways in which legitimation occurs (and new principles of legitimation can be advanced) within the subfield of restricted cultural production, and also deepens our understanding of the social history of jazz in postwar West Germany.

A Word about Sources

Written sources for this study included the wealth of Berendt's books, articles, radio typescripts, program- and record cover notes, and correspondence housed at the Jazzinstitut in Darmstadt. The Berendt papers contain a great deal of material but are nevertheless not as complete as one might hope, particularly in relation to Berendt's correspondence.[8] Contemporary reviews of Berendt's books, productions, and activities (some of which came from his own pen!) were located in a range of German print media—particularly the jazz periodicals *Jazz Podium*, *Die Gondel/Jazz Echo*, *Das Schlagzeug*, and *Sounds* as well as the scholarly

---

8. The Institut's director, Wolfram Knauer, laments that many of those papers that Berendt retained after selling his collection in 1983 did not ultimately find their way to the Jazzinstitut after his death, as originally planned. Other reasons for the incompleteness of the Berendt papers can only be surmised: perhaps some of his dealings were oral. Perhaps he was a poor record keeper. Perhaps he retained or destroyed papers, which might have reflected unfavorably upon him (although it must be said that the archive does include some such materials).

Jazzforschung, the highbrow music magazine *Melos*, generalist periodicals such as *Merkur* and *Der Spiegel* and newspapers including the *Berliner Tageszeitung*. In addition, reviews were sought in the American *Downbeat* and the French *Jazz Hot* periodicals. Inquiries with the Goethe Institut—whom Berendt advised for almost two decades in relation to its sponsorship of touring German jazz musicians—yielded other material. However, the SWF's archives were not searched. Given that Berendt worked for the broadcaster for over forty years—and was responsible for thousands of jazz programs—searching their archives would have been a mammoth task. It was also far from clear that this would yield considerable *new* material, given the volume of Berendt's articles at the Jazzinstitut. I assumed that his written articles must also be representative of the themes he advanced in his radio programs.

Berendt's own memoir, *Das Leben: Ein Klang* (1996), is written from a New Age perspective and remains distanced from his earlier jazz work. It proved to be of limited value. His treatment of the "jazz years" is quite scant and often tangential; impressions also count more than descriptions of "hard facts."[9] Like many of his writings, it is inadequately attributed (cf. Hunkemöller 1977: 187; Kumpf 1979; Jeske 1983: 58, 64; Budds 1990: xi). In addition, there is the question of the reliability of Berendt's recollections. There are demonstrable instances elsewhere where he got the facts wrong,[10] and "unreliability" was also a criticism raised by Werner Wunderlich, a former colleague at the SWF (1998: 4; 2004). Finally, one must consider Berendt's early advice to Günther Huesmann—a budding critic who, in 1989, would become his collaborator on the *Jazzbook*—that, as a jazz writer, style was more important than truth (Huesmann qtd. in Rüsenberg 2002: 4).

Given Berendt's controversial nature and the issue of reliability, it was essential to test my hypotheses with musicians, critics, and Berendt's former colleagues. I established contact with key musicians such as Albert Mangelsdorff, George Gruntz, Manfred Schoof, Alexander von Schlippenbach, Peter Brötzmann, and Karl Berger as well as with former colleagues including the impresario Ralf Schulte-Bahrenberg, Werner Wunderlich, former *Spiegel* culture editor Siegfried Schmidt-Joos, and with the most important figures from the now defunct Saba/MPS record label. Contact was also established with a range of international musicians and critics who had worked with Berendt on the *JMTW* series, including Bubi Chen (Indonesia), Terumasa Hino (Japan), Keshav Sathe

---

9. This is a criticism also raised in relation to others of his books: see, e.g., Hunkemöller 1977: 187.

10. See, e.g., Silvert 1979, where Berendt both embroiders the story and gets the facts wrong.

(UK), Irène Schweizer (Switzerland), and Salah El Mahdi (Tunisia).[11] However, these individuals' recollections also needed to be interpreted with a certain degree of caution, as they "represent individual interpretations of experiences that are filtered and influenced by the biography lived before and after the [relevant] events, by collective models of interpretation and narrative, and also through the interview situation" (Maase 1992: 39).

Structure

The first part of this book (chapters 1–4) is devoted to an analysis of how Berendt set about legitimating jazz during the 1950s. Chapter 1 sketches the contours of the West German jazz scene and gives a brief history of jazz in Germany up until 1945. It focuses on why and how Berendt sought to elevate jazz to the level of "serious" music and examines the extent to which these efforts were racked with ambivalence. Chapter 2 analyzes how he contended with the rowdy behavior of some jazz enthusiasts, whom various commentators thought were giving jazz a bad name or even feared might be the fascists of tomorrow. It also outlines the spiritual dimensions he discerned in jazz and explores his attempts to proselytize the music to religious audiences. Chapter 3 considers the political aspect of postwar German debates about jazz and analyzes how jazz was made the subject of ideology during the Cold War. It also takes into account how and why Berendt interacted with and fostered Eastern European jazz during the 1950s and beyond. Chapter 4 examines how Berendt's writings about African Americans and jazz throw into relief some of the complicated ways that race and ethnicity were discussed in the wake of the "Third Reich."

The second part (chapters 5–9) examines significant developments in German and European jazz during the 1960s and 1970s and Berendt's involvement in them. Chapter 5 begins by analyzing the malaise felt in the West German jazz scene by the early 1960s. It also profiles two important new institutions that (paradoxically) emerged at this time and that became central to Berendt's activities during the next two decades—the Berlin Jazz Days and the Saba/MPS label. Chapter 6 considers the fresh imperative felt among European musicians to "find their own voice" and examines how some engaged with homegrown folkloric traditions as a way of making jazz their own. It also delineates the ideo-

---

11. Some of these informants corresponded with me. Others I spoke to by telephone. Wherever possible, however, live interviews (tape-recorded and transcribed) were conducted. Transcripts and notes are in the possession of the author.

logical difficulties encountered in West Germany with such an approach. Chapter 7 examines how some European free jazz musicians engaged instead with techniques familiar from modern European concert music as they too strove for valid forms of artistic expression. Chapter 8 brings the focus squarely back to Berendt. After outlining the increasing politicization of the arts during the late 1960s, it focuses on why and how parts of the West German scene began to emancipate themselves from the Jazz Pope. The second part concludes—in chapter 9—by analyzing the ways in which terms such as "German" and "European" jazz, and the notion of the free jazz orchestra, were discursively employed as a way of constructing a cultural identity equidistant from the United States and the nationalist German past.

The third part (chapters 10–15) is a study of Berendt's and various key musicians' engagements with world musics in the 1960s and 1970s. The book branches out at this point in order to cover the breadth of those activities. Chapter 10 examines Berendt's increasing drive, beginning in the early 1960s, to travel to exotic destinations in Asia, the Caribbean, and South America. It analyzes his written depictions of these destinations and considers his efforts to promote the reception of world musics he encountered. Chapter 11 contemplates the liberal motivations behind the Goethe Institut's jazz tours to Asia, South America, and Africa which began in the mid-1960s. It contrasts these with the attitude towards jazz and Western popular culture exhibited by "Third World" nationalists such as Indonesia's President Sukarno. Chapter 12 examines Berendt's engagement with Japanese jazz as it came to fruition in the 1965 performance by the Hideo Shiraki Quintet and a koto trio at the Berlin Jazz Days. Chapter 13 focuses on his ambivalent attitude towards Brazilian bossa nova, which he brought to Berlin in 1966. Chapter 14 analyzes a series of three intercultural "encounters" he engineered between jazz musicians and Indian, Tunisian, and Indonesian musicians in 1967. Chapter 15 concludes the third part by examining two of the last records in the *JMTW* series, which showcased ways in which African American musicians engaged with the non-Western world. The chapter also surveys Berendt's worried reflections on what he identified as the protofascist "roots" discourse concurrently being advanced by some African Americans, among others.

My concluding chapter commences with an analysis of Berendt's New Age turn during the 1980s, and of the notion of *Weltmusik* that he advanced in that context. The chapter evaluates critical responses to *Weltmusik* and offers some conclusions about intercultural musical appropriation, as well as about Berendt himself and the postwar reception of jazz in Germany. A chronology of Berendt's life and key dates in postwar German history and in the jazz scene is included to help orient the reader, as is a discography of Berendt's intercultural music productions.

Figure 2 | Berendt at the typewriter. From the Jazzinstitut Darmstadt. Used with permission.

PART I

Joachim-Ernst Berendt and the Postwar Legitimation of Jazz

CHAPTER 1

Jazz and the Divide between Serious and Entertainment Music

If culture functions as a battleground for ideas, jazz provided such a battleground in postwar Germany, just as it did elsewhere in the world.[1] However, it did so for specifically German reasons. In the wake of defeat, Berendt and his fellow publicists sought to legitimate the music they admired, in a context where it had been widely disapproved of by many Germans from across the spectrum—including National Socialist ideologues, cultural conservatives, and critical theorists. This not inconsiderable task took over a decade until, by the late 1950s or early 1960s, jazz had become more or less socially accepted (Berendt 1957c; 1996a: 312; Fark 1971: 237; Schwab 2004: 140). It also took a great deal of energy and a range of resourceful strategies.

The West German Jazz Scene (1945–1961): A Sketch

The social "arrival" of jazz was not simply a result of the activities of jazz publicists. It occurred in the context of a modest boom in interest among many younger Germans during the mid- to late 1950s (Schwab 2004: 137). The scale of this boom ought not be overestimated, however: the historian Michael Kater estimates that fewer than 10 percent of young Germans became jazz enthusiasts in the postwar era (2006).

---

1. Cf., e.g., Starr 1994 (on jazz in the Soviet Union); Atkins 2001 (Japan); and Ansell 2004 (South Africa).

Their interest was, in turn, served by various media. Among these, radio was of critical importance. Following 1945, jazz was broadcast both on stations run by the occupying forces and on the newly established West German public broadcasters, including Berendt's employer, the SWF (Lange 1996: 145, 190–1). However, until the mid-1950s, jazz programs were broadcast solely in late-night time slots (Hoffmann 2000: 8). The print media were also important. During the late 1940s and early 1950s, however, most of the jazz periodicals that were established died a quick death (Hoffmann 1994: 91–2; Lange 1996: 192). Longer lived was the *Jazz Echo*, a supplement to *Die Gondel*, a Hamburg "girlie" magazine, which was first published in 1950 and continued into the mid-1960s.[2] Then, in 1952, the still-extant *Jazz Podium* was introduced, first as a supplement to a Viennese magazine and, by the following year, as an independent periodical in its own right (Lange 1996: 193).

At the grass roots level, enthusiasts banded together into so-called Hot Clubs, which were designed to share access to recordings, organize jam sessions and lectures, and—just as importantly—to lobby for the recognition of jazz as an art form. In 1950–51, three such groups formed the German Jazz Federation (DJF), an umbrella organization intended to continue these ministries on a broader scale and act as a "bulwark against [anti-jazz] defamation." Soon the number of affiliated clubs had risen to forty. In 1952, it launched the *Jazz Podium* as its press organ, and in May 1953 it organized the first annual German Jazz Festival in Frankfurt am Main ("DJF: Bollwerk" 1953; Wunderlich 1968; Lange 1996: 187–9; Hoffmann 1999: 2; 2003b: 22–3).

When it came to live music, West German enthusiasts were entertained by touring American jazzmen—beginning with Duke Ellington's trumpeter Rex Stewart, who flew in to a blockaded Berlin in 1948, and increasing in the early 1950s with Norman Granz's Jazz at the Philharmonic and other visitors—as well as by local professionals and amateurs (Pfankuch 1988; Lange 1996: 202–03). German musicians found temporary engagements in a range of locations during the late 1940s and 1950s, including in so-called "Ami-Clubs" catering to U.S. soldiers stationed in the Federal Republic as well as in the clubs and jam sessions run by Hot Clubs and private entrepreneurs (Jost 1988a: 368–70; Lange 1996: 186). Many obtained regular employment in light music orchestras on the payroll of the public broadcasters. These orchestras catered to broad tastes and by no means restricted themselves to "pure" jazz, however that was to be understood. As in other parts of the world, jazz was not understood as just one style, either. In the late 1940s most Ger-

---

2. This supplement was largely carried by *Die Gondel*'s larger non-jazz readership (Lange 1996: 193).

man jazzmen largely played in the Swing style familiar from before the War (Jost 1988a: 367–9). During the 1950s, some adopted earlier-still "trad" (traditional) styles. On the other hand, those interested in modern jazz typically had to undergo a phase of catching up with the rapid stylistic developments in American jazz. Years later, the pianist Michael Naura aptly dubbed this a "plagiatory epoch" (qtd. in Jost 1988a: 371).

Berendt's relationship with the jazz scene sketched here was a complex one. As the SWF's so-called "Jazz Editor"—a role he assumed when the position was created in 1949—he was well known to radio listeners. An active writer, he was also no stranger to those interested in reading about jazz. He was the author of numerous books, including the bestselling *Jazzbook* (1953); he edited the *Jazz Echo* under the pseudonym "Joe Brown" (Schwab 2004: 103; Schmidt-Joos 2005); and he contributed regularly to the *Jazz Podium*—except during one period in the mid-1950s when his relationship with its editor soured. Considering himself much too much of an individualist, he resiled from active membership of a Hot Club and also criticized such groups from time to time. However, he was still a member of the DJF and, indeed, acted as its press consultant during the 1950s ("Jazz und theoretische Physik" 1953; Schwab 2004:118). Berendt was also an active public speaker, and throughout the 1950s he gave numerous talks at Hot Clubs and—perhaps more importantly—at other venues around Germany, including on behalf of the DJF. Through his employment, Berendt also had regular contact with many musicians: the SWF employed a big band, which performed regular radio concerts and, from 1952 to 1957, enjoyed considerable fame under the baton of Kurt Edelhagen (Lange 1996: 156). He was involved with various other engagements and commissions (including for his pioneering television series, *Jazz – Heard and Seen*) and also with awarding jazz prizes. When circumstances permitted, Berendt also engaged American musicians for radio programs, television broadcasts, and other events with which he was associated. Through both the radio and print media Berendt commented on and criticized American and German musicians as well. Hence, as his position as West Germany's preeminent jazz authority became assured during the 1950s, he had considerable power to "consecrate" musicians. Although it is not entirely clear when the term "Jazz Pope" first emerged, it may well have been during this era.

Jazz in the Weimar Republic and Nazi Era

To gain a proper appreciation of the cultural context in which Berendt operated, jazz's checkered history in Germany needs to be recalled.

What was understood to be "jazz" may have been performed and recorded there in the disordered years following World War I. However, the first American performers were only heard live in the mid-1920s, after the German currency had stabilized (Jost 1988a: 357–9; Robinson 1994: 4). During the 1920s and early 1930s, the music enjoyed a certain vogue, but was never a mainstream success (Poiger 2000: 16).[3]

The new music polarized commentators. Conservatives often associated it with the idea of decadence, suggesting, for example, that it was "socially acceptable barbarism and stimulated propaganda, displaying only inner emptiness and abandonment" (Halfeld qtd. in Poiger 2000: 19). As Poiger points out, leftists "were perhaps most ambivalent about American cultural imports." The gist of their criticism was that it was a "bourgeois product designed to manipulate the proletariat and to dissipate its revolutionary potential" (2000: 20, 21). On the other hand, there was also considerable enthusiasm for jazz during the Weimar years. Some progressive voices—including Alfred Baresel and H. H. Stuckenschmidt, who both continued to be critics in postwar West Germany—considered jazz to be a new art form worthy of respect. For them, it represented "potential for rejuvenating classical music gone stale in the works of postromantic epigones" (Kater 1992: 16–17). Various younger composers also engaged with jazz during the late 1920s: Ernst Krenek's popular (1927) opera *Jonny Strikes Up* was influenced by the music, as was Brecht's and Weill's 1928 collaboration *The Threepenny Opera* (Jost 1988a: 362; Poiger 2000: 21). From 1928 until 1933, the respected Hoch'sche Conservatorium in Frankfurt am Main even offered a jazz course under the tutelage of the Hungarian émigré Mátyás Seiber, which was the first of its kind in the world (Kater 1992: 17; Steinert 1992: 64–5; Smith Bowers 2002: 121–5, 129).

"Nigger-Jew-Jazz"

Hitler's accession to power in 1933 represented a sharpening of tension in the climate surrounding jazz, and it was during this era that Berendt was first exposed to it. Conservative anti-jazz polemic had often been transfused with anxieties about the exaggerated, "primitive" sexuality of the Negro (Kater 1992: 22). However, National Socialist ideologues now included an extra dimension: jazz was also played and marketed by Jews. Accordingly, labels such as "Nigger-Jew-Jazz" and "jewified Nigger-music" were employed (Jost 1988a: 362; Kater 1992: 20, 32). A low

---

3. On the "German Jazz Age," see Kater 1992: 3–28; Robinson 1994: 4–7; Partsch 2000.

point in this Nazi campaign came with the 1938 Düsseldorf exhibition of "degenerate music," which located jazz alongside the modernist music of composers such as Paul Hindemith and the Jewish Arnold Schoenberg (Dümling and Girth 1988; Dümling 1994).

The objection to "Nigger-Jew-Jazz" was clearly not simply an aesthetic one. The music also symbolized "a Jewish-Negro plot to undermine Germanic culture" (Kater 1992: 24). As Kater observes, Blacks were seen as being naively responsible for the sexual component of jazz, whereas Jews were thought to be using jazz as part of a plan to poison the blood of German women by "seducing them through acts of 'musical race defilement'" (1992: 33). Indeed, it was partly jazz's racial indeterminacy that made it so offensive. Tellingly, the National Socialist Richard Litterscheid noted in 1936: "It was only after the 'white' American bands picked up the stimulus of Nigger-Jazz, that the actual Anglo-American-Negro hybrid product of jazz came into being" (qtd. in Hoffmann 1996: 99). Jazz was considered dangerous because it was an aural version of—and bodily temptation toward—the miscegenation that the National Socialists sought to outlaw under the Nuremberg Laws and that offended their ideology of "pure" racial (and cultural) essences.

Various piecemeal bans on radio broadcasts and jazz dancing were instituted in the name of National Socialism. Nevertheless, there was never a blanket ban, and the National Socialist position was characterized by both persecution *and* ambivalence, as Poiger observes (Jost 1988a: 362–6; Lange 1988: 391; Fackler 1994: 441–3; Poiger 2000: 22). Indeed, jazz and jazzlike light music were actually used at various times by the Third Reich, both as anti-British propaganda and as so-called "German Dance- and Entertainment Music" (Kater 1992: 111–35; 1994: 72–3; Bergmeier and Lotz 1996; 1997). For various reasons—including economic ones—ideological opposition to jazz was not pursued to the hilt: often jazz was turned into "German Dance Music" simply by changing a song title or swapping a saxophone for a violin (Dümling 1994: 60; Fackler 1994: 452–8).

Opposition to Jazz and Postwar Liberalism: A Program

After the defeat of 1945, many Germans continued to voice their opposition to jazz. The public expression of such views reached an early highpoint in 1947–48, when the newly established radio magazine *Hör Zu* published a slew of readers' letters objecting to broadcasts of the music (Fark 1971: 178–80). Berendt also observed in 1950 that arrogant, ill-informed opposition to jazz manifested itself in many letters received by the broadcasters (1950a: 89). In the late 1940s he even received a warning from a disgruntled SWF listener stating that unless he stopped broadcasting jazz, "a pair of good German male fists (!) would introduce the right rhythm to him" (Berendt 1996a: 313). In this context, he all but equated Germanness with being opposed to jazz (1950a: 88).

Vehemently anti-jazz attitudes survived well into the 1950s. In December 1953, for example, a correspondent to the *Konstanz Südkurier* referred to jazz as "a music carried primarily by impulses of the blood and the will," and which was "fundamentally foreign to our being, [it is] subterranean and inflammatory." It might be appropriate for a "Negro-milieu," this writer opined, but not for the Occident (Münz 1953). It was only between 1954 and 1958 that anti-jazz tirades gradually tapered off and the balance of media coverage shifted from value-laden position taking such as this to more informative reporting (Fark 1971: 274–5).

In the context of this vociferous opposition, Berendt and others took the understandable view that there was an ideological hangover from National Socialist anti-jazz indoctrination (Berendt n.d.d.; Schreiber 1958; Zimmerle 1960). Overcoming postwar anti-jazz sentiment was therefore practically raised to a moral duty: as Berendt observed in 1950, exposure to radio listeners' anti-jazz letters was reason itself to be pro-jazz (1950a: 89). Although such moralizing comments were partly just another way of lobbying for the recognition of jazz, the stakes were also understood to be considerably higher.

Indeed, for Berendt, the task of legitimating jazz was located within the project of liberalizing German society after 1945:

> It concerned something [that was] societal, [something] fundamentally political. It concerned making the cultural life—and with it the consciousness—in our land more worldly, open and tolerant, [and] less nationally circling around itself, less oriented towards itself. (1996a: 314)

This task was consistent with Berendt's harrowing personal experience of having lost his father to Dachau, and also with his background as a soldier who witnessed (at least) the atrocities of the Eastern Front.[4] The desire for a new, liberal Germany was also consistent with a characteristically postwar West German *Weltanschauung* conditioned by the trauma of National Socialism. According to Peter O'Brien, this *Welt-*

---

4. Unfortunately, it was not possible to uncover official sources relating to Berendt's career as a junior officer in the *Wehrmacht*. His memoir, however, contains several reflections on his military career and reveals that he participated in the siege of Leningrad (1996a: 269–70, 399).

anschauung interprets modern German history as a drawn out struggle between German nationalism and Western liberalism, and is based on an anxiety caused by the memory of the Weimar Republic's failure. Seeking to explain this failure, some West German intellectuals argued that Germans were somehow "philosophically predisposed" to welcome a dictator promising a "utopian community" (O'Brien 1996: 24). Historians and sociologists posited a *Sonderweg* (special path) to modernity, which involved a "modernized society without a modernized (that is, liberal) citizenry" (O'Brien 1996: 30–1). Accordingly, German illiberalism was a "dormant virus always capable of revival" (O'Brien 1996: 39). The result was a strong investment in (technocratic) liberalism and a compulsion to "keep vigilant watch for the slightest traces of nationalist revival" (O'Brien 1996: 3).

This philosophy manifested itself in much of Berendt's discourse about music. However, his arguments often contained paradoxes, and there were contradictions between the liberal position he took as a writer and the practices he sometimes pursued. Berendt was a complex man: if he was touched by a liberalizing zeal, he was also a highly ambitious individual who wished to establish himself as West Germany's leading jazz authority. As will be seen, he wished to provoke thought, and ostensibly embraced the stance of the tolerant liberal humanist, yet he also reacted aggressively to the slightest criticism, and wished to maintain his authority by having the last word in debates.

"Jazz in a Tuxedo"

With a strong emotional attachment to jazz—first sparked when he chanced on a broadcast of Swing music in 1936—and with his liberalizing project and his ambition to motivate him, Berendt answered postwar opposition first and foremost by pointing out jazz's artistic credentials. This is a recurrent theme in his first two books, *Jazz: A Time-Critical Study* (1950) and *The Jazzbook* (1953), the very writing of which was partly an attempt to have the music taken *seriously*.

Berendt's attitude was not without precedent. Indeed, jazz had a history of being treated seriously, both on the continent and at home. During the 1920s and 1930s, the francophone "founding fathers of jazz studies"—Robert Goffin, Hugues Panassié, and Charles Delaunay—had each written about "authentic," "hot" jazz as a folk music with artistic merit (Gioia 1988: 19–49, 28). Weimar writers had also published books devoted to jazz (cf. Pollack 1922; Baresel 1926; Bernhard 1927; Egg 1927). The first Carnegie Hall jazz concert, in 1938, marked jazz's "coming of age" in the United States and led to increased jazz writing and research there (Gioia 1997: 152. See also Gennari 2006). Stylistic changes in the jazz world also contributed to the trend toward seriousness: indeed the avant-garde beboppers of the 1940s, and many of the modernists who followed them, were increasingly associated with a *"l'art pour l'art"* perspective (Gioia 1988: 71–2).

Berendt's deadly serious *"time-critical study"* was written in a remarkable year for the 27-year-old. The Federal Republic was only a year old, and, on the personal front, he had married, become a father, and just been appointed jazz editor at the SWF. His was not the first postwar German-language jazz book, but it was the first to be published in Germany (cf. Back 1948; Slawe 1948). It is short—more like an extended essay, really—and deliberately pitched at an intellectual audience, albeit one with no particular love for the nineteenth century and its cultural manifestations. The book is notable for what it avoids, namely any strict musical analysis of jazz pieces—never Berendt's concern, given his lack of academic training—or any chronicle of jazz musicians or stylistic changes in the idiom. Instead, it is unique in the international jazz literature—an overwhelmingly ambitious and speculative attempt to link jazz with a range of twentieth-century phenomena, including existential philosophy, modern art, literature, historiography, participatory democracy, and—Berendt's particular hobby horse—theoretical physics![5] In this way, *Jazz* attempted to gain legitimation for its subject by association.

Although *Jazz* received a lukewarm reception from some fans, was rejected by conservative music pedagogues because of its celebration of ecstasy, and Berendt himself was later dissatisfied with it, it was regarded highly enough by the U.S. administration to garner him a three-month trip to the United States as part of the Cultural Exchange Program (Kaestner 1951; Kleber 1953: 63; Berendt 1996a: 291; Lange 1996: 195).[6] It is difficult to overestimate the value of this debut American trip for Berendt. In addition to spurring a taste for international travel that would grow and inform his production activities over the following decades, he gathered valuable experience of jazz in its home environment—like other Europeans before him, including the important critic Leonard Feather, Berendt made a beeline for Harlem. During the trip, he assembled a wealth of material which he then worked through for his epochal *Jazzbook*. It was presumably also at this time that he began to develop his philosophy regarding jazz writing—like Feather and Nat

---

5. He actually began to study theoretical physics shortly before his conscription into the *Wehrmacht* in 1941 (Berendt 1996a: 267).

6. On the program, see, e.g., Ermarth 1993: 13–14.

Hentoff, he regarded a proximity to, and indeed intimacy with, the musicians about whom one was writing to be essential (see, e.g., Berendt 1977a: 408 ff). This philosophy would be further cemented on Berendt's second extended trip to the United States in 1960, when he and the Californian photographer William Claxton made a three-month road trip across the country, visiting jazzmen in their home environments. Being a European helped Berendt gain proximity to the musicians too. Claxton observes that "most of [the American musicians whom they encountered] took to him right away. It helped that he was from another country, which made him even more interesting to them" (2005: 28).

The *Jazzbook* differed markedly from its predecessor. A work of greater maturity, and more of a piece with other works of jazz history being written in the United States and Europe during this era, it also seemingly had less to prove. While still avoiding any rigorous musicological approach, it was far more informative about jazz itself—with the result that it was much more readable. Berendt gave clear treatments of what, for him, were jazz's essential characteristics. He also included musicians' biographies, descriptions of the typical jazz instruments and their leading exponents, a discography, and—most importantly—a plausible outline of the way in which jazz had developed in accordance with a "decade-by-decade" model. This quality of stylistic development was, for him, the most imposing thing about jazz: "it has proceeded with the

Figure 3 | Berendt and the Modern Jazz Quartet's John Lewis enjoy a meal. Courtesy of the Jazzinstitut Darmstadt. Used with permission.

same degree of consistency and logic, necessity and completeness, which signifies the development of genuine art since the beginning" (1953a: 14). The "jazz development" was one of the central bases upon which Berendt made jazz's claim for high art status. However, this progressivist notion of the jazz tradition was not his alone—as Scott DeVeaux shows, it is a common trait of many jazz histories (1997: 5–8). In the United States, it had been advanced during the postwar era both by the Marxist-minded Sidney Finkelstein (*Jazz: A People's Music* [1947]) and by his fellow critic, Barry Ulanov (*History of Jazz in America* [1952]), albeit to satisfy differently weighted interpretations of the jazz phenomenon (Gennari 2006: 140 ff). In Europe, it was likewise formulated in the Frenchman André Hodeir's *Jazz: Its Evolution and Essence* (1954). The *Jazzbook*'s eye-catching family tree diagrams, which neatly illustrated the way in which jazz had developed over the years also resembled those used by the American historian of jazz, Marshall Stearns in 1952 (cf. Gennari 2006: 206).

The *Jazzbook* was a cheaply priced Fischer paperback. This, together with its informative nature and authoritative tone, and the fact that it was pitched at both enthusiasts and skeptics, contributed to the astonishing success of the book. Although there were a number of other German-language jazz books by 1953, the *Jazzbook* was the market leader (cf. Finkelstein 1951; Schulz-Köhn 1951; Twittenhoff 1953; Usinger 1953). It clearly struck a chord: as one reviewer noted, it was a book that was long overdue and it became, as Lange observes, the basis for many young Germans' knowledge about jazz (Harth 1954: 45; Lange 1996: 195). More so than its obscure predecessor, the *Jazzbook* contributed to legitimating jazz. However, Berendt by no means let his pen rest with the *Jazzbook*. Yet another way in which he continued to advance his task was to delineate various links between jazz and "classical" music, extending beyond a shared notion of progressive stylistic development.

Jazz and New Music

In postwar West Germany, the parameters of debates about jazz were set by a landscape made up of the rigid opposites of *Ernste-Musik* ("serious" music) and *Unterhaltungs-Musik* ("entertainment" music) (Berendt 1950b: 216; Adorno 1962: 21). As will be shown, there were many reasons why an association between jazz and *U-Musik* was considered undesirable. However, there were also positive reasons for associating jazz with certain types of *E-Musik*—beyond the bald symbolic capital residing in the latter. Firstly, various composers—from Ernest Ansermet, Darius Milhaud, and Igor Stravinsky to Hindemith, Krenek, and Weill—had engaged with jazz in the past (Berendt 1959f; Widmaier 1966; Schatt 1995). For Berendt, making an association between jazz and *E-Musik* must also have seemed rather natural. For one, he had a modest background in *E-Musik*, having taken piano lessons as a boy, and even occasionally played the organ in his father's church (T. Koch 1985). His work at the SWF also brought him into close contact with Heinrich Strobel, who was head of music there and who resuscitated earlier *E-Musik* institutions, including the highbrow music journal *Melos* (in 1946) and the famed Donaueschingen Music Days (1950) after their demise under the Nazis (Häusler 1996:133–5). Strobel acted as a mentor to the young Berendt, and in all likelihood encouraged his first music criticism, which included several pieces on New Music (Berendt 1996a: 286–9).[7]

The association with Strobel was particularly fruitful (Berendt 1996a: 286–9). Importantly, the older man was open to jazz; during the Weimar era, he himself had written positively about it (Robinson 1994: 7). As editor of *Melos*, he now published articles by Berendt on jazz and a wide range of other subjects, including *U-Musik*, the radio, and "Americana." As artistic director of the Donaueschingen Music Days, he also welcomed jazz into the program in 1954 and 1957 (Berendt 1996b: 408–9; Häusler 1996: 133–5). "Symphonic Jazz" was also granted a presence at an international music festival hosted by Strobel and the SWF in 1955 (Berendt 1996a: 286). In 1954 and 1955, Strobel and Berendt even commissioned compositions combining jazz and contemporary concert music, an idea that had intrigued Berendt since 1952 at least (cf. Berendt 1952d: 103).

In 1954, they commissioned the Swiss Rolf Liebermann to compose a *Concerto for Jazz-Band and Symphony Orchestra* (Berendt 1996b: 408). This hybrid composition was well received by audience and *E-Musik* press alike, and was subsequently performed in the United States, where the musician and musicologist Gunther Schuller was about to start his own "Third Stream" proselytizing (Ruppel 1954; "Jazz auf den Donaueschinger Musiktagen" 1954; "Jazz News" 1955b; Berendt 1996b: 408).[8] Nevertheless, there was debate—including from Berendt himself—about whether the combination was meaningful, given that the jazzmen had been given no room to improvise ("Brown" 1954c; Berendt and Claxton 1961: 238). Regardless, Berendt considered experiments

---

7. The Jazzinstitut's catalogue of Berendt's articles indicates that many of the articles he wrote between 1947 and 1949 related to New Music rather than to jazz.

8. Schuller developed his famous concept of a "Third Stream" of music independent from—but drawing on—the jazz and concert music traditions in the mid- to late 1950s (see, e.g., Schuller 1961; Kumpf 1975b 16–18; Hellhund 1986).

such as these *necessary*, given that critics—he was uncharacteristically modest enough not to mention himself—had long theorized about the matter (1955b: 11). Putting the question of aesthetic success to one side, the West German jazz press rightly recognized the symbolic importance of the Donaueschingen concert: it marked a victory in jazz's strive for recognition as an art form ("Brown" 1954c; Lippmann 1954).

Just as important for the acceptance of jazz in West German cultured circles was the performance of America's Modern Jazz Quartet (MJQ) at Donaueschingen and elsewhere in 1957. Berendt had neatly paved the way for this. In 1955, he had championed its sophisticated music to *Melos* readers (1955d). The following year he invited it to perform at a Freiburg concert celebrating the SWF's one thousandth jazz program, after which it embarked on a lengthy national tour organized by the DJF (Nass 1956; "Jazz News" 1956e; 1957c). That tour culminated in a performance at Donaueschingen in October 1957—where jazz was again squarely featured (Curjel 1957: 328). If the MJQ's dinner suits, serious demeanor, and performances in high art venues aided the bourgeois acceptance of jazz in West Germany (Schwab 2004: 124), then the presence of jazz at Donaueschingen in 1954 and 1957 surely also contributed to its "arrival."

While Donaueschingen provided an opportunity for experimentation, a pair of extended articles and accompanying lecture tours gave Berendt the opportunity to theorize extensively on the links between jazz and *E-Musik*. These articles were published in a 1959 volume co-edited by Berendt in which they rubbed shoulders with serious *E-Musik* criticism by the likes of Theodor Adorno (!), a coup that was not lost on jazz critics (Schmidt-Joos 1959b). In "Jazz and New Music" (1959f)—which, in its lecture format, was accompanied by music from the Hans Koller combo, one of West Germany's leading modern groups—Berendt made perhaps the first sustained attempt to analyze the links between those two idioms (cf. Schmidt-Joos 1959c). In retrospect, the parallels explored—including a joy in playing, and an interest in rhythm and linearity—seem somewhat simplistic. The assertion that some modern jazzmen improvised solos that corresponded closely, yet unconsciously, with Hindemith's theories in *The Craft of Music Composition* (1941–5) is also highly speculative. Berendt is on much stronger territory, however, when examining the ways in which musicians and composers from each of the two camps had engaged with the other over the years. While critical of these efforts—New Music composers failed to grasp the peculiarities of jazz (i.e., improvisation, an individual tone and "swing") and jazzmens' improvisations lacked the superior form of *E-Musik*—Berendt posited that both New Music and jazz were now arriving in similarly atonal territory. Arguing against a conflation of the two (based on an again somewhat simplistic dichotomy between *emotional* jazz and *intellectual* New Music[9]), he nevertheless urged that each idiom should retain an awareness of and "longing" for the other—whatever that might mean in practice.

The fact that Berendt and his co-editor Jürgen Uhde won an article from Adorno for the same volume in which such ruminations appeared is remarkable, given that they would have been anathema to the older man. Only a few years earlier, Adorno had taken Berendt to task in the journal *Merkur* for allying jazz with Stravinsky's and Hindemith's modernism, and with the avant-garde generally. There he argued that autonomous *E-Musik*—in particular his favored school of Viennese modernism—was far more advanced than jazz in just those areas that Berendt claimed it was "modern," namely tonal variation, atonality, and polyphony. By comparison, jazz was thoroughly "tame" (Adorno 1953a: 891–2. See also 1962: 25).

Jazz and Old Music

Berendt's other attempt to link jazz with the *E-Musik* tradition was similarly controversial, but clearly struck more of a chord among the populace. "Jazz and Old Music"—the brainchild of pianist Wolfgang Lauth—was a collaboration between Berendt and the music historian Dr. Josef Tröller, with music from Lauth's combo, J. S. Bach, and the MJQ. The lecture tour, which teased out parallels between jazz and Baroque music, quickly became a success. After premiering in Mannheim in January 1956, it toured throughout the rest of the year. A commercial recording was released and won the German Critics' Prize in 1957–8, and a film version was even made and selected to represent West Germany at the Venice Biennale (Lauth n.d.: 22–5; "Debatten um" 1956; "Jazz News" 1956a; 1956f; 1957a; 1957c; 1958b; Berendt and Tröller 1959). *Jazz Podium* praised the record highly and stressed its value as a tool for the jazz enlightenment of (older) cultured citizens: "[It is a] record which one ought to own, in order to play it to one's parents and teachers, during discussions at universities and in [one's] circle of friends, simply everywhere where a lack of clarity about jazz exists" (Rev. of *Jazz und Alte Musik* 1958).

However, the project also had its critics within the jazz scene. Some complained that the parallels identified—such as the commonality of

---

9. Cf. Gioia 1988: 33.

improvisation—tended to be superficial. Others perceptively observed that the whole concept implied that jazz only had value insofar as it could be related to art music ("Debatten um" 1956; Ganns 1956). While Berendt strenuously dismissed this criticism at the time, it did have a grain of truth to it; he later confessed that the comparisons he made with Bach et al. were indeed a strategy intended to "justify" jazz ("Jazz News" 1956b; Berendt 1996a: 154).

Jazz and Musical Romanticism?

If Berendt was keen to draw parallels between jazz and New and/or Baroque music, then he showed a distinct ambivalence toward the Romantic concert music of the nineteenth century. Musical Romanticism was, according to one musicologist, not so much a "definable style" as a "spiritual attitude." In this scheme, the composer was revered as all-important, an artistic genius able to transform primal sound into music. Particularly in late Romanticism, the performer was supposed to submit unquestioningly to the free artistic will of this composer (Blume 1979: 103, 112). It was about just such Romantic precepts that Berendt expressed his distaste (see, e.g., Berendt 1957d: 23–4). In general, he took the view that jazz evaded the *Weltanschauung* that beleaguered Romantic music. In his first book, he even opposed jazz to the Romantic conception of music (1950a: 91. See also Berendt and Tröller 1959: 174, 182; Berendt 1957d: 26; 1959f: 184; 1959h).

The critical attitude toward Romantic music was possibly inherited from Heinrich Strobel, who himself was decidedly anti-Romantic (Häusler 1996: 134). It may also have been too much of a stretch to simultaneously profess one's interest in modernist New Music *and* the Romanticism against which it rebelled. But the distaste was also typical of a postwar West Germany, in which some considered that Romanticism had contributed to the rise of National Socialism (O'Brien 1996: 24). Late German Musical Romanticism did have distinct nationalist connotations (Blume 1979: 175–6, 178; Longyear 1988: 212, 283). Moreover, the music and anti-Semitism of the Romantic composer Richard Wagner had directly influenced National Socialism (Sontag 1980: 149–50; Van der Will 1995: 133–5). As Susan Sontag puts it: "Hitler has contaminated Romanticism and Wagner, ... much of nineteenth-century German culture is, retroactively, haunted by Hitler" (1980: 151). It is therefore unsurprising that Berendt was uncomfortable with the concepts of a Romantic composer dictating a performer's interpretation, or pre-programming a listener's emotional responses (see, e.g., Berendt and Tröller 1959: 174).

Nevertheless, his interpretation of jazz was not without its Romantic elements. In 1963, his fellow critic Baldur Bockhoff diagnosed a thoroughly Romantic tendency in Berendt's and others' focus on "truth," "vitality," and "authenticity" in jazz: "What is this if not a weak echo of that Romantic longing for the Blue Flower?" (1963: 916). As Ted Gioia has also shown, it can certainly be argued that jazz—with its focus on the individual musician and the way in which improvisation is thought to lay bare his or her soul—is a thoroughly Romantic art form (1988: 81–4).

Jazz and *U-Musik*

Berendt's 1950s discourse about the aesthetic location of jazz had another complicating dimension. While negotiating a complex line in relation to the links between jazz and *E-Musik*, he was also involved in shoring up a by-no-means-clear distinction between jazz and *U-Musik*.

Initially, the distinction was one that seemed to be of comparatively little interest to him. From 1946 until 1949, he was responsible for all *U-Musik* programming at the SWF and even penned several would-be *Schlager* (pop songs) in the era (Berendt 1996a: 290–91). Around this time he also professed a desire to remove what he called the "theoretical, to all intents and purposes 'bureaucratic' cleavage" between *E-Musik* and *U-Musik* (1950b: 216). Indeed, he noted in 1953, "it does not so much depend on the distinction between 'culture' and 'entertainment' as that between good and bad music, and there is good and bad in both fields" (1953c: 44).

Berendt might have occasionally opined during the late 1940s and early 1950s that "authentic" jazz bridged the divide between *E-* and *U-Musik* (see, e.g., 1950b: 217). Under pressure, however, it clearly fell for him on the *E-Musik* side, particularly as the 1950s progressed. And so he went to lengths to distinguish between "true" jazz and the commercial *Schlager*. The former was said to be emotionally honest, the latter insincerely sentimental. Jazz also had the swing, improvisation, and individual tone that the *Schlager* lacked. In fact, the *Schlager* was nothing more than a commercialized derivative of true, artistic jazz (1950a: 38–43; 1953a: 10; 1959f: 188).

This theoretically clear dichotomy between art and commerce broke down, however, not only if one took the past into account but also within the context of the 1950s West German jazz scene, as even Berendt was sometimes forced to concede. For example, while he considered George Gershwin to have been a purveyor of commercialized "lemonade-like" symphonic jazz (that is, not true jazz), he acknowledged that Gershwin's melodies still had artistic merit (1951: 80; 1959f: 189–91). He also had to admit that jazz had often had a very close relationship with popular music. Notably, the jazz of the 1930s "Swing" era had been very popular, as he conceded to Adorno in 1953 (1953b: 888).

No wonder, then, that not all members of the West German jazz scene wished to make—or were capable of making—a sharp distinction between "true" jazz and popular music. Some older jazz authorities such as Alfred Baresel were accused of being unable to distinguish between the two ("Brown" 1953c). To make matters worse, musicians refused to respect the border, "straying" from jazz into the pop domain despite the imperious protestation of critics like Berendt.[10] By performing quite mixed repertoires, the radio orchestras, too, did not alleviate the situation (cf. Jost 1988a: 367–8). As the first *Gondel* readers' poll—conducted in late 1952—indicated, there was considerable confusion among fans as to whether particular musicians might be counted as jazz musicians or not. Prior to the poll, "Brown" urged readers to bear in mind the difference between jazz and dance or *Schlager* music. Despite this, he acknowledged that the *Gondel* team could not afford to be too harsh on those who got it wrong, particularly when it came to selecting singers in the "German" category ("Brown" 1952a: 62). In 1950s West Germany, the distinction between popular music and jazz was therefore clearly not as demarcated as Berendt might have declared. Why then was it insisted upon?

The Stigma of *U-Musik*

There were several reasons why Berendt eschewed links between jazz and *U-Musik*. He was interested in installing jazz on the same level as *E-Musik*, which militated against elaborating links with *E-Musik*'s schematic opposite, in a context where *U-Musik* was a priori second-rate (see, e.g., Berendt 1950b: 215). Secondly, the established jazz literature already exhibited a deep anticommercialism. In addition, since the advent of bebop, many musicians and critics were interested in distancing modern jazz from dance and the mass market (DeVeaux 1997: 8, 12–15). There was also a pragmatic motivation to dissociate jazz from

---

10. Cf "Brown's" urging that Caterina Valente ought to keep her jazz and her *Schlager* singing strictly separate ("Jazz News" 1954b: 45) or his warning to Wolfgang Sauer that once jazz singers started singing *Schlager*, they damaged their ability to sing jazz ("Jazz News" 1954c). Paradoxically, Berendt himself enthused occasionally about singers such as Lena Horne, who crossed the line and succeeded in singing *Schlager* without disowning the jazz tradition (1952b: 26).

popular music: in the Federal Republic, concerts and film screenings were taxed at different rates depending on the artistic rating assigned to them. If jazz could be designated the status of art music, it would be exempt from the entertainment tax.[11] Another important reason militating against too close an association between jazz and popular music was the notorious position taken by Theodor Adorno, who steadfastly located jazz as a form of popular music within an insidious Culture Industry.

Adorno comprehensively registered his opposition to jazz in 1932, and his last major word came thirty years later. However, there is an internal consistency within his essays, which justifies their being considered together (Schaal 1983: 19; Robinson 1994: 2; Partsch 2000: 250–1). The essays have caused much consternation and, as Heinz Steinert observes, the secondary literature on Adorno tends not to take them altogether seriously (1992: 22–3). Hence, they are often dismissed as racist, elitist, and ignorant (Schönherr n.d.: 2). Adorno's interpretation has several dimensions: a musicological analysis investigating jazz's relationship with *E-Musik;* a sociological study of jazz's affinity with totalitarianism and its relationship with the Culture Industry; and a psychoanalysis of the jazz musician and recipient (Schönherr n.d.: 4). Adorno's interpretation of the relationship between jazz and *E-Musik* has been considered above, and his sociological study and psychoanalysis will be examined in the next chapter when I analyze postwar debates about young Germans' "jazz enthusiasm." Here I will focus solely on his positioning of jazz as a form of *U-Musik*.

For Adorno, "even in its more sophisticated forms jazz is popular music" (1962: 33). He established this by noting that jazz often employed a *Schlager* melody (or something similarly banal) and that the same basic rhythm was to be found in both jazz and popular music (see e.g. 1953a: 891–2). Moreover, jazz was produced and distributed by the commercial music industry: hence, it was "a commodity in the strict sense" (1936: 473). Jazz was also properly to be seen as a functional (dance) music, rather than as having any inherent aesthetic value: "Jazz is not what it 'is' … it is what it is used for" (1936: 472). Despite jazz's ostensible stylistic change (codified in Berendt's "decade model"), Adorno considered it static, a "perennial fashion": with "the periodic revivals of hot jazz under different names merely vitamin injections into the monotony of mass production" (1953a: 891; 1953b).

---

11. I thank Bernd Hoffmann for pointing this out to me. On this topic, see Hoffmann 2003b. This was a live issue for Berendt: his 1953 short film *Jazz – Yesterday and Today* fell foul of the tax, in that it was unable to get an artistic rating high enough for West German movie houses to be interested in showing it ("Brown" 1954b).

As Cornelius Partsch observes, the strength of Adorno's jazz essays is his analysis of the production side of what he and Max Horkheimer in 1947 called the Culture Industry (2000: 268 n.137). This term refers to "the standardization and rationalization of the methods of dissemination and not ... to the actual process of cultural production" (Burns 1995b: 2). The standardization ensured that cultural products were the same despite the appearance of individuality. Hence, the totalizing Culture Industry promised consumers an escape from everyday drudgery, yet it was the same old drudgery they found in culture (Adorno and Horkheimer 1947: 150). Art renounced its own autonomy and proudly took its place among consumer goods (Adorno and Horkheimer 1947: 166). Moreover, fusions of *E-* and *U-Musik* abounded (Adorno and Horkheimer 1947: 144). On the reception side, the "dumbing-down" effect was clear: "the mass phenomenon of popular music undermines the autonomy and independence of judgment" (Adorno 1962: 38). This was a matter of no little concern in postwar Germany: my next chapter will show how the Culture Industry (and jazz in particular) was understood to link in with authoritarian behavior and fascist potential.

Berendt versus Adorno

While this interpretation seems dated now, it commanded serious attention in postwar Germany and elicited a prominent response from Berendt. After Adorno's return from the United States, he made a renewed contribution to West German jazz discourse in a June 1953 article in the highbrow journal *Merkur* (1953b). Berendt—who had already contributed an article on racial discrimination in the United States to the journal in 1952 (1952e)—was encouraged by the editor Hans Paeschke to respond and agreed not only because he wanted to establish jazz's credentials, but also because it represented another prestigious publication for him. He may even have had in mind the publicity that the controversy might create for his forthcoming *Jazzbook*. However, the tussle with Adorno and the fact that Paeschke gave the elder man the final word upset Berendt. Nor did the exchange cause Adorno to revise his ideas about jazz, despite Berendt's latter suggestion to the contrary (Broecking 2002: 43–9). Indeed, Adorno may well have had Berendt in mind when he spoke disparagingly of the "Jazz Expert" type of fan in his 1962 *Introduction to the Sociology of Music* (1962: 12–14).[12] More importantly, the *Merkur* debate represented an opportunity to think through

---

12. Cf. Adorno's comments about Berendt in 1953 (1953a: 891).

Adorno's theory about the Culture Industry, yet Berendt did not make the most of that chance (Steinert 1992: 20).[13]

Berendt's reply consisted mainly in invoking the distinction between "true" jazz and commercialized *Schlager* music. Hence, "true" jazz was neither dance music nor the stuff of the hit parade: "Since the beginning, jazz has been a music of the few for the few, whereas *Schlager* music has perhaps the largest audience that anything existing today has." Having thus created a special place for "true" jazz, he then paralleled it with *E-Musik*, particularly the music of Stravinsky, Hindemith, and Bach (1953b: 887–9). He did not engage in any significant way with the idea of the Culture Industry itself. As Steinert asserts, Berendt's type of argument does not challenge the inherited notion of art, it simply reapplies it. Moreover, it erects a false divide between "true" jazz and "pure" commerce (Steinert 1992: 137). There is, however, a dialectical relationship between jazz, art, popular music, and commerce. Jazz is, in David Horn's words, "in a dialogue with both 'art' and popular culture" (1991: 103).

* * * * *

In 1950s West Germany, jazz was in the process of legitimation. This was partly a result of the rise of a new habitus held by a segment of educated young West Germans, who were well disposed to (certain) American popular culture (Maase 1992: 177). Jazz's potential to challenge some of the received conceptions of high art was immanent within the music itself. As Nicholas Evans notes, "jazz's aesthetic status cannot easily be labelled. … [It] blurs the lines between commonly accepted ideas about … art, thereby raising questions about those ideas" (2000: 11). However, in the 1950s, the high/low dichotomy remained influential with opponents of jazz as well as with lobbyists like Berendt, even if, occasionally, they were critical of it or suggested that jazz might transcend the border. The strategy of allying jazz and *E-Musik* was more than understandable given the symbolic capital residing in the latter, yet the attempt was fraught with ambivalence and a sense that the rules of *E-Musik* did not really apply (see e.g. Berendt 1953b: 889. Cf. Adorno 1953a: 891; Bockhoff 1963: 914–6, 919). It also had the whiff of an inferiority complex. The distinction between jazz and *U-Musik* was also problematic in that it failed to take into account the links between jazz and the music industry. In retrospect, it can be seen that a new mode of legitimation was required: a critical vocabulary for talking about those qualities that gave the music equivalent artistic status to that of *E-Musik* while maintaining

---

13. Note that later in the 1950s, Berendt did attempt to critique Adorno's theory about the authoritarian nature of the Culture Industry recipient—see chapter 2.

that jazz was not *E-Musik* in the traditional sense (cf. Bockhoff 1963: 919; Steinert 1992: 18–19). But this may have been asking too much in the 1950s.

As we will see, during the course of the 1960s these earlier debates quickly became historical. While Adorno's views became more and more outdated after jazz had "arrived," a new generation of musicians and critics also began, by the mid- to late 1960s, to view the attempts of Berendt and his colleagues to "force [jazz] into a tuxedo [and] onto the concert hall podium" and to rope it off from *U-Musik,* as dated and having unfortunate consequences (Bockhoff 1963: 919. See also Schmidt-Joos 1965a: 321; Brötzmann 2004).

CHAPTER 2

Dance as Escape?

> I come from a pastor's house ... I set a great deal on this background—because I assume that is why I ... came to the conclusion that much in our European (and especially German) culture is awry. That which belongs together is asunder: mind and soul, body and mind.
> —Berendt quoted in "Jazz und theoretische Physik" (1953)

Aesthetic debates about jazz did not occur in a vacuum during the 1950s. An increasing number of young Germans took to the music with an unbridled passion that, for many older commentators, was downright worrying. Some regarded this as a false escape from society's problems, others saw it as symptomatic of a lost generation, while others still drew on Adorno's interpretation of the fascist potential residing within the jazz enthusiast. Explaining "jazz enthusiasm" therefore became vital in the battle to legitimate jazz.

Swingheinis and *Halbstarken*

In the mid-1950s, a spate of so-called *Halbstarken* ("half-strong") youth riots took place in both East and West Germany. These riots—the high point of which was in 1956—were often associated by commentators with "young rebel" American movies and with rock 'n' roll. However, one of the first riots occurred at an October 1955 Louis Armstrong concert in Hamburg, when fans vented their annoyance at the brevity of the concert and the cancellation of a second event by starting fights and causing property damage ("Zum Armstrong-Skandal" 1955; Poiger 2000: 71 ff). This was not an isolated incident: "rowdy" behavior by so-called *Swingheinis*—a derogatory term deriving from the Nazi era and similar in meaning to the later term *Halbstarke*—was reported at other jazz events too, including the first Jazz at the Philharmonic tour in 1953 (Berendt 1953a: 203–5; "Brown" 1953b; Lange 1996: 186–7). As Poiger notes: "In spite of the efforts by West German jazz clubs to make the music acceptable, jazz became extremely controversial after 1955 in the wake of the *Halbstarken* rebellion" (2000: 148). To the dismay of "serious" jazz enthusiasts, much of the media coverage of the *Halbstarken* referred to rock 'n' roll as a form of jazz or otherwise "defamed" jazz (Lange 1996: 187; Poiger 2000: 148–9).

With this outbreak of rowdy behavior, numerous West German commentators expressed concern about what the *Halbstarken* and their musical enthusiasm represented. Their interpretations built upon earlier anxieties expressed by pedagogues and others in relation to jazz. In a 1951 review of Berendt's *Jazz*, for example, the music pedagogue Heinz Kaestner had interpreted jazz as supplying a form of false "flight into the unconscious through intoxication" (1951: 43). Two years later, in a book intended to inform music teachers about jazz, so that they might steer young enthusiasts toward more worthy (and less harmful) musics such as European folk music or *E-Musik*, the former National Socialist music pedagogue Wilhelm Twittenhoff similarly interpreted jazz as being "in its background and its deepest essence magic music" and as representing "an irruption of the magical, the dionysian, nay the subterranean-chaotic" (1953: 5, 73, 111, 112. Cf. Fuchs 2002: 30).

A common theme related to the seemingly machinelike nature of jazz/rock 'n' roll and its reflection of modernity. In a 1956 article, for example, Adolf Theobald saw jazz as a nonintellectual music reflecting the alienated existence of the young city dweller. Its constant, motorlike rhythm corresponded to the monotonous work life of young Germans (1956). A related line was developed by the cultural philosopher Günther Anders in an address at the 1957 Dortmund Jazz Salon titled "Jazz and the self-mechanization of man." That address drew on his 1956 opus, *The Antiquatedness of Man*, which advanced the thesis that modern man had been outstripped by and was subservient to technology. For him, jazz involved "ecstatic sacrificial dances, which are cultically celebrated in honor of the Baal of the machine." Dancers might be genuinely ecstatic, but not in a redemptive sense: they were "'beside themselves,' not in order to unite themselves with the chthonic powers, but rather with the god of the Machine: Industrial Dionysos-Cult" (Zimmerle 1957: 7; Anders qtd. in Miller 1968: 102; and in Dauer 1961b: 195).[1]

Commentators also used their writings on jazz enthusiasm to express broader concerns about postwar West-German materialism. In Theobald's opinion, for example, jazz involuntarily filled a hole in the soul, which was symptomatic of a more general poverty of feeling among postwar West German youth in its drive for material possessions (1956). In another essay from 1956, Helmut Kotschenreuther similarly diagnosed a "loss of the middle" in postwar German mass society. Accordingly, jazz was a form of substitute religion (1956: 202).

In line with the "liberal watchdog" *Weltanschauung*, commentary was often infused by anxieties informed by Germany's National Socialist past. Hence Walter Abendroth and others drew a parallel between the enthusiasm exhibited by jazz fans and that of the National Socialist hordes (Poiger 2000: 95–8). A similar interpretation was advanced by Kotschenreuther, who regarded jazz as placing totalitarian demands on the individual, not unlike the terror exercised by a dictatorship: "[in jazz concerts], fans get 'beside themselves.' Differences in individuality vanish, thinking is extinguished and replaced by a sensual willingness for abandon." In this "mass psychosis," jazz itself became irrelevant: it was simply the "gate through which the fan enters the collective, the hearthwarmth of the anonymous mass" (1956: 199–201). It was little wonder that Kotschenreuther quoted Adorno in support of this interpretation: this style of thinking was clearly indebted to Adorno's views on the authoritarian nature of jazz and the Culture Industry.

The Jazz Recipient and Fascism

Adorno first drew a link between jazz and fascism during the mid-1930s, but also advanced it again during the early 1950s, albeit before the *Halbstarken* riots. The basis for this link was partly the affinity he discerned between jazz and military march music: "the entire arrangement of the jazz orchestra … is identical to that of a military band. Thus jazz can be easily adapted for use by fascism." In order to support his argument he pointed to the functionalization of jazz by fascist Italy. The nominal jazz ban in Nazi Germany, on the other hand, was an exception to the rule, based simply on the Nazis' predilection for precapitalist-feudal aes-

---

1. On German cultural critics' anxieties about technology during the postwar era, see Mausbach 2006: 176 ff.

thetics, and did not prevent the music from continuing to exist under a pseudonym anyway (1936: 485). At heart, jazz enthusiasm reminded him of "the brutal seriousness of the masses of followers in totalitarian states" (1953b: 129). Or, as he put it in 1937, "jazz and the pogrom belong together" (1937: 116).

Adorno's interpretation was based on an analysis of jazz's syncopation and improvisation, and a psychoanalysis of the jazz subject (a term applied to both musician and listener). Syncopation was aimless and, because it was understood to occur before the beat, represented premature ejaculation (1936: 490). Improvisations were "merely ornamental in their significance, and never part of the overall construction or determinant of the form" (1936: 477). The freedom in improvisation was therefore only fictive: "He who is reproducing the music is permitted to tug at the chains of his boredom, and even to clatter them, but he cannot break them" (1936: 480). Effectively, it was this false sense of freedom that prevented the jazz subject from attaining enlightenment.

Psychoanalytically, the jazz subject was therefore understood to have a troubling authoritarian, sadomasochist character trait. Indeed Adorno had no doubt:

> that everything unruly in it [jazz] was from the very beginning integrated into a strict scheme, that its rebellious gestures are accompanied by the tendency to blind obeisance, much like the sado-masochistic type described by analytic psychology, the person who chafes against the father-figure while secretly admiring him, who seeks to emulate him and in turn derives enjoyment from the subordination he overtly detests. (1953b: 122)

This interpretation of jazz keyed in with Adorno's thoroughly pessimistic interpretation of the operation of the Culture Industry, in terms of preventing independent thought in the recipient.

"The Overcoming of a Generational Tragedy Out of the Spirit of Jazz Music"?

There were several—sometimes contradictory—strategies adopted by Berendt to counter critiques such as these. Firstly, like other jazz lobbyists, he made a distinction between the *Swingheinis* and serious, true jazz enthusiasts, who listened to jazz in earnest (see, e.g., 1953a: 203). He also continued to distinguish between "true" jazz and commercialized popular music, including the "primitive" rock 'n' roll associated with the

Halbstarken ("Jazz News" 1958d; Poiger 2000: 149, 257 n.34; Berendt n.d.g.). Finally, Berendt attempted to discredit Adorno's psychoanalysis of the jazz subject. In their 1953 debate, he may have expressed unwillingness to engage in Adorno's interpretation at a philosophical or sociological level, yet he still accused Adorno of stooping to psychoanalysis because he could not appreciate the jazz rhythm's "ingenious combination of force and freedom." He also implied that Adorno's analysis was racist, in that it imposed the sadomasochist trait on the already discriminated-against African American, and he disputed any link between jazz and totalitarianism by pointing out that jazz fans had been hounded both by the Nazis and by Eastern European regimes (1953b). Although he did not do so in his 1953 reply to Adorno, Berendt also sought to revalorize the dionysian enthusiasm of the *Halbstarken/Swingheinis*. His argument here was based in an entrenched critique of Western society, but was actually increasingly consonant with a broader liberal reinterpretation of the *Halbstarken* phenomenon.

By the second half of the 1950s, West German social scientists and politicians increasingly accommodated the consumption of American popular culture by young people. As Poiger observes, conservative sociologists such as Helmut Schelsky and politicians including Chancellor Adenauer's treasurer and successor, Ludwig Erhard, "employed psychological theories to explain rebellious adolescent behavior and to define it as nonpolitical" (2000: 11, 106–36). She places this more relaxed attitude toward the consumption of popular culture within a broader West German "Cold War liberal consensus" (2000: 110). Berendt's writings about jazz enthusiasm and dance ought to be read within that context.

These writings exhibit a distinct ambivalence toward the *Swingheinis/Halbstarken*. He disapproved of their excesses—their "hellish" screaming and blaring on sirens at jazz concerts—which only spoiled the experience for true jazz fans ("Brown" 1953b). Berendt doubtless perceived such behavior—and the way in which it was reported in the press—as damaging the program to establish jazz as high art. In this context, he urged the more serious and sedate jazz enthusiasts to accept the *Swingheinis* into their Hot Clubs. By being accepted rather than excluded, the *Swingheinis* could learn what jazz really was. This would also nip their excesses in the bud (1953a: 203–5; 1956e: 174–5). As Poiger points out, "these ideas had class implications: Berendt wanted jazz fans to shed styles associated with lower-class culture and to assume a more bourgeois demeanor" (2000: 145).

However, Berendt's *Swingheini* discourse had another important dimension. This was revealed both in his understanding of young people's desire to achieve ecstasy through rock 'n' roll and in his ambivalence toward "serious" jazz fans' asceticism (cf. 1955b: 11; 1956e: 173–4; 1959i: 23). For while he disapproved of excessive forms of *Swingheini* behavior, Berendt by no means objected to "enthusiastic participation" ("Brown" 1953b). This stance was part of an attempt to rescue ecstasy and dionysian enthusiasm as legitimate experiences in what Berendt considered a "late" and overly rationalized society. That broader concern played itself out in many locations, including in his 1950 "*time-critical study*" of jazz; in an essay on drug use and ecstasy in the jazz scene (1956e); in his many talks given during the 1950s to church organizations; and also in his attitude toward the tricky matter of jazz dancing.

In 1950, Berendt observed that jazz was only secondarily dance music, yet when one did dance, it was neither society dancing nor mere entertainment but rather "existential escape" (1950a: 14). This attitude was subsequently fully explored in a 1956 essay "Dance as Escape."[2] Here he professed to understand those who danced to jazz, given the highly organized nature of modern society: "young people who live in such a world need an escape from it." Just as he did with the *Swingheini*, Berendt humanized the jazz dancer, who was just participating in a natural process of reaction to a bourgeois world with which (s)he was unable to identify. But there was no cause to be alarmed by this escapism, since it was analogous to the escape into nature favored by the *Wandervögel* ("birds of passage") youth subculture earlier in the century, although he quickly pointed out that dance escapism was not antimodern like the *Wandervögel* had been.[3] Instead, the jazz dancer was firmly anchored in the modern world (1958b: 131).

For Berendt, jazz dancing had broader significance too, even if the dancers may not have been aware of it. Drawing on the Nietzschean juxtaposition of the apollonian, rational art of sculpture and the dionysian, emotional art of music, he interpreted the dancing phenomenon as a counterweight to the unfortunate, progressive suppression of the dionysian since ancient Greece (1958b: 135–6). Jazz dancers signified "a—certainly frequently very uncontrolled [and] necessarily unconscious—escape from a tradition in which it is, at most, only now a literary discovery that there is also a dionysian art and cult experience in addition to an apollonian" (1956e: 172–3). A visit to a jazz club pro-

---

2. This lengthy article was serialized in the *Deutsche Woche* in late 1956 and then published in a volume devoted to the place of dance in modern society (Berendt 1958b).

3. On the perceived reactionary, protofascist nature of the *Wandervogel* movement, see, e.g., Mosse 1975: 133–5; Linke 1991: 46.

vided the enthusiast with a moment of dionysian intoxication that was otherwise missing from his or her systematized life. However, there was no cause for alarm:

> Even where it becomes ecstatic, the enthusiasm "functions." For that reason it can never become orgiastic. It sets in with the first beat of the drummer and ends with his last. One is astounded by oneself when the concert is over. And one is also pleased that one has, in an almost childlike way, shaken things off that are problematic to those who are unable to shake them off in this way. The jazz fan is namely a problem in our problematic world because he insists on not having those problems, which it is practically good form to have. (1956e: 177)

The notion of "authenticity" in jazz, and the immediate expression of unscripted feelings through improvisation could also be related back to Nietzsche's concept of the dionysian, as a reviewer of one of Berendt's 1957 lectures observed. It was this dimension that appealed to young people who opposed the "paralyzed, frozen and schematized Occidental civilization." By neatly paraphrasing the title of Nietzsche's first book, Berendt's reviewer posited the promise of jazz: "The overcoming of a generational tragedy out of the spirit of jazz music" ("Im Jazz" 1957).

This type of interpretation has been explored more recently by John Carvalho and others who have applied Nietzsche, in part to counter Adorno's anti-jazz arguments. Carvalho has sought to demonstrate how modern jazz coincides with Nietzsche's "new aesthetic of music" (as reconstructed by Frederick Love). He argues, for example, that jazz's emphasis on improvisation gives musicians "the special capacity … to give style to the chaotic images and dangerous tendencies swirling around them." Further, "by virtue of its origins, its structures and its sound, [modern jazz] exhibits the … southern affinities" that Nietzsche came to admire in the Mediterranean music of Bizet (1998: 199). He concludes: "had Adorno listened to jazz more for the flute song of Nietzsche's aesthetics than for the percussive march of dialectical or psychoanalytic redemption, he would have heard how wrong he was" (1998: 199). Notwithstanding this, it should be pointed out that Adorno had a distinct aversion for what Steinert calls the "myth of authenticity" and for hopes of a new beginning (1992: 67, 72. Cf., e.g., Adorno 1953a: 893). He may well also have agreed with Günther Anders's assessment that the dionysian ecstasy in jazz was a false one, or with the music pedagogue Heinz Kaestner, who bluntly observed in his review of Berendt's *"time-critical study"*: "we cannot deal with the problem of existence by [applying] magic" (1951: 43).

Jazz and the Churches

An important venue for Berendt's musings on the dionysian aspects of jazz were, curiously enough, the lectures he gave at religious institutions around West Germany between 1954 and 1958. This pastor's son was not the first postwar West German jazz critic to consider jazz from a religious perspective (cf. Zenetti 1953a; 1953b); however he became quite adept at it and the two mainstream churches became another important venue for his jazz proselytizing. Apparently he also found speaking to this audience more rewarding than addressing the jazz scene ("Jazz-Tage einer Evangelischen Akademie" 1954). The churches, which during the late 1940s and early 1950s "seized the moral vacuum left by National Socialism" (Poiger 2000: 46), were also clearly increasingly interested in jazz, despite an apprehension in the early 1950s that a large proportion of German Christians were opposed to the music, viewing it either as an expression of the Godlessness of the current day or as something liable to drive young people wild (Zenetti 1953a; Kahl 1954; Fark 1971: 240).

Chief among the churches' reasons to engage with jazz was a desire to comprehend its attraction to young Germans, in order to then determine what stance to take in relation to it (Kahl 1954; Schmidt-Garre 1954; Fark 1971: 241). However, jazz also represented an opportunity. Though theologians ostensibly resisted the suggestion that jazz could be used for "Christian missionary activities," Berendt's interpretation hinted at ways in which the churches might be able use jazz to bolster their appeal among German young people (Altgelt 1958). He portrayed this as a music with religious roots that offered an authentic, ecstatic "body and soul" experience that might be lacking in the European churches but was alive and well in African American churches—churches that he had had the opportunity to visit on his first trip to the United States in 1950. He interpreted this form of charismatic Christianity as being close to the forms of worship of the first Christians, and by inference more authentic (Kahl 1954; Schmidt-Garre 1954; Berendt and Knesebeck 1955: 82; Berendt 1963e: 452–3).

Particularly as the 1950s progressed, Berendt's church audiences did begin to entertain applying jazz in their work. Some theologians identified it as a useful "heightening of life" (Kahl 1954). Some called for it to be used in youth work ("Korrespondenten berichten" 1958). In 1955, the Evangelical theologian Dr. Heidland saw in it a possibility for the renewal of liturgical forms ("Brown" 1955b). Other more conservative Christians remained skeptical, however, taking the view that attempts to use jazz in church services would not increase the religiousness of young Germans but would damage the churches' credibility and introduce a harmful foreign element (Fark 1971: 241). Finally, some theologians tried to take a balanced view. For example, while advocating that Christianity should learn from jazz, the director of the Catholic Academy of the Diocese of Rottenburg expressed concern in 1958 in relation to the dangers of a lapse into "total emotion" (Schreiber 1958).

Jazz was indeed used in a religious context during the mid- to late 1950s and subsequently (Fark 1971: 240–1). Berendt even had an active hand in fostering some such activities. For the 1955 international music festival in Baden-Baden, for example, he commissioned Heinz Werner Zimmermann, a composer of sacred music who was also inspired by jazz, to compose a "Sacred Concert" for the Edelhagen Big Band ("Jazz News" 1955d; Zimmermann 2002: 183–4).

* * * * *

Berendt's meditations and hopes in relation to jazz sought to make sense of and point ways out of a strong cultural pessimism. From his perspective, jazz offered a "healing moment in the confusion of our times" (qtd. in "Im Jazz" 1957). While it reflected the fracturedness of modern times, it was nevertheless thought to contain the possibility of ordering the disorder of modernity.[4] Adorno et al. might have agreed with Berendt's other conclusion that bodily jazz enthusiasm offered a (brief) escape from the highly rationalized existence of the individual in modern society. However, for them it was a false escape. For his part, Berendt would have agreed with those who claimed that jazz was a *vital* or *emotional* rather than an *intellectual* activity. However, rather than being a frightening gateway to fascist potential, he categorized jazz enthusiasm as far less sinister, even though it was "mindless." His attitude toward jazz enthusiasm was—somewhat paradoxically, given his critique of rationalized modern society and his millenarian predictions if society continued down that path (see, e.g., 1958b: 132)—in tune with the increasingly liberal consensus attitude toward jazz and toward the consumption of American popular culture in 1950s West Germany.

Though he found an interested audience among church organizations during the 1950s, Berendt undoubtedly placed too much hope in the healing potential of jazz. In reviewing his talk to the Protestant Academy of Berlin in February 1958, Erika Altgelt added a refreshing note to the rhetoric expounded by him and other West German jazz publicists: "The world will neither cure itself by means of jazz, as a few gushers seem to assume, nor can one accuse it … that it has not succeeded in doing so over [the last] sixty years" (1958).

---

4. This was indeed a central thesis of the "time-critical study" (1950a: 85).

Even the more modest notion of using jazz to reinvigorate organized religion was, on Berendt's view, unfulfilled: by the early 1960s, he seemed disappointed that the established churches had not learned properly from the jazz lesson. He now expressed skepticism about their superficial attempts to use jazz for proselytizing. What was really needed, he urged, was a more fundamental embrace of the ecstatic and vital (i.e., dionysian) religious experience in the African American Gospel Church (1963e: 452–3; 1966a). This general disappointment with organized religion in Germany no doubt contributed to his subsequent embrace of Eastern spirituality the following decade, which in turn would influence his musical productions.

CHAPTER 3

Jazz Greetings to and from the East?

If Berendt's writings about jazz reflected cultural and spiritual concerns, they also engaged in important, yet complex, ways with West Germany's recent political past, as well as with its infant democracy and with the Cold War. At heart, jazz was characterized as embodying freedom and as being a liberal and inherently democratic art form. These tropes helped draw a distinction between current-day (West) Germany and the Nazi past. Together with the related idea of jazz's internationality, they also played on Cold War ideologies even while they professed not to.

Jazz as True Freedom and the Rhythm of Democracy?

Aware that many bourgeois opponents of jazz regarded its freedom as representing an implicitly dangerous lack of restraint, Berendt was keen to show that the music was actually imbued with what he called a restrained or "true" form of freedom. According to his philosophy, there was a distinct—almost Heideggerean—restriction in true freedom, which was not meaninglessly chaotic but rather possessed a certain form and frame of reference. Jazz's freedom was likewise guided by a frame of reference:

> When improvisation is performed contemporaneously by several musicians—as a "collective"—it does not just represent independence, but also [a] constant reference between the musicians, on the one hand,

and the structure of the tune, on the other hand. The same can be said of the variation principle, which is so essential for jazz music, and of rhythm. (1950a: 41–2)

Discussions about the freedom in jazz also had a political dimension in postwar Germany, which was sometimes made explicit. In 1950, for example, in the midst of his musings on the nature of freedom—in jazz and in general—Berendt observed that from the American perspective, jazz was the most democratic music of the century. He admitted that this was a slogan, yet also observed that there was a grain of truth to it. Citing Alfred Döblin, he asserted that jazz was a "climate" or "era, in which democracy plays itself out" (1950a: 35).[1] For Berendt, jazz's "democratic" dimension was to be found both in its freedom and its deepest rhythmic essence, which was seen to embody the tolerance of opposing standpoints. He drew heavily here upon an idea attributed to the cultural philosopher Rudolf Kassner, namely, that rhythm "understands the dialectical art of bridging opposites, balancing them, mediating them," and is a symbol "of connection, tolerance, and the possibility that opposing opinions can exist side-by-side" (1950a: 31–2). In watchdog fashion, he also pointedly observed that Germans frequently lacked this rhythmic dimension (1950a: 92–3).

In this way jazz was cast as the ideal soundtrack to the postwar democratization and liberalization of West Germany. The pairing of jazz with a democratic mindset was advanced not only in *Jazz: A Time-Critical Study*, but also, in a somewhat schoolmasterly fashion, in various other locations, including in relation to *Die Gondel*'s 1952 readers' poll as well as in his appeals to sectarian West German jazz enthusiasts to "get" the "jazz message" and tolerate those with taste preferences different from their own.

Jazz Polling and Sectarianism: Democracy on Trial

In August 1952—exactly three years after the first federal election—*Die Gondel* announced the inaugural German jazz poll. The principle, borrowed from jazz magazines published elsewhere, including the United States where such things had existed since the 1930s, was straightforward: readers were to nominate their favorite musicians, and a German "All-Star" orchestra would then be assembled to make a recording. This recording would do important work: it would be evidence to the world

---

1. In the postwar years, Berendt had professional contact with Döblin, who was also associated with the SWF (Berendt 1996a: 42, 293, 451).

that jazz in Germany was no worse than elsewhere in Europe! ("Brown" 1952a: 62).

The way in which the poll proceeded, however, was not entirely happy. In his commentary, "Brown" (a.k.a. Berendt) implied that the presidents of certain Hot Clubs had attempted to get their members to vote *en bloc* (in protest against the "commercial" choices which it was anticipated other *Gondel* readers would make). He queried whether such a president might not be "a little 'dictator'" and singled out the president of the Koblenz Jazz Club, who had threatened that his Club members would stop subscribing if certain musicians won the poll: "Does one know so little about the idea of a poll, that one has forgotten that such a "musical democracy" [as jazz] requires generosity and tolerance even when one is not in agreement... ?" (1952c: 60). Several months later, "Brown" also accused Alfred Baresel, the older German jazz critic—and hence his rival—of authoritarian thought patterns. Baresel had proposed that, rather than *Gondel* readers selecting the German "All-Stars," a panel of German jazz experts should do so. "Brown" noted acerbically: "[so then] each year the *Gondel* will [have to] ask Mr *Reichs*- (Sorry!) Mr. Federal Jazzdirector, whom Baresel's number-ones are" (1953c).

Enthusiasts were also "encouraged" to be tolerant and desist from indulging in sectarian (or what Berendt simply called "ideological") behavior. This occurred within the context of vehement disputes between "moldy fig" "trad" jazz enthusiasts and "sour grape" fans of modern jazz, which racked the jazz scene in Germany just as they did elsewhere in the jazz world (cf., e.g., Gendron 1995). Although he himself had a constitutional interest in avant-garde styles and thought modern jazz enthusiasts less ideological than the "trad" enthusiasts, he urged his readers to understand jazz as a "whole" and to tolerate all styles from its history (Berendt 1952g; 1953a: 206–8; 1956e: 108–9; "Brown" 1952b). This too was a trope that was advanced by American jazz scholars, including Marshall Stearns (Gennari 2006: 152).

Despite this doctrine of tolerance, however, Berendt's behavior in relation to some of his critics—and, in particular, his messy clash with Dr. Leo Waldick of the Düsseldorf Hot Club in 1954—suggests another story: that of an increasingly powerful critic, vigorously guarding his post (and his reputation) in the field.

Criticizing the Jazz Pope

The dispute with Dr. Waldick began as a mere difference of opinion about the measure of success enjoyed by the Kurt Edelhagen Orchestra (then in the employ of the SWF) at the Salon International du Jazz in Paris in May 1954. Berendt had introduced the group in Paris and broadcast the performance on the SWF. Then, in a *Jazz Podium* review, Waldick made a point of disagreeing with a certain "someone" who had labeled the performance an outstanding success (1954a: 9). Although he was not expressly mentioned, Berendt quickly responded by disputing Waldick's account and calling for objective journalism (1954f). Not to be outdone, Waldick retaliated by "criticizing the critic," which he justified on the basis of Berendt's position of authority within the jazz scene (i.e., because readers were inclined to take what he said at face value). He queried the soundness of Berendt's evidence for the Orchestra's success. Moreover, he inferred that Berendt had misled readers by a selective quotation of reviews and opened up the question of journalistic dishonesty (1954b).

As this debate raged in the pages of *Jazz Podium*, Berendt was also engaged in a telling behind-the-scenes counterattack. Considering that Dieter Zimmerle, the editor of *Jazz Podium*, was the person really responsible for the controversy, Berendt first of all refused to make further contributions to the magazine and threatened the editor of the Viennese parent newspaper with a media campaign should Zimmerle continue with his troublemaking (Berendt 1954c; 1954d; 1954e). After Waldick's sharp critique (and given that Zimmerle wished to give Waldick the last word), Berendt also engaged lawyers to threaten defamation proceedings (Berendt 1954d; Schrimpf 1954; Ziegler 1954). Although he was prepared to compromise a little, Berendt rejected the intercessions of those members of the jazz scene who—in order to head off a potentially scandalous court case—proposed a joint "goodwill" statement from the parties and a panel of jazz experts (Berendt 1954d; 1954e; Buchholtz 1954). By continuing to threaten legal action, he ultimately obtained from Waldick a public declaration that he had not intended to belittle Berendt's reputation, although Waldick did not retract, in as many words, his inference about Berendt's misleading readers (Berendt 1954e; cf Waldick 1954d).[2]

Berendt's actions in this dispute not only reveal a critic keen to maintain his reputation and position of authority but also call into question his rhetoric of tolerance of opposing opinions. On the other hand, Waldick's action, as well as *Jazz Podium*'s coverage of both sides of the debate and its encouragement of readers to make up their own mind about

---

2. This solution represented a compromise for both men: Waldick also wanted Berendt to apologize for having slandered him (Waldick 1954c), something that Berendt found preposterous (1954e), and Berendt wanted Waldick to retract expressly the suggestion of a conscious misleading of readers (Berendt 1954d).

it, indicate that regardless of Berendt's concern about the survival of authoritarian or "ideological" behavior within the jazz scene, free-thinking, democratic patterns were indeed in existence ("Das Forum" 1954).

Dictators Don't Swing: Jazz, Resistance, and Postwar Moralizing

An important plank in Berendt's association of jazz with democracy was his notion that rhythm was inconsistent with the aesthetic feeling of the dictator (see, e.g., 1950a: 32). In the 1953 debate with Adorno, for example, he elaborated:

> Is Adorno's sense so poorly equipped that he is unable to detect how this music "inoculates" completely safely against all varieties of totalitarianism with each jazz beat? Did one ever see a functionary or miltarist who was simultaneously a jazz fan? Where does this deeply rooted disinclination of all the military against jazz come from? (1953b: 890)

In one fell swoop, jazz became the opposite of totalitarianism and, by extension, the jazz enthusiast was rendered antifascist. Berendt's rhetorical questions may have been characteristically (and polemically) overstated. Their tenor was not, however, atypical for the postwar West German jazz lobby, including when representing itself in the international press (see, e.g., Berendt 1957f: 35. Cf. Hoffmann 1994: 84).

This interpretation was hardly pulled from thin air, given that National Socialist ideologues did have an official aversion to jazz. As we will see, there were also groups of German jazz enthusiasts who were subjected to Nazi chicanery during the "Third Reich" and who took up an oppositional position toward the regime. From a sociopsychological point of view, the postwar attitude is also thoroughly understandable: it offered the jazz enthusiast a way of drawing a distinction between him- or herself and the Nazi past, and provided comfort at a time when many Germans continued to reject jazz. More critically, Bernd Hoffmann calls this a "collective exculpation strategy" (1994: 83). He argues that such blanket statements long hindered a differentiated historical analysis of jazz under National Socialism from taking place (Hoffmann 1994: 84–5).

The relation between jazz and fascism was indeed more complex than some postwar jazz publicists would have had their audiences believe. This is evident both in the way in which the National Socialist regime dealt with jazz and in the way in which musicians and enthusiasts interacted with the regime. As observed in chapter 1, the opposition to jazz by National Socialist ideologues was ostensibly clear-cut, yet various exigencies ensured that Goebbels' actual policies were ambivalent, with jazz and jazzlike music actually being accommodated and functionalized. Furthermore, at the individual level, Berendt's supposedly absurd notion of a jazz-loving militarist was not all that far-fetched.[3]

As Michael Kater's research shows, there *were* individuals who could indeed accommodate membership of the NSDAP, SS, or SA with a love of jazz (1992: 98–101; 1994: 76). The opportunist musicians who played "propaganda jazz" for the Nazis—hot jazz recordings which were combined with anti-British lyrics and broadcast to tempt British soldiers to defect—could also hardly be classified as resistance fighters, and while there might have been individual exceptions among jazz enthusiasts, Kater concludes that the "ideal type of a person who predicated his or her active involvement in the jazz culture on a pronounced antagonism to the Nazi regime—never existed in the flesh" (1992: 96. Cf. Jost 1988a: 365–6). Even members of the famous "Swing Youth," who formed regional countercultures during the "Third Reich" and were persecuted by the authorities, did not necessarily *initially* view their behavior as oppositional to the regime. The Swings' steadfast refusal to join the Hitler Youth or comply with bans on Swing dancing often started out as hedonist and nonconformist and only became politicized over time, as a result of Gestapo persecution (Kater 1992: 153–62; Fackler 1996: 64). Kater notes that for some this process was only complete when they found themselves incarcerated (1992: 162). As he concludes, "jazz proves to have possessed an ambiguous potential for resistance against the ... Third Reich" (1994: 78. See also Fackler 1994: 468–9).

Jazz and Domestic Politics

Notwithstanding their undifferentiated nature, "jazz = democracy" and "dictators don't swing" were powerful political tropes in West Germany, particularly after public concerns about the dangers of jazz to young people had been assuaged. For various publicists and politicians, "jazz came to symbolize the new pluralist society espoused increasingly by West German politicians in the second half of the 1950s" (Poiger 2000: 166). By 1957, the music had been used by both major West German

---

3. He was in fact confounded on just this point in 1958, when the West German Defense Minister Franz Josef Strauß proposed a jazz band within the Bundeswehr. In this controversy, Berendt ostensibly clung to his binary opposites of "jazz" and "military"; however, he also took the opportunity to sell an article on jazz to the Bundeswehr itself (Berendt 1958c; Hund 1958; Poiger 2000: 166–7).

political parties as a way of attracting youth votes (Berendt 1957f: 35; R. Willett 1989: 91). For example, in 1956 the SPD financed the Berlin leg of the "Jazz and Old Music" tour ("Jazz News" 1955f; 1956b; Berendt and Tröller 1959: 162). Future SPD chancellor Willy Brandt also used jazz during campaigning in Berlin in the 1950s (Kater 1992: 209; Poiger 2000: 167).

An August 1958 interview given by the West German Defense Minister Franz Josef Strauß (initiated by Berendt, as press consultant for the DJF) indicated how even the conservative CDU/CSU coalition government used the "dictators don't swing" trope. Echoing Berendt's own discourse, Strauß used the notion to distinguish between his own government and the "Third Reich" (as well as East Germany):

> [The totalitarian governmental systems] see in jazz an inimical, destructive element. ... Of course, we experienced that in the Third Reich. Verily the "free elements" of jazz do not get on well with the regimentation that totalitarian governmental systems care to apply. With its individual musicality, its *joy* in improvisation, its *freedom* to have many forms, and its *power* to build communities of the like-minded, jazz does not fit the picture, according to which the dictators wish to change the world by brutal force. (qtd. in Berendt 1958c)

As Strauss's use of the present tense makes clear, the "dictators don't swing" trope was not just useful in distinguishing between postwar West Germany and its past—it was also especially useful within the context of the Cold War.

Jazz in the Soviet Zone

British Field Marshall Montgomery apparently once remarked that if it were not possible to conquer the communist east with weapons, then it would be possible to do so with the jazz trumpet (Noglik 1994: 149). After the hardening of the Cold War in the late 1940s, Eastern-bloc cadres also began to excoriate jazz as an agent of American cultural imperialism. Just as Germany became a hot spot in the Cold War, jazz also now served as a site of cultural contestation.

The U.S. Information Service (USIS) and State Department were quick to recognize the productivity of the "jazz = democracy" trope and actively promoted the ideology. From 1945, the USIS broadcast international "Voice of America" (VOA) radio programs, which contained some jazz. In 1955, VOA host Willis Conover also started a jazz program directed at young Soviets (Starr 1994: 210, 243–4; Kofsky 1998: 189–94).

Then from 1956 the State Department also began to send so-called "Jazz Ambassadors" on tours of the communist and unaligned world (Von Eschen 2004). It did so with clear political aims. As a cultural affairs officer at the U.S. embassy in Moscow put it in 1956: "The whole business of jazz was a political question, not cultural" (qtd. in Starr 1994: 244). Conover also candidly admitted in 1965 that "our music helps maintain contact with people already inclined to sympathize with the United States" (qtd. in Kofsky 1998: 190). Under the circumstances, the Marxist historian and jazz critic Frank Kofsky labeled jazz a "Cold War secret weapon" (1998: 189). By the late 1950s, jazz had also become an ideal Cold War weapon within Germany. The reasons for this included that psychologists no longer viewed jazz enthusiasm with anxiety, that German audiences were inclined to take jazz "seriously" and, importantly, that jazz was subject to suppression in the East (Poiger 2000: 163).

This suppression has a relatively complicated history, however. As Frederick Starr and others have shown, Eastern European communist regimes, including the German Democratic Republic (GDR), alternated between denigrating jazz as an agent of U.S. cultural imperialism and accommodating it (Starr 1994: 204–34, 261–75; Noglik 1996; Poiger 2000: 150–62). After a period of grace in the first few years after the war, the situation hardened with the Berlin Blockade, and the music was subjected to an ideological clampdown in the early 1950s (Lange 1996: 198; Poiger 2000: 150). Characteristic of this campaign were the East German musicologist Ernst H. Meyer's words in his 1952 book, *Musik im Zeitgeschehen* (*Music in the events of the day*): "The present-day 'Boogie-Woogie' is a conduit through which the barbarianizing poison of Americanization intrudes and threatens to anaesthetize the brains of the workers. This threat is just as dangerous as a military attack with poison gases" (qtd. in Noglik 1996: 208). Subsequent turns in the Cold War, such as the June 1953 uprising in East Berlin or the unrest in Hungary in 1956, brought about ideological changes in tack in relation to jazz. Even after the construction of the Berlin Wall in August 1961 staunched the flow of young Easterners to the West and the regime could afford a thaw, the cultural politics of the SED toward jazz and other Western popular culture continued to be characterized by ambivalence (Goodbody, Tate, and Wallace 1995: 172 ff; Noglik 1996: 209 ff).

Within these shifting cultural politics, attempts were made by East German enthusiasts, in particular Reginald Rudorf, to carve out an "authentic" folk jazz (as opposed to "commercial" modern jazz) which might be acceptable to cultural cadres. Such efforts were tolerated by the regime for a time, but were then subjected to recrimination—Rudorf was imprisoned for two years in 1957—when the Communist Party changed its tack (Rudorf 1964; Poiger 2000: 150–62). Part of the problem was that jazz presented an unresolvable ideological dilemma for the Eastern bloc. As Martha Bayles succinctly points out in relation to earlier debates in the Soviet Union: "[jazz] sprang from an extremely oppressed people in an extremely capitalist country. The dilemma for the Party, therefore, was whether to praise jazz as the rallying cry of the black masses, or to denounce it as a tool of capitalist domination" (1994: 74).

Berendt's Jazz Greetings To and From the East

In many ways, Berendt was an enthusiastic Cold Warrior. As the debate with Adorno demonstrates, he happily used the repression of jazz in East Germany as a strand in his "dictators don't swing" argument (cf. Berendt 1953b: 890). However, he did not stop there. During the 1950s, he was a keen reporter on the East German campaigns against jazz (see, e.g., Berendt 1952g; 1952h; 1956a 17; n.d.d.). Articles also lampooned the GDR's efforts to promote a "new progressive dance music" in its stead (1952h; n.d.d.; "Brown" 1955a). He drew attention to the Eastern European jazzmen who defected to the West in protest, and, in 1955, he attacked Reginald Rudorf's attempt to bill "true" jazz as the music of the Afro-American victims of capitalism (1952h; "Brown" 1955a; Berendt 1965f). Berendt was also peripherally involved in the activities of the USIS and the State Department. In 1960, he contributed two programs to Willis Conover's "Jazz Hour" on the VOA ("Jazz News" 1961a). His lengthy 1960 trip to the United States was also intended to be cofunded by the State Department, yielding a documentary to be shown by the SWF in West Germany and then distributed elsewhere in the world by the State Department. For unknown reasons, however, the State Department withdrew its support, which caused *Downbeat* to lament the loss of a film that would have "constituted excellent public relations for America" ("Berendt dreht Jazzfilm in den USA" 1959; "Überraschend abgesagt" 1959; "Joachim Berendt's American Journey" 1960).

Nevertheless, Berendt's activities extended beyond commenting on the repression of jazz in the Eastern bloc or opportunistically working for the USIS: he also took a keen interest promoting the music of Eastern-bloc musicians, writing (often hard-won) articles about them, making broadcasts and recordings with them, and extending invitations to them to perform in the West. His motivations to do so were complex. In 1981, he asserted that this work was altruistic (1981c: 23). However, Berendt was also partly motivated by a desire to establish himself as *the* West German expert in Eastern European jazz and by the prospect of marketing his jazz publications in the East (Berendt 1996a: 317; Wunderlich 2004). It is also likely that Berendt felt some moral obligation to foster the Eastern European jazz scenes. In this respect, he may well have been influenced by the (Cold War–tinged) sentiment of the director of the Frankfurt *Amerika-Haus*, whose May 1953 address at the inaugural German Jazz Festival he quoted at length in *Die Gondel:*

> We know that during the Nazi era and also now in the Soviet Zone of Germany an underground movement has developed which is secretly supporting jazz. This is just proof that there are people around the whole world who will not allow themselves to be forbidden their art and who are defending themselves against the regimentation of their lives. They are the people to whom those of us who are lucky enough to live in a free civilization must give our support. ("Brown" 1953a: 63)

Certainly, Berendt's writings from the late 1950s reveal a sense that the set-upon Eastern-bloc musicians were in an analogous position to German jazz enthusiasts during and after the "Third Reich" and therefore deserving of all the assistance possible (see, e.g., 1957e; 1957g). However, he was also influenced by guilt in relation to Germany's—and his own—recent past in Eastern Europe. As he noted in his autobiography, whenever he came into contact with musicians from Leningrad, for example, he was always particularly accommodating toward them, imagining that they might have been in the city at the time when he and his army were bombarding it during World War II (1996a: 399). This complex cocktail of guilt, altruism, and ambition can also be detected in his crucial experience of the 1957 Jazz Festival in Sopott (Poland), which formed the foundation for his later activities promoting Eastern European jazz.

Jazz Builds Bridges

In July 1957, a West German contingent including the Joki Freund Quintet from Frankfurt am Main, the Spree City Stompers from Berlin and several DJF luminaries attended the Polish Jazz Festival in Sopott, a town on the outskirts of Gdansk (formerly Danzig). The festival was the second to be held there since a thaw in the mid-1950s had rendered jazz ideologically acceptable (Berendt 1957e; 1981c; "Polish Writer Calls for More Jazz Diplomacy" 1966). The impetus for the West German attendance came from Werner Wunderlich, the DJF's "Poland consultant," who had learned Polish during a four-and-a-half-year stint in a prisoner of war camp and who had been approached by the Polish *Jazz* magazine to attend with his own amateur group. After much lobbying, Wunderlich persuaded Joki Freund and his colleagues to go instead. At this point, Berendt approached Wunderlich and asked to join the contingent (Wunderlich 1987; 2004; Paulot 1993: 42–4; Schwab 2004: 125–6). From the German perspective, the trip was momentous, not only because it was among the first international tours by a group of West German jazz musicians (cf. Reiniger 1983: 66–7) but also because of the location.

Freund's trombonist Albert Mangelsdorff approached the trip with a sense of guilt, only too aware of what Germans had done in Poland during World War II (Paulot 1993: 42; Schwab 2004: 126). Another member of the party, Olaf Hudtwalcker—a Frankfurt am Main broadcaster and the DJF's president—felt distinctly uncomfortable when the group arrived in Kunowicze, as he tried to remember "whether old Fritz had won or lost a battle here back in his day" (Hudtwalcker 1957: 5). Berendt also had a bad conscience on the trip (Berendt 1981c). Despite the general trepidation, the reception was overwhelmingly positive. Leopold Tyrmand, a Polish writer and jazz enthusiast, celebrated the occasion as one of the first genuine cultural contacts between Polish and German young people in almost twenty years (Hudtwalcker 1957; Berendt 1981c). Mangelsdorff, who also participated in various jam sessions with Polish musicians, considered the warm reception he received as among the finest moments in his career (Paulot 1993: 43; Schwab 2004: 126). The experience was also beneficial for the Polish musicians, whose exposure to jazz during the recently ended era of repression— what they called the "catacomb" period—had been largely restricted to listening to the VOA as well as to German broadcasts (Berendt 1957g; Paulot 1993: 43). For these reasons, the German attendance at Sopott has subsequently been called a "key experience for the whole Polish jazz scene" and a new beginning in German-Polish jazz history (Paulot 1993: 44; Schwab 2004: 126).

The trip was also particularly productive for Berendt. Aside from broadcasting the festival on SWF and writing several articles about it, he established contacts with various Polish musicians, whom he subsequently invited to perform and record in West Germany (Hudtwalcker 1957; Schwab 2004: 126).[4] In 1965 he also included a quota of Polish

---

4. His first invitation was extended in August 1957 to the pianist Andrzej Kurylewicz to perform at the German Radio Exhibition in Stuttgart. He later invited the pianist Kryzsztof Komeda—subsequently to gain fame as Roman Polanski's film composer of choice—to West Germany. Berendt worked with Komeda on several projects, and also championed the saxophonist Zbigniew Namyslowski, another Pole who went on to find international fame (Berendt 1965a; 1981c). In 1961, he invited the bassist Roman Dylag

jazz on *Jazz Greetings from the East*, a landmark record compilation of Eastern European jazz. These invitations continued with a vengeance after Berendt was appointed artistic director of the Berlin Jazz Days in 1964 (see chapter 5).

Philosophically, Berendt took from Sopott a sense that jazz was an important force in liberalizing the Eastern bloc: following Tyrmand, he even asserted that jazz was a "bloodless Poznan [where an uprising took place in October 1956]" (1957e; 1981c). Accordingly, the Eastern European jazz scene was a social movement that German enthusiasts should support. Recalling the postwar bandstand fraternizing between American troops and German jazzmen, Berendt urged that jazz was a congenial medium for bridging social and political divides and encouraged West German enthusiasts to take up correspondence with their counterparts in the Eastern bloc (1957e; "Jazz News" 1957d). Even if fans could not understand each other too well linguistically, jazz's "universal" essence would come to the rescue.

Jazz Is Universal?

> In the final analysis, jazz is a universal language—perhaps the first truly [sic] universal of our time. (Berendt 1964d)

As early as 1950, Berendt advanced the idea that, apart from technology, there was nothing as "international" as jazz (1950a: 47). Hence, there were no national varieties of jazz: "That is ... the good thing about jazz, that there is neither German nor Chinese nor I-don't-know-what [jazz], but always only good or bad" (1955b). This international—or as it was often stated "universal"—trope was also advanced by Marshall Stearns in the United States, including in the context of the State Department's Jazz Ambassador tours, and was shared by many postwar jazz writers, American, German and otherwise (cf. Starr 1994: 210; Poiger 2000: 165; Gennari 2006: 150ff). It was based partly on jazz's undeniable appeal around the globe, vociferous opposition notwithstanding. Indeed, in this context UNESCO even took an active interest in the possibilities of using jazz as a medium for international dialogue, setting up in 1952 an International Federation of Jazz, of which Berendt was the West German delegate (Berendt 1952c; Soufflot 1952).

---

to participate in a group he was assembling for the Berlin Jazz Salon, but the Polish Government refused to grant Dylag a visa (Berendt 1961d). In 1964 he invited Polish musicians to participate in the SWF session at the German Jazz Festival in Frankfurt.

The international personnel of various big bands of the late 1950s and early 1960s also prompted jazz writers to have recourse to jazz's "universality." Particular candidates included the Kurt Edelhagen Orchestra—especially after it transferred in 1957 to the WDR in Cologne[5]—and the Kenny Clarke–Francy Boland Big Band, whose debut 1961 album was even titled *Jazz is Universal*. Tags such as these may have been heartfelt or programmatic; but they could also be a marketing ploy. When, in 1958, the American impresario George Wein assembled an international youth jazz band to play at the Newport Jazz Festival, for example, he intended this "Tower of Babel Band" to "foster a sense of cross-cultural unity, employing the universal language of music," although as he observed in his memoir, this was also a shrewd tactic to publicize the festival throughout the world (2003: 183). In Germany, "Joe Brown" (a.k.a. Berendt) also assiduously propagated the view that this Newport Youth Band was "a symbol of the collegial character of jazz music" (1958).

Berendt's embrace of jazz's internationality was clearly influenced by the broader American discourse, but also inflected by the characteristic West German liberal opposition to nationalism. He did not simply parrot an imported notion. Rather, he Germanized it by investing jazz with a suitably cleansed Romantic program. This resuscitation of one of (early) Romanticism's projects represented a positive dimension of Berendt's thoroughly ambivalent relationship with Romanticism, the negative dimension of which has been explored in chapter 1. Hence, in 1950, he seized upon the internationality of jazz as allowing a continuation of the task set for music during the German Romantic era, but which, paradoxically, Romantic music had been unable to deliver:

> Music was regarded not only by Romanticism's musicians but also its poets and philosophers as the most important of the arts, which had the task of uniting all peoples of the earth in the same universally understood language. (1950a: 46)

According to Berendt, Romantic music not only became ideologically beleaguered and nationalistic but also neglected rhythm, which undermined its appeal to non-Europeans.[6] And since jazz—like the music of

---

5. In 1957 Berendt and the *Jazz Echo* dubbed the orchestra "almost a symbol of jazz's internationality" and a "UN in Jazz" (Berendt 1957f; "Jazz News" 1957b).

6. On the notion of music as a "universal language" favored by humanist and Enlightenment thinkers, see, e.g., Blume 1979: 28–9. He too observes that Romanticism eventually ended up emphasizing national differences and thus impinged upon cosmopolitan and humanist ideals (1979: 176).

"primitive" peoples—gave primacy to rhythm, it held the key to universal musical understanding and to the realization of the Romantic hypothesis of music as a universal language (1950a: 45–7).

Besides the neo-Romantic project, which writers such as Berendt invested in the "jazz is universal" trope, it had a clear Cold War political value too. For the VOA's Willis Conover it was consonant with the aims of the U.S. State Department to win over foreign hearts and minds through popular culture (Conover 1961). Other American commentators were quite frank about the matter, too: one observed in 1955, for example, that "American jazz has now become a universal language. It knows no national boundaries, *but everyone knows where it comes from and where to look for more*" (qtd. in Kofsky 1998: 189; my emphasis). In the cover notes for a 1963 recording by the Clarke–Boland Big Band, another pointed out that jazz might be "the universal language of our time" but it clearly had an American accent—it was a *"lingua americana"* ("Clarke–Boland Big Band *Big Band*" cov. notes 1963). For the VOA's producer, Tahir Hakki Sur, the Clarke–Boland Big Band was even the musical equivalent of the "Multi Lateral Force" proposed by NATO (Sur 1963).

By the late 1950s, German politicians also drew on the trope when criticizing the illiberalism of the GDR. For example, in his August 1958 interview with Berendt, Defence Minister Strauß observed that:

> Everyone [knows] the supranational character of jazz and the fact that jazz friends around the world are a "one big family." Totalitarian systems of government only refrain from making use of the repression of jazz at times when it seems opportune to display a "more liberal" attitude to the outside world. Then jazz—or what is understood to be jazz—is abused for propaganda purposes, in order to use enthusiasm for jazz as a political alibi. (qtd. in Berendt 1958c)

* * * * *

During the 1950s, jazz was laden with considerable political baggage by its publicists, as well as by its Eastern-bloc opponents. In the West, it was a music of democratic tolerance and even antifascism, equidistant from the evils of the National Socialist past and the totalitarian regimes of the Eastern bloc. While these tags were useful in the context of legitimating jazz and offered a comforting way of distinguishing between the present and the recent past, they tended to be overstated. Rhetoric about the international, "universal" nature of jazz also fed into and drew upon Western Cold War tropes and was political, even when it appeared not to be. However, these tropes—together with Berendt's ambition and the guilt associated with the National Socialist past—primed him to encourage and promote Eastern-bloc musicians in the West, which undoubtedly ranks as a significant achievement. As he began to travel further afield in the 1960s and 1970s, similar motivations also began to drive his championing of other jazz scenes too, as part 3 will show. All of these activities were soon to bear important musical fruit.

CHAPTER 4

Jazz, Race, and Colorblindness

> One encounters [the racial problem] constantly whenever one is thinking or writing about jazz.
> —J. E. Berendt, from his papers at the Jazzinstitut, 1956

Uta Poiger has observed that "'race' has hardly been a category of analysis in histories of the German post-Nazi period," which is no doubt partly a result of the fact that "race" became a taboo in Germany after 1945 (2000: 7. Cf. Sieg 2002: 2). However, jazz discourse offers a perspective on the ways in which race *was* able to be discussed in postwar West Germany, despite the taboo. The role race played, particularly within Berendt's writings, was nevertheless a highly complicated and paradoxical one, incorporating both a romantic essentialization of difference and a humanist desire to transcend that difference.

Berendt on U.S. Racial Discrimination

Berendt did not discuss race only within the context of the jazz scene. Charged in particular by his experiences in the United States in 1950 while participating in the Cultural Exchange Program and researching the *Jazzbook*, he also wrote on racial discrimination and the civil rights movement. This is not surprising given the way in which various of Berendt's counterparts in the United States, going back to the critic and producer John Hammond, combined an interest in jazz with a solid commitment to the civil rights movement (see, e.g., Gennari 2006). Berendt actually became something of a minor authority on the matter, contributing articles in the early to mid-1950s to respected West German print media including *Der Spiegel* (1952), *Merkur* (1952), the *Frankfurter Hefte* (1955), and the *Frankfurter Allgemeine Zeitung* (1956). These articles drew attention to segregation, discrimination, and inequality as well as to the manner in which some progress was being made (Berendt 1952e; 1955e; 1955f). Perhaps even preempting his American colleagues, Berendt also identified the racial discrimination suffered by jazz musicians (see, e.g., 1952b; 1956b; 1960c).[1] He felt that the jazz world threw racial issues into particularly sharp focus, given the debates that existed about whether whites were able to play jazz as well as blacks, and whether they had any right to do so (1956b).

From the security of an outsider's vantage point, Berendt gave vent to a range of African American attitudes toward discrimination, civil rights, and the cultural ownership of jazz, including more strident views. For example, in his 1953 *Jazzbook*, he quoted an unnamed Californian musician who told him that the stylistic development of jazz was a result of African Americans needing to keep one step ahead of the white musicians who were constantly copying them (1953a: 93–5). However, in keeping with both the mainstream civil rights movement of the day and his own liberal philosophy, Berendt gave his approval to "calmer" approaches. His articles on discrimination favored the "nonviolent good will direct action" position taken by the NAACP, or what he himself called "a calm overcoming of the differences" (1955e: 798. See also 1955f: 739 ff). This approach was in keeping with what he saw as the essential "unshakeable calmness of the [Negro] race" (1952e: 197). Later, in the early 1960s, he also expressed regret at the militant turn taken by black jazzmen, which had the tragic effect of excluding white musicians from their circle (1962j: 41).[2]

Berendt's model for the overcoming of racial discrimination also had a distinct sexual dimension, although given the sexual mores of the 1950s, this was expressed in a somewhat oblique way. In his articles, he paid attention both to the interracial romantic encounter and to the possibility of the offspring of such encounters ultimately "passing" for white (see, e.g., Berendt 1952e: 197–8).[3] In a 1952 *Spiegel* cover story

---

1. Charley Gerard notes that the American critic Nat Hentoff (in 1959–60) was one of the first critics to break the silence about racial prejudice in jazz (1998: xv).

2. We will return to Berendt's attitudes on this matter in chapter 15.

3. A draft of this article contains further unpublished passages dealing with the eroticized relationship between whites and blacks in the United States (1952f). See also Berendt 1955g: 33–4.

about the "café au lait" singer Lena Horne, for example, he noted how she had supported interracial "mixing" in a number of ways, not least in her marriage to a white man (1952b). In his 1996 memoir, Berendt expressly elaborated upon the link between the interracial sexual encounter—which, of course, had been anathema to Nazi ideologues—and his utopian post-racist vision: "We—particularly the Europeans—considered it an antiracist act when we slept with black women; we thought

Figure 4 | "Café au lait beauty" Lena Horne graces the cover of *Der Spiegel* in 1952. © *Der Spiegel*. Used with permission.

that in this way we were contributing to forming a new mankind, in which there were no more races" (1996a: 106).

At this point, at the very latest, it is necessary to make some observations about Berendt's sexual life. Married four times, he makes no secret in his autobiography and elsewhere that he also enjoyed numerous relationships, extramarital and otherwise.[4] William Claxton, with whom Berendt traveled around the United States for three months in 1960, observes that one of Berendt's "vices" was a desire "to meet young 'schwarze girls' … with the idea of dating them. He considered them so beautiful and exotic" (2005: 28). For his part, Claxton felt compelled to warn him:

> this was not a good idea. The civil rights movement had not yet begun, and one had to be very careful about such relationships. Being a visiting European was not novel enough to escape a possible bad scene and put a quick end to our relatively innocent jazz-seeking trip. (2005: 28)

Berendt was not simply interested in the sexual encounter at a private, if perhaps erotomanic, level; later in life, he also published a short piece in *Mein Heimliches Auge*, an erotica yearbook, (Berendt 1985d; Rüsenberg 2004). These are not simply titillating details. As can be seen here, and as will also be demonstrated elsewhere, Berendt's cultural theories often had a sexualized dimension, which cannot be easily removed from his personal libertinism.

While on the subject of Berendt's private life, it is also worthy of note that his mother Frieda left his father when he was only three years old, and that prior to his father's death in Dachau, he and his rather stern father had a strained relationship, disagreeing over various things, including the younger Berendt's interest in jazz (Berendt 1996a). It is possible that Berendt's sensitivity to criticism, which for one of his critics bordered on a persecution anxiety, related to the sense of abandonment he must have felt as a result of his father's untimely death and his mother's estrangement (Kumpf 2007). Berendt's only child, Christian, born in 1949 to his first wife, Inge, died at a relatively young age in 1978. The guilt that Berendt in turn felt toward his son, based on his own failings as a parent, is palpable in his autobiography (1996a: 403ff).

---

4. Berendt married Inge, his first wife, in 1949. He was divorced from her in 1957. He married his second wife, Gigi, in the early 1960s and then divorced her several years later. He was married to Vera in the late 1960s and 1970s. He married his fourth wife, Jadranka, in 1988. As he observes in his memoir, he regularly engaged in extramarital relationships during his first two marriages (1996a: 424 ff. See also Berendt 1985d).

Postwar Jazz Interest as Philosemitism?

The historian Frank Stern, who has examined the phenomena of anti-Semitism and philosemitism in postwar West Germany, observes that the philosemitic gesture involved publicly disavowing the anti-Semitism of the past—and indeed inverting it—and thereby seeking to make amends for the Holocaust. Stern shows that, in the postwar era, philosemitism unintentionally instrumentalized the Jewish people's suffering as a way of assisting the Federal Republic's political integration into the West (1992). During the 1950s, this philosemitic gesture was also reflected in quite complex ways in various West German debates, attitudes and cultural practices about a range of other ethnic Others.

Tina Campt and her colleagues have shown, for example, how a generation of Afro-German children—offspring of African American GIs and German women—who entered school in the early 1950s, were also functionalized in a philosemitic-like way. By analyzing parliamentary debates about the schooling deemed appropriate for these children, they reveal how West German politicians anxiously regarded the treatment of the children as being a beacon to the world of the Federal Republic's political maturity and democratic progress, and as being "an opportunity to work off some of the guilt that the burden of Nazi racism had left on the German people." This was a matter that was initially as important as their welfare and actual pedagogical needs (Campt et al. 1998: 222–9; 224).

Philosemitic-like practices could also be found within the cultural field. For example, in her study of American Indian impersonation ("ethnic drag") practices in postwar Germany, including in the theatrical adaptations of Karl May's *Winnetou* novels, Katrin Sieg advances the notion of a "triangulated surrogation," a psychological mechanism that allowed postwar Germans who identified with the victims of American Indian genocide (and/or with their white avengers) to avoid identifying with the perpetrators of Jewish persecution. In a context where "race" and the Holocaust were effectively excised from public discourse, these fictional Native American victims took the place of Jewish victims, who could now be "forgotten" while fantasies of racial harmony reworked the terms of the trauma (Sieg 1998: 300–02; 2002: 10, 13).

In a similar way, jazz—and the African American—acted as a site at which an identification with another "triangulated surrogate" could be made, although I do not suggest that this was necessarily conscious, or by any means the only factor at play. In fact, a "triangulated surrogation" was potentially rendered quite easy. As shown in chapter 1, Nazi ideologues had made extensive use of the "Nigger-Jew-Jazz" label and, in the postwar era, Berendt and his colleagues continued to refer to the association, albeit non-pejoratively. Accordingly, the link between Jews and Blacks was stressed, not only in articles about jazz but also in pieces on the civil rights movement.

In his writings on civil rights in the United States, for example, Berendt identified that the majority of white civil rights advocates were Jews. Indeed, for him the civil rights movement was characterized by a "notable combination of Negroid vitality and Jewish intelligence" (1955f: 749). In relation to this Black-Jewish link, he posed the question:

> [Is it] a coincidence or [something] more? [Is there] a social, perhaps even psychological affinity? I am led to think about this because most of the white musicians who come close to holding a candle to the Negroes in their own artistic field—that of jazz music—are Jews. One has tried to name reasons for this: [is it] because no one can play truly felt jazz music without having the feeling of being oppressed, unjustly disadvantaged, or hated? (1952e: 198. See also 1955f: 749)

He also interpreted Miles Davis' 1949 recording "Israel"—which, in 1953, he rated among his favorite six tunes—as a sign of the typical jazz musician's solidarity with the Jewish cause. He argued that giving a tune such a title could only be a protest against the anti-Semitism rife in the United States in the postwar era. In doing so, he expressly equated being a jazz musician with having sympathy for Jews and for minorities in general (Berendt n.d.f.; "Jazz und theoretische Physik" 1953).

Berendt—who in his memoir entertains the idea that his forebears were Jewish and identifies a characteristically "Jewish" trait in his activities promoting jazz—was not the only postwar West German jazz writer whose writings bore the hallmarks of a form of philosemitism, however (1996a: 167–176). In the late 1950s, for example, Alfred Rosenberg also reveled in the notion of jazz being a "musical *Mischling* [half-caste]," thereby repeating but inverting the trope used by the Nazis (1959). Beyond this re-evocation of the link between jazz, Blacks, and Jews however, postwar West German jazz discourse intersected with preexisting discourses about race in other complicated ways.

The "Whole" Negro

At the heart of Berendt's Nietzschean interpretation of jazz—and its ability to heal the sadly over-rationalized denizen of the modern world—was a romanticized view of the African American, who was seen not to distinguish between Western dualisms such as the body and the soul, the secular and the religious:

> For him, the world has not fallen apart into the "secular" and "religious," the "sensual" and the "intellectual," or however else you wish to describe the dualisms, between which the dialectic play of Occidental reactions move. Music speaks to him "totally" ... or not at all, insofar as he has not reacted by taking the option open to many a modern big-city Negro—that of a consciously complete assimilation to the white pattern of behavior. The [Negro's] musical experience emerges from a completeness and unspoiledness, a totality, of which most modern Europeans scarcely even possess a memory any more. (1956e: 171)

The Negro was also regarded as "naïve"—in a non-pejorative, Schillerean sense—and "authentic," compared with the rational Westerner (see, e.g., Berendt 1952a; 1952e: 199). Art and life were more a matter of a rhythmic "conjuring-up" than European-style rationality, and literature did not exist "in that rarified atmosphere of exclusive intellectualism ... which surrounds the significant bearers of modern European literature" (Berendt 1955f: 748. See also 1950a: 72; 1952a). In this way, Berendt constructed an idealized image of blackness, which was seen to offer Europeans a way of reconnecting with a lost dionysian element and a more authentic state of being.

Such a romantic attitude is, from today's perspective, dated, to say the least. It can certainly be argued that, though positively intended, it paints the African American as premodern and incapable of "suffering" from the evils of rationalized civilization, that it has little to do with the complex reality and diversity of black existence(s), and that it denies the African American his or her subjectivity. Furthermore, it does not reject the paradigm of race as a biological fact, or the stereotypes of the instinctual black man advanced by Nazi ideologues, but simply inverts them by giving them a positive weighting. And yet, the view advanced by Berendt during the 1950s was not entirely out of keeping with other attitudes current at the time.

Firstly, this negrophilic trope had clear forebears within earlier European jazz writing. The writing of the francophone critics Delaunay, Panassié, and Goffin was shot through with the early-twentieth-century "primitivist myth" that cast the "authentic" jazz musician as an instinctual noble savage (Gioia 1988: 20–49; Gennari 2006: 57–8). Charley Gerard has also observed the presence of a negrophilic "black mystique" within much jazz literature written by those whites whose contact with blacks may have been little more than peripheral (1998: 97 ff). Secondly, there were parallels between Berendt's jazz discourse and the *négritude* advanced during the 1930s, 1940s, and 1950s by francophone black thinkers such as Léopold Senghor and Aimé Césaire, who countered racist attitudes by enshrining and idealizing the black experience. Senghor, for example, asserted that black Africans had a more intuitive approach to the world (McLeod 2000: 77–8). Berendt can hardly have been unaware of the *négritude* discourse. In the late 1950s, he broadcast at least one program in which poems by Césaire were recited against a backdrop of Dizzy Gillespie's music ("Jazz und Dichtung" 1958).

Finally, one must read Berendt's race discourse in the context of the perceived ideological hangover from National Socialism. For many years, jazz continued to be rejected by numerous West Germans, sometimes in terms not dissimilar to those employed by Nazi ideologues (see, e.g., Schreiber 1958; Zimmerle 1960). Racial Others also continued to prompt anxieties and periodic outbursts. As the historian Maria Höhn has shown in her study of American GI garrison communities in the Rhineland Palatinate during the 1950s, African American GIs (and interracial relationships) generated "widespread racism that existed side by side with the overall tolerance towards black soldiers" (2002: 93). She also observes that, despite the philosemitic rejection of racism and anti-Semitism at the official level, "popular anti-Semitism … was widespread during the 1950s and receded only by the end of the decade" (2002: 221). Therefore, to borrow Scott DeVeaux's remarks in relation to the United States, we can equally observe that in postwar Germany "to insist on the dignity and inherent worth of the black expressive arts was in itself a risky political act in the 1940s and 1950s" (1997: 20).

In an important way, Berendt's racial discourse had a paradoxical dimension too: while it betrayed a romanticized negrophilia, it was also framed by his broader liberal humanist habitus. Hence, even while essentializing the Negro, he urged his audience to see the common elements between black and white (see, e.g., 1952a: 20).

For a Colorblind Society

For Berendt, jazz offered a utopian vision of an integrated society in which race no longer mattered. Given on-stage and audience "mixing" in Southern U.S. jazz concerts when "Jim Crow" segregation was still the rule, he asserted that jazz had contributed more to overcoming segregation than anything else, and quoted Louis Armstrong with approval: "jazz is a great tool in the racial question. It makes people wonderfully colorblind" (1956b). This idea that jazz is a way of creatively surmounting racism was—and, to an extent, remains—a common trope within the liberal jazz literature tradition. It was pushed in the United States by Leonard Feather and others, and it seems likely that Berendt was at least partly influenced by that discourse (DeVeaux 1997: 18–19; Sudhalter 2001: xvii; Gennari 2006: 55 ff, 151).

Jazz's colorblinding effect was based in Berendt's interpretation of the music's racial genealogy, which, it should be noted, he made in the absence of detailed musicological analysis. He summed this up in 1953: "jazz only emerges and exists in the juxtaposition of 'black' and 'white'" (1953a: 13). By maintaining this line, he came to hold a mediating position in Germany between what he called the "African Party" of jazz writers, such as the musicologist Alfons M. Dauer, who—like Marshall Stearns in the United States—had by the late 1950s made detailed analyses of the African roots of jazz, and the discographer Horst H. Lange, who, somewhat bizarrely, published an article in 1960 declaring that jazz was a creation of whites (Dauer 1958; 1961a; Lange 1960). Just as he had earlier sought to distance himself from the feud between "trad" and "mod" (modern) jazz fans, Berendt now distanced himself from this debate about the racial heritage of jazz and insisted on a radical relativism:

> The question of what is "African" and what is "European" in jazz is without objective meaning ... It can only be answered subjectively-relatively-psychologically ... Jazz is something new, of itself, and in itself complete and... as with all such art forms, critics and musicians project into it that which suits their own situation. ... And everyone can prove his view "scientifically." (n.d.e.)

Within the context of billing jazz as an intercultural hybrid, Berendt showed an interest in those musicians who confounded the descriptors "black" and "white" traditionally used in the jazz literature. There were, as he observed in 1956, strange reversals of musical responsibilities and it was sometimes no longer possible to determine just by listening whether a black or white musician was playing (1956b).[5] He also called on jazz fans and writers to speak less about skin color and more about music (n.d.a.: 4.), an appeal echoed by other like-minded German jazz writers at the time (see, e.g., Rosenberg 1961).

And yet, there was an unresolved tension in Berendt's discourse. Just as he also advanced a romanticized reading of the Negro, he continued to apply the epithet "black" as a musical descriptor (see, e.g., 1960b:

---

5. He may well have been thinking here of the famous blindfold test conducted by Leonard Feather with the black trumpeter Roy Eldridge in 1951 for *Metronome*. Despite his claims to be able to identify a player's color from his or her tone, Eldridge was unable to do so when put to the test by Feather (Gennari 2006: 56).

40). In the very article in which he appealed to fans not to focus on skin color, he engaged in a speculative analysis of the ways in which black musicians were "better" than white musicians and vice versa. While concluding that each was better in their own way—black musicians tended to be more innovative, but white musicians tended to be more technically proficient—one must nevertheless query why, if it was necessary for others to focus less on race, Berendt himself entered into an analysis of the intersection between race and jazz aesthetics (n.d.a.: 4)

* * * * *

Berendt's discourse both overturned *and* reproduced preexisting racial premises. Following the earlier French school of jazz criticism, he essentialized the Negro, attributing to this fantasy picture instinctual, "whole" qualities that were absent or suppressed in rationalized Western civilization. In doing so, he inverted the racist paradigm of the Nazis. Yet he also sought—while perhaps never quite succeeding—to move beyond questions of race: jazz nominally represented a utopian vision of a world in which race did not matter. There were non-German precedents in the jazz literature for each of these tropes. However, in the West German context they were inflected by the trauma of National Socialism. In particular, Berendt's interest in the plight of the Negro and his or her music was consistent with a broader philosemitic attitude. For him, and no doubt for many young postwar West Germans, jazz was partly a site at which, to borrow Arlene Teraoka's words in another context, West Germany could "redeem its fascist past and forge a new identity for the future." (1996: 78) This was a powerful motivator and would also drive his *Jazz Meets the World* and *Weltmusik* activities in the coming decades.

PART II

Europeanizing Jazz

CHAPTER 5

The Blues of German Jazz

By the late 1950s or early 1960s, a number of important changes could be detected in the West German and international jazz scenes. In the United States modern jazz was beginning to develop in radical and expansive directions. At the same time, a newly politicized discourse was being formulated. By contrast, despite the social acceptance of jazz in West Germany, musicians and critics increasingly began to detect a malaise in the scene. Thanks to his travels, Berendt had a keen eye on developments on both sides of the Atlantic and was now able to use the facilities at his disposal—in particular handsome funding from the *Berliner Festwochen* and the backing of Saba, an independent German label with a strong interest in jazz—to intervene and begin to make his mark on the development of jazz.

Modal and Free Jazz

As Ted Gioia has noted, "new sounds were in the air [around 1960]" (1997: 312). Firstly, a modal approach to improvisation was developed by the trumpeter Miles Davis and his colleagues. This was used in particular on Davis's recording "Milestones" (1958) and on his 1959 album *Kind of Blue*. It freed up improvisation, which now was no longer based on the diachronic chord progressions in a composition, as it had been with the earlier hard bop style. Instead, the improviser could make use of all sorts of different, and often unusual, musical scales (Litweiler 1984: 110–12; Budds 1990: 44–50). This development often coincided with an interest in Other musical traditions, from Spain to Africa and India. In 1960 and 1961, for example, Davis and the saxophonist John Coltrane separately recorded albums that applied modal techniques and took Spanish music as a cue (Davis's *Sketches of Spain* and Coltrane's *Olé*). Coltrane, in particular, explored Other musical traditions during this era, and freely drew inspiration from or paid tribute to them (Porter 1998: 199–213). In this respect, a selection of his titles from the early 1960s—"Liberia," "Africa," "Dahomey Dance," and "India"—is revealing, yet it should not be construed as evidence of a close musical synthesis of those Other musics (cf. Jost 1973/74: 144).

The adoption of a modal approach did give jazz musicians a basis upon which to engage with various world musics. By 1963, at the latest, they recognized the similarities between modal improvisation and the "melodic orientation of other world musics" (Budds 1990: 50–51). Nevertheless, one should be cautious when interpreting "modality" as Coltrane and Berendt did—as a universal cutting across different musical cultures (cf. Berendt 1973/74: 155–6; Porter 1998: 211). This approach downplays the differences in function, for example, between an Indian raga and (most) jazz.[1]

"Free jazz"—so named after the title of the saxophonist Ornette Coleman's 1960 album—represented another more radical reaction to the perceived clichés of hard bop. It was characterized by a "subversion of the various jazz conventions—chord changes, tempos, song forms, structured solos, and the like" (Gioia 1997: 344). The focus was now on what Budds calls "free group improvisation, [i.e.] the simultaneous creation of melodic lines with little or no concern for the production of 'harmonious' vertical composites" (1990: 59). Free jazz might have just been "the act of qualified spontaneous creation of music by a group of sympathetic musicians" yet it was also highly controversial at the time, both with critics and enthusiasts (Budds 1990: 83; Porter 1998: 203). This was for aesthetic as well as political reasons.

---

1. Martin Pfleiderer observes that the commonality of "modality" to modal jazz and other musical cultures makes sense only if one has a very general definition of modality—a residual category erected by music theory that contains all of those melodic structural principles that are neither based on functional harmony nor atonal. In fact, the modal approach to jazz improvisation has more to do with eighteenth- and nineteenth-century European music theory than any of the practices used in Asian musical traditions. Nevertheless, many of the scales used in modal jazz improvisation are shared by non-European cultures, which has allowed for a point of contact between jazz and certain Other musics (1998: 104–10).

(Free) Jazz and (Black) Politics

The 1960s saw an increasing politicization among many American musicians and critics, particularly in the second half of the decade. This tendency was often paired with a marked preference for free jazz. Since the notion of freedom was being raised within the contexts of both avant-garde jazz and the civil rights movement, it is not surprising that the one found reflection in the other (Gioia 1997: 338). The titles of some modern jazz compositions—including Sonny Rollins' *Freedom Suite* (1958), Charles Mingus's "Fables of Faubus" (1960) and Max Roach's *We Insist: Freedom Now* Suite (1961)—clearly referred to the civil rights movement (Jost 1973). Increasingly, however, a newly critical, sociologically grounded jazz discourse began to discern links between (free) jazz *aesthetics* and the politics of African American emancipation.

The sociohistorical context driving this development is significant. It included an administration that was committed to the war in Vietnam and that increasingly neglected the welfare of domestic minorities, a growing disillusionment among African Americans with the possibility of a peaceful integration into white American society, and the rise of Black cultural separatism and militant Black Nationalism. These phenomena now manifested themselves in the stance adopted by various African American musicians and critics toward what they strongly regarded as *their* musical property (Jost 1982: 176–77; Budds 1990: 116–27). Charley Gerard has coined the useful term "Black music ideology" to encapsulate this stance (1998: 1–37).

According to Gerard, "Black music ideologists are offended that each style of jazz ... has been appropriated from the African American community almost from the day after it was first heard there." On this approach, stylistic change "is not the result of musical development per se but of sociopolitical events affecting the African American community" (1998: 6, 35). The American critic who contributed the foundational text to the Black music ideology was the Black Arts Movement playwright and poet Amiri Baraka (LeRoi Jones), who published his influential study *Blues People* in 1963. As John Gennari notes *Blues People* recuperated "African culture as the core of African American identity [and] was a brief for racial solidarity that anticipated the black nationalist agenda" (2006: 271). During the mid-1960s, Baraka's writing became even more polemical — and exclusionary — as he adopted Islam and a new name, and left his white wife, Hettie. In the process, he became what Gennari calls a "lightning rod of cultural combat" (Gennari 2006: 279 ff, 279). Following on from his lead, the links between free jazz, the Black music ideology, and a critique of the predominantly white-run Culture Industry were forcefully advanced by musicians such as Archie Shepp in 1965, as well as by white writers including the American Frank Kofsky in 1970 and, in Europe, the Frenchmen Philippe Carles and Jean-Louis Comolli in 1971 (Shepp 1965; Carles and Comolli 1971; Kofsky 1998 [1970]. See, generally, Gennari 2006: 251 ff). At the same time as these critical perspectives were being advanced, some musicians were also attempting to form alternative models for the diffusion of their music, including "rebel" festivals—for the first time in 1960 at Newport—and collectively run record labels (Jost 1982: 211–22; Gerard 1998: 90–6). One should be wary of simplistically equating free jazz with political protest, however. As Ekkehard Jost lamented in his epochal 1975 study of free jazz, this tendency has meant that the "autonomous musical aspects of the evolution of free jazz" have been ignored (1975a: 9).

Berendt Hears a New Avant-Garde

At the aesthetic level, free jazz's approach to meter and rhythm "destroyed the foundation that was conditional for the existence of the property of swing" (Budds 1990: 70). It thereby eroded one of the three defining elements of jazz that Berendt had held to throughout the 1950s. However, he enthusiastically picked up on the beginnings of the paradigm shift to free jazz, as well as on modal jazz. In 1959, he attempted to invite Ornette Coleman's Quartet to the Donaueschingen Music Days (Anders 1975). Early the following year, he praised Coleman's music in *Jazz Echo* (1960e). What seems to have been most influential for crystallizing Berendt's interest, however, was his second extended trip to the United States, which he made in mid-1960, ten years after his debut trip and just a couple of years after an acrimonious and traumatic split with his first wife, Inge. Over three months, he and the Californian photographer William Claxton traveled around the country by car, observing, photographing, and recording the jazz scene. During this odyssey, they found time to spend an afternoon in the Guggenheim Museum with John Coltrane and also to attend both the official Newport Jazz Festival *and* the landmark "Newport Rebels" festival, at which Ornette Coleman, Max Roach, and Charles Mingus and other members of the avant-garde performed. In Berendt's and Claxton's encyclopedic 1961 book *Jazz Life*, Berendt's enthusiasm for free and modal jazz is palpable (1961: 236–8. See also Berendt 1960a; 1960d). Nor was this a passing fancy. In a series of two important 1962 articles, he now took leave from earlier modern jazz styles (from cool and west coast to soul jazz and hard bop, all of which he now considered to be too "safe"). They had allowed jazz to "catch its breath" but were backward looking. Avant-gardists, including Coleman and Coltrane, were finally entering new, unknown territory again. As far as he was concerned, it was "one of the most interesting periods in jazz history. The developments are toppling over each other. Everything is in flux" (1962b). He clearly welcomed this situation. In the progressivist conception advanced in the *Jazzbook*, the jazz tradition needed to be renewed, not simply maintained. Before long, he would have the means at his disposal to contribute to this process.

The Blues of German Jazz

Despite the enthusiasm shown by Berendt and other critics toward the musical innovations in the United States, and despite the increasing social acceptance of jazz in West Germany, a distinct malaise manifested itself in the West German jazz scene at this time (Berendt 1959d; Jost 1988a: 376; Pasquier 2000: 73–4). This had various causes. Firstly, the jazz "boom" of the mid- to late 1950s was receding, partly as a consequence of the popularity of rock 'n' roll (Berendt 1959b; Jost 1988a 376; Schwab 2004: 159). As Berendt put it in a 1959 article on the German jazz scene, the music was lacking a broad fan base (1959c). This was something for which critics were not entirely blameless, however. Indeed, the "jazz as art" view propagated by Berendt and some of his colleagues no doubt contributed to the marginalization of jazz, in terms of its popularity ("Deutscher Jazz" 1965: 76; Schmidt-Joos 1965a). While embracing the more challenging avant-garde styles, they continued to distance themselves from more popular forms of "commercial" or "pseudo" jazz, such as Dixieland revival music (see, e.g., Berendt 1961b; Roth 1961).

The marginalization had various consequences for the jazz scene. Firstly, the number of professional jazz musicians who could support themselves by playing full time dwindled (Berendt 1962g: 22–3; "Deutscher Jazz" 1965: 75). This situation was exacerbated by the introduction of jukeboxes in the early 1960s and the resulting demise of many live venues, as well as by the presence of amateur jazz bands, which were prepared to play for very low fees (Schmidt-Joos 1960; Berendt 1962a; Jost 1988a: 376–7). Secondly, the priorities of the recording industry were such that recording possibilities were also extremely restricted (Berendt 1959b 35; 1962e; "Deutscher Jazz" 1965: 76). It is understandable in the these circumstances that, among the small cohort of professional modern jazz musicians able to eke out an existence, there was a growing introspection and dissatisfaction with their own musical activities to date—a significant change of mood that will be analyzed in detail in chapter 6.

Berendt's role as jazz writer was also undergoing a change. Even if, at the close of the 1950s, he observed that reading about jazz seemed to be more important to some West Germans than actually listening to it, by the early to mid 1960s he faced the reality of an increasingly exhausted market for German jazz literature (Berendt 1959c; 1966n: 136; Prieberg 1963: 294). As journalist Klaus Fischer perceptively observed at the time: "Today's twenty-year-olds want to own new and interesting jazz records and visit exciting jazz concerts, not listen to jazz theorizing delivered in a pedagogical tone" (1965). This comment also reflected the fact that the long-running upturn in the West German economy had increasingly delivered a disposable income to twenty-something Germans which could be spent on things such as records and concerts (Schildt and Siegfried 2006b).

On Berendt's own account, he felt it necessary at this time to do what he could to ensure that the music that he admired was performed and recorded (1966n: 136). Fortuitously, two new avenues opened to him in the early 1960s that allowed this to happen, despite the countervailing contraction of the jazz scene. In 1962, he was approached by the artistic director of the *Berliner Festwochen* (Berlin Festival Weeks) to organize a jazz festival for West Berlin. He also renewed contact with Saba, a fledgling West German record company that was about to launch a new jazz series. These two events would give him an important platform for the next decade.

Berlin JazzFest 1964–72

The JazzFest (originally called the Berlin Jazz Days) is an annual festival, which in 2004 celebrated its fortieth anniversary. Since the beginning, it has been associated with the *Berliner Festwochen*, a cultural festival founded in 1951. The *Festwochen* were initially financed directly by the Western Allies but subsequently were run by the State of West Berlin and then through the *Berliner Festspiele GmbH*, a company funded by (West) Berlin and the Federal Republic (Eckhardt 2000a: 9–10; 2000b: 150). During the Cold War, they fulfilled several purposes. Until the early 1970s, they were regarded as a type of "shop window for the Free World," intended to demonstrate the strength of pluralist-democratic culture to the East (Eckhardt 1975; Traber 2000: 169). This function also continued after the construction of the Berlin Wall in August 1961, when a so-called "radio-bridge" was created to broadcast the *Festwochen* to East Berliners (Eckhardt 2000a: 29). The political dimension of the *Festwochen* was not lost in the GDR either, where cadres were irked by the official involvement of the Federal Republic in financing the festival (Traber 2000: 169). The *Festwochen* also fulfilled a compensatory function during the Cold War: by presenting cultural events which might otherwise have passed the city by, they furnished West Berliners with a method for overcoming the isolation felt in the former capital (Eckhardt 1975; 1979: 5–6; 2000b: 150–1). The task of making Berlin a cultural metropolis during an existential crisis naturally came at the price of high subsidies, however (Chervel n.d.).

Berendt was approached in 1962 by the intendant of the *Festwochen*, Professor Nicolas Nabokov, with the proposal that he act as artistic director for a one-off jazz festival to be held during the 1964 *Festwochen* (Berendt 1969a; "Gespräch mit Joachim-Ernst Berendt" 1988). This was not the first time that the *Festwochen* had run a jazz event—there were smaller "Jazz Salons" in 1959 and 1961, with which Berendt was tangentially involved (Lange 1996: 189; Eckhardt 2000a: 26–7)—however the 1964 Jazz Days were a coup in terms of funding and high art setting—architect Hans Scharoun's recently constructed Berlin Philharmonic—and further sealed the "arrival" of jazz in West Germany. Despite the success of these inaugural Jazz Days, Nabokov had no interest in continuing them as part of the *Festwochen*. At this point, the Jazz Days team of Berendt, the German concert agent Ralf Schulte-Bahrenberg, and the Newport Jazz Festival impresario George Wein seized the initiative and approached the Berlin Senator for Science and the Arts, Professor Werner Stein, who had ultimate responsibility for the *Festwochen*.[2] Stein agreed to continue to support the Jazz Days in 1965 but stopped short of underwriting them—that would have to be done by Schulte-Bahrenberg and Wein (Schulte-Bahrenberg 2004). The Jazz Days were then also given their own date in November, independent of the *Festwochen*.

Over the next few years, the Jazz Days continued to flourish. The relationship between Berendt and Wein became more established, as Wein used the Jazz Days as a springboard from which to launch Euro-

---

2. Initially, the Jazz Days were to be answerable to an advisory panel and run directly by the *Festwochen*. However, Berendt nominated an independent team, including Schulte-Bahrenberg and Wein as "co-producer." Berendt had previously advised Schulte-Bahrenberg on the latter's (financially unsuccessful) 1960 and 1961 Essen Jazz Days (Broecking 1995: 74; Gruntz 2004). Wein, who had run the Newport Jazz Festival since 1954, was responsible for engaging the American jazz musicians (Berendt 1969a). He and Berendt had known each other since at least 1958, when Wein had traveled to Europe to recruit musicians for Marshall Brown's International Youth Band, which performed at Newport that year. Berendt had given assistance to Wein and Brown in auditioning German musicians for the band.

pean tours for some of those musicians who were engaged for Berlin.[3] In addition to the subsidies from West Berlin, Berendt secured lucrative funding from a range of West German public broadcasters in return for radio and television broadcast rights (Broecking 1995: 74; Schulte-Bahrenberg 2004).[4] He also garnered financial support from the Saba record label (see below), as well as support in kind, such as free or discounted airfares for international invitees (see, e.g., Berendt 1965e; 1966l; 1967n: 33; 1968g: 3; 1969d: 4; 1970d: 7). In the event, the total funding behind the Jazz Days was rumored to rival that of Bayreuth's Wagner Festival and was such that, during the mid- to late 1960s and early 1970s, they enjoyed a reputation as the most significant European jazz festival and, indeed, the most important jazz festival outside the United States (Ohff 1967b; 1971a; Wilmer 1970; Schade 1971; Graves 1972; Broecking 1995: 74).

Berendt's Vision for the Jazz Days

Another reason for the Jazz Days' reputation was Berendt's "competence and authority" as artistic director, as the Berlin critic Heinz Ohff put it (1971a). Other critics also praised the creative impulses "emitting from Berlin" during Berendt's heyday (Schmidt-Joos 1971). Berendt's artistic direction was, in turn, influenced by various factors. In the first three years, it was the annual theme of the *Festwochen* that provided an impetus. In 1964, for example, the *Festwochen* were devoted to "Black–White, Africa–Europe: Interactions between the cultures of the Occident and black Africa" (Eckhardt 2000a: 32).[5] In keeping with this theme and with the inclusive approach promoted in his *Jazzbook* as well as in his attempts to foster tolerance within the jazz scene, Berendt assembled

---

3. Berendt also produced a recording of George Wein's in 1969, when he invited the piano-playing impresario and a group of "Newport All-Stars" to perform a tribute to Duke Ellington at the Jazz Days. Over the years, the two men also worked together outside of the bounds of the Jazz Days—in 1982, Berendt curated a "Jazz and World Music" concert for Wein's Kool Jazz Festival in New York, for example.
4. The WDR, SWF, ZDF and SFB broadcasters supported the inaugural Jazz Days. In subsequent years, other broadcasters also contributed. By 1970, the umbrella ARD organization became involved (Berendt 1964c; 1965e; 1968g 3; 1970d: 7).
5. The *Festwochen* theme provided direct inspiration to Berendt until 1966. In 1965, it was the encounter between Japanese and Western culture, which gave the impetus for *Sakura Sakura–Japan Meets Jazz* (see chapter 12). The 1966 *Festwochen* were dedicated to the Baroque, hence the inclusion of the Swiss jazzman George Gruntz's "Jazz goes Baroque" (Berendt 1965e; 1966l: 16; Eckhardt 2000a: 33–5). In both instances, the *Festwochen* theme also coincided with concepts that had earlier held Berendt in their thrall.

a "representative" festival, including various different styles of jazz, from traditional to avant-garde. This desire to present "the whole jazz" would continue until his last Jazz Days in 1972 (Ohff 1971a; Schulte-Bahrenberg 2004).

Figure 5 | Günther Kieser's poster for the 1968 Berlin Jazz Days. © Günther Kieser. Used with permission.

Berendt also actively experimented with ideas. This was because—as opposed to the "American" approach to festivals—he eschewed the idea of *only* presenting groups that one could otherwise hear in a jazz club (Berendt 1961c; "Gespräch mit Joachim-Ernst Berendt" 1988: 679). In the program notes for the inaugural Jazz Days, he outlined this philosophy:

> A jazz festival ought to be more than a collection of famous names. It should:
> a) give the musicians the possibility to imagine and introduce new ideas, which they would not otherwise be able to realize,
> b) it should also propose its own ideas,
> c) and, above all, it should, in all its various manifestations be devoted to a single governing idea. (1964c)

True to this mission, Berendt tried hard to assemble the Jazz Days around a single notion. In 1965, it was the idea of sustaining a "jam-session atmosphere" by presenting a number of new groups and "workshops" assembled especially for the Jazz Days. In 1966, it was the encounter between jazz and other art forms (in particular dance, folklore, and modern concert music). In 1967 it was *JMTW*. Thereafter, the concept of a central theme broke down for reasons that are fully explored in chapter 8. Even in the absence of a unifying theme, however, Berendt used the Jazz Days to pursue his own ideas. As he noted in his autobiography: "Nowhere else could I realize so many of the ideas dear to my heart in such a short period of time" (1996a: 326). Among these ideas were "Jazz in Church" sessions (in 1968 and 1969), which reprised his activities in the 1950s interpreting jazz for Church Academies, as well as Eastern European showcases (in 1964, 1968, 1970, and 1971).

The Jazz Days and Thinking beyond the Cold War

The presence of Eastern European musicians at the Jazz Days was partly a consequence of Berendt's long-standing interest in and engagement with the jazz scenes in various Eastern-bloc countries. However, the location of the Jazz Days was especially significant and no doubt further encouraged his invitation policy. Berendt was very conscious of West Berlin's precarious geopolitical position and, in his way, was as interested as ever in finding ways of using the eminently "international" jazz to communicate across the East-West divide. This desire manifested itself in his 1964 program notes, in which he pointed to the value of jazz as a model for bridging tense political boundaries. In so doing he transposed free jazz ideas and the concerns and tribulations of the civil rights movement onto Cold War Berlin:

> Nowhere has the encounter between black and white become as fruitful as here [in jazz]. In this respect jazz anticipates that which remains to be achieved in other areas and which, especially in recent years has proven itself to be an extremely difficult, highly current and strangely ambiguous problem: the overcoming of an encounter, in the course of which it [difference] becomes self-evident. These Jazz Days are a manifestation of the encounter between black and white and the overcoming of [those categories]. *What jazz musicians call their "freedom movement" will strike a chord in a city like Berlin, where the problem of freedom is more urgent than in other European cities.* (1964c; my emphasis)

In a similar vein, Berendt commissioned the African American saxophonist and arranger Oliver Nelson to write *Berlin Dialogues for Orchestra* in 1970, a piece intended to reflect on and musically explore Berlin's position. Nelson—who visited the GDR during rehearsals—scored a big band suite including hectic passages titled "Confrontation" and "Over the Wall." These were intended to reflect the senselessness of a world divided between East and West (and, in the United States, between North and South) (Nelson 1970b). Patently embittered by the failures of the civil rights movement, Nelson felt that his insight as an African American "could be a better presupposition to consider Berlin's situation than many things the politicians have said" (qtd. in Berendt 1970d: 11).

Although Berendt's talk of artistic and political freedom and his provocative brief to Nelson may well have been inflammatory in the context of Cold War debates about culture, his invitation policy toward Eastern-bloc jazzmen anticipated the cultural political thrust of the *Festwochen* in the early 1970s, which was intended to sound out whether that which was beyond the reach of high politics might be achievable in the cultural field instead (Müller-Wirth 2000: 244). For some of those audience members who listened to Eastern European musicians in the Philharmonic, Habakuk Traber's gloss about the cultural politics of the *Festwochen* preparing Berliners for the situation after 1989, may also have held true—although, of course, no one was predicting such an outcome at that time (2000: 177).

Jazz in the Black Forest: Saba/MPS

If the Jazz Days gave Berendt a live platform for realizing some of his own ambitions (and those of selected musicians), the Saba record label gave him a medium for disseminating the results to a broader audience. For a number of years there was close symbiosis between the Jazz Days and the record label, with the label releasing records of Jazz Days invitees and enlisting Berendt as producer.[6] This was also something in which the State of West Berlin had an interest during the Cold War. Senator Stein expressed the wish to the Jazz Days team that as many "Live in Berlin" records as possible be released and marketed as such (Schulte-Bahrenberg 2004).

Together with the Frankfurt jazz promoter Horst Lippmann's productions of modern West German jazz for the CBS label, Saba was responsible for increasing the international exposure of German (and European) jazz during the 1960s (Pasquier 2000: 58–65. See also Gerard 1998: 147–8). It was therefore not entirely untrue, when, in 1967, Berendt claimed, with characteristic boosterism: "Before Saba began with its jazz work it was a truism: European jazz is unsaleable. In the meantime some of the most interesting jazz records in Europe have come into being—and Saba has played a significant role in that." (1967h: 14) This is a statement with which many of the collectors around the world who pay exorbitant prices for original Saba records would doubtless agree.

As a label, Saba had an independent status, which granted it—and Berendt as a producer—considerable latitude. During the late 1950s and early 1960s, its owner Hans-Georg Brunner-Schwer—an heir to the Saba firm of radio manufacturers—had begun producing jazz recordings in the town of Villingen in the Black Forest (K-G Fischer 1999: 80–1). He was motivated by a combination of factors. Firstly, he wished to document the jazz he loved, which he felt was being neglected by the major record labels in their reorientation toward "beat" music. However, there was also a material reason for the productions: the development in 1961 of the *Sabamobil* car hi-fi system created the need for a special stock of recordings (Tormann n.d.: 4, 12; "10 Jahre MPS-Records" 1974: 21).

---

6. From 1964 until 1971, Saba contributed to the running costs of the festival in return for the rights to release live albums or to record Jazz Days invitees in its studios (Berendt 1967h: 14; 1968g: 16; 1972a: II; Schmidt-Joos 1972: 198). From 1967 until 1969, it contributed a group to the "Jazz Party," which traditionally concluded the festival (Berendt 1967n: 25; 1968g: 15; 1969d: 4). By late 1971, however, the close relationship had broken down. The Jazz Days' organizers now requested larger contributions from the label. As a result, the label staged an event to rival the opening concert of the Jazz Days (Berendt 1972a: II; Schmidt-Joos 1972: 198, 200–01). In 1972, it also provided documents and critical comments to the Spiegel critic Siegfried Schmidt-Joos, who then wrote a piece of investigative journalism highly critical of Berendt's practices (Schmidt-Joos 2005). See chapter 8.

Berendt's first documented contact with Brunner-Schwer occurred in 1959, when the two collaborated on a recording of the Hans Koller–Oscar Pettiford Quartet (K-G Fischer 1999: 81; 209). Then, in 1964, in the context of the approaching Jazz Days, Berendt offered to produce additional records for the firm. Given his links with a stream of international visitors, the offer was quickly accepted (Fruth 2004). Saba's jazz series was billed at its 1965 launch as being supervised by Berendt; however he remained at all times a freelancer ("Saba bringt Jazz-Plattenserie" 1965; K-G Fischer 1999: 82; Fruth 2004). Nor was he the sole producer for the jazz series: Brunner-Schwer and others also produced numerous records. In addition, Brunner-Schwer, being owner of the label, had the final say over whether a particular proposal of Berendt's went ahead (Berendt 1999: 123; Schoof 2004).

Berendt's intention as supervisor of the jazz series was to record and promote musicians who had been overlooked by the commercial labels or who were at the beginning of their careers ("Saba bringt Jazz-Plattenserie" 1965). Hence, the Saba recordings included European (but mainly German) jazz groups as well as expatriate "Americans in Europe" and international visitors to the Jazz Days (Berendt 1967h). From the beginning, the Saba recordings ran the gamut from traditional jazz to the avant-garde, which also fitted with Berendt's holistic conception of jazz and his Jazz Days invitation policy, as well as with the differing personal tastes of Brunner-Schwer and Berendt (K-G Fischer 1999: 82).

According to Saba's former recording director Willi Fruth, the label—and its successor Musik Produktion Schwarzwald (MPS), which existed from 1968 until 1983—were never large money making concerns. Some releases—including Brunner-Schwer's productions of the Canadian pianist Oscar Peterson—were commercially successful, whereas others—including many of Berendt's productions—were not. In any event, jazz recordings accounted for a very small section of the West German market for recorded music. Until the early 1970s, when the market for jazz recordings picked up somewhat, the label also suffered from inadequate international distribution. It is perhaps telling that the American investor that took over the Saba radio business in 1968, was not interested in taking on the record-production wing. It was at this point that Brunner-Schwer, a man of independent means, made the decision to continue running that business in its own right ("10 Jahre MPS-Records" 1974: 21; Pasquier 2000: 63; Fruth 2004; Tormann n.d.). His activities subsequently earned him the title "patron" of jazz (Hoehl 1968; Tormann n.d.: 5). Notwithstanding this, it would be wrong to cast Saba/MPS as being independent of commercial concerns. As Brunner-Schwer pointed out in 1968: "in addition to [having] a passionate engagement with the music, the economic viability ... also has to be set right, for only in this way can a healthy relation between art, technology and business be found" (qtd. in Hoehl 1968).

Between 1964 and 1981, Berendt either produced or coproduced 130 records for Saba/MPS, by which he did quite well, financially (K-G Fischer 1999: 15; Fruth 2004).[7] He also produced recordings for other firms before, during, and after this period. In many ways however, the thirteen records in the extended *JMTW* series are representative of his production work, notwithstanding that they do not contain any recordings of Eastern European jazz, nor any combinations of jazz and poetry, which was another pet project of his (cf Meifert 1999). Nor are there any "Free Jazz/New Jazz Meeting" recordings (see chapter 7), "Jazz in Church" productions, or subsequent New Age productions in the series.

* * * * *

Berendt's motivations to diversify into festival direction and record production—a diversification that was consonant with the activities in the United States of critic-cum-producers such as John Hammond and Leonard Feather—were multifaceted. On the one hand, they reflected both his ever-present ambition and his growing dissatisfaction with the mere role of jazz writer. This new field of activity represented a fresh stream of income in an increasingly exhausted market for jazz literature. However, it also reflected an enthusiasm for exciting new developments in the American avant-garde jazz scene. During his heyday as a producer and festival director (1964–72), Berendt's ability to realize musicians' and his own artistic visions was itself the result of a confluence of factors. These included his position of power and authority within the West German jazz scene, the healthy subsidies deriving from the geopolitical situation of Berlin, the patronage of the network of West German public broadcasters and of Brunner-Schwer's Saba/MPS label, the experimental ethos held by various modern jazz musicians (and Berendt), and, not least, his own toil.

Berendt's *modus operandi* was quite interventionist. He regarded himself on the one hand a mere "catalyst" and on the other hand an

---

7. Siegfried Schmidt-Joos observed in 1972, on the basis of information received from MPS, that Berendt received between 1500 and 2,000 DM as producer's fee and 5 percent royalties on wholesale sales. He calculated that, by then, he had earned almost 250,000 DM in total (1972: 198). Berendt disputed this, however, noting that the royalties only cut in after three thousand records had been sold (and this was seldom reached with his avant-garde productions) and that, in relation to international sales, they were set at only 2.5 percent (1972b: 2).

active "player" (1996a: 327). Indeed, he relished the role as producer as one that satisfied his own need to be musically creative: "Whenever I produced records, I was always also, in a small way, one of the players. … That's why I did this work … : because I could always act 'like' a musician" (1996a: 389). Although he did not play an instrument during these sessions, he considered himself to be "playing" the musicians (1996a: 389). This had some truth to it, given that he often put musicians together into ensembles according to his own predilections rather than according to already existing bands. Berendt's mode of production tended to antagonize musicians, as will be demonstrated in chapter 8. His difficult manner also succeeded in antagonizing some of his colleagues at Saba/MPS (Schmidt-Joos 1972: 198). However—before these differences are taken into account—it remains to examine some of the musical changes afoot in European jazz in the 1960s and to explore how and why the musicians and Berendt fostered those changes.

CHAPTER 6

Emancipation and the Dilemma of *Volk*-Jazz

Since the 1970s, it has been customary in Germany to speak with pride of the European jazz "emancipation" (cf. Berendt 1977a; Jost 1978; 1987). According to this narrative, there was a sea change in modern European jazz from the beginning of the 1960s. A change of mood led to European musicians now seeking to break free from blindly following American jazz models. In this context, some musicians engaged with domestic folk music traditions—a strategy that had its pitfalls, however, particularly in West Germany.

Toward the European Jazz Emancipation

Jost refers to the period between 1945 and the early 1960s as the epigonic epoch of postwar European jazz (Jost 1987: 202). Or, as the pianist Michael Naura put it, "we blew our nose every time an American musician had a cold" (Naura 1988: 406). From the early 1960s, however, playing epigone came to be seen as inadequate: formerly a source of inspiration, having an American jazz idol was now seen as dominating and even crippling for the West German musician. Among other factors—including broader sociopolitical ones explored in depth in chapter 8—it was this self-reflection that initiated the much-vaunted European jazz emancipation that unfolded during the late 1960s and 1970s (Berendt 1977a: 213; Jost 1978: 55; Knauer 1996a: 146 ff). The soul-searching itself had various causes. It must surely have been partly a consequence of the increasingly straitened position of professional West German jazz musicians. The increasing legitimation of jazz as an art form must also have contributed. After all, how could jazz discourse sustain a claim to high art status and simultaneously allow plagiarism? For many musicians, a significant trigger for the self-reflection actually came, somewhat paradoxically, from developments in the United States itself (Berendt 1977a: 215; Jost 1978: 55). Wolfram Knauer has observed that the rhetoric of free jazz was received in Europe in a dual sense: as in the United States, it called into question the traditional rules and norms that governed jazz technique, but in Europe it now also questioned the notion that all jazz innovation must necessarily come from the United States (1996a: 141).

The trombonist Albert Mangelsdorff (1928–2005)—perhaps Germany's best-known jazzman—offers a classic example of this increasing self-reflexivity. Mangelsdorff's desire to find his own voice dated back to his first trip to the United States in mid-1958, when he took part in Marshal Brown's Newport Jazz Festival International Youth Band (Jost 1987: 201). When, some years later in 1963, his quintet recorded the landmark album *Tension* for Horst Lippmann's CBS series, Mangelsdorff had a clear message to impart to his fellow Europeans: "I think that many European jazz musicians don't make enough use of this freedom [in the new jazz] to express themselves and THEIR personality—even if only to separate themselves musically from a model or idol, whom they admire" (qtd. in Knauer 1996a: 147).

At least in part, *Tension* did diverge from the sort of music that American free jazz musicians were creating (Knauer 1996a: 148–9).[1] At this time, however, the European jazz emancipation was very much in its infancy, and Knauer locates *Tension* within an initial phase of awakening self-awareness. By the late 1960s, the self-awareness was well established and the rhetoric of finding one's own distinct voice was replaced by a more stridently rebellious rhetoric (Knauer 1996a: 150–55). This shift is explored more in following chapters. As will also be explored, there was a raft of additional sociopolitical factors that drove the European jazz emancipation in the latter part of the 1960s. Ekkehard Jost sums these up succinctly: student protests; anti-authoritarianism; the politicization of art; the questioning of norms and idols; and a latent Anti-Americanism, fueled not only by the Vietnam War but also by oppositional artistic movements within the United States itself—including, of course, much free jazz (1994: 235).

---

1. The degree of divergence is a moot point. Knauer admits that, if one is so minded, it is open to debate whether there were American models for the novel parts of the album (1996a: 149). Mangelsdorff also admitted that his music from this era "was not *very* different from American jazz" (Mangelsdorff 2004; emphasis in original).

Figure 6 | Albert Mangelsdorff in the SWF studio, Baden-Baden, 1966. © Paul G. Deker. Used with permission.

Euro-Folk and the Emancipation of European Jazz?

Both European and American jazzmen had engaged with European folk music prior to the 1960s. In general, they tended to do so by simply borrowing a melody (Noglik 1990: 229).[2] During the 1950s, for example, the Swedish saxophonist Lars Gullin began to adapt Swedish folk melodies (Kjellberg 1994: 225–7). Some isolated attempts were also ventured in Germany. In 1957, Werner Heider performed an impression of the German folk song *"Mein junges Leben hat ein End"* at the German Jazz Festival, and, as Berendt observed in 1961, some of the amateur German Dixieland revivalists also jazzed German folksongs (Berendt 1957a: 43; 1961b). American musicians—particularly those who visited Europe— were also involved in the business. Most famously, the saxophonist Stan Getz performed an adaptation of the folk theme *"Ack Värmeland du Sköna"* when he visited Sweden in 1951 (Kjellberg 1994: 225). Swing bandleader Lionel Hampton also developed a "Flamenco-Sound" after a European tour in 1956 ("Jazz News" 1956d). As has already been observed, modally oriented jazzmen such as Miles Davis and John Coltrane both engaged with Spanish music a few years later as well. In the early 1960s, other Americans such as Jimmy Giuffre and Paul Horn were also involved in folk-jazz activities (Berendt and Claxton 1961: 249). From the early to mid-1960s, however, European jazz musicians, in particular, began looking to their folkloric traditions with renewed interest (Noglik 1990; Kjellberg 1994; Knauer 1994b: 185, 190).

The reasons for this more thoroughgoing folkloric turn—which was rendered possible by the freeing up of jazz norms in the 1960s—were various. Many musicians were indeed influenced by the growing self-reflection discussed above and an engagement with local folklore offered a way of reflecting one's environment and expressing one's own voice (Noglik 1990: 229). Again somewhat paradoxically, this identity-based strategy may have been partly informed by American jazz practices: Knauer observes that the European gesture of engaging with one's folkloric "roots" paralleled African American free jazz's Afrocentric rhetoric (1994b: 190). However, engaging with domestic folklore could also be driven by a jazzman's earlier musical socialization or simply by curiosity. Another possible cause related to changing musical fashions. Matching the decline in popular interest in jazz in West Germany during the 1960s, was an upsurge in interest in folk music (see below). Some mu-

---

2. The notable exception was the French guitarist Django Reinhardt, who in the 1930s had drawn on gypsy traditions in a more thoroughgoing manner (Gioia 1997: 171).

sicians and producers may have been inspired by or wished to benefit from that reorientation. However, the new recourse to folklore was not unproblematic. As Bert Noglik points out, many European jazz musicians considered much local folk music to be too "dead," ideologically burdened, or clichéd to be suitable (1990: 232 ff).

Two records in the *JMTW* series illustrate well the European musicians' new recourse to folkloric roots, as well as Berendt's location at the forefront of fostering such activities. They also indicate how the well-traveled producer's reach and influence extended well beyond the confines of the West German jazz scene. *Flamenco Jazz* and the quaintly titled *From Sticksland with Love* (both 1967) engaged with Spanish and Swiss folklore respectively. The Swiss pianist George Gruntz (born 1932) was the leader of *From Sticksland with Love*, a mammoth concert financed by Saba, in which a battery of Swiss and expatriate African American jazz musicians performed in various combinations and permutations with two Swiss folklore groups, George Mathys' fife corps and Alfred Sacher's drum clique. These two groups performed regularly during the famous *"Fastnacht"* (carnival) celebrations in Gruntz's native Basel, which is home to a lively folkloric tradition. Gruntz moved well beyond the mere borrowing of a folklore melody. He *did* do this, but he also gave the folklore groups space to perform independently of the jazz musicians. Hence, the two musical idioms are constantly juxtaposed.

Gruntz was motivated by various factors, the predominant one being a curiosity about the combination (Gruntz 2004). His recent engagement with Other music—on the *Noon in Tunisia* project (see chapter 14)—also encouraged him to compensate by engaging now with the Self; that is with his local folk music traditions (Gruntz 2002: 65). The project's realization also had a mundane cause: the success of *Noon in Tunisia* had led Berendt and Gruntz to consider other experimental collaborative projects that might be suitable for the incipient *JMTW* series (Gruntz 2004). Gruntz's proposal clearly appealed to Berendt, who some years earlier had reflected on Switzerland's healthy folkloric drum culture and the possibility that it was why there were so many good Swiss jazz drummers (1965b). He had also, since at least 1962, been enthusiastic about unorthodox combinations of jazzmen and folklore musicians (see chapter 12). And, of course, the experimental ethos also went right back to his and Heinrich Strobel's commissioning of Rolf Liebermann's *Concerto for Jazz Band and Symphony Orchestra* for the 1954 Donaueschingen Music Days.

From Sticksland with Love gives a perspective on the ambiguous nature of the "emancipation." As with other attempts by Europeans to use local folklore, Gruntz's recourse to Basel's drum and fife traditions was actually not a complete innovation: the American Swing drummer Gene Krupa had already performed briefly with Basel drum cliques when he passed through on tour (Berendt 1967o). Nevertheless, *From Sticksland with Love* was the most ambitious and comprehensive such project to date, and has been followed by other Swiss musicians who have undertaken similar activities (see Solothurnmann 1994). While Gruntz considers that the record has its place within the European emancipation and observes that, at the time, he too had developed a new self-confidence, his attitude toward the term is not uncritical. Unlike some of his European contemporaries from the late 1960s—see chapter 8—he himself did not wish to pursue any dogmatic rejection of American models (Gruntz 2004).

The Spanish saxophonist Pedro Iturralde (born 1929) was the leader of the *Flamenco Jazz* ensemble—a polyglot group of European musicians that included, at Berendt's instigation, the Andalusian flamenco guitarist Paco de Lucia. Like Gruntz, Iturralde does not seem to have had a dogmatic desire to distance himself from American models.[3] Indeed, Olaf Hudtwalcker, in his cover notes for *Flamenco Jazz* quite plausibly pondered whether Davis's *Sketches of Spain* and Coltrane's *Olé* might not have actually encouraged the Spaniard in his own efforts (1967). Iturralde—who is actually a Basque rather than a native of Andalusia, the home of flamenco—was apparently initially motivated to draw on Spanish music by "subconscious homesickness" he felt while touring in Europe during the early 1960s (Berendt 1967n: 34). Beyond this, he wished "to demonstrate that our music, without losing its personality, can integrate itself into another culture as universally actual as is jazz." In doing so, Iturralde attempted to "take flamenco as a source of inspiration and, using its peculiar feeling, ... express [him]self freely and sincerely through improvisation and according to the rhythmic conception of jazz" (Iturralde qtd. in Montes and Cifuentes 1967).

Berendt probably first heard of Iturralde's flamenco jazz in a concert broadcast from London by the European Broadcasting Union in November 1966, at the very time that he was making plans for the *JMTW* series. Given the widely regarded efforts of Miles Davis et al. and the North African influences in Andalusian flamenco—which includes jazz-like principles such as improvisation and the *falseta*, or "break"—he no doubt thought that a flamenco jazz recording would be an ideal inclusion in the series (cf. Berendt 1967n: 34; Montes and Cifuentes 1967; Noglik 1990: 243–5). He was presumably partly inspired by the comparative

---

3. If this was a concern, then it was not referred to in the liner notes for his three *Flamenco Jazz* albums recorded in the 1960s, nor in more recent articles about him.

popularity of flamenco in West Germany at the time (see below). In inviting Iturralde to perform in Berlin, Berendt also expressed himself to have been motivated by a moral consideration. As he observed in his program notes, "After all these American and international Flamenco Jazz experiments, it seemed called for to question the Spaniards themselves on the subject" (1967n: 34).

Nevertheless, the recourse to flamenco was not unproblematic, particularly for German commentators. It was important for Olaf Hudtwalcker to distinguish between Iturralde's artistic flamenco jazz and the clichéd, touristy nature of much Spanish flamenco. Indeed Hudtwalcker even observed that *Flamenco Jazz* might succeed in "freeing flamenco from its folklore trappings and nightclub image." With one eye on the need for self-respecting European jazzmen to be doing their own thing, elaborate efforts were also made to distinguish *Flamenco Jazz* from Davis's and Coltrane's recordings (Hudtwalcker 1967. See also Berendt 1967n: 34). Despite these efforts, it was perhaps inevitable that some critics and reviewers, like Heinz Ohff of the *Berliner Tagesspiegel*, would draw the comparison (Ohff 1967a).

The Ideological Taint of Folklore in West Germany

It might be thought that, in the midst of such activities as Iturralde's and Gruntz's, a record on which West German jazz musicians engaged in depth with German folklore would have been an obvious inclusion in the *JMTW* series. However, this was not to be. While the clichéd or hackneyed nature of some folklore could hinder jazz musicians, ideological associations also blocked the path (Noglik 1990: 232 ff). And, as Berendt noted in 1961, folklore was a controversial thing in (West) Germany (Berendt and Claxton 1961: 249).

The German words *Volkslied* and *Volksmusik* carry a long history of extra-musical connotations. *Volkslied* collectors like Johann Gottfried Herder and his nineteenth- and early twentieth-century successors (the "musical folklorists") sought to preserve a "pure" folk heritage they perceived to be disappearing (Steinbiß 1984: 15–17; Cooley 1997: 9). These activities were often accompanied by nationalist sentiment; indeed, Herder was the founder of a form of German cultural nationalism. As Timothy J. Cooley observes, there was no great conceptual leap between the notions of a pure national music and a pure political nation (1997: 9). This ideological link between folklore and nationalism has persisted even though, as Knauer observes, on closer inspection folklore actually tends to be regional rather than national (1994b: 188). Folklore nevertheless supplies important material through which the nation can be "imagined."[4]

Since 1945 in particular, German folklore has had a strong ideological taint. It has been perceived by many members of the West German jazz scene, and others, to be compromised by association with National Socialist *völkische* (folk) ideology.[5] Among others, the critic Günther Huesmann has noted that "German folk music is inaccessible for jazz musicians—and not only because it is so banal. The Nazis had laid a claim to this music as a 'treasure of the Aryan folk,' and ever since it has had an unmistakably chauvinistic quality" (1986. Cf. Berendt 1977a: 229, 241–4). The bassist Peter Kowald (1944–2002) has also expressed that "if one grew up in the 1950s, you couldn't actually sing a German folk song any more because Hitler had used all that" (qtd. in Wilson 2001: 112). On the other hand, not all Germans shared the unease: the amateur jazz musicians who "Dixielandized" German folk songs presumably felt no particular compunction in doing so.

Global Folklore as a Surrogate for a Lost German Tradition?

For many young West Germans, the folklore of other countries—folk songs of the British Isles, flamenco from the Iberian peninsula, or indeed blues songs from the U.S. deep South—provided a kind of surrogate for tainted German folklore, particularly during the years of the folk music revival of the 1960s and 1970s. Colin Wilkie, an English folksinger resident in Germany, a participant in the first *Burg Waldeck* folk festival in 1964 and a collaborator, in 1969, with the Hessischer Rundfunk (HR) jazz ensemble, observes in relation to the 1960s West German folk scene, that "most of the Germans we knew sang Irish, Scottish, English, American, Greek, Russian [folk songs]—anything but German" (Wilkie and Hart 2004).

It is within the dual context of the 1960s folk music revival and the ideological ballast of much German folk music that the West German impresarios Horst Lippmann and Fritz Rau (L+R) assembled a range of so-called "authentic documentations" of international folklore. The most important of these were the "American Folk Blues Festivals" that were organized annually from 1962 to 1970, initially under the aus-

---

4. For a discussion of the way in which flamenco was used in Franco's Spain, for example, see Washabaugh 1996: 162.

5. On the broader attitude toward German folk music in the postwar era, see, e.g., Steinbiß 1984: 33.

96 | THE RETURN OF JAZZ

pices of the DJF (Brigl and Schmidt-Joos 1985: 128 ff). Again, it was Berendt—freshly returned from his long American trip with William Claxton—who provided an initial impetus (Lippmann 1962). Steeled

Figure 7 | Günther Kieser's poster design for the first American Folk Blues Festival, 1962. © Günther Kieser. Used with permission.

by the success of the Folk Blues Festivals, L+R soon began mounting various other "authentic documentations," including "Spiritual and Gospel Festivals" (1965 ff), "Flamenco Gitano Festivals" (1965–70), a "Festival Folklore e Bossa Nova do Brasil" (1966) and a "Festival Musica Folklorica Argentina" (1967) (Hudtwalcker 1966; Brigl and Schmidt-Joos 1985: 144–52). For a short while they had a considerable significance within West Germany's cultural life and Brigl and Schmidt-Joos point out that, on the strength of these tours, the name "L+R" became synonymous, among intellectually minded West German young people, with the distinctive notions of "openness to the world, sincerity and honesty" (1985: 144).

Lippmann and Rau assembled their documentations with a pedagogical zeal, which was no doubt influenced by their backgrounds as jazz enthusiasts. Moreover, this folklore was interpreted as having direct links or being otherwise analogous to "authentic" jazz: folk blues was seen, for example, as being a semirural precursor of jazz. Authentic flamenco, like gospel, was viewed as being a vital music ignored by official cultural circles, just as jazz had been early in the 1950s (Brigl and Schmidt-Joos 1985: 128 ff). Some of the tours, particularly the blues, gospel and flamenco ones, were financially successful. As Rau noted, the latter benefited from that West German demographic whose interest in Spain was primarily linked to its being a tourist destination. However, the success of the "authentic documentations" tailed off noticeably in 1967, as the public's interest passed to pop music and soon L+R's folklore packages were a thing of the past (Brigl and Schmidt-Joos 1985: 149–52).

Despite their enthusiasm for these musics, jazz critics still found it necessary to dissociate international folklore from notions attached to the German species. In 1966, Hudtwalcker pointed out, for example, that authentic flamenco was an art form "that extended far beyond that which we know as folklore" (1966: 10). The HR's Ulrich Olshausen, in his cover notes for the *JMTW* record *Wild Goose*, a 1969 collaboration he initiated between the HR jazz ensemble, Colin Wilkie, and Wilkie's partner Shirley Hart, noted that Anglo-American folk song was nowadays "the sophisticated music of the city and of the city-dweller" (1969). This put paid to the idea that an enthusiasm for folk music might involve a reactionary flight into an imagined preindustrial world, such as that of the *Wandervogel* movement of the early twentieth century. Berendt went one step further in his cover notes for *From Sticksland with Love*. There he advanced the concept of an international folklore:

> Folklore today no longer stands for Germany's nineteenth-century "Volkslieder" as typified by [the musical folklorist] Friedrich Silcher, nor

does it stand for old chansons in France, or for flamenco in Spain. Folklore today truly means global folklore to all of us, regardless whether it is Balkanese or Brazilian, Yiddish or Javanese, Central European or South African. Modern man is more of a world citizen when it comes to folklore than in most other areas. (1967o)

In this way, folklore became a suitable ideological bedfellow for jazz, which Berendt had sought to establish during the 1950s as the universal music *par excellence*. Hence, he saw it as perfectly natural that jazz musicians were now able to work with folk musics from around the world (1967o). This appealing notion of a global folklore provided a philosophical underpinning for the whole *JMTW* series, and the moderate popularity of international folklore in West Germany during the mid-1960s at least potentially supplied it with an expanded audience.

Navigating the Pitfalls of German Folklore

The notion of "global folklore" was also de facto pursued on the one *JMTW* record where jazz musicians actually did engage with German folklore. *Wild Goose* (1969) contains an adaptation of *"Ich armes Maidlein klag mich sehr"* (*"Armes Maidlein"*), among an album otherwise comprising versions of Colin Wilkie's compositions and his adaptations of English folksongs. *"Armes Maidlein"* was in fact a last remnant of a largely unsuccessful attempt by Lippmann and Rau, as managers of the Albert Mangelsdorff Quintet, to encourage musicians in the circle around Mangelsdorff to engage with German folklore. The story behind this and behind the Mangelsdorff Quintet's earlier adaptation of *"Es sungen drei Engel"* (*"Drei Engel"*), recorded on its 1964 *Now Jazz Ramwong* album illuminates even more clearly the fate of German folk music within West German jazz. *"Drei Engel"* is a true rarity (cf. Berendt 1977a: 239; Huesmann 1986; Noglik 1990: 238–40). It was also created for a very specific context, which called for special measures to be taken to Germanize jazz: *Now Jazz Ramwong* showcased tunes played by Mangelsdorff's Quintet on the first large-scale international jazz tour to be financed by the West German government's cultural outreach arm, the Goethe Institut.

Jazz for Goethe?

The Goethe Institut was founded by the Federal Republic in 1952 and charged with the responsibility of conducting language courses for non-Germans, particularly those from underdeveloped countries, intending to study in West Germany. In 1960, the Department of Foreign Affairs gave the organization the additional task of administering cultural institutes overseas. Such institutes were soon established in a wide range of locations, where they gave language courses and presented events such as music concerts, theatre performances, exhibitions and lectures (Ross 1965).

From the outset, the cultural institutes had a specific political brief. At a basic level, this involved representing West German culture to the world at large. Karl-Ernst Hüdepohl, the head of the Goethe Institut's programming division, elaborated on this task in 1968. According to him, it involved providing factual information about West Germany, garnering sympathy for the country by staging cultural events and providing services, collaborating on joint projects, advancing a reciprocal understanding of the Other, and consciously working toward a complementation of the world's cultures (1968: 19).

The question of cultural representation was a vexed one in the context of postwar Germany, however. On the one hand, it was deemed necessary to rehabilitate Germany's international reputation. As the president of the Goethe Institut, Peter H. Pfeiffer, remarked in 1965, Germany needed to win back "that reputation which she possessed in her great days and which she [had] forfeited by means of the madness of her self-overestimation" (1965). However, given that the cultural politics of the Nazis and those of the institute could both be seen, in their way, to be celebrations of German culture, it was necessary for the institute to distinguish strongly between the two and proceed with caution. Hence, the institute's Werner Ross expressly criticized the concept of cultural imperialism (1965: 13). In 1968, Pfeiffer stipulated that West Germany should rather present its culture "as collaboration and stimulus, as model or possibility." (1968) This task was placed in an expressly cosmopolitan context. The institute's work was understood as part of a broader project of cultural exchange aimed at "an unreserved opening up to One World," whereby Germany would take its place in a "*Weltkultur*" (world culture) (Ross 1965: 15). Not inappropriately, given the institute's activities, Pfeiffer employed a musical metaphor to express the aim; Germany's gaining "a worthy place in the concert of Peoples" (1966).

Such laudable statements of high principle nevertheless left open the question of what sort of offerings the institute should actually finance. In the early 1960s, it took a narrow and conservative approach, which Berendt summed up as "Mozart, Beethoven, Goethe, etc." (1980a). However, as Werner Ross pointed out as early as 1965, "diligent journalists hurried to discover in this 'baroque music by candlelight' yet another fundamental restorative tendency in the Federal Republic" (1965: 8). Such criticism caused the institute to reexamine the notion of "culture" as a passively received thing (Ross 1965). As the 1960s progressed, the institute continued to express the desire to liberate itself from elite notions of culture, a task which gained special urgency in the wake of 1968 (see, e.g., Pfeiffer 1968; Von Herwarth 1970; Goethe Institut n.d.).

In the event, jazz concerts provided one opportunity for the institute to reflect a more up-to-date notion of culture. However, the programming of jazz was not uncontested. Throughout the 1960s, jazz continued to be regarded by some critical voices as not being "German" enough and therefore, in the context of representing German culture abroad, as being a *"Falschspiel"* (wrong play) (Goethe Institut 1968: 60. See also Mangelsdorff 1964a: 159). By the late 1960s, the institute's detractors were also suggesting that its programming of jazz was simply an "alibi" for conservative, business-as-usual programming (Goethe Institut 1969: 115).

The beleaguered institute's domestic concerns did not exist in isolation, however. There was also the matter of audience attendances at Goethe Institut events abroad. Indeed, the new policy of jazz programming was partly motivated by a desire to broaden these audiences. By the mid-1960s, the institute had identified that its concerts tended to attract a rather small "high society" crowd. As such, there was an unfortunate gap between those up-and-coming young professionals who attended the institute's language courses and the elites who attended its concerts. Increasingly, it wished to attract the former to its cultural events (Ross 1965: 14–15). The desire to broaden the appeal of the institute's cultural events only went so far, though, and stopped short of the so-called "mass public." It was clearly proud of the large, young audiences that the jazz concerts attracted and was excited by the possibilities of telecasts of its jazz concerts reaching even larger numbers (see, e.g., Hömberg 1965: 50–1; Goethe Institut 1965: 41; 1966: 80–2; 1968; 1969: 66, 86). However, German pop music remained a bridge too far for some years yet (cf. "Jazz aus Deutschland für Südamerika" 1968: 277).

Of course, this reorientation in the institute's cultural policy coincided with the broader legitimation of jazz in West Germany. Nevertheless, the institute's embrace of jazz was initially quite tentative. It took considerable persuasion on Berendt's part for the institute to countenance financing a jazz tour, and when it finally did agree to send the Mangelsdorff Quintet to Asia in 1964, it made it clear that this trip was to be a one-off experiment (Berendt 1964b: 138; 1980a; Paulot 1993: 206–7). The expectations placed on the group, not only to attract a larger, younger audience, but also to represent West Germany in an appropriate way, must have been considerable—indeed the future of other such tours was effectively riding on it. No wonder that Ralf Hübner, the drummer in Mangelsdorff's Quintet, recalled feeling like a guinea-pig (Paulot 1993: 211).

"*Drei Engel,*" or How to Combine Modern Jazz and German Folklore

Mangelsdorff's group made a number of deliberate repertoire decisions for the Goethe Institute's maiden jazz tour. At the suggestion of Berendt—who travelled with the Quintet and announced its concerts—it adapted local music from the countries it was intending to visit (see chapter 11). Secondly, it also enlarged the German dimension of its repertoire by adapting *"Drei Engel"* (Paulot 1993: 207). Mangelsdorff—who was now more interested in writing original material than in creating adaptations of others' compositions—recalled *"Drei Engel"* also being Berendt's idea (Berendt 1977a: 228–9; Paulot 1993: 233; Mangelsdorff 2004). It seems likely that the institute was at least partly responsible. Given the significance of the tour as an officially sanctioned act of German cultural diplomacy, one can assume that there was some pressure exerted on the group by the institute that their music be distinctly German, rather than simply a *"Falschspiel"* imitation of an American art form. This assumption is borne out by the fact that Mangelsdorff, after returning from the trip, publically observed that his group's music was received in Asia as being specifically *German* and that that must have been gratifying for the institute (Mangelsdorff 1964a: 159).

Prior to departure, Berendt assembled a number of German folk themes that he thought might be suitable. Mangelsdorff selected *"Drei Engel,"* although even here he was reticent, partly because of the clichéd nature of the song, which he thought sounded too "Christmassy"—a reference to the fact that the song was known as a Christmas carol (Berendt 1977a: 229). Another source of Mangelsdorff's hesitance was the ideological ballast perceived to inhere generally in German folklore (Mangelsdorff 2004). In this respect, *"Drei Engel"* was a special case, however. For various reasons, it evaded the taint of National Socialism.

With much *Volksmusik* thought ideologically off limits, Berendt had looked to folkloric material from the twelfth to fourteenth centuries (Berendt 1977a: 229). There was a musical reason for this: like some of the band's own compositions and the Asian themes adapted for the tour, this older German folklore was modal (Berendt 1964a; Knauer 1996a: 148). However, there was also an ideological reason: "buried" musical folklore can avoid the taint of some living folklore (Noglik 1988a: 516). And as Mangelsdorff told me, he deliberately avoided adapting a song "which was everyday, which one often heard in the Nazi era" (2004). "*Drei Engel*" was ideologically safe for additional reasons alluded to by Berendt in his cover notes for *Now Jazz Ramwong*:

> ["Drei Engel" was] originally a fighting song and grew out of the battle against the Mongols on the Lechfeld Plain. However, as I noted when announcing the concerts in Asia, "because Germany has now become a peace-loving country, it has come in the meantime to be sung as a Christmas carol." Paul Hindemith wove the song into his opera "Mathis der Maler." [The American jazzmen] Roland Kirk and Benny Golson took it from the Opera. (1964a)

These carefully selected comments reveal a great deal. Berendt represented the tune as a metaphor for what had happened to (West) Germany over the course of the twentieth century: like "*Drei Engel*," he urged, West Germany had had a militaristic past, but since the war, it too had become peace-loving. Furthermore, "*Drei Engel*" had been appropriated by Hindemith, the composer whose atonal modernist music had been labelled "degenerate" by the Nazis and who, after a complicated period, had eventually left Germany in exile. More specifically, it had been used in Hindemith's opera *Mathis der Maler*, which was based on the life of Matthias Gruenewald, a medieval German artist with a social conscience. Ultimately, the National Socialists forbade the opera and, in 1936, all performances of Hindemith's work were outlawed. In 1937, he left the country (Kennedy 1988: 299–300). Far from being tainted by Nazi ideology, then, "*Drei Engel*" could be associated with a victim of Nazi persecution, a fact that was not lost on Mangelsdorff (Mangelsdorff 2004). To an informed listener familiar with Hindemith's work, the song might also have been associated with the theme of the artist exercising a social conscience.[6] In this way, "*Drei Engel's*" antifascist credentials were on a par with those which postwar West German jazz lobbyists had claimed for jazz itself.

In addition, "*Drei Engel*" had just been adopted into the jazz canon by two African American musicians, Roland Kirk and Benny Golson (Kirk and Golson 1963). On that basis, Mangelsdorff's group could not

---

6. The question of the complicity or otherwise of the *Mathis* opera with the tenets of National Socialism has, more recently, become a contested one. Early in the postwar years, Berendt's mentor at the SWF, Heinrich Strobel, advocated the view that it represented the artist engaging in "inner emigration" against an oppressive regime. More recently, Claudia Zaenck has advanced the view that the libretto is more consistent with the idea of the artist accommodating National Socialist cultural policy (see Kater 1997: 178 ff).

be accused of seeking to nationalistically glorify German culture: "*Drei Engel*" had already been put on a (jazz) pedestal by Kirk and Golson. This was an instance in which copying the Americans was, paradoxically, very much in the interests of the West German jazz musician, despite all contemporary discourse to the contrary.

Finally, Mangelsdorff's engagement with the folk tune was not somehow dangerously "stuck" in the past. The Mangelsdorff Quintet's music was firmly planted in the avant-garde jazz idiom. As Berendt termed it, "*Drei Engel*" was an "Old-German Soul-Waltz," metamorphosed into Mangelsdorff-music (1964a). His engagement with German folklore could not therefore be classified as what Berendt later disparagingly referred to as a typically German approach to tradition, namely, using it as an "alibi" for ignoring the contemporary (1977a: 228).

"*Drei Engel*" was in all respects an ideal vehicle for the presentation of "German" jazz by a group sponsored by the Goethe Institut. Particularly once it had been explained from the bandstand by Berendt, it was neatly distanced from the nationalistic ideological associations of German folk music and could even be used to draw a distinction between the "Third Reich" and the Federal Republic. It matched the Goethe Institut's cultural policies and brief perfectly.

After "*Drei Engel*"?

In the years following "*Drei Engel*," Mangelsdorff continued to strive for a personal style emancipated from American models. With the sole exception of "*Armes Maidlein*," arranged by his colleague Joki Freund for *Wild Goose*—an album on which Mangelsdorff also performed—these efforts focused on the writing of original material as well as on the techniques of free jazz, rather than on a renewed engagement with German folklore (Jost 1987: 200–10). Despite the urgings of Lippmann and of Rau—who was particularly enamored of "*Drei Engel*" and who also wished to rescue *Volksmusik* from the province of the Right—Mangelsdorff could not be persuaded to record an album consisting entirely of adaptations of German folk music (Paulot 1993: 185, 187). Few other West German jazz musicians were much interested either. As will be seen in the following chapters, there was a far greater comfort with free jazz, European New Music, and non-European world musics.

Tellingly, the most concerted effort to engage with German folkloric material occurred in East Germany in the early 1970s. In 1972, the East German pianist Ulrich Gumpert recorded one such album titled *Aus Teutschen Landen* (sic). This reflected a greater ease with the German folkloric tradition on the Eastern side of the inner-German border (Heffley 2000a: Ch. 2: 66–8). It also indicated, perhaps, a specifically Eastern European dimension to the desire for emancipation from *American* jazz models (cf. "Ost-Jazz" 1964). Certainly, many Eastern European jazz musicians did engage with folk music during the 1960s (see, e.g., Various Musicians 1965; 1968). However, while Gumpert's approach was partly colored by "affection and respect," it was also tinged with irony and *Verfremdung*—which suggests that he too wished to maintain a certain distance (Jost 1987: 248; Noglik 1988a: 521; Heffley 2000a: Ch. 2: 68).

CHAPTER 7

Globe Unity
Free Jazz Meets European New Music

If German folklore was largely unsuitable for adaptation, then an engagement with contemporary European New Music provided another, more attractive pathway to emancipation. Indeed, jazz had much more in common with New Music from an ideological perspective, given that both had been labeled degenerate by National Socialism. The concept of a combination of jazz and New Music was actually by no means a new one in the early 1960s. As we saw in chapter 1, Berendt had been drawing parallels between jazz and New Music and fostering various "Third Stream" type activities since the mid 1950s—well before "emancipation" entered the discourse. However, these opportunities dried up when, after 1957, Heinrich Strobel placed an embargo on the programming of jazz at Donaueschingen, an embargo lifted only once in 1967. Indeed it was only after Strobel's death in 1970, that avant-garde jazz became a regular fixture at Donaueschingen (Berendt 1996b).[1] Together with the Berlin Jazz Days, Donaueschingen now gave Berendt a fresh opportunity to promote new combinations of jazz and New Music. The enthusiastic uptake among German musicians of free jazz—with its questioning of norms and its openness for other approaches and material—provided the musical basis for those combinations.

---

1. Berendt reports that Strobel put a stop to jazz at Donaueschingen because he thought that jazz's popularity might inundate the festival's true focus: avant-garde concert music (1996b).

Berendt and West German Free Jazz

After rave reviews of Ornette Coleman's early albums by Berendt and other critics, it took some time for West German musicians to work through the radical aesthetic innovations of free jazz: indeed Ekkehard Jost writes of a "phase interval of five years" between the first U.S. free jazz and its beginnings in Europe (1978: 55). Predictably, Berendt put a great deal of energy behind promoting this domestic variant. In 1965, for example, he used his influence at Saba to realize the Gunter Hampel Quintet's desire to record *Heartplants*, an album partly in the free jazz idiom (Jost 1978: 55–6; Schoof 2004). Then, in 1966, he likewise proposed that the label record the pathbreaking Globe Unity Orchestra (see below). Berendt's efforts here should not be dismissed lightly. As Orchestra alumnus Manfred Schoof recalled, free jazz was far from the label owner Brunner-Schwer's personal taste (2004).[2]

During the 1960s and early 1970s, Berendt also regularly programmed the cream of European (and American) free jazz at the Jazz Days and at other events he organized, including at Donaueschingen.[3] Just as important as these formal concerts—if not more so—were the annual "Free Jazz Meetings" he instituted at the SWF, however. The Free Jazz Meeting began life in December 1966 as a three-day event at the SWF's Baden-Baden studios. Highlights were recorded especially for radio broadcast, and, in 1970, for telecast. In 1969, the meeting even resulted in a commercially released MPS recording, *Gittin' to know y'all*. However, as this title suggests the end result was strictly secondary, with the major focus being on *process* ("Avantgarde-Treffen beim Südwestfunk" 1966; Zimmerle 1967a, 1969a; "Free Jazz in Baden-Baden" 1968; "Das Free Jazz Treffen des SWF" 1970; Panke 1971a). A focus on process over result is, as Ted Gioia observes, one of the primary principles of jazz, and it was also an important aspect in other contemporary art practices in the 1960s, such as the "happenings" (Kultermann 1971: 11; Gioia 1988: 104–5).

The idea—which was soon adopted by other German broadcasters like the NDR and Radio Bremen—was to create an opportunity for the invitees, up to twenty-five young members of the international and domestic jazz avant-garde, to test out new ideas and "socialize" in different

---

2. Brunner-Schwer was presumably influenced in his decision to record *Globe Unity* by the unexpected commercial success of the *Heartplants* album (cf. Schwab 2004: 171).

3. He invited the British free jazz pioneer Joe Harriott to participate in the SWF session at the 1964 German Jazz Festival, thereby giving the German audience its first taste of live free jazz (Schwab 2004: 162). Early Jazz Days invitees included Ornette Coleman (1965); the GUO and Albert Ayler (1966); Archie Shepp and *Jazz Meets India* (1967); and Sunny Murray, Don Cherry, and Fred van Hove (all 1968).

combinations for a period of between three days and a week (Olshausen 1967; Mümpfer 1974). This concept was related to the "jam session" theme that Berendt had pursued at the 1965 Jazz Days, but was intended to be removed from the concert hall setting and from questions of commerce (Panke 1971a; Bachmann 1975c). As critic Klaus-Robert Bachmann noted, the meeting was philosophically based on a dialectical combination of organization and spontaneity (1975c). Like the Jazz Days and Berendt's wider production style, it reflected his interventionist approach, at least in relation to invitations (Olshausen 1967). Despite this, the editor of *Jazz Podium* observed in 1967 that "no one felt pressed into an undesirable framework" (Zimmerle 1967a). Not that everyone always agreed: in 1969, for example, some of the American invitees—members of the so-called expatriate "Chicagoans in Paris"—resented that some of their colleagues had been excluded ("Das Free Jazz Treffen des SWF" 1970). Various other issues, including the brevity of the meeting, the short rehearsal times, and the lack of a precise schedule were also occasionally criticized (Zimmerle 1967a; 1969a; Mümpfer 1974: 24). However, these aspects tended not to detract from the undeniable benefits accruing to the European invitees. As Ulrich Olshausen observed in 1967: "five minutes playing with [free jazz pioneer] Don Cherry ... would have to be more valuable than listening to a hundred records" (1967).

Sometimes, the meetings also yielded more tangible results. Some invitees began to plan new collaborations (Zimmerle 1967a; 1969a). Others recorded raw material to be put to use later (Olshausen 1967; Zimmerle 1969a). Grand ideas—such as the *JMTW* projects *Jazz Meets India* and *Eternal Rhythm*—were also germinated at the meetings, and then fully realized in Berlin and/or Donaueschingen (Broecking 1995: 76). It would be wrong to conclude that the meetings were always unmitigated successes, however. Some of the musical experiments misfired (Olshausen 1967; Zimmerle 1969a). Occasionally, Berendt's failure to invite particular musicians, the Black music ideology of some of the invitees, or what the Europeans saw as aggressively "American" play was also thought to have cast a pall over the Meeting ("Das Free Jazz Treffen des SWF" 1970; Lewis 2002; Schoof 2004).[4] Nevertheless, such things were probably inevitable with an activity so experimental, and for those

---

4. Lewis suggests that one significant reason for the antagonism or lack of cooperation (in 1969 and subsequently) between the "Chicagoans in Paris" and the European avant-gardists, was that the two groups were effectively in competition for the same financial opportunities (2002: 239). On the divergence between the "American" and "European" approaches to performance, which Manfred Schoof observed on occasion at the Free Jazz Meetings (2004), see chapter 9.

Figure 8 | The 1966 Baden-Baden Free Jazz Meeting. *From left to right:* Albert Mangelsdorff, Manfred Schoof, Alexander von Schlippenbach, Buschi Niebergall, Berendt. © Paul G. Deker. Used with permission.

fortunate enough to be invited, the meetings provided a welcome, paid venue to perform and broadcast. German free jazz pioneer Peter Brötzmann has observed that "these Meetings ... were very important just for all of us to develop a kind of togetherness ... a feeling for 'Yes, we can do it!'" (2004). His colleague Alexander von Schlippenbach has also noted that they were beneficial for the New Jazz, particularly because they were broadcast (2004). For the expatriate Americans, on the other hand, the meetings contributed to the "European circuit," which "became an essential means of support for Free musicians" (Litweiler 1984: 241). Ulrich Olshausen was therefore not without justification when he observed in 1967 that Berendt had done a great service to jazz by instituting the meeting (1967).

Berendt Writing on (German) Free Jazz, 1966–73

Though he was not the only critic to do so, Berendt was comparatively early to write about West German free jazz, and he also called on a new generation of younger critics to attempt to come to grips with the music (1966b; 1966f; 1966n; 1967p). His own interpretation was most comprehensively set out in a *Melos* article published in 1967 and in the 1968 (third) edition of the *Jazzbook* (1967d; 1968c: 32–46). While predominantly focusing on musical aspects—atonality; intensity; the emancipation from meter, beat, and symmetry; and the engagement with both world musics and with noise—Berendt was also interested in free jazz's deeper message, namely, that "we have to stop viewing music as the medium of our self-affirmation" (1968c: 45. See also 1967d: 343). Adopting a critical tone, he urged that free jazz was a medium against bourgeois society's single-minded interest in security, and married this attitude with his own longstanding, almost apocalyptic convictions about a crisis in the modern consciousness:

> A bourgeois world which is no more unified than in its constant scream for security stands in great need of a consciousness of the chaos which encircles it—unless it wants to completely cease to exist. One of the possible ways of mediating this consciousness—in so far as it orders the chaos and gives it artistic form—is free jazz. (1967d: 352)

This comment, which was vaguely consonant with the critical climate of the times, also echoed, to an extent, the notion that he had earlier advanced in *Jazz: A Time-Critical Study*—that jazz had the ability to order the chaos of modernity (1950a). However, it was significantly removed from the Black music ideology of a Leroi Jones/Amiri Baraka or an Archie Shepp.

Globe Unity: A Fruitful Combination of Free Jazz and New Music

One of Berendt's most significant free jazz productions in the 1960s was *Globe Unity* (1966), the debut album by the Globe Unity Orchestra (GUO), a recording he included for a time in the *JMTW* series. The GUO—which premiered at the Jazz Days in 1966, performed at Donaueschingen in 1967 and 1970, as well as at the New Jazz Meeting in 1975, and has been active ever since—is often referred to by Europeans when discussing the emancipation; it is regarded as "independen[t] of American models" and as even "dismiss[ing] ... the child-parent relationship between American and European Jazz" (Burde 1978: 48; Jost 1978: 56). This is no coincidence; for the GUO's pianist and composer Alexander von Schlippenbach (born 1938) as for other core members, questions of emancipation, and playing their "own thing" were indeed very significant concerns ("'Own Thing'" 1966: 69).

Early in 1966, von Schlippenbach received a commission from the West Berlin broadcaster RIAS—one of the Jazz Days' sponsors—to compose a piece for the upcoming festival (Jost 1987: 77). That year, Berendt was assembling the Jazz Days around the idea of an encounter between jazz and other art forms, including modern concert music (Berendt 1966l: 2). The initial brief was for von Schlippenbach—a graduate of Cologne's Musik Hochschule and well trained in composition—to collaborate with the renowned New Music composer, Boris Blacher, to come up with a "Third Stream" type of work for jazz soloists and string quartets. However, he did not find the proposal sensible and instead suggested that he alone compose a work solely for free jazz orchestra, an idea with which he had been toying for some time ("'Own Thing'" 1966: 69; Noglik 1981: 102–3). Berendt quickly acceded to the proposal, and also suggested that a recording be made for Saba (Schoof 2004).[5]

Inspired equally by European New Music, including Schoenberg, as by American free jazz, von Schlippenbach developed his own innovative approach to the task (Storb 1978: 4–5). In his two 1966 composi-

---

5. For his part, Blacher continued with his own commission and composed "*Improvisation über Plus Minus Eins für Jazz-Quintett und Streich-Quartett*," which, like Globe Unity, premiered at the first concert of the 1966 Jazz Days but which was not particularly well received (Berendt 1966l: 13; Miller 1966: 324).

tions for the GUO, "jazz themes in the traditional sense play a negligible role" (Burde 1978: 48). Rather, collective jazz improvisation is combined with a serial technique borrowed from New Music composition (Kumpf 1975b: 57 ff; Burde 1978: 48 ff). Not that all listeners could identify the serialism: the veteran *E-Musik* critic H. H. Stuckenschmidt, who reviewed the GUO's performance at the 1967 Donaueschingen Music Days, for example, pointedly remarked that even a schooled listener was able to detect this only by reading the program notes (1967: 458). In any event, von Schlippenbach reserved considerable leeway for the musicians to improvise. In doing so, he relativized his own role as composer, and for this reason Ekkehard Jost prefers to call "Globe Unity" a *collective composition* (1987: 78). This is in keeping with Schlippenbach's own radical conception of the GUO at the time, where "the whole spirit is in revolt against any form of subjection in music" (von Schlippenbach 1966). Rainer Blome concurred when he boldly opined in the newly established West German free jazz periodical *Sounds* that the record should be played in all European music schools as it was far more instructive than "a hundred readings about harmonic theory" (Blome 1967).

Berendt himself was quick to identify a considerable advance beyond the "Third Stream" activities with which he had been associated a decade earlier: "the blending of jazz and contemporary music has been an undertaking quite as problematic for both sides as it has been attractive—but here it has been perfected" (1966o). With ten years' hindsight, the Berlin critic Wolfgang Burde was not quite so sure: "One might doubt whether avant-garde music and jazz were really integrated in this work, whether they really merged to form a new entity." "Nonetheless," he continued, "it is undeniable that in this historic first work a new realm of expression had been conquered which had far-reaching consequences for the further development of European jazz" (1978: 48). Indeed, many European jazz musicians have continued to be influenced in a like manner by modern *E-Musik* traditions (Jost 1987; Noglik 1990: 263–314). Just why the long-lived and dynamic GUO fitted so well with the notion of a specifically "European" jazz will be revisited in chapter 9.

Auto Jazz

As Berendt's compilation *Jazz Greetings From the East*, and his productions of *Flamenco Jazz* and *From Sticksland with Love* indicate, his active involvement in European jazz extended far beyond German borders. Another non-German JMTW production was *Auto Jazz* (1968) by the French saxophonist Barney Wilen (1937–1996), who became well known through his masterful participation in Miles Davis's 1957 sound track to the Louis Malle film *Lift to the Scaffold*. Though *Auto Jazz* also combined free jazz and New Music techniques, it took quite a different tack from *Globe Unity* and further indicates the breadth of approaches made possible by free jazz during the 1960s, approaches enthusiastically taken by the European musicians whom Berendt fostered.

Auto Jazz applied techniques of "electro-acoustics"—combining standard instrumentation with taped sounds, in this case of the Monaco Grand Prix—and "preparation"—changing the notes and timbres produced by an instrument, in this case by putting objects in the strings of the piano.[6] In its live performances, it also relied on nonmusical art forms: the filmmaker François Conrad de Ménil's film of the 1967 Monaco Grand Prix, and the visual artist Etienne Oléary's light effects (Berendt 1968a). This type of approach to the integration of the arts was characteristic of much avant-garde "intermedial" art in the 1960s, and it therefore should not surprise that *Auto Jazz* was performed, during 1967 and 1968, at modern art venues in Europe and the United States, including at Berlin's *Akademie der Künste* in conjunction with the 1968 Jazz Days.[7] The New York premiere was even attended by modern art luminaries such as Andy Warhol and Robert Rauschenberg (Berendt 1968a; 1968d; Le Bris 1968).

Wilen's primary motivation for *Auto Jazz* was a fascination with motor vehicle noise and the possibility of using it musically (Le Bris 1968).[8] For his part, Berendt was well aware of Wilen's electro-acoustic ideas, having invited him to participate in the 1966 Free Jazz Meeting, on which occasion, and very much with the producer's encouragement, Wilen had performed a "duet" with a tape recording ("Avantgarde-Treffen beim Südwestfunk" 1966; Zimmerle 1967a). Electro-acoustic jazz clearly attracted Berendt at this time. Not only did he encourage Wilen's efforts at the Free Jazz Meeting, and then leap at the opportu-

---

6. Electro-acoustics were used within the New Music tradition by the German composer Karlheinz Stockhausen as early as 1959–60 for his composition *Kontakte* (Kumpf: 1975b 46–7). The preparation technique was developed in the 1930s by the American avant-garde composer John Cage.

7. On the intermedial art of the 1960s, see, e.g., Kultermann 1971: 40, 77.

8. Wilen had been interested in this concept since 1964. Then, in May 1967, he had the opportunity to make professional quality recordings of the Grand Prix. It was during this process that he met the filmmaker de Ménil and formed the idea for the *Auto Jazz* project. The project premiered at the *Musée d'Art Moderne* in Paris during the October 1967 *Biennale de Paris*. In December of the same year, it was performed at a "Man and Machine" event organized by New York University. George Gruntz also presented the piece at a series of jazz events he programmed in 1968 at the Basel Theater under the title "Contemporary Sound Focus" (Le Bris 1968; Anders 1972: 16; Gruntz 2004).

nity of producing a record version of *Auto Jazz*, and presenting it live in Berlin in 1968, he also programmed the American George Russell's *Electronic Sonata for Souls Loved by Nature*—which likewise combined taped sounds with live jazz—at the 1970 Jazz Days (Berendt 1967g: 4, 1970d: 14; Zimmerle 1967a). Just why this type of music appealed is evident from his cover notes for *Auto Jazz*. While drawing parallels and distinctions between Wilen's use of taped sounds and the French composer Pierre Schaeffer's *musique concrète*—a technique devised in 1948 whereby music was assembled from recorded "concrete" sound objects, such as snippets of taped birdsong—he took the opportunity to revisit an argument that he had first raised a decade earlier. According to him, Schaeffer abstracted individual sounds from their environment, and his music was therefore actually alienated and "un-concrete" (1968a). On the other hand, Wilen's saxophone and the undoctored vehicle noise stood on their own terms; they were equal partners that performed as a "duo" (1968d). In this way, Wilen wrestled with the sounds and noise of modern technology and rendered them into music. In the process he humanized that noise, and—by implication—he humanized modernity itself (1968a). This was a sentiment also held by George Russell at the time (Berendt 1970d: 14; Shapiro 2000: 52). In Berendt's case—informed, as he was, by an opposition to the bloodless rationalism of modernity and by Günther Anders' anxious notion of the "antiquatedness" of mankind in the face of technology—this was part of an artist's moral obligation:

> Should the artist ever stop to make his art penetrate the technical world and quit incorporating it into his work, then the world of art and of the spirit shall be reduced to elementary, hardly recognizable "reduits," shrinking in proportion to the expansion of the technical world. …
>
> That exactly is a duty of the contemporary artist: to make sure our technical world of today remains accessible and comprehensible, and musically possible, including everything within it that becomes sound, tone, or noise. It's a human task in a world which has functionalized and manipulated man to such a degree that often only the artist has retained the possibility to inject human dimensions into the computerized anti-humanity of the machine. (1968a)

This was a reprise of an argument first put in his 1959 address at the Berlin Jazz Salon, in which he had debated Anders in person and sought to establish that modern artists were capable of rendering human the technology that was indeed outstripping humanity (Berendt 1959g. See also 1957d). It was also consonant with Berendt's broader ideas about (free) jazz being able to order the chaos of modernity. By 1968, however, this was an interpretation which was roundly rejected as ideological clap-trap by some younger European critics (see, e.g., Renaud 1968).

* * * * *

Schlippenbach's and Wilen's combinations of free jazz and New Music clearly appealed to Berendt, who had long been interested in encouraging such things. They were performed in the highest of high art venues and were consistent with earlier efforts to legitimate jazz. Made possible by the innovations of free jazz, these types of activities clearly represented to him a significant front of jazz's avant-garde, particularly in Europe, and one well worth supporting. Despite adopting a tone occasionally critical of bourgeois society or the "anti-humanity of the machine," his accommodating attitude to free jazz—which he sought to contextualize within the jazz tradition, suggesting that earlier styles such as bebop had also been received as "chaotic" at the time, only to be later received into the canon (1968c 44)—was largely in keeping with the modernist aesthetic of novelty and perpetual artistic progress, which essentially accepted the place reserved for art within bourgeois culture (cf. McCormick 1991: 8; DeVeaux 1997: 22).

Almost inevitably, Berendt's enthusiasm for free jazz waned. As Peter Brötzmann has observed: "he was one of the first who said 'Okay, this music is dead'" (2004). By the 1973/74 edition of the *Jazzbook*, he asserted that the perpetually evolving "jazz development" had continued beyond free jazz. True to the "decade" model, which he had been espousing since the first edition of the *Jazzbook*, free jazz was properly to be seen as the historical jazz style of the 1960s. 1970 had heralded a "cooling-off of free jazz" and a new, as yet nameless, post–free jazz. Free jazz had indeed involved a process of liberation; however, it was the post–free jazz musician who was now "really free, free to play all the things that were taboo for many creative musicians of the free jazz period." He also chided those who had not moved on: "aimless freedom is nothing but the inconsistent, misunderstood freedom of the fashionable emancipation movements—in politics, society, and the arts" (1973/74: 37–40). It was in this context that Berendt dropped the Free Jazz Meeting in 1972 and—when it returned in 1973—renamed it the *New* Jazz Meeting (cf. Mümpfer 1974: 23).[9] The emphasis of the Donaueschingen jazz concerts in 1973 and thereafter was also less exclusively on free jazz (Kumpf 1974; K-G Fischer 1999: 48).

---

9. The Free Jazz Meeting had been scrapped in 1972 due to a lack of funds at the SWF, brought about by its financial contribution to the Munich Olympics Jazz Festival, of which Berendt was artistic director (Weidemann 1972a).

Peter Brötzmann suggests another reason for Berendt's declining interest in free jazz, namely, the refusal of many European free jazz musicians to cooperate with him and his practices: "he wanted it to be dead because he couldn't make his influence clear [among them]" (2004).[10] Increasingly, Berendt also found his "aestheticist" interpretation of free jazz challenged by a more radically politicized one. Beginning in the late 1960s, the Jazz Pope himself became the object of a process of emancipation, as criticism of his theories, his invitation policies, and his practices mounted. This occurred within the context of an increasingly polarized jazz scene, which was symbolized by the combination of loud boos *and* cheers that met the Globe Unity Orchestra's 1966 debut in Berlin (cf. Jost 1987: 77).

---

10. It is possible that a joke made at Berendt's expense by several employees of the Saba/MPS record label may have contributed to his waning interest in free jazz. After recording themselves randomly performing on instruments on which they had no training or ability, these employees then persuaded Berendt that their recording was actually of an undiscovered Eastern European free jazz group. After Berendt fell for the ruse and expressed his interest in producing an MPS album by this unknown "group," the MPS employees revealed their joke. Berendt was not amused! (Baur 2006).

CHAPTER 8

Emancipation from the Jazz Pope

As the 1960s and 1970s proceeded, free jazz was claimed by some younger West German musicians and critics, who were influenced by the concerns of the 1968 generation. Just as issues such as the older generation's acceptance of National Socialism, postwar West Germany's "Adenauer restoration," the lack of an adequate parliamentary opposition during the Great Coalition of 1966–69, and the United States's foreign policy came in for hefty criticism, so too did Berendt's interpretation of jazz and his rather autocratic tone and style.

The Berlin Booers

As has already been noted, the Globe Unity Orchestra's audience at the 1966 Jazz Days included numerous booers. This was not an isolated incident, however. Indeed, between then and 1972, almost all reviewers observed booing at the Jazz Days. Various reasons were identified. In 1967, it was Miles Davis's failure to return for an encore (Morgenstern 1968: 22). In 1969, Sarah Vaughan had performed for too long (Berendt 1969a: 398). Older, less avant-garde musicians—including Red Norvo and Stan Kenton—drew rebukes such as "This is not for a jazz concert, it's for a museum," or "Get back to Disneyland!" (Feather 1969: 19; Wilmer 1970: 26). However, being young did not create immunity either. Pop jazz musicians such as Brian Auger and jazz rockers like Burnin' Red Ivanhoe and Tony Williams were also booed (Feather 1969: 19; Wilmer 1970: 27; Sandner 1971: 433; Hultin 1972: 35). Nor did free jazzmen escape ire: like the Globe Unity Orchestra in 1966, the Cecil Taylor Quartet was also booed in 1969 (Zimmerle 1969b: 394).

The booing phenomenon soon warranted the sustained reflection of critics, particularly in 1968, and again in 1969 when the "Jazz Party" that concluded the Jazz Days culminated in a riot in which instruments were seized by members of the audience (Boas 1969; Zimmerle 1969b: 395). In 1968, Berendt put the booing down to a generalized "frustration of Berliners confined to a split city" (Feather 1969: 29). Manfred Miller concluded in 1969 that the booing phenomenon represented a renewed outbreak of 1950s "moldy figs" versus "sour grapes" sectarianism (1969). This certainly had a grain of truth to it, and Berendt was not entirely blameless here. True to the spirit of the "whole jazz," he often programmed his concerts in a deliberately provocative fashion. In 1966, for example, he programmed both the uncompromisingly avant-garde GUO and the elderly traditionalist Willie "The Lion" Smith in the one concert (Berendt 1966l). By contrast, concerts dedicated to one style—such as the "Now! Music Night" in 1971—were more uniformly well received (cf. Hultin 1972: 32).

Clearly there was an ideological dimension to the booing phenomenon, particularly for younger enthusiasts (cf. Zimmerle 1968b: 375; Feather 1969: 29). Indeed, various critics even wondered whether this ideological aspect was more important for some fans than the music itself (Zimmerle 1968b: 375; Berendt 1969a: 398; Schreiner: 1969). It did not take long for the booing to be expressly linked with the increasingly politicized youth of the 1968 generation, which—given the attraction of West Berlin to conscientious objectors for whom a domicile there signified exemption from conscription into the Bundeswehr—had a particularly strong presence in the city. Some commentators even began to speak of an "extra-parliamentary opposition in the concert hall" (Schreiner 1969).[1] In 1968, one Otto Gmelin, the author of a philosophy of television, went so far as writing to Berendt about the rowdiness at the Jazz Days: "that is exactly what we want!! Finally! Aggressivity = Emancipation" (qtd. in Berendt 1969b: 47).

Although free jazz had a range of connotations in West Germany in the late 1960s and most members of the 1968 generation probably actually preferred music by the likes of Bob Dylan and the Rolling Stones, free jazz did have a clearly political dimension for some, which goes part way to explaining how it could be associated with philosophies such as Gmelin's (cf. Kriegel 1998: 167; Pasquier 2000: 95–6). One musician

---

1. As is well known, the so-called "extra-parliamentary" opposition was formed by members of the SDS in response to the absence of an adequate parliamentary opposition during the era of the Great Coalition between the CDU/CSU and the SPD.

for whom this was so was the saxophonist Peter Brötzmann, who was making a name for himself as a leading avant-gardist as early as 1965 and who was one of the founding members of the Globe Unity Orchestra (Schmidt-Joos 1965a: 321).

Peter Brötzmann and the "*Kaputtspiel*" (Playing Things to Pieces)

Brötzmann (born 1941) is both a musician and an accomplished visual artist, who has been influenced as much by figures from the world of conceptual art such as John Cage, Nam June Paik, and the Fluxus movement, as he has been by the avant-garde jazz of Charles Mingus, Ornette Coleman and others (Schmidt-Joos 1968: 129; Corbett 1994: 251). Like Barney Wilen—with his musical use of motor vehicle noise on *Auto Jazz*—he has also been interested in incorporating noise into music (Schmidt-Joos 1968: 129). Brötzmann's music is intended to be challenging for musician and recipient alike. For the musicians, "each person has the greatest possible freedom, which he must also exploit" (qtd. in Blome 1966). As Jost observes of the listener, Brötzmann's eschewal of "tonal centres, discernible melodic runs and themes," as well as swing and "'workmanship' in the traditional meaning," means that his music can be "'destructive' ... of an experience that has become dear and familiar to the listener, an experience not only of Jazz but of Music in general" (1978: 56).

In the early years in particular, Brötzmann's approach was purposefully destructive (cf. Blome 1966). His colleague, the bassist Peter Kowald, summed it up with the controversial rubric "*Kaputtspielphase*," which he used to refer to European free jazz during the mid- to late 1960s: "The main objective was to really and thoroughly tear apart the old values, this meaning to omit any harmony and melody; and the result wasn't boring only because it was played with such high intensity" (qtd. in Jost 1978: 57).[2]

---

2. Some free jazz contemporaries of Kowald's held similar beliefs about the necessity of destroying elements of the jazz tradition in order to create a tabula rasa (see, e.g, Schoof qtd. in Kumpf 1975b: 11). However, others, such as Alexander von Schlippenbach, maintain that their music has always had a constructive aspect and reject the notion of a "*Kaputtspielphase*" as a "stupid slogan" (Storb 1978: 7; von Schlippenbach 2004). Brötzmann also distances himself from the idea that there was simply a "phase," but rather maintains that a new way of playing was initiated then, which has continued to be important well beyond the 1960s (Noglik 1981: 193).

Figure 9 | Peter Brötzmann, Baden-Baden, 1967. © Paul G. Deker. Used with permission.

Machine Gun, Free Jazz, and Politics

One of the high-water marks of this energy-filled free jazz was Brötzmann's second record, *Machine Gun*, an album that Wolfgang Burde memorably described as "[a] powerful thumping, scarcely comprehensible 'chaos,' remote fringe-realms in which savagery and music reigned" (1978: 50). Recorded in May 1968—as rioting occurred on the streets of Paris—and bearing a suggestive title, the record quickly prompted the question as to whether it was program music to accompany or evoke a revolution. Brötzmann strenuously denied that either the title or the music was programmatic "in a foreground sense" (qtd. in Noglik 1981: 198).[3] However, while he eschewed a *direct* link between his music and the radical leftism of the 1968 generation, he did admit "that one could scarcely deny that the political movements and atmosphere of those years have also influenced our musical development in a certain way" (qtd. in Noglik 1981: 198).

Brötzmann was aware that his music shocked some listeners, a side-effect he found not altogether undesirable: "one [ought to] know in what times one is living and that many things have to be changed. And for that reason, one naturally doesn't just noodle around." He hoped that he could thereby contribute toward waking up "50 million sleepy people" and fostering social change (qtd. in Schmidt-Joos 1968: 129). In this and other respects, Brötzmann exhibited strong hallmarks of the 1968 generation's habitus and offers a perspective into how that habitus could manifest itself in and around free jazz.

As a "kid of the war," he was motivated by a sense of shame about those generations which had supported National Socialism: "Naturally I am not to blame for the shit, but I have always felt ashamed of what my fathers and grandfathers did. ... And that is really a fundamental basis for all we did in my generation" (2004). Like other members of his generation, he was also critical of the Adenauer "restoration," which saw the rehabilitation of tainted figures like Adenauer's close associate Hans Globke. In addition, he was influenced by a critical attitude toward developments in Cold War and postcolonial world politics, in particular the wars in Korea, Algeria, and Vietnam:

> That made us so full of, not hate, but we were fucking desperate. And we wanted to change the world. And we had the feeling, we are young enough. We are able. ... and so that is why, especially [for] the German part of the improvised or free jazz—for that years [sic] I would say the

---

3. The title "Machine Gun" actually derived from the appellation Don Cherry had given to Brötzmann's rapid staccato style of playing the saxophone (Noglik 1981: 199).

name *free jazz* was the right name, because for me, I thought free ... '*eine Art von Befreiung*' [a way of freeing] from old stuff, from rules in the arts, from rule in politics. (2004)

The "very aggressive way and means of expressing ourselves back then" was, as Brötzmann has observed, partly a way of conveying this combination of anger and desire for freedom he felt, which was further exacerbated by the fact that some non-Germans also tended to hold his generation responsible for what had happened in the recent past (Brötzmann 2004). Looking back, Brötzmann has noted that the "feeling that we could take a little part in changing the world, the society" was "very naïve." Nevertheless, he regrets that in the interim, free music has become depoliticized (qtd. in Corbett 1994: 249–50).

Anti-Festival/Total Music Meeting

One further way in which some West German free jazz was politicized in the late 1960s lay in the way it was organized; hence, musicians were involved in setting up both an "Anti-Festival" in opposition to the official Berlin Jazz Days, and a collectively run label, intended to record and distribute music through channels independent from established labels such as Saba/MPS. This movement started in September 1968 when, during the famous Essen Song Days, a group of musicians decided to stage an Anti-Festival during the upcoming Jazz Days (Margull 1971). This Anti-Festival represented one of the first times since the 1954 controversy with Dr. Waldick that Berendt's practices were openly called into question. Hence, a *Sounds* article heralding the Anti-Festival denounced the 1968 Jazz Days as "a commercial event, from which the organizers wish to enrich themselves." One problem was with the festival's quota of free jazz. *Sounds* conceded that there was going to be some free jazz at the Jazz Days—including Barney Wilen's *Auto Jazz* and American luminaries such as Don Cherry, Pharoah Sanders, and Sonny Sharrock!—but complained that it would be "presented in such a way that no one felt shocked" ("Anti-Festival Berlin" 1968).

The Anti-Festival—which in later years was renamed the less inflammatory Total Music Meeting (TMM)—was in many ways the polar opposite of the Jazz Days. Like the original "Newport Rebels Festival" in the United States in 1960, the first difference lay in the organizers, who were a collective of musicians rather than the Jazz Days' impresarios Ralf Schulte-Bahrenberg and George Wein, together with Berendt as artistic director. The focus was entirely on avant-garde jazz, rather than on something for everyone, as at the Jazz Days (Margull 1971: 210; Schulte-Bahrenberg 2004). In addition, the musicians presented at the TMM were predominantly *European* (Gebers 1972). As Brötzmann, who was heavily involved from the beginning, has noted: "It was a political thing. Because all the money at that time in Berlin ... went to some American. What we thought at that time—Bullshit! We don't need that shit anymore. And so we had to set up something and we did it" (2004).

Rather than actively assembling groups as the interventionist Berendt was wont to do, the TMM's philosophy was to present preexisting groups (Margull 1971: 210). The atmosphere was also quite different: as bassist and TMM organizer Jost Gebers observed, the idea was to reduce the whole "festival business" to a minimum (Jänichen 1979: 16). Instead of being in the high art Berlin Philharmonic, TMM concerts took place in a club. Performers were not required to wear suits, as Berendt had stipulated for the Jazz Days as late as 1968 (Margull 1971: 209). "Disruptive factors," like the television cameras present during the Jazz Days concerts, were also avoided (Jänichen 1979: 16). This modest setting was, of course, partly a necessity: unlike the Jazz Days, the TMM did not initially receive any public funding (Gebers 1972).

Berendt's first reaction to the 1968 Anti-Festival was to attempt to defuse the critique. He pointed out that the Jazz Days had always presented free jazz, and that many of the musicians who would be appearing at the Anti-Festival had previously performed at the Jazz Days. Hence, "Anti-Festival" was actually a misnomer. Instead, it should be called a "Co-Festival" (Berendt 1968e; 1968g: 7). This outwardly liberal stance did not, however, take into account the TMM's divergent principles, as rapidly became clear when, in 1971, there was a failed attempt to integrate the TMM into the Jazz Days.

This attempt, which took the form of a so-called "Now Music Night," came about as a result of a forum held during the 1970 Jazz Days to discuss the booing phenomenon and other criticism. Berendt agreed during the forum to devote a whole concert to the avant-garde in 1971, and it was also mooted that that concert would be run by a musicians' collective (Ohff 1971b; Schmidt-Joos 1971; Gebers 1972: 6). In the event, however, Berendt simply conferred the concert's organization upon Manfred Miller, one of the younger critics and an avid free jazz enthusiast (Berendt 1971e: 40; Gebers 1972: 6). The "Now Music Night" did diverge from a typical Jazz Days concert, given that it took place in the TU Berlin's dining hall and the audience was able to move around during the performance. However, the venue was roundly attacked by critics and the failed concept of the "Now Music Night" was not revisited in 1972 (Ohff 1971b; Sandner 1971; Hultin 1972: 32).

The experience of the "Now Music Night" clearly created bitterness on the part of the TMM's organizers, who now seized the initiative. In mid-1972, they sought a portion of the Jazz Days' funding from the ARD—the umbrella organization of West Germany's public broadcasters (Gebers 1972: 6). This bid proved unsuccessful, yet aggravated Berendt, who then threatened to stop the Jazz Days' invitees from moonlighting at the TMM as well, a practice which was hitherto common (Gruntz 1972a: 22–3). This again indicated that Berendt's stance was only liberal in so far as it did not involve questions of competitive funding.

Figure 10 | The European avant-garde and select American guests at the 1968 Anti-Festival/TMM. *From left to right:* Sonny Sharrock, Pharoah Sanders, Gunter Hampel, Evan Parker and Han Bennink. © Paul G. Deker. Used with permission.

It was only after Berendt's departure as artistic director in 1971–72 that a thaw developed between the Jazz Days and the TMM (Gruntz 2004). Indeed, a symbiotic relationship soon developed with the Jazz Days eventually even contributing to the running costs of the TMM. Despite the financial arrangement, arm's length was maintained and the TMM retained its fierce artistic independence (Brötzmann 2004; Schulte-Bahrenberg 2004). Official Jazz Days invitees continued to moonlight at the TMM if they were comfortable in the free idiom, and TMM stalwarts such as Brötzmann also continued to perform from time to time at the official festival (Brötzmann 2004; Mangelsdorff 2004; Schulte-Bahrenberg 2004). It was clear, however, that the two festivals had separate sets of parameters. The TMM's musicians could do their own thing, and Schulte-Bahrenberg could avoid programming as much uncompromising—and, from his perspective, comparatively unremunerative—free jazz (Schulte-Bahrenberg 2004).

Free Music Production

Six months after the 1968 Anti-Festival, the same nucleus of musicians formed a collective record label, Free Music Production (FMP), whose activities similarly contrasted with Berendt's productions for Saba/MPS. Rather than assembling groups, FMP's concept was to document existing ensembles (Margull 1971: 210; Jänichen 1979: 15). Unlike Berendt's productions, which covered the gamut of jazz styles, FMP was—as the name indicated—dedicated to free music. But it was more than just a record label. Along with recording and distributing self-produced records, FMP was also associated with a range of innovative events, including the TMM, concerts for children and music workshops (Gebers 1972; 1978; Jänichen 1979: 15–17).

The motivations to form FMP were many. On the one hand, this was a self-help organization which gave musicians the ability to release and distribute records which were uncompromising and of comparatively little interest to the commercial record labels (Gebers 1972: 6; Brötzmann 2004). In this way, FMP granted additional public exposure (and money) to *European* musicians who were not getting the festival invitations it was felt they deserved (Jänichen 1979: 17; Brötzmann 2004). On the other hand, the collective also had a political dimension, at least for some of the musicians. Hence, Gebers noted in 1972 that FMP was interested in "co-decision and democratization within our musical fields" (1972: 7) Brötzmann has also observed that "as good old Marxists, we wanted to have our own tools ... our own business. So that was the idea of FMP. And in the first years it was working" (2004). The political dimension was not something which all of the FMP musicians shared over the lifetime of the label, however. By the late 1970s, the question of politics was expressed to be entirely a matter for the individual musician:

> It is difficult enough within the framework in which we work to settle on criteria of musical quality which apply to all people. If one also tried to bring [this approach] to bear on a political opinion, then we would be doing something other than what we are doing today. The only organ of control should be the person who is making his or her own music. (Gebers qtd. in Jänichen 1979: 15).

Berendt's Jazz Days Draw to a Close

The polarized audiences and the Anti-Festival had an indirect outcome in relation to Berendt's role as artistic director in Berlin. Most importantly, there was a change in the dynamic between him and the members of the ARD, which by dint of their purchase of the broadcast rights, were the Jazz Days' principal backer (Schmidt-Joos 1971). Despite concessions designed to still critics, such as the creation of an "advisory board," and the forum held in 1970, Berendt was forced to submit to an additional level of accountability in 1971. This took the form of a panel of ARD representatives (Schmidt-Joos 1971; Berendt 1971e: 2).[4] As early as 1969, he had signalled that he was opposed to the idea of a panel with any substantive power (Berendt 1969a: 397). And almost as soon at it was appointed, the ARD panel made its presence felt.

The difficulties featured a clash over Berendt's programming, for the second time in three years, of the Duke Ellington Orchestra, which was considered by various parties to be past its prime. The *Spiegel*'s culture editor, Siegfried Schmidt-Joos, inferred that this meddling upset the cosy relationship between the Jazz Days and their American coproducer, George Wein—who had a financial interest in tours made by the Ellington Orchestra (cf. Wein 2003: 173)—and that Berendt was effectively beholden to Wein. According to Schmidt-Joos, Berendt had reacted in an offended manner to the involvement of the ARD panel and promptly tendered his resignation (1971).

Although Berendt was not without his supporters in complaining about the stifling effect of the panel (cf., e.g., Ohff 1971b), it was a legitimate body. There were significant public funds invested in the Jazz Days. There was also the reputation for booing, which was constantly mentioned in domestic and international reviews. Under these circumstances, it was hardly surprising that the primary sponsor instituted a panel. It is also clear that this would have rankled with Berendt, who was accustomed to enjoying a free hand. While he claimed that his retirement from Berlin was a result of health concerns and of a spiritual awakening, his unwillingness to share his power with the panel must also have been a significant factor ("Berliner Jazztage 71" 1971; Berendt 1985a: 270; "Gespräch mit Joachim-Ernst Berendt" 1988: 679).

---

4. George Gruntz, Berendt's successor as artistic director, observes that the panel was intended to make sure that there was no duplication between the engagement of musicians to perform at the Jazz Days and the regular employment of those musicians at the radio stations which funded the Jazz Days. According to him, the panel did not meddle in the programming of the festival but did have an advisory capacity (2006).

And yet, Berendt's "retirement" was not a true departure. He was soon approached by the West Berlin Senate—the festival's other major backer and the body responsible for appointing its artistic director—and requested to stay on (Gruntz 1972a: 19). Berendt ultimately agreed to retain responsibility for the "program conception," although it was never quite clear how this role would differ from that of the artistic director. However, between the appointment of George Gruntz as the new artistic director in 1971, and the publication in *Der Spiegel* of a fresh attack in October 1972, the division of labor worked well (Gruntz 2004). It was only after this *Spiegel* article that Gruntz began to reflect on the possibility that Berendt was trying to retain de facto control over the Jazz Days, something which was long suspected by Berendt's primary critic at the time, Siegfried Schmidt-Joos (Schmidt-Joos 1971).

Schmidt-Joos Holds *Der Spiegel* to Berendt

Schmidt-Joos (born 1936) knew Berendt well. In the mid-1950s, he had been involved with East German jazz clubs and with Reginald Rudorf, but had had to flee the GDR in 1957 after the regime clamped down on jazz enthusiasts. By 1958, he had established himself as a jazz critic in West Germany and was soon asked by Berendt to edit the second edition of *The Jazzbook*. Over the following few years, he and Berendt collaborated on various radio programs for the SWF and for Schmidt-Joos's employer, Radio Bremen. Both men contributed articles to the *Jazz Echo*, which Berendt edited, and which he ultimately handed over to Schmidt-Joos to edit (Brigl 2001: 7–8; Schmidt-Joos 2005). Schmidt-Joos was also associated for a time with the Jazz Days, co-announcing one of its concerts in 1964 and making significant contributions to the program notes in 1965.

In 1968, Schmidt-Joos became culture editor for *Der Spiegel* (Brigl 2001: 8). Shortly thereafter, he began to use the magazine to criticize Berendt. According to Schmidt-Joos, he objected not only to the way Berendt big-noted himself but also to his humorless manner (Brigl 2001: 10; Schmidt-Joos 2005). Although Berendt and others suggested that envy might have been a cause of Schmidt-Joos's attack, it would be wrong to conclude that his motivations were simply psychological: Schmidt-Joos points out that he was comfortable with his role as a journalist and had no desire to become the artistic director of the Jazz Days (Berendt 1972b: 4; Kühn 1972b; Schmidt-Joos 2005). Schmidt-Joos's critique had two main strands. The first derived from a reappraisal during the mid- to late 1960s of popular music and of jazz's relation to it. The second strand concerned Berendt personally.

Pop Jazz and the "Guardians of the Jazz Grail"

Schmidt-Joos began his campaign to (re)position jazz within popular culture in the mid-1960s, in the wake of jazz's declining popularity in Germany and concurrent with the rise of free jazz, which was hardly likely to reverse the trend. His efforts took place within the context of an increasingly sophisticated pop music, such as that of the Beatles, and of a growing reappraisal of popular culture in West Germany (Bullivant and Rice 1995: 248–9). He commenced his lobbying in a 1965 article that drew attention to high-quality American "pop jazz." Schmidt-Joos lamented, however, that German jazzmen were barred from this field. The postwar reception of jazz in Germany—with its focus on jazz as art—was responsible for this unfortunate state of affairs. For him, the answer was clear: a dismantling of the barriers between jazz and pop culture (1965a: 321). He set about this highly controversial task by pointing out the pop credentials of jazz and by attacking attempts to combine jazz with high art forms, such as ballet, concert music, and the opera (1967a; 1967b; 1967c; 1967d). The subject was brought to a head in late 1968, when Schmidt-Joos presented a television special on jazz and pop. He concluded the program with the gloss: "The fusion of jazz and pop may not be taking place among critics for the time being, but among musicians it is being completed day by day." Such a flourish was bound to incense older critics, who now publically took Schmidt-Joos to task for his heresy.

Not wishing to stop at a curtly worded rejoinder in *Jazz Podium*, the jazz-loving Duke of Mecklenburg convened a conference of older critics and scholars at which the matter could be seriously debated (Herzog zu Mecklenburg 1968; "Positives Resultat der Hechinger Gespräche" 1969).[5] The upshot was an open letter, in which they denounced talk of a fusion of jazz and pop as a misrepresentation of the facts, and, what's more, one with base commercial motivations. Those cases where pop musicians played jazz or vice versa were isolated exceptions, and musics with both jazz and pop elements were, at best, an "encounter" rather than a "fusion" ("Jazz und Pop. Ein Offener Brief" 1969; Schmidt-Joos

---

5. In addition to the Duke of Mecklenburg, the following critics and scholars attended: Berendt, Alfons M. Dauer, Werner L. Fritsch, Wolfram Röhrig, Alfred Rosenberg, Dietrich Schulz-Köhn, Joe Viera, and Dieter Zimmerle.

and Schmidt 1969: 118). At the heart of this pedantry was a conviction that jazz had a much higher value than disposable popular music, a point that Berendt and others had been driving home since the 1950s (Schmidt-Joos and Schmidt 1969: 118).

In a rejoinder, Schmidt-Joos and Felix Schmidt, his colleague from *Der Spiegel*, now attacked the older critics' purism. Turning the moralizing tables on those who had once used the Nazis' opposition to jazz to support their jazz lobbying, they declared that the open letter reminded them "of the declarations of Bavarian song societies and hunting associations … which, ostensibly in order to keep the German *Volkslied* pure, lambasted jazz as perverse Negro music" (Schmidt-Joos and Schmidt 1969).

Berendt's position on the question of pop jazz was characteristically ambivalent. He was one of the signatories of the open letter, and yet he also programmed and produced music that straddled jazz and pop/rock.[6] This surely had many reasons. As we have seen, he wished to present the "whole jazz" in Berlin (Berendt 1969d: 5; 1970d: 7; 1971e: 3; 1972c: 9). He was also criticized at the 1970 forum for not programming enough pop jazz (Schmidt-Joos 1971). In addition, including pop jazz may have been calculated to maximize ticket sales in Berlin, as some critics suggested ("Anti-Festival Berlin" 1968; P. Baumann 1968). Finally, as the progressively minded Jazz Pope he clearly did not wish to be left behind by any new developments in modern jazz. Nevertheless, accepting pop jazz and jazz rock called for fancy footwork. In 1969, he noted that a "healthy" relationship between jazz and pop had been restored, but quickly added that this was mostly one-sided; jazz almost always remained the donor, and pop the beneficiary (1969d: 41). He also felt it necessary to stress the jazz dimension of the pop jazz and jazz rock groups that he presented at the Jazz Days (1967n: 40; 1968g: 6, 16, 20–1; 1969d: 44). Clearly, he was reticent to give too much credence to the possibility that artistic achievement might be possible within pop music, or that jazz was a part of popular culture.

"A Bit Hacked Off?"

Schmidt-Joos did not stop at attacking the older critics' elitist attitudes toward popular music. He also made a personal attack against Berendt.

---

6. Invitees to the Jazz Days that fell into the category included the Gary Burton Quartet (1967 and 1968), Brian Auger and Julie Driscoll, Barney Wilen's Free Rock Band—whose album he also produced for MPS—and a pop-soul group (1968); Burnin' Red Ivanhoe (1969); and Association P.C., Soft Machine, and Tony Williams' Lifetime (1971).

This had been brewing for some time before it culminated in 1972. In 1970, for example, he criticized Berendt's programming of the highly eccentric Sun Ra's Arkestra in Donaueschingen and Berlin, suggesting that he had lost touch (1970: 228). In 1971, he gave voice to other critics who thought Berendt sensitive, ambitious, and vain (1971). The attack was then stepped up in an October 1972 *Spiegel* article titled "*Etwas Abgezapft*" (a bit hacked off).[7] In it, Schmidt-Joos identified that Berendt—a full-time SWF employee—had profited handsomely from his record productions and activities as the artistic director of the Jazz Days, and of the 1972 Munich Olympics jazz festival. In addition, he questioned whether the Jazz Days' accounts were in order, suggesting that they did not reflect contributions made by MPS and that some musicians had been asked to sign receipts for higher amounts than they actually received. Finally, Berendt was identified as being far too powerful for many musicians to be comfortable corroborating the claims against him (1972).

Berendt—who was in Brazil when the article was published—and Schulte-Bahrenberg quickly retaliated with a letter to *Der Spiegel* and a longer response to the Evangelical Press Service—which, in an unprecedented move, was also printed in the program notes for the 1972 Jazz Days (Berendt 1972a; 1972b; 1972c 11–13; Berendt and Schulte-Bahrenberg 1972). They explained that Berendt's fees were at or below international standards and that record production royalties did not cut in where sales were low. The Olympic Organizing Committee had approved his fee for the Munich Olympics jazz festival. It was also pointed out that the Jazz Days' accounts were audited regularly. More generally, Schmidt-Joos was accused of inaccurate quotation, and of carrying out a malicious personal vendetta (Berendt 1972a; 1972b).

It is hard to fully evaluate Schmidt-Joos's attack without inspecting the records of MPS and the Jazz Days, and comparing international practices at the time. Berendt certainly had a plausible answer for many of the criticisms. His acceptance of fees in relation to production and artistic direction were in themselves unobjectionable: he was hardly accepting a fee for no work at all. As to whether they were in accordance with international standards, it is difficult to say. Certainly, former colleagues of Berendt's have observed that he was a good businessman and earned a great deal of money through his jazz activities, something which no doubt rankled with freelance musicians (and critics) who were scuffling around, trying to make a living (Fruth 2004; Schulte-Bahrenberg 2004). As Schmidt-Joos himself observed, it was not easy to furnish proof of

---

7. The article was initiated after the MPS record label presented documents to the *Spiegel* relating to Berendt's activities as record producer (Schmidt-Joos 2005).

Berendt's abuse of power within the German jazz scene, as musicians were reticent to offend someone who had the ability to determine who performed at prestigious events such as Berlin, Donaueschingen, and the Baden-Baden Free Jazz Meetings, and who was also a well-known broadcaster and writer—i.e., who was the Jazz Pope. Nevertheless, it should be noted that the director of the *Berliner Festwochen* was reportedly satisfied with the explanations given and that other critics thought Berendt had answered the charges (Kühn 1972b; Weidemann 1972b).

Inevitably, the attack had its outcomes. For one, Berendt fell ill and was unable—or unwilling—to attend his last Jazz Days. If he had harbored the expectation that he would be able to remain in de facto control of Berlin, it was soon dashed. Gruntz—who was unaware of the polemical attacks on Berendt at the time of his appointment as artistic director—was rudely awakened by Schmidt-Joos' article. He swiftly conveyed to Berendt that he would not allow himself to be used as a puppet. From that point on, Gruntz took effective control of artistic direction, although he remained open to Berendt's informal suggestions for a number of years yet (Gruntz 2004).[8] However, Berendt's sidelining from Berlin only silenced his critics for a period.

Wilhelm Liefland: Free Jazz, Adorno, and the Search for the Jazz Killers

In 1977, the Frankfurt critic Wilhelm Liefland used a review of Berendt's latest book, *A Window out of Jazz*, to launch an acerbic polemic against him, which in turn initiated a curiously public exchange of letters that neither man seemed inclined to conclude. Liefland (1938–80) was, like Berendt, a rather sensitive pastor's son. He was not only a jazz critic but also a poet and writer with a sharp turn of phrase. He wrote freelance reviews for the *Frankfurter Rundschau* between 1970 and 1980, although during the first half of the decade he was an alcoholic and his output was intermittent. By 1975, however, he had dried out and was living an almost ascetic life (Dillmann 1992; Jungheinrich 1992). With his "thickly laid-on 68er Attitude," Liefland personified what Volker Kriegel has called the political typology of German jazz critic. For this type of critic, the American equivalent of which might be a Frank Kofsky, jazz criticism was a form of social criticism, and Liefland's favorite topic was

---

8. The complete break came only in 1976, when Berendt offended Gruntz, from which point on he rebuffed all further input from Berendt. Gruntz subsequently discovered that Berendt continued to draw a fee, even after this point, when his input was reduced to zero (Gruntz 2004).

the dialectical connection between art, morality, and society (Kriegel 1998: 186).

Liefland was an uncompromising champion of free jazz (Sandner 2004: 285). Citing Carles' and Comolli's 1971 Black music ideological study *Free Jazz—Black Power*, he stressed the political significance of free jazz. He argued that the jazz literature typically ignored this broader significance, and that Berendt's aestheticist *Jazzbook* was a primary offender. Hence, Berendt was responsible for a:

> trust in the eternal fact that jazz *qua* jazz just keeps on running regardless of its form (and he quantifies this is decade blocks, free jazz therefore from 1960 until 1970) and regardless of the negations. That [trust] destroys the ability to see the singularity of musical happenings at a particular historical moment and the incommensurably new quality of free jazz, which certainly is not "made" in order to fit a historico-critical family tree. (1976: 11)[9]

According to Liefland, this type of approach was responsible for some free musicians losing touch with the idiom's "political culture-medium," and developing a false consciousness (1976: 11).

Liefland's critique escalated with the review of *A Window out of Jazz*. This was actually a sequel to an earlier article in which he had criticized the Frankfurt jazz cellar's proprietor Willi Geipel's commercial practices, and appealed to musicians to self-organize along the lines of FMP (Liefland 1977a). Berendt had sent a long letter to Liefland haranguing him for using the media to exact a personal revenge against Geipel, which was surely wide of the mark and doubtless only served to aggravate the younger critic (Berendt 1977c). Liefland's review of *A Window out of Jazz* now charged Berendt with responsiblity for jazz's wasting away into "an expensive knick-knack." He was accused of having disregarded Marxist perspectives and the critique of capitalism inherent in musicians' collectives like FMP. Other failings were also singled out. Firstly, there was Berendt's self-aggrandizement and his "profit praxis." Secondly, there was the way in which he tried to gain credibility from his father's death in Dachau, and used the spectre of neo-fascism as an ill-thought-out basis for discussing "beauty" in 1970s jazz.[10] Finally, there was the book's tone, which Liefland memorably described as "false,

---
9. It should be observed, however, that Liefland respected the book in its historical context—namely, for the way in which, when first published in 1953, it had won over many followers (including himself) by providing a "legitimation of jazz as an artform worthy of being taken seriously (however that was to be understood back then" (1975).

10. For an account of Berendt's important 1975 "New Fascism" essay (also included in *A Window out of Jazz*) and the controversy that it unleashed, see chapter 15.

whining, authoritarianly rasping, [and] schmalzing in the scales (modes) of love, humanity, tolerance, love and, once again, love" (1977b). Elsewhere, he took issue with Berendt's tendency to see jazz as religion (Liefland 1977c). These elements all prevented the reader from thinking critically for him- or herself (see, e.g., Liefland 1977e). This was important—according to Liefland, (free) jazz and its discourse ought to promote independent, critical thought. In this respect, Liefland acknowledged that he had profited from Adorno's notions of criticism, while rejecting his actual theories about jazz (Liefland 1977f). Leaving to one side Adorno's deep dislike of jazz, there was an irony in this. As Burns and van der Will have noted in relation to the broader uptake of critical theory among the 68 generation: "The very thesis which denied the possibility of critical citizenship itself helped trigger developments that led to the quantum leap in the advancement of active, participative democracy"—and, in this case, to the willingness of critics like Liefland to speak out (1995: 274).

Liefland's review prompted a controversy over the following weeks as *Frankfurter Rundschau* correspondents took up positions both pro and contra (see, e.g., Bodenstein 1977; C. Farrell 1977; Kille 1977; Kleinschmidt 1977; Krauth 1977; Mais 1977). Significantly, the bassist Eberhard Weber concurred with Liefland and—echoing Schmidt-Joos five years earlier—agreed that many German musicians were critical of Berendt's practices, but were unwilling to speak out (Weber 1977). They had good reason not to. Subsequently, others have confirmed that Berendt "punished" or threatened to hinder the careers of those who offended him. Manfred Schoof—who is otherwise an admirer of Berendt's—has observed, for example, that:

> He was not always honest. He also harmed some people. If they said something against him ... , then he consciously disregarded them or did not work with them ... good musicians like Peter Trunk ... a legendary bassist, with whom I worked a lot. ... and he totally [avoided working with him] or said "I will ruin you!" or something like that. Expressions like that also crossed his lips. (2004)[11]

It would be wrong to conclude that Liefland's polemic was motivated simply by personal animosity, though some thought so at the time (cf. Liefland 1977d). In fact—through his own choice—Liefland had little to do with Berendt professionally (Liefland 1977c; 1977d; 1977e). Nor was this simply an inter-generational conflict, although Liefland did consider

---

11. The pianist Michael Naura also observes, for example, that after an occasion when he had lampooned Berendt, the critic punished him by dropping his name from the next edition of the *Jazzbook* (2000a).

himself, in a sense, to be Berendt's student (Liefland 1977e). Rather, he was committed to the "long march through the institutions" and regarded himself to be doing his duty as a writer and democrat (Liefland 1976; 1977d). In his view, Berendt had too much power, and his self-aggrandizing, "schmalzing" discourse hindered clear, critical thought. This was anathema to a man so committed to the concerns of the 1968er generation.

Tragically, Liefland died by his own hand in 1980. Brötzmann, who was a good friend of his, observes that "he was anyway too sensitive for this world" (2004). Opinion about the critic is divided today. Albert Mangelsdorff, who as a Frankfurter also knew him well, considered his attack on Berendt fanatical and mostly unjustified (2004). Manfred Schoof recalled Liefland as being "simply too ... dazzled ... 68er generation. ... For me he was too deeply anchored in that to have enough perspective. Critics also have to be a bit objective, after all" (2004). On the other hand, critics such as Wolfgang Sandner have praised the cathartic power of Liefland's sharp analysis of the jazz scene and its agents (2004: 285).

* * * * *

Berendt's involvement in the West German jazz scene was far from selfless. However, even his staunch critics had to recognize his contributions. Brötzmann recently observed, for example, "I don't blame him for everything. I think he did good work. But he was not the only one" (2004). Schmidt-Joos respected Berendt's achievements in Jazz Days past (1971). He would have liked to praise Berendt in the early 1970s, but found that Berendt had already done so himself! (Brigl 2001: 7; Schmidt-Joos 2005). Even at the height of his dispute with Berendt, Liefland also found praise for the way the 1953 edition of the *Jazzbook* had contributed to legitimating jazz (1977b).

Berendt did assist some of the younger critics (including Schmidt-Joos, Manfred Miller, and Claus Schreiner).[12] He also tried to accommodate some of the criticisms of his Jazz Days programming. However, these initiatives—which did not really delegate power—were unable to still his critics. Berendt's detractors were motivated by various factors, and it is not possible to completely discount the personal element. As Mangelsdorff observed: "He was enormously active and it is only natural that that gives rise to envy; he was also, shall we say, not always very approachable in his character, particularly regarding his colleagues. ... He

---

12. Miller contributed to the program of the Jazz Days in 1966, 1969 and 1970. In 1971, he coedited the program with Berendt and coordinated the "Now Music Night." He also coedited the program in 1972. Claus Schreiner contributed to and assisted Berendt with the program editing for the 1969 Jazz Days.

also provoked resistance" (2004). There were certainly what Gerhard Koch called "oedipal" reasons for the revolt against the "super-father-figure" Berendt (2000). Nevertheless, psychological reasons should not be overstated. During the late 1960s Berendt's theses became contentious, in a context both where popular culture was being reevaluated, and where art and culture became increasingly politicized. Even more than this, his egocentric, authoritarian style and (mis)use of power to promote his own productions rankled. What Jost has called the Berendtian "we"—namely his speaking of the projects which he assisted as if they were his own creations—naturally irritated many musicians and colleagues (cf. Berger 2004; Gruntz 2004; Jost 2004; Wunderlich 2004).[13]

Unfortunately, Berendt flexed his muscle against those whom he perceived had crossed him. It is difficult to ascertain the full extent of his threats—including whether he always carried them out and, if so, whether they were effective. Although he continued to have power as a producer, broadcaster, and critic during the 1970s, it was increasingly possible—like Eberhard Weber and Volker Kriegel—to avoid working with him (cf. Weber 1977). Others, such as Brötzmann, maintained careers largely independent from Berendt, yet knew how to engage him for their own purposes when required.[14] By the early 1970s, it was also possible for younger critics to carry on careers independent of Berendt (Rüsenberg 2004).

The reasons why Berendt's influence had already diminished by the time Liefland launched his polemic in 1977 were many. Contributing to the erosion of his power base and the "democratization" the West German jazz scene were various factors including the ARD's insistence on having an advisory panel to the Jazz Days, former colleagues and critics such as Schmidt-Joos speaking out, the independence of musicians like Brötzmann, a souring of relations with MPS, and the rise of independent German record labels including FMP and ECM, which had no wish to enlist him as a producer.[15] This was a concrete way in which one "long

---

13. Werner Wunderlich, Berendt's latter-day colleague from the SWF, was particularly offended, for example, that Berendt had given the public the impression that it was he (rather than Wunderlich) who had been instrumental in organizing the West German delegation's attendance at the Second Polish Jazz Festival in Sopott in 1957 (Wunderlich 1987, 1998, 2004). See chapter 3.

14. He and Han Bennink secured Berendt's support, for example, for their 1977 *"Schwarzwaldfahrt"* project (Brötzmann 2004).

15. The Munich independent ECM was founded in 1969. Berendt apparently offered to produce records for the firm (suggesting that it wouldn't be possible to run such a firm without him), but its proprietor Manfred Eicher refused, observing that one of the reasons that he had set up ECM was so that there was an alternative to Berendt. Offended, Berendt then started to publicly attack the company (Gruntz 2002: 90). The matter even

march through the institutions" manifested itself: here in the West German jazz scene, the "emancipation" ultimately also involved emancipation from the Jazz Pope. It does not surprise then that, when Berendt was publicly thanked as outgoing artistic director of the Jazz Days in 1971, he too raised a chorus of boos! (Hultin 1972: 32).

---

came to litigation after Berendt intended to publish a critical article in *A Window out of Jazz*. The parties ultimately came to a settlement of the dispute (Liefland 1977b).

CHAPTER 9

On the Uses of European Jazz

The ideology of emancipation focused new—and, to a certain extent, unwelcome—attention on the possibility of national characteristics existing in European jazz (Jost 1987: 18). If German musicians were no longer copying American models, what could their music now be called? Was it "German," something more broadly "European," or was it simply the music of creative individuals? How were these epithets used in the West German jazz scene, and when were they best avoided?

Domestic Opposition to "German" Jazz

As my discussion of adaptations of German folklore indicates, the idea of a distinctively "German" jazz was—and is—a fraught one. Musicians and critics avoided the notion for various reasons. For one, there was still an adherence to the cherished notion of jazz as an international musical language. That was so despite the efforts of critics such as Frank Kofsky in the United States to reveal how this trope was capitalized upon by the State Department in its use of jazz as a "Cold War secret weapon." By the late 1970s, there was a recognition in the West German jazz scene of the way in which the trope had been used in this fashion (see, e.g., Jost 1978: 62). However, the "universal" view proved unshakable and still holds much influence within the German jazz scene. To give but one example, Manfred Schoof has recently stated: "For me it is the most universal music that exists these days" (2004).[1]

---

1. See also Mangelsdorff 1964a: 159; 2004; and "'Own Thing'" 1966: 68.

Also militating against the idea of "German" jazz was the Romantic-tinged view that jazz is an individual music par excellence. Albert Mangelsdorff observed, for example, that:

> I was always of the opinion that jazz does not necessarily have anything national to do with it: for example [that it is] typically German, or typically American or anything. For me, jazz is a music of individuals. And you [can] hear that in jazz as well. There is not any American style and so on, but rather it is always the personalities who bring forth and express jazz. That most of them are in the USA, or come from the USA, is in the nature of the beast. That is where [jazz] came into being. (2004)

Alexander von Schlippenbach is even more outspoken: "There are German jazz musicians, even a few very good [ones]! But there is no 'German jazz'" (2004).

Various other factors discouraged adherence to the idea of "German" jazz. Within the scene, the attribute "German" had been used pejoratively when a musician did not have the requisite sense of swing (Paulot 1993: 154). Incidents abroad must also have contributed to the stigma of "German" jazz—as well as to the general sense of discomfort with being German. For instance, when the Kurt Edelhagen Orchestra appeared at the Salon International du Jazz in Paris in May 1954, the audience had to be "encouraged" by the host Charles Delaunay to welcome the Germans in an appropriate manner (Waldick 1954a: 9). A decade later, the Albert Mangelsdorff Quartet was subjected to a "joke" in extremely poor taste when it performed in London at the 1965 Richmond Jazz Festival. When the English compere announced that the group would play the "Auschwitz Blues," Mangelsdorff longed for the stage to open up and swallow them: "[the announcement] was so unexpected that I could not react. What could I have said anyway? Just imagine—the Auschwitz Blues. What a challenge that would have been. … You just cannot play that well" (qtd. in Paulot 1993: 166). Incidents like this can hardly have encouraged West German musicians to identify with the notion of "German" jazz. However, as their efforts became increasingly audible beyond the borders of West Germany, questions of "Germanness" and jazz began to be raised, first by international and then—in catch-up mode—by German critics themselves.

International Critics Tune In

Mangelsdorff was among the first West Germans to have his work gain international attention. His mid-1960s recordings for the German CBS label, and his schedule of touring, including for the Goethe Institut, propelled this exposure. And, almost inevitably, international critics began to reflect on the "German" qualities of his music.[2] In these critics' opinions, Mangelsdorff and his fellow musicians owed a debt to America, but were in the process of finding their own, distinctively "German" voice. For example, when *Downbeat* editor Don DeMichael reviewed Mangelsdorff's 1963 *Tension* album, he noted that "the group's horn men tend to sound like their American models," but there was "no blatant imitation." He even detected "a slight Germanic flavor—a solidity, a heaviness, if you want, that makes the group something unto itself" (1964: 29). The American critic Gilbert Erskine, who reviewed Mangelsdorff's and the MJQ pianist John Lewis's album *Animal Dance* a short time later, observed that Mangelsdorff "at this point ... sounds perhaps too American to be described as original," yet observed that the trombonist "comes on like a new Teutonic wind" and concluded that "it is clearly possible that important developments in jazz may soon be taking place overseas" (1964a). When Erskine's colleague Pete Welding reviewed *Now Jazz Ramwong* in 1965, he did not expressly use the epithet "German," yet he did consider the group's "balance of discipline and freedom" might "provide American groups a fascinating and instructing object lesson" (1965: 30).

Live performances also provided international critics with an opportunity to comment on "German" jazz. When Mangelsdorff's Quartet played in England in 1965, for example, local critics thought the music "undeniably German, if not to say 'gothic.'" (Berendt 1965d). The Mangelsdorff Quintet's tour of Asia the previous year also had signal importance for the discovery of "German" jazz. On this occasion, various Asian critics considered the group's music either "German" or "German-styled" (Mangelsdorff 1964a: 159; Berendt 1964a). One Manila critic elaborated: "Albert's grand, freely swinging cadences derive from German Romanticism. His polyphony differs from the polyphony of a Charlie Mingus simply by the fact that it is tied to the German polyphonic tradition from Bach to Reger and Hindemith. Albert's ballads have the interiority of a Schubert *Lied*" (qtd. in Berendt 1966d: 106). Political circumstances sometimes also mandated that the group play up the "German" dimension, notwithstanding their distaste for the idea. Such was the case, for example, in Burma, where a decidedly anti-American sentiment was noted. Mangelsdorff recounted, "under no circumstances

---

2. Mangelsdorff was actually not the first to have his music labelled "German" by international commentators. Berendt observes that the Kurt Edelhagen Orchestra was identified during the 1950s as having an "aspect of drill ... and this seemed to international critics to signify the German psyche" (1977a: 177).

were we to give the impression that [our music] was American-inspired. It had to stand out as 'German'" (2004).

"German" Jazz and the Germans: Take Two

By 1966 at the latest, Berendt had softened his own position on the notion of "German" jazz, which he had formerly rejected in his defence of the idea of jazz's internationality. He now noted that musicians might disown the idea—that was their prerogative as artists engaged with more or less unconscious acts of creation—however, as a critic, he was inclined to agree with overseas colleagues who identified a "German" dimension in German jazz. Accordingly, he discerned that the leading German jazzmen of the day were influenced by German traditions: with the *Heartplants* Quintet, it was German Romanticism; with the organist Ingfried Hoffmann, it was Beethoven's sonatas. This was still a risky strategy and he was quick to distinguish the idea of "German" jazz from the nationalism of the past. He did so by deliberately placing the German developments within a *European* context: "Now don't go thinking that I am associating jazz with *Blut und Boden* [blood and soil]. That is loathsome to me. We are not dealing with German, but rather European developments here." He also sought to maintain the international aspect: "wherever there is a conflict between the national and the international, one ought to forget the national—here [in jazz] as elsewhere" (1966d).

The question of "German" jazz was not isolated to the mid-1960s, however. If anything it became more pressing the following decade. In particular, free jazz of the "*Kaputtspiel*" variety and beyond led critics to wonder whether there might not be something characteristically German about it. By the late 1960s, Peter Brötzmann's intense music was coming to the attention of international commentators. It too was associated by some with Germanness. In the opinion of one British critic, for example, his music had "berserker" and "teutonic" traits typical of German jazz (Berendt 1977a: 236). Brötzmann also recalls a caricature of himself in the British press from this time depicting him wearing a spiked World War I helmet (Brötzmann 2004). This sort of international attention, together with a prevalence of free jazz in Germany during the late 1960s and 1970s, prompted Berendt to consider the matter of "German" jazz again.

In a 1977 article, he observed that free jazz had maintained a disproportionately strong foothold in Germany. By advancing the simplistic idea that a musician's eschewing of melody represented a rejection of his or her society, he pondered whether the comparative popularity of melody-less free jazz signified a broader rejection of German national identity and society (1977a: 236–40). This, then, was another way in which it was acceptable to canvass the notion of "German" jazz: as something paradoxically opposed to the German nation at the very moment it was announcing itself as characteristically German! Certainly, some free musicians like Brötzmann did have a critical attitude toward German society. However, Berendt's speculation was also a little simplistic.

A contrasting analysis was put by the younger academic musicologist Ekkehard Jost. While he eschewed the idea of *single* national jazz varieties, he thought it "obvious that in the course of the last 10 years, some Free Jazz-'languages' have developed that diverge in their characteristics, promoted by the different social conditions" (1978: 62). Unlike Berendt, Jost avoided nebulous ethnopsychological questions of "national identity" when explaining the success of energy-laden free jazz in West Germany at the beginning of the 1970s. Instead, he preferred an economic analysis, arguing that free jazz had succeeded in West Germany because jazz received a comparatively high level of public funding, which, in turn, had caused a high presence of free jazz, and that, in turn, had created a receptive public for it (1987: 111–12). Of course, as we saw in chapter 8 there were also ideological reasons for the uptake of free jazz (cf., also, Jänichen 1979: 15), but Jost's analysis added an important corrective to Berendt's.

In the end, Berendt and Jost shared more than seems apparent at first reading. They both raised the notion of a typically "German" jazz, but each distinguished between this idea and nationalist chauvinism in a way that is characteristic of the postwar era (cf. Jost 1987: 18). Significantly, they also spoke of "German" jazz within the context of a broader *European* phenomenon.

Globe Unity and the Idea of "European" Jazz

For over thirty years, the Globe Unity Orchestra and similar "collectives" from the late 1960s have supplied one important focus for reflecting on "European" jazz. Not that this term has been used uncritically. For commentators such as Jost, this format does not represent the be-all-and-end-all of "European" jazz (1994: 241–2, 249). Likewise, Jost and Berendt both observe that similar formations were not unknown in the United States (Berendt 1973/74: 404; Jost 1994: 239). The notion of the "European" free jazz collective was also far from a baseless phantasm: ensembles like the GUO did have (largely) European personnel, and, as demonstrated in chapter 7, an approach to composition that borrowed occasionally from European New Music (see also von Schlippenbach 1966; 1975: 13; Jost 1987: 117).

Perhaps the most important aspect of the GUO's "Europeanness," however, centred around its collective philosophy. As Jost points out, ensembles like the GUO were based on "a democratic group-concept aimed at musical and economic equal rights." The important concomitant of this philosophy was that the "European collective" could be contrasted with the materialist "star syndrome" of the American jazz scene (Jost 1994: 239. See also Brötzmann 2004; Schoof 2004). For his part, Berendt expressly contrasted a "specifically European attitude toward the collective" with the American "nineteenth century glorification of [individual] liberty" (1973/74: 404–6). As these comments suggest then, the "emancipation" was also partly an emancipation from an erstwhile love affair with the United States and its culture.

In fact, this mood was entirely consistent with a broader reevaluation of the postwar relationship between West German and American culture, a process particularly marked in members of the 1968 generation. As Gerd Gemünden has observed, the attitude to America was now marked by a paradox:

> it became apparent that America had mapped itself in complex ways over specifically German problems. The voices in this debate displayed a paradoxical attitude toward American politics and the country's popular culture: on the one hand an attraction toward a culture that had been decisive in furnishing and shaping childhood images, tastes and desires and, on the other hand, a rejection of American politics and the colonizing effect of its mass culture. (1998: 23–4)

The notion of an emancipated European jazz neatly accommodated a distancing from aspects of the United States—including its capitalist "star syndrome" and its foreign policy—to which musicians and critics took an increasingly critical attitude. Brötzmann recalls, for example, that "it was the time of Vietnam ... there was a big anti-American movement going on." In this spirit, he even scaled a flagpole at the 1967 Donaueschingen Music Days—where he was performing with the Globe Unity Orchestra—and removed a flag hanging to honour American guests, including, by the way, the Black music ideologist Archie Shepp, who probably did not mind Brötzmann's gesture at all (Brötzmann 2004). However, "European" jazz was also a branding device that musicians could use to lever themselves into a better market position. Again, Brötzmann recalls: "I think the main thing for us to get together [under the banner of European jazz] was because the American part of the music, of course, was always stronger ... stronger in the way of financial possibilities. I mean these guys got paid 3-4-5 times as [much as] we did. And we had to fight against that" (2004).

"European" jazz was therefore useful in that it simultaneously profiled domestic musicians, allowed a critique of American (jazz) practices and had the added benefit of avoiding the stigma of "Germanness" by being associated with a positively weighted supranational entity. Indeed, the notion of European jazz dovetailed perfectly with parallel discourses on West Germany's place within a united (Western) Europe, which was considered by many postwar West Germans as a bulwark against the dangers of resurgent nationalism (see, e.g., Huyssen 1992: 71; Friedrichsmayer, Lennox and Zantop 1998: 5; Gemünden 1998: 197). By committing themselves to the notion of "European" jazz, there could be no suggestion that West German musicians and critics were toying with cultural nationalism, a danger that persisted if one overly stressed the notion of "German" jazz, or did so in the absence of umbrella concepts like "European" or "universal" jazz.

But Is the Free Jazz Collective Really European?

The "Europeanness" of the free jazz collective is far from uncontroversial. There were also collectives in the United States, such as the Jazz Composers Orchestra Association (JCOA), although these admittedly tended not to be as long-lived as the Globe Unity Orchestra. George E. Lewis identifies how Berendt's account of the "European" free jazz collective also crucially neglected to mention the Association for the Advancement of Creative Musicians (AACM), an important Chicagoan collective whose various members sojourned in France in the late 1960s and early 1970s, and some of whom Berendt actually invited to participate in the 1969 Baden-Baden Free Jazz Meeting (2002: 232). Free jazz ensembles of this sort were even regarded by some Black music ideologists as being specifically African American. In 1970, for example, Frank Kofsky claimed that free group improvisation was symbolic of "the recognition among musicians that their art is not an affair of individual 'geniuses' but the musical expression of an entire people—*the Black People in America*" (qtd. in Budds 1990: 83; my emphasis). Clearly, Black music ideologists may have taken a dim view of the notion that the free jazz collective was typically "European."

From the German perspective, however, comparisons with America were now a little beside the point. By the late 1960s, a level of self-awareness and self-confidence pertained among West German musicians

Figure 11 | European and free: Fred van Hove, Han Bennink, Albert Mangelsdorff and Peter Brötzmann perform at the 1975 Total Music Meeting, Berlin. © Paul G. Decker. Used with permission.

that rendered moot comparisons with the Americans (Knauer 1996a: 150–7). As Schoof observes: "I don't know whether [the JCOA] or we [the GUO] came first. ... It is also basically irrelevant because the one did not come into being because of the other" (2004).

By the same token, attempts to completely dissociate "European" from "American" jazz make little sense, particularly from today's perspective. Consistent with the ambivalence toward America displayed by his generation, Brötzmann observes: "I always [had], as we say in German, *'zwei Herzen in meiner Brust'* ... I mean, of course I always was very fond of American music and American musicians, and, on the other hand, we had to go our own way" (2004). As the 1970s progressed, and the ideology of "emancipation" faded a little, West Germans also began to reengage with their American colleagues (Noglik 1990: 222–4; Knauer 1996a: 156; Heffley 2000b). Indeed, Brötzmann nowadays spends as much time performing with Chicagoan musicians as he does with Europeans, and has even succeeded in exporting the "European" approach to dividing profits (Brötzmann 2004. See also Heffley 2000b). For his part, Alexander von Schlippenbach has also distanced himself from the idea that the "collective" form of the Globe Unity Orchestra is or was something typically "European," given that there were similar groups in the United States and that American musicians often performed with the GUO over its long lifetime (2004).

* * * * *

To the extent that they make any sense at all in relation to a highly individualized art form, terms such as "European" jazz are surely no more than stereotyped generalizations. However, some labels can be extremely useful. In the 1960s and 1970s, in particular, the notion of "European" jazz contributed to increasing the market share of local musicians, as well as to reflecting and strengthening the self-confidence of German musicians—something which spurred a great deal of creative activity—and, finally, to helping them and the jazz scene to construct an identity equidistant from the German past and the American present.

PART III

Jazz Meets the Other

CHAPTER 10

The Marco Polo of Jazz

It would be wrong to suggest that European jazz musicians have only been interested in questions of emancipation, and in engaging with their own traditions, folkloric or "high." Since the 1960s, many have also engaged with world musics. This was a development particularly dear to Berendt and one which he was anxious to promote and document in the *JMTW* series and beyond. To a significant degree, Berendt's interest was borne by a thirst for travel and new experiences, musical and otherwise. Beginning in mid-1962—when he spent three months in the Middle East, India, Southeast Asia, and Japan—he began traveling to Asia, North Africa, South America, the Caribbean, and other "exotic" destinations. These travels, which occurred on an almost annual basis until the mid-1970s, were highly productive, yielding radio specials, articles, and commercial recordings (Berendt 1996a: 339). And, before long, the Jazz Pope was also being referred to as "the Marco Polo of Jazz"—a title which is surely unrivalled among the ranks of international jazz critics (K. Fischer 1965).

Why Asia?

Berendt's motivations to travel to Asia in 1962 were various. On the one hand, he had reached something of a saturation point in his jazz excursions to the United States. In 1950 and 1960 respectively, he had spent several months in the States. On the latter occasion, he made a veritable odyssey with William Claxton, and, as *Jazz Life*, their 1961 collaboration aptly demonstrates, they thoroughly plumbed the depth and breadth of the American jazz scene. While he continued to travel to the

United States thereafter—an August 1962 trip was his sixth—Berendt was clearly focusing on other horizons too ("Visiting Jazzman" 1962; "Jazz News" 1962b). In fact, by 1964 he said that he was more interested in visiting Asia than the United States, despite the jazz attractions of the latter (Berendt 1964b: 138).

Figure 12 | John Coltrane on the set of *Jazz - Heard and Seen*, Baden-Baden, 1961. Hanns E. Haehl; courtesy of the Jazzinstitut Darmstadt. Used with permission.

Earlier trips also gave him a brief taste for "exotic" musics. In 1950, he had been impressed by live Native American music (Berendt 1951: 81). Then, on a side trip to Argentina in 1960—which took place during a break from his road trip with Claxton—he was exposed to bossa nova, a music still to make its splash on the international popular music market (Berendt 1963c: 38). He also made recordings during the 1960 trip with Claxton, not only of jazz and blues musicians, but also of Sea Islands' folk music, which he considered to be closely related to the early music of African American slaves, and a precursor to jazz (Berendt and Claxton 1961). Berendt's catholic musical curiosity coincided with that of several avant-garde U.S. jazz musicians who, as we saw in chapter 5, were now taking a keen interest in world musics. It was John Coltrane—with whom Berendt had not only spent time on his 1960 U.S. trip, but also produced a 1961 SWF television special when the saxophonist toured Germany—who exerted a particular influence on him, including in relation to his decision to travel to Asia (Berendt 1978: 6, 270–1; 1985a: 327; Broecking 1995: 76).

Curiosity coincided with other material realities. As we have also seen, by the early 1960s the West German market for jazz books was saturated. However, as the disposable income of young West Germans increased and international travel came within reach, other new markets beckoned.[1] By the early 1960s, Berendt had joined the staff of *Twen*, a smart new magazine, not unlike America's *Esquire*, pitched at young, well-to-do West Germans (Glaser 1997: 264). In 1961, Pan American placed an advertisement in *Twen* and donated airline tickets to Asia to the magazine's editors. When his colleagues failed to show any interest, Berendt availed himself of the opportunity. And so, in late February 1962, he set out for Asia, full of expectations, both musical and sexual. As he later reminisced: "I was a young man and the pretty Japanese, Thai, and Vietnamese women interested me greatly. It was still before the Vietnam War and so I set off to experience the sensual side of Asia" (qtd. in Broecking 1995: 76).

Just how Berendt did experience and reflect on his travel to "exotic" destinations over the next fifteen years will now be explored, given that his travel writings may well have colored young West Germans in *Twen*'s demographic in their own attitudes to international travel, and that these essays were inextricably linked with his interpretation of world musics.

---

1. On the increasing international travel of young Germans during the "long 1960s," see Schildt 2006.

Berendt's Travel Journalism

Berendt's essays about locations such as Bali, Brazil, and the Carribbean—which were published in a variety of media between 1962 and 1977—did not only, as one might expect from a man with open ears, comment on the music that he "discovered" in these far-flung locations; they also contained a range of more general "popular ethnographic" reflections.[2] Notwithstanding the difficulties pointed out by James Clifford in relation to historical studies of ethnography—namely, the "limited and foreshortened evidence" available to the historian, who is not able to see what the ethnographer saw, and is also unable to get to the informants' side (1988: 59)—it is possible to discern some recurring themes in Berendt's travel journalism. Much like his earlier writings on the Negro, these essays are characterized by a cultural critique of the West and also colored by the trauma of the recent German past.

Bali—An Unspoiled Paradise with an Amicable Approach to Alterity

Berendt first visited Bali in 1962 and, clearly enchanted by it, returned time and again over the coming decades (Berendt 1977a: 374). In 1981, he even indicated that he would dearly like to live on the island but that its climate did not agree with him (Holleufer 1981: 10). His image of the country was somewhat contradictory. On the one hand, Bali was a "last, unspoiled paradise" (1962c: 22). It was full of strange and marvellous sights, such as the *Barong* dance, which culminated in the head of a live chicken being bitten off. Of additional interest to him was Bali's saturation with music and spirituality (1962c: 22; 1962d). In all of these respects the Balinese were seen as having an "authentic" existence: or, as he wrote in 1977, they were "civilized *and* wild. In a proximity and combination the like of which can be found nowhere [else]" (1977a: 377; emphasis in original). Berendt's Bali was therefore partly an Other, valued as a repository for qualities such as spirituality, and a marriage of civilization and vitality which, in the 1950s, he had diagnosed as being lacking in the inauthentic West. Hence, the Balinese were akin to the Negroes in his earlier writings about jazz.

Berendt, however, was also fascinated by *change* in Balinese culture. He identified that the Balinese had a "smiling" approach to external influences and to the maintenance of their own culture: "They cosset them-

---

2. I adopt this term from Lisa Gates, who considers "popular ethnography," with its accessibility and compelling narratives (as typified in the U.S. by *National Geographic*) to be scientific ethnography's "commercial cousin" (1998: 235–6).

Figure 13 | Berendt in Indonesia, 1967. Pabel Stern, Hamburg; courtesy of the Jazzinstitut Darmstadt. Used with permission.

selves away but, despite this, remain the most lovable ... people one can imagine. In the midst of all their isolation they remain receptive and approachable if it involves something suited to them." Berendt pointedly contrasted this stance with that of *other* peoples—and although he did not mention Germany, there was no mistaking whom he meant—"[the Balinese] keep their culture pure without becoming refutory or angry in relation to the Other—as other peoples had to do in order to keep their culture pure" (1962c: 23).[3] In this way, Bali functioned partly as a site at which to be critical of the recent German past. Subsequent writings on Brazil and the Caribbean took a similar tack by stressing the notions of syncretism and cultural hybridity and—if anything—were even more explicit on the lessons to be learned by the Germans.

---

3. Berendt ultimately revised somewhat his account of the Balinese smiling at external cultural influences. In 1977, he referred to the way in which they could also become aggressive when they saw their culture endangered—as they had done during the war against the Dutch and also during the putsch at the end of the Sukarno era (1977a: 373).

Aestheticizing the Creole

Berendt first visited Brazil in 1966 on a scouting mission for Lippmann and Rau's upcoming *Folklore e Bossa Nova do Brasil* tour, and returned in 1972, when he was invited to participate as a judge in a popular music competition (Brigl 2001: 17). He was attracted not only by the country's music—with which he became intimately acquainted, as we shall see in chapter 13—but also by what he saw as the racial equality between Negro, indigenous South American, and European. Hence, his 1977 sketch of Brazil's cultural history—which reads as a tribute to the achievements of African Brazilians, as well as to miscegenation and the aesthetic of "coffee-brown" skin—noted that it was not race per se that divided Brazilians, but rather socioeconomic inequality (1977a: 338–40). That he focused on the notion of interracial equality was not surprising. As Barbara Browning has shown, the idea of Brazil's so-called "racial democracy"—first posited by the Brazilian sociologist Gilberto Freyre in the 1930s—continues to hold sway in the Brazilian popular imagination (1995: 3–34).

The notion of a "racial democracy" must have appealed to a postwar West German only too conscious of the racist policies of Germany's recent past. However, particularly from today's perspective, Berendt's rosy interpretation might be criticized for glossing over more critical readings of Brazilian society. Commentators such as the historian Thomas Skidmore have argued since the mid-1970s that "racial democracy" talk has a downside. They assert that while it was originally antiracist and progressive, nowadays it misrepresents the facts and obscures actual racial inequality (namely, the fact that black Brazilians are overrepresented among the country's poor). For the Brazilian Carlos Hasenbalg, it is part of a "wider matrix of ideological conservatism where the preservation of national unity and social peace are the paramount concerns" (qtd. in Browning 1995: 6). Berendt did gush about racial democracy; however, to his credit, he also observed that the blacks were Brazil's poorest (cf. 1977a: 340).

Berendt's 1977 essay on the Caribbean—which he preferred to call the "Creole" region, and to which he also reckoned both Louisiana and French Guyana—covered similar ground, but also went further. He praised the cultural hybridity and post-racial Creole identity that he observed there, and also laid bare a link between these phenomena and interracial desire. While conceding that the Creole region was not altogether idyllic—a certain racial fanaticism existed, for example, in Trinidad—he discerned a transcendent tendency toward interracial desire, miscegenation, and hybridity, which ensured that racial markers were being erased: "Every young man in Trinidad sees, if he has eyes in his head, that the most attractive girls on his island are the 'Douglases': mixes of Indians and Negros. Even today every second Trinidadian can no longer say with certainty to which race he belongs" (1977a: 360). According to Berendt, this Trinidadian example could not be admired enough, particularly as it contradicted all European experience. Citing a Trinidadian politician, he even implied that it could be instructive for overcoming difficulties within Europe, including those faced by *Gastarbeiter* in Germany! (1977a: 361).

Berendt was not alone among his countrymen (and women) in reflecting on interracial desire. Katrin Sieg argues that the relative absence of postcolonial Others in postwar West Germany meant that there was greater latitude to explore this territory (2002: 189–90). She observes that the trope of interracial love—one of the "standard tropes of contact"—represents a utopian desire for wholeness and for a transcendence of difference (2002: 215). The problem is that—as in the account of the Balinese "smiling" in the face of external influences, or in the aestheticization of "coffee-brown skin"—it can reduce the encounter between ethnic groups to a benign love story. At a symbolic level it paints the Other as a woman who is a sexual initiator and obscures alternative accounts of the mixed-race child as born of rape and repression (Browning 1995: 21–2).

For someone who came of age during the Nazi era, Berendt's paean to Brazil's racial democracy and the culturally indeterminate Creole identity did contain an antiracist dimension. However, although he referred to the catastrophic history of colonialism (see, e.g., 1977a: 366), his focus on interracial desire—which neatly legitimized his own sexual adventures—had the potential to gloss over more critical interpretations of the encounter with the Other. He also neglected to mention critical interpretations of the post-racial Creole identification, including its tendency to break down when the (black) "Creole" was transplanted to Europe.[4]

"Third World" Illiberalism

And yet despite all of this, Berendt's accounts of exotic locations were not exclusively romanticized. At times he was also highly critical. In particular—and not surprisingly—he demonstrated a heightened sensi-

---

4. In this respect, he might have mentioned the Martinique-born Frantz Fanon's theories. He cited Fanon in the Creole essay (1977a: 371), yet did not delve into his highly critical attitude toward the legacy of French colonialism on the psyche of the black man.

tivity to the nationalism that was so instrumental in the nation building of the postcolonial era. This came to the fore in his accounts of Southeast Asia. Once again stressing the well-worn opposition between jazz and nationalism, Berendt asserted, for example, that the standard of the Thai King Bhumipol's *Royal Jazz Sextet*—which he heard in 1962, when granted an audience with the saxophone-playing regent—was restricted by its all-Thai makeup, which, as he also pointed out, was a consequence of purely nationalist considerations. If only, he lamented, the band contained some of the excellent Filipino musicians in Bangkok, it would be truly "regal" (1963a: 25).

The Indonesian President Sukarno's nationalism was also singled out for vigorous criticism. As he observed, Sukarno was seeking to instate Javanese culture as hegemonic throughout the Indonesian archipelago (cf. Ramstedt 1991: 111–13). In this campaign, he vocally sympathized with minorities such as the Balinese and the ethnic Chinese (1962c 23; 1963a: 23–4). Berendt's allergic response was consistent with his attack during the 1970s on cultural nationalism elsewhere in the Third World (see chapter 15) and was surely borne by his "liberal watchdog" attitude. However, siding with the Balinese and the ethnic Chinese—who were explicitly described as cultural minorities suffering under the yoke of a nationalist dictator—had an extra significance (1962c: 23; 1963a: 23). This status rendered them, too, stand-ins for the Jewish victims of the Third Reich. Indeed, in a 1967 article on jazz in Southeast Asia, Berendt expressly made a link between the ethnic Chinese and German Jews: "'The Chinese are to us what the Jews were to you,' one is often told, 'no one likes them but they do the big business'" (1967i: 2). By sympathizing with the "Jews" of Indonesia then, one could yet again demonstrate that one had overcome the cultural chauvinism of the Nazi past.

Musical Souvenirs

Experiences that could be written up for the press represented only one form of souvenir that the "Marco Polo of Jazz" brought back with him from his travels. When he returned from Asia in 1962, Berendt also carried a palpable enthusiasm for world musics, as well as numerous recordings of the same: the *Jazz Echo* reported that he had sufficient material from the trip to assemble thirty-two (!) separate SWF radio programs covering, *inter alia*, Indian, Thai, Balinese, Chinese, and Japanese musics ("Jazz News" 1962c). In addition, he was able to negotiate the commercial release of recordings he made of Balinese gamelan music.

The Music from Bali, which was released in 1962 on the Dutch Philips label, takes its place beside other recordings of world musics that—parallel with the expansion of the academic discipline of ethnomusicology, and the rise of the LP record format—were increasingly being sold onto Western markets from the mid-1950s onward (Pfleiderer 1998: 62–3). Although these records were seldom commercially very successful, they were well received in some quarters: indeed, many of the jazz musicians who engaged with world musics from the 1960s onward were inspired by such recordings (Berendt 1977a: 382–3; Seeger 1991: 292; Pfleiderer 1998: 63). These records were often culled from field recordings made by academic ethnomusicologists and accompanied by quite detailed notes. While Berendt himself was fond of long cover notes, and referred to the work of ethnomusicologists from time to time, he was nevertheless keen to promote quite a different, nonacademic approach to world musics such as *The Music from Bali*.

Berendt beseeched *Twen* readers and music fans to discover for themselves the music of Southeast Asia—which he thought the equal or better of Western art music, yet shamefully undervalued in the West (1962c; 1962d). Through applying what he called a jazz perspective, he promised that listeners would be better rewarded than by "the thought processes of certain Professors, who have written books about the music of China, Bali, Thailand or India from the standpoint of the European music tradition" (1962c: 17, 20). In his view, academic approaches focused too much on technique and context—and national differentiation—with the result that they missed out on the emotional power of the music (1962c: 23).

As a counter-suggestion, Berendt advanced a rather vague "jazz" approach, which essentially involved responding to the music at just that emotional level. This had distinct similarities to his romanticized interpretation of the "naïve" attitude to Western music displayed by early African American jazz musicians, and by Southeast Asian musicians, and also resembled the aesthetic approach to music advocated by some German Romantics (cf. Berendt 1962c: 17; Blume 1979: 109; Longyear 1988: 17). In so doing, Berendt turned the European layperson's lack of knowledge about the specifics of an Other music into a virtue: "We are unconstrained by the external trappings of a music and hear in it that which is its fundamental substance: *primal messages which are the same everywhere [in the world]*" (1962c: 23; emphasis added).

As Pfleiderer observes, and as we will see again in the conclusion, this type of notion has become rather controversial indeed. The question of musical "universals"—such as the existence of singing in most musical cultures or the connection between music and dance—was historically of interest to comparative musicologists; however, the academic focus shifted over time to questions of *difference* rather than similarity. There are doubtless similarities between musical cultures from around the world, but, as Pfleiderer points out: "The actual similarities which exist between different musical traditions have, time and again, been willingly mystified into musical universals and anthropological constants, into indicators of generalized deep structures of human musicality." Such postulates are, of course, difficult to either prove or disprove (1998: 13–14).

In Berendt's case, the universalizing approach was motivated by a genuine and laudable interest, as well as by his own lack of ethnomusicological training, and by a general dislike of overly scientific methods. It surely rendered strange musics more easily digestible for the lay public, and contributed to raising the profile of those musics. However it also had the tendency to encourage an exoticizing mode of interaction with the music: although Berendt himself gave relatively extensive—if occasionally inaccurate or speculative—background information to his audience, the local context and significance of the music was, *ipso facto*, rendered less important.[5] In an extreme situation, such an approach might have unfortunate consequences, as, for example, in the case of blythely recording and disseminating music sacred (and secret) to a particular culture.[6]

Contacts with Other Jazz Scenes

In addition to the recordings and travel experiences that Berendt took with him from these trips, he also established yet more valuable contacts with jazz scenes around the world. On two occasions, this led to requests that he lobby for West German jazz musicians to tour those locations: when he travelled to Buenos Aires in 1960, for example, he was requested to assemble a group to tour Argentina the following year ("Jazz News" 1960d). This project was never realized, nor was King Bhumipol's entreaty two years later that a band form part of the retinue of the West German president, who was soon to visit the Thai court (Berendt

---

5. The ethnomusicologist Wolfgang Laade criticized Berendt, for example, for the errors in his liner notes, although he conceded that these were only natural given that he was no expert in relation to world musics (1970: 141).

6. For an example of one such case, in which the sacred/secret music of Australian Aborigines was recorded and intended for public release, only to be saved from this fate at the last minute by a court injunction, see Shakespeare 1999: 418.

1964d: 13). His Majesty's request nevertheless gave the impetus for the Albert Mangelsdorff Quintet's inaugural Goethe Institut–funded jazz tour in 1964.

Berendt's many contacts with musicians and critics would prove very useful not only when he accompanied the Mangelsdorff Quintet on its 1964 tour, but also for the *JMTW* series and beyond. In 1962, for instance, he met some of the Japanese musicians, whom he would later invite to Berlin for the 1965 *Sakura Sakura* project. He also met the Indonesian musicians Bubi Chen and Jack Lesmana, who would take part in the 1967 *Djanger Bali* concert and recording. His trip to India elicited contact with the critic Niranjan Jhaveri, who, many years later, would invite him to participate in the 1980 Jazz Yatra festival in Bombay (Berendt 1962c: 20; 1980c).

* * * * *

Berendt's travels in Asia, South America and the Caribbean were highly productive, yielding a wealth of articles, recordings, and contacts as well as a heightened enthusiasm for world musics. Reading his travel journalism, it is easy to see why these destinations appealed to him. Not only did they provide a great many new and exciting experiences to the restless critic; they also supplied another Other to the Germany of which he was critical. It was as a direct consequence of these travels—and in particular of his debut trip to Asia in 1962—that his career as an engineer of intercultural encounters now came into being. If Berendt's embrace of world musics—and his advocacy of an emotional, "universalizing" approach to them—set an important conceptual basis for these activities, then King Bhumipol's request for German jazz set in train the circumstances under which that music making received a kick start.

CHAPTER 11

The Goethe Institut's Jazz Ambassadors Strike Up

The Albert Mangelsdorff Quintet's 1964 tour of Asia—the background of which has already been discussed—encompassed fifty concerts in locations from Iran to Japan and was clearly regarded by the Goethe Institut as a resounding success. So much so that it was soon regularly sending jazzmen overseas (Berendt 1977a: 227–8; 1980a). Indeed, by 1968 it had financed twenty-six tours to all continents but Australia and was spending almost one-fifth of its annual 1 million DM–music budget in this way ("Jazz aus Deutschland für Südamerika" 1968). Some commentators even thought that the Germans were taking over the international jazz-proselytizing work of the Americans. Hence, when an "All-Star" West German band traveled through South America in 1968, a critic with the *Jornal do Brasil* noted: "It is no longer the Americans who are bringing the quintessence of the art form with them; it is the Germans" (qtd. in Dilloo 1969). In 1981, Berendt also reported that the USIS had expressed admiration for the institute's jazz work, which made the United States's efforts seem pale by comparison (1981b: 10).[1] The Jazz Pope was intimately involved in all of this, of course—not only did he lobby hard for the institute to countenance financing such tours in the first place, he also advised it during the 1960s and 1970s on whom to send (Von Schlippenbach 1981; Berendt 1996a: 324, 396–8). At a material level, the tours provided an important source of income for

---

1. In 1978, the USIS took over the "Jazz Ambassador" tours from the State Department, where they had been languishing since the mid 1970s. Von Eschen observes that the tours tapered off markedly from this time, as funds were cut and the foreign policy objectives of the tours receded (2004: 249, 251).

musicians—and for critics like Berendt who occasionally accompanied the tours. Symbolically, they offered another opportunity to advance a modern, liberal image of West Germany, not least by way of the tourists' adaptations of local musics. However, given the postcolonial status of many of the countries on the itinerary, some of the intended recipients were inclined to take a dim view of these sorts of activities.

Tolerance and Respect in Action

As we saw in chapter 6, the institute's jazz tours presented a novel avenue through which to represent West Germany as a tolerant country. Musicians and critics projected the institute's guiding philosophy in various ways. Berendt, for example, explicitly used his concert announcements during Mangelsdorff's Asian tour to emphasize that West Germany was a peaceful country. Others were less blatant and took comfort from the view that just by playing *jazz*, they were representing West Germany as distanced from its burdened past. The singer Willi Johanns, who traveled to North Africa in late 1965 and early 1966 with the Kurt Edelhagen Orchestra, offers one such example. In a *Jazz Podium* article written on his return, Johanns proudly observed that the Orchestra's music had caused North African audiences—who were surprised "that such a lively and contemporary music could be heard from the land of Wagner and the Nibelungen"—to rethink "outmoded images of Germany" (1966: 94).[2] Given Germany's military aggression in North Africa during World War II, this was no idle matter. In addition, the tours offered a concrete opportunity to demonstrate respect for Other cultures—both in discourse and by way of the practices adopted by the tourists. Hence, in addition to praising indigenous musics which they encountered along the way, musicians such as Mangelsdorff also paid musical tribute by performing jazz adaptations of local songs (Mangelsdorff 1964a: 158).

Now Jazz Ramwong

In preparation for its 1964 tour—and again at Berendt's initiative, but following a pattern already established by the American Jazz Ambassadors—Mangelsdorff's Quintet adapted music from India, Vietnam, Indonesia, and other countries on their itinerary (Mangelsdorff 1964a: 159;

---

2. It is unfortunately difficult to assess the veracity of such claims given the paucity of available evidence about how the tours were received by overseas audiences.

Paulot 1993: 233. Cf Von Eschen 2004: 46, 107). To this end, Berendt supplied the group with recordings he had collected in Asia in 1962 and it then selected suitable pieces for adaptation, including Ravi Shankar's composition "Pather Panchali," a composition by the Thai King Bhumipol, and the Thai folk song "Nau Djay Ramwong" (Berendt 1964b: 138; 1980a; Paulot 1993: 207). Mangelsdorff viewed these adaptations as a way of building a bridge to local audiences who might otherwise have had little exposure to jazz (Mangelsdorff 1964b). For his part, Berendt billed them as special musical greetings to the countries visited, and *Jazz Podium* concurred when it reviewed *Now Jazz Ramwong*, the Quintet's recording of these adaptations, observing that the album involved a "respectful bow to the admired musical culture of Asia" (Berendt 1964b: 138; "Now Jazz Ramwong" 1964).

The diplomatic strategy was clearly appreciated by some Asian audiences. After the Quintet performed at King Bhumipol's court, for example, the King invited it to jam with him and his Royal Jazz Sextet (Berendt 1964a). The reviewer from the *Bangkok Post* also thought that the Quintet had done a "marvelous job transforming the folktune ['Nau Djay Ramwong']" (qtd. in Berendt 1964a). In addition, the Indonesian musicians Jack Lesmana and Bubi Chen interpreted Mangelsdorff's version of the Indonesian folk song "Burungkaka Tua" as a special greeting (Berendt 1967a; Chen 2004). However, some were more ambivalent about these sorts of efforts: the Japanese trumpeter Terumasa Hino thought, for example, that adaptations of Japanese folk songs performed by visiting Western groups like the Mangelsdorff Quintet were a bit gratuitous and not very interesting, although he was still able to "tune out the actual song itself and just appreciate the musicianship of the performers" (Hino 2004).

For Mangelsdorff, the significance of these adaptations was also not to be overstated:

> I do not consider that our music could be influenced by Asian music. Both musics are too different in their nature for that. Similarly, it would scarcely make sense just to appropriate Asian themes. You can only take [them] on for the purposes of adaptation … But that is just an external activity, which in no way should be misunderstood as a true process of musical melding. Naturally the personal experiences of a musician are reflected in his music, but it by no means changes itself in its character. (1964a: 159)

Mangelsdorff's focus was clearly on remaining true to himself and to his personal conception of jazz. Set as he was upon following his own path toward emancipation from American models, any extensive engagement with Asian musics would have been a distraction. As he wrote after returning from the trip: "[The trip to Asia] was not of decisive meaning for our music making. Leading a regulated life in one set location, working on yourself and practicing is important for that. That is the only way to get results that count. Above all it is finding yourself that is the thing" (1964a: 159).

The pattern of engaging in what might be called acts of musical diplomacy became common among the institute's jazz tourists over the coming years. For example, the saxophonist Klaus Doldinger, who travelled to South America in 1965 and to Asia in 1969, frequently adopted the approach ("Das Klaus Doldinger Quartet in Südamerika" 1965; "Jazz zwischen Icking und Indonesien" 1969: 164). On its 1975 Asian tour, Manfred Schoof's Sextet also performed a concerto in which the group engaged with Indian, Thai, Korean, Malaysian, Indonesian, and Filipino musics (Berendt 1975e). However, particularly as time passed, some German musicians distanced themselves from the idea: for instance, the bassist Eberhard Weber, who participated in Schoof's 1975 tour, reportedly compared the group's attempt with that of Chinese musicians playing "My bonnie lies over the ocean" while touring Scotland! (Berendt 1977a: 235). In early 1981, freshly returned from the Globe

Figure 14 | Klaus Doldinger and his Quartet take time out during their 1969 Asian tour for the Goethe Institut. Courtesy of the Jazzinstitut Darmstadt. Used with permission.

Unity Orchestra's belated debut tour for the institute (and in the context of a dispute with Berendt, who had now retired from advising the institute[3]), Alexander von Schlippenbach expressed the view that such activities "demonstrate an embarrassing superficiality and courtesy—as if the political component of the Goethe undertaking were supposed to directly transfer onto the music." Instead, he advocated maturity on the part of the musicians, and like Mangelsdorff before him, inferred that they should hold true to their own course (1981).[4]

Collaborations and Developmental Aid

Occasionally, the institute's jazz tourists also had an opportunity to engage in musical exchanges with musicians whom they met on tour. This was usually in the form of a fleeting jam session, or during spontaneous discussions between musicians in which they swapped ideas and techniques. The tours' boosters did not hesitate to laud such events as instances of genuine cultural exchange ("Doldinger füllt Titelseiten" 1965: 175; Hömberg 1965: 50; Goethe Institut 1966: 81; Johanns 1966: 95). However the "close collaborations" to which Berendt referred in 1980 were certainly not yet a reality when Mangelsdorff's group first travelled to Asia in 1964 (1980a). As Mangelsdorff observed, they were simply too busy rehearsing, traveling, and performing to have time to really get to know the locals (1964a: 158). Longer-term collaborations would only come later—for example when the Dave Pike Set traveled to Brazil in May 1972 and resided in Bahia for two weeks, sharing a house with the Brazilian group Grupo Baiafro. This stint resulted in joint performances and the recording *Salomão* (Schreiner 1972; 1993: 83–4; Kriegel 1998: 169–70). It also reflected a 1970 change in Goethe Institut policy, which now increasingly focused on dialogical and partnership-based cultural work (Goethe Institut n.d.).[5]

---

3. The dispute related to Berendt's criticism of the Goethe Institut for programming the Globe Unity Orchestra. He thought that its brand of avant-garde jazz was not entirely appropriate for the Asian locations to which it traveled (Berendt 1981b).

4. Recently von Schlippenbach has observed that "'*Now Jazz Ramwong*' was a good production, about which no musical complaints can be made," while still maintaining that some musicians' engagement with world musics—such as Eberhard Schoener's 1975 *Bali Agung*—had been dreadfully tasteless: "I tend to be skeptical about such adaptations because cheap effects are often used: in a word, kitsch gets produced" (2004).

5. It should be observed, however, that as early as 1965 there had been calls for musicians to stay in one location for a longer period. It was understood that only under such circumstances could more effective cultural exchanges between the Germans and the locals take place (Hömberg 1965: 49).

Regardless of the actual extent of collaborations, the feeling that one had made a contribution was one that was savored by the tourists and by Berendt. On the return of Mangelsdorff's Quintet in 1964, Berendt expressed with renewed vigor the conviction that jazz—and by extension the institute's tours—could make a valuable contribution to intercultural understanding (1964b: 140). No doubt recalling his positive experiences in Poland in 1957, Mangelsdorff also reported that "the most rewarding [part] of this trip [was] that we were allowed to feel that we had given something to others" (1964a: 159). Willi Johanns even went as far as labeling the Edelhagen Orchestra's tour of North Africa "musical developmental aid" (1966: 95). This was a notion that the institute itself advanced at various times during the 1960s (Hömberg 1965: 49; Goethe Institut 1967: 91; Hüdepohl 1968: 19–20; Pfeiffer 1968; 1970).

When Berendt glossed that "[more] jazz ensembles certainly ought to be sent to Eastern countries ... as messengers of the lively musical happenings in the Western world," he summed up a widespread attitude in the West German jazz scene and beyond that saw this type of "musical diplomacy" as a contribution to better intercultural understanding, and he was also subconsciously (or otherwise) expressing a desire to make up for the chauvinism of the Nazi past (1964b: 140). However, there were other ways of interpreting such activities. This much can be seen if we turn our focus, for example, to Indonesia in the early 1960s. Mangelsdorff's group had been unable to enter the country in 1964 because of the "Confrontation" between Indonesia and Malaysia (Berendt 1967a). However, had they done so, they would have encountered an attitude on the part of some Indonesians that did not see jazz as a medium toward a conviviality between countries and that may well have held their adaptation of the Indonesian folk song "Burungkaka Tua" to be something more harmful than a musical greeting.

President Sukarno and Jazz

By early 1964—when Mangelsdorff's Quintet was waiting in Singapore hoping to gain entry to Indonesia—the recently established Malaysian Federation had become a burning issue both for President Sukarno and the Indonesian Communist Party (PKI), which increasingly had the president's ear. The Federation was seen as an imperialist creation of Great Britain, the former colonial power, and concurrent with this view there was an upsurge in general anti-imperialist militancy, including in relation to American popular culture (Mortimer 1974: 203–46; SarDesai 1989: 237–9).

The Indonesian concert organizer and jazz writer P. R. Sudibyo has observed that the PKI spoke out against Western popular music generally, and only spared lambasting jazz by name because it was a minority music (Sudibiyo 2004a). However, jazz did not escape President Sukarno's criticism. His attitude manifested itself in several ways: firstly, he asked the guitarist Jack Lesmana and the pianist Bubi Chen to desist from improvising in his presence (Berendt 1967n: 33; Chen 2004). He also ordered the American jazz clarinettist Tony Scott, who resided and performed in Indonesia in 1960, to leave the country (Berendt 1967n: 33).[6] Nevertheless, despite an unfavourable climate, it was not impossible to play jazz—just as it had not been impossible in the Third Reich or during periods of repression in the Eastern bloc. Sudibyo organized jazz concerts during the early 1960s; however, so as to escape unwelcome attention from the authorities, he expressly avoided references to jazz by billing the gigs simply as "parties" (Sudibyo 2004a).

In explaining Sukarno's opposition, Berendt relied on his tried-and-true "dictators don't swing" philosophy: "Jazz, of course, is 'political' music everywhere in the world, and during the Sukarno era, it was blacklisted the same as under most other dictatorships, whether of leftist or rightist persuasions" (1967a). However, this convenient aphorism did not explore the specifics of Sukarno's and the PKI's broader opposition toward American popular culture.

On the one hand, the PKI's 1963 objection to U.S. "cultural penetration" (Mortimer 1974: 244) resembled the position advanced at different times by its communist counterparts elsewhere in the world, including in the Eastern bloc. And if the United States was thought to be perpetrating "cultural penetration" in Indonesia, then there was no logical reason why other "imperialist" Western countries—the imperialist charge was also expressly leveled at West Germany (cf. Mortimer 1974: 210)—could not be accused of something similar: from this perspective, the Goethe Institut's jazz tours might have been seen as ancillary "Cold War secret weapons," as it were.

However, Sukarno's opposition to Western popular culture was consonant with a deeper-running cultural nationalism independent of his association with the PKI. Indeed, nationalism was one of the *Pantja Sila* (five fundamental principles) he formulated in 1945 as guiding the newly established Indonesian Republic, and which acted as a rallying

---

6. Sudibyo and the Indonesian journalist and jazz historian Alfred Ticoalu both intimated, however, that Scott's being advised to leave Indonesia was unrelated to jazz but based, rather, on personal reasons—namely, a clash with the president concerning the affections of a certain Indonesian woman (Sudibyo 2004a; Ticoalu 2004b). On Scott, see also chapter 14.

point during the struggle against Dutch rule, particularly during the turbulent years of the late 1940s (Wertheim 1959: 228). Writing in 1959, the Dutch scholar W. F. Wertheim noted that this cultural nationalism was "still an important source of the spiritual strength needed to build a new Indonesian society." He also observed that while nationalist phenomena "may sometimes smell of chauvinism," from the Indonesian perspective they were "only too understandable reactions to a colonial past and at the same time conditions to free themselves from an inferiority feeling" (1959: 331–2).

It is therefore unsurprising that Sukarno's nationalism had little room for Western music and dance, which as early as the 1950s he had considered an affront to young people's Indonesian identity (Mortimer 1974: 244).[7] The exact source of irritant to this "imagined" Indonesian identity—be it American Jazz Ambassadors, Goethe Institut tourists or the Twist—was presumably a little beside the point. And had President Sukarno been aware that some West German musicians and critics—and the Goethe Institut itself—regarded their jazz tours as cultural "developmental aid," he would presumably have been incensed, since the very notion of cultural aid inferred that the recipients of that aid were culturally underdeveloped.[8]

The German Perspective

Objections like Sukarno's and the PKI's were not infrequently encountered by the Goethe Institut's jazz tourists. In 1964, for example, Mangelsdorff had to deal with a distinct anti-Americanism in Burma, which denigrated American jazz as corrupting of young people (Mangelsdorff 1964a: 159). Subsequent jazz tourists, like the Manfred Schoof Sextet in 1975, also observed anti-Americanism in various parts of Asia, and Berendt noted in 1981 that on one of his trips to Indonesia, he had been confronted with complex arguments about latent colonialism in the Western understanding of culture (Berendt 1975d; 1981b: 11).

---

7. It should be noted, however, that the President's attitude was not without its paradoxes: Alfred Ticoalu observes that, based on interviews he conducted with associates of Sukarno, whatever his official ideological objections might have been, in private he was an admirer of European classical music (Ticoalu 2004b).

8. According to Ticoalu, there is no evidence that Sukarno was aware of Mangelsdorff's attempts to enter Indonesia in 1964 or of his version of the Indonesian folk song "Burungkaka Tua." He observes that, in any case, these matters would have been rather minor concerns at the time, given the more pressing matter of the escalation of the Confrontation with Malaysia (2004b).

And yet these critical views tended to be downplayed. There were several reasons for this. Firstly, musicians and critics were hardly likely to criticize the philosophical basis of what had become an important source of income for them. Moreover, the institute expressly understood itself to be avoiding all forms of cultural imperialism. In addition, as we saw in chapter 10 nationalism such as that displayed by Sukarno was thought inherently suspect, given the German experience, and so there was an unwillingness to enquire as to its value in a postcolonial setting. The tone of these arguments against jazz and American popular music were also presumably all too familiar from the Nazi and Eastern-bloc propaganda directed at jazz. Finally, and perhaps most importantly, the idea that jazz could be an agent of dangerous Western "cultural penetration" was simply inconsistent with the image that the postwar West German jazz scene held: if jazz was fundamentally "international" and anti-ideological, how could it be an agent of penetration? Hence, Mangelsdorff dismissed the Burmese attitude in the following terms: "one can see that in the play of politics the most astounding observations can be arrived at, and the plainly obvious, namely the truly international, collegial character of music gets overlooked—or ignored" (1964a: 159). For his part, Berendt thought that charges of latent colonialism should simply be met with a policy more attentive to the musical tastes of the target audience: "clever and sensitive cultural work ought to strive toward curing these sorts of allergies and not exacerbate them" (1981b: 11).

Beyond the Musical Greeting

Musical diplomacy like that recorded on the Albert Mangelsdorff Quintet's 1964 album *Now Jazz Ramwong* was partly aimed at demonstrating critics', musicians'—and, ultimately, West Germany's—modern, liberal credentials. Whether it was received in this way by all the intended recipients is, of course, another matter entirely. On the musicians' side, there was often a sense that while these were worthwhile activities, they did not necessarily represent the main core of one's musical trajectory. Although, as we will see in chapter 15, the staunchest criticisms were yet to come, there was also a dawning uneasiness on the part of some critics about the appropriation of world musics. However, a critic such as Richard Chand, writing in *Downbeat* in 1961, did not take issue with the appropriation per se. Rather, he objected to jazzmen getting the credit for what they had taken: "Exotic musicians and musicologists are glad that modern jazz-musicians have taken their recent influence from 'exotic' music or else 'accidentally' play it. We only ask that proper credit be given to exotic music and that musicians playing it are no longer called innovators" (1961: 8).

For his part, Berendt by no means objected to the idea of Western musicians adapting or otherwise engaging with world musics—indeed, as we will see, he continued to strongly encourage such activities in the coming years. However, by the mid-1960s, he also began to promote activities in which Other musicians were given a voice too. The first such opportunity was in 1965, when the Japanese Hideo Shiraki Quintet was invited to perform in Berlin with three performers on the koto, the traditional Japanese psaltery. This too was an activity that grew out of Berendt's 1962 Asian trip.

CHAPTER 12

Japanesing Jazz, or, Kimono Today, Swing Tomorrow

Berendt was fascinated by Japan at a number of levels, musical, cultural, and spiritual. Indeed, between 1962 and 1980, he visited the country seven times (Berendt 1980b: 9). Here was a country that, like Germany, had been defeated in the Second World War and that had also seen a strong influx in jazz culture in the postwar years. From Berendt's perspective, postwar Japan was also peculiarly bicultural: traditional Japanese and modern Western culture appeared to happily coexist, sometimes within the one person.[1] It is therefore not surprising that Japan provided the first real opportunity for Berendt to experiment as a producer of a more thoroughgoing intercultural music making.

Jazz in Postwar Japan

As the jazz historian E. Taylor Atkins has shown, the reception of jazz in Japan has a long and complex history. This, in turn, exhibits distinct parallels with the plight of jazz in (West) Germany—particularly in the War and postwar years. During the War, jazz was subjected to ideological imperatives, where, as in Germany, it faced a complex mixture of repression and accommodation. Likewise, in the 1950s, it experienced a

---

1. I adopt the term *biculturalism* from the ethnomusicologist Mantle Hood, who used it to describe individual musicians who were familiar with several different musical cultures (Stroh 1994: 337).

boom—and again for similar reasons as in West Germany (Atkins 2001: 128–59, 184 ff; Minor 2004: 8). Atkins observes that the "production and consumption of jazz ... were decisively shaped in the first two postwar decades by institutional, psychological, and sociocultural impulses set in motion by the Occupation," and that jazz's strong appeal to young Japanese lay "in an ethos of rebellion and anomie traceable to 'the confusion era' and the disparagement of the inherited value system" (2001: 167; 169). However—just as in West Germany—jazz was in the doldrums in the early 1960s, its popularity surpassed by rock 'n' roll (Atkins 2001: 212). Such was the scene Berendt encountered when he first visited in 1962, eager to sample the jazz which Japan had to offer.

Berendt found things to both criticize and admire in the Japanese jazz scene. On the one hand, jazz appeared to be just another variety of Western music: a young Japanese person might listen to jazz, but he or she also listened to rock 'n' roll, Latin-American, and Hawaiian music (Berendt 1963b: 18, 20). Jazz's lack of special status had the result that Japanese musicians did not take it seriously enough:

> Japanese musicians lack what the Americans call "dedication." They do not have the devotion to one—and only one—type of music which all great musicians have possessed, regardless of what they might have played. What the Japanese play is perfect and often also imaginative and it is always elegant and convincing, but their jazz lacks that which art must have: [the necessity] that it is so and not anything different, and that it cannot be anything different. In Japan everything can always be different. (1963b: 20)

This capricious attitude—Berendt likens it to the way one might approach fashions—was implicitly incompatible with the idea of jazz as art (1963b: 20). Given that in his debate with Adorno a decade earlier, the older man had rejected jazz as a "perennial fashion," it was important for Berendt to maintain the distinction between serious artistic "style" and modish musical "fashion." Publically criticizing the Japanese approach to jazz was therefore a way of bolstering its art status in West Germany. And yet, there was a material reason for Japanese musicians' diversity: the depressed market for jazz ensured they had to be versatile in order to make a living (Atkins 2001: 212).

On the other hand, Berendt was also intrigued by the way in which Japanese tradition and Western modernity seemed to coexist, or, as he put it in the title to a piece he wrote for *Die Welt* in 1962, "Kimono today, Swing tomorrow" (1962f). Following the musicologist William P. Malm, he observed that Japan had been able to maintain both its traditional music *and* Western music, although he did concede that nowadays more

Japanese were inclined to express themselves in a European rather than traditional Japanese mode (1963b: 16–17, 20. Cf. Malm 1959: 23; Laade 1970: 144). Citing Malm again—and echoing his contemporaneous assertions about the Balinese—he further noted that the Japanese were capable of weathering even the most intensive cultural invasions and possessed enough independence to apply these foreign cultures in a new way (1963b: 18). Not that this sunny optimism was shared by all Japanese at the time: in the same year as Berendt's first visit to Japan, one local commentator expressed his disgust at the hybridization of national culture, even as he hoped that something worthwhile might one day come of it (Atkins 2001: 218). These reflections logically led Berendt to consider whether there might be such a thing as a peculiarly "Japanese" jazz, a topic that, as we shall see, was also beginning to occupy Japanese critics.

Some years before he was comfortable advancing the notion of a characteristically "European" or "German" jazz, Berendt therefore entered into a discussion of the characteristics he perceived in Japanese jazz. In this respect, he walked a complicated line. While attempting to distance himself from a common stereotype, which also had some purchase in the Japanese jazz scene at the time, he too found himself discerning a certain Japaneseness in the thorough way in which Japanese musicians copied their American models (cf. Atkins 2001: 210, 217–18). On the aesthetic front, however, he considered that there was a distinctively "melancholic and elegant" Japanese jazz sound. Finally, he referred to the novel way in which jazz was beginning to be combined with Japanese traditional music (1963b: 18). This latter development was of great interest to Berendt, and one to which he would give his own special imprimatur.

Jazz and Japanese Music: Paths toward an Encounter?

During his 1962 trip, Berendt produced a television special on jazz in Japan for his *Jazz–Heard and Seen* series, which was by now almost a decade old. On that occasion, he commissioned "The Sharps and Flats," a renowned big band, to perform an extended piece in which a koto folk song was transformed into jazz (Berendt 1963b: 18). Reprising a recording it had made the previous year, Berendt also had the Hideo Shiraki Quintet play another traditional song "Matsuri no Genzo," on which it was accompanied by a koto player.

This was by no means the first occasion on which a jazz musician had engaged with Japanese folklore. During the late 1930s and early 1940s, jazzmen had drawn on Japanese folk music for cultural nationalist reasons (Atkins 2001: 131–9). In the postwar years, both Western and Japanese musicians also performed adaptations of Japanese folk songs (Atkins 2001: 242–3; Minor 2004: 1). The trumpeter Terumasa Hino recalls that it was common during this era for Western jazz tourists to perform versions of folk songs when visiting Japan and, true to this model, the Mangelsdorff Quintet performed "Sakura Waltz," its adaptation of the Japanese chestnut "Sakura Sakura," when it visited in 1964 (Hino 2004).

What made the Shiraki Quintet's activity innovative was the way in which it performed with a practitioner of traditional koto music. This in itself was not entirely new either—notably, the Californian producer Richard Bock recorded an album in 1960 on which the koto player Kimio Eto and the American jazz flautist Bud Shank played together, and the expatriate American clarinettist Tony Scott had also improvised with the koto player Shinuchi Yuize in Japan as early as 1959 (Berendt 1963b: 18; Scott n.d.). However, those efforts involved a stylistic compromise on the part of the jazzmen, who adapted their style of playing significantly in order to accommodate themselves to the Japanese idiom (Berendt 1963b: 18; Laade 1970: 140–1, 145; Pfleiderer 1998: 71–2). The Shiraki Quintet's "Matsuri no Genzo" and *Sakura Sakura*, its album recorded with three koto players and conceived for a performance at the Berlin Jazz Days in 1965 attempted a more exploratory combination of the two idioms.

Sakura Sakura is quite a mixed bag. Three of the songs are adaptations of Japanese folk songs, whereas the other three are originals written by the jazzmen, albeit mostly in the spirit of folk music. One adaptation involves Hideo Shiraki on drums together with the koto trio. The koto players perform with the Quintet on three of the other songs, and on the remaining two songs the jazzmen perform by themselves. Bert Noglik has aptly observed that as the *Sakura Sakura* recording progresses the koto players are "added, first of all only as an asset, 'framing,' and finally getting stronger and becoming a part of the mutual course of the music" (1997: 2). The jazzmen *do* hold their ground to a greater extent than either Shank or Scott had done. For their part, the koto players do not simply assimilate by playing jazz on unorthodox instruments either. Nor do they play "authentic" Japanese traditional music, even if Berendt might have asserted this at the time of their Berlin performance (1965e). On at least one of the tracks, they "step out of their conventions, making it possible for the archaic and the avant garde to meet on a virtual level" (Noglik 1997: 2).

For Berendt, this encounter was one that both symbolized, "in the most heightened way," the broader engagement between East and West, and was undertaken with the greatest of respect on the part of the jazz-men (1965e). In many ways, this type of live encounter was the logical next step in Berendt's vision for musical diplomacy. But how did the musicians and German and Japanese critics interpret it?

To Synthesize or Not

The critical reception of the Jazz Days concert and the subsequent Saba recording was, in a word, rather mixed. In the *Berliner Zeitung*, Barbara Rose observed that "the confrontation of Japanese tradition and occidental modernity is fascinating," and Horst Windelboth of the *Berliner Morgenpost* was reminded "of the masterpieces of Japanese painting: Tender, refined and like drawn with china ink" (qtd. in Yui 1965). However, the jazz press was somewhat less positive. *Jazz Podium*'s reviewer was of the view that the two idioms ran in parallel rather than fusing in a convincing fashion ("Berliner Jazztage 1965": 289). Ingolf Wachler thought that the performance had misfired (1966: 45), and Siegfried Schmidt-Joos observed that

> the proclaimed synthesis between modern jazz and Nippon's century-old music tradition [just] did not want to take place. The Japanese blew robust Hard Bop on top of saccharine koto-accompaniment on two of the numbers. On the third ... , the band-leader Shiraki conjured forth tender drum and cymbal colors for the very Japanese performance of the three ladies, and, beyond that, forgot to swing. (1966: 40)

Reviews and analyses of the Saba recording also demonstrated some reservations. Wachler thought the record an improvement on the live performance and *Jazz Podium* praised the striking mix of Japanese music and hard bop—while remaining most impressed by the pure jazz parts, it must be said (Wachler 1966: 45; "Rev. of *Sakura Sakura*" 1966). The musicologist Wolfgang Laade took the view that both groups played together well, but also noted that the whole affair was rather Western (1970: 144). Most recently, Martin Pfleiderer has identified that "the different musical components ... largely stand side by side without connecting" (1998: 75).

However, if commentators have failed to be convinced that *Sakura Sakura* involved a fully integrated synthesis of two musical forms, contemporary German reviewers were nevertheless impressed by its exotic novelty. Hence, *Jazz Podium* praised the "optical" aspect of the Berlin performance, where the koto players performed in kimonos ("Berliner Jazztage 1965": 289). Others stressed the color and prettiness of the

Figure 15 | Manufactured biculturalism? The front and back covers of the 1965 *Sakura Sakura* recording. Design: Hans Pfitzer; photos: Berendt and K. Hucke; courtesy of Universal Music. Used with permission.

event (Ohff 1965; Rev. of *Sakura Sakura* 1966). Schmidt-Joos even got ahead of himself by referring to the koto players as attractive *geishas*, a term used for professional female singers, dancers, and entertainers of men (or, in common parlance, prostitutes) (1966: 40). Like the kimono-wearing Japanese pianist Toshiko Akiyoshi on her 1956 tour of the United States, the exotic appeal of the "koto Girls" clearly contributed to the positive side of *Sakura Sakura*'s German reception.[2] Ingolf Wachler appears to have been alone among critics in wondering whether all of these trappings might have actually inhibited the reception of the music qua music (1966: 45).

"Japanese Jazz," Folk Music and Emancipation

Berendt encouraged the Shiraki Quintet to perform with the koto players and adopt a "Japanese" repertoire for several reasons.[3] In 1965, the *Berliner Festwochen* bore the overarching theme of the encounter be-

---

2. Atkins suggests that Akiyoshi's wearing of a kimono on the tour was "in keeping with the exoticism which propelled her to celebrity" (2001: 208).

3. Terumasa Hino, who was a member of the Quintet, recalled that it was at Berendt's instigation that it performed with the koto players. He also noted however that "the Quintet did not feel constrained while in Berlin to play the jazz versions of the folk songs" (2004).

tween Japanese and Western culture (Berendt 1965e; Eckhardt 2000a: 33). This conveniently gave him the opportunity to continue within the context of the Jazz Days those experiments with which he had earlier been involved in Japan. Perhaps he also wished to put on a concert which would have exotic appeal to German audiences. However, it is simplistic just to dismiss *Sakura Sakura* on that basis, given that it was also warmly received by various Japanese musicians and critics.

The critic Masahisa Segawa thought, for example, that "the combination worked successfully" (qtd. in Minor 2001: 13). His fellow critic Shoichi Yui also embraced the concept:

> Shiraki is intelligent enough to know that it is necessary to create own dimensions in Japanese jazz. The result is on this record. It excels anything Shiraki has recorded in Japan so far. It is modern jazz in the sense of Elvin Jones and John Coltrane and yet, it is so very Japanese, on the other hand, in the sense of the tradition of our country as you can imagine. I feel that it is not without symbolism that this recording—with its splendid meeting of old Japan and modern jazz—was not done in our own country but in Germany. This country always showed a deep understanding for and interest in Japan. (1965).

Yui—who was a friend of Berendt's and also active as a producer (Berendt 1977a: 14, 135; 1996a: 390)—had been urging Japanese jazz musicians to search for a "Japanese" voice since the late 1950s. Indeed, he became one of the champions of the notion of *Nihonteki jazu* (Japanese jazz), which became influential—if not uncontroversial—within the Japanese jazz scene, particularly in the late 1960s and early 1970s, but which still holds sway among some commentators and musicians today (Atkins 2001: 38–9; Hino 2004; Minor 2004: 51, 58, 178). Atkins has shown that Yui's "jazz nationalist" concept retained the notion of jazz as a universal language and sought to locate "Japanese jazz" within a broader global trend, but also was wedded to the idea of an essentialized Japanese cultural identity. Put bluntly, "Japanese jazz" was something that only Japanese people could play (2001: 240 ff). This trope served a range of useful purposes. It "demonstrate[d] Japanese creativity and personal authenticity, reverse[d] the jazz community's alienation from the cultural mainstream, and render[ed] moot comparisons to an ethnic standard of authenticity established in America" (Atkins 2001: 37–8). In this respect, it was—much like the concurrent European "emancipation" discourse, one might add—an empowering "authenticating strategy," but as Atkins observes, it "artificially homogenize[d] an unruly assemblage of highly individualistic artistic voices" (2001: 262). And, as the examples of Bud Shank and Tony Scott suggest, the Japanese did not have a monopoly on the styles and approaches that could be regarded as "Japanese jazz."

Like the notion of "Japanese jazz" itself, recourse to Japanese folklore was of somewhat ambiguous value to Japanese musicians. The late Hideo Shiraki was an enthusiastic participant in *Sakura Sakura*: as his colleague the trumpeter Terumasa Hino recalled, "Shiraki was always crazy about the koto and traditional Japanese drums. So ... the leap to recording folk songs as jazz was not a big one for him to take" (2004. Cf. Atkins 2001: 240). However, Hino himself had mixed feelings. While it would have been a little clichéd to perform jazz adaptations of Japanese folk songs *within Japan*, he felt more comfortable doing so *in Germany*, where he appreciated that audiences might be genuinely interested to hear such things. Personally he did not find *Sakura Sakura* very stimulating, however, and also noted that the record received a lukewarm reception among the Japanese jazz scene (Hino 2004). As William Minor notes, "some native musicians were suspicious of Shiraki's motives for using indigenous elements, seeing this as a ploy to gain international favor" (2004: 13). This hints at the central dilemma involved in activities such as *Sakura Sakura*: they both "pandered to Western audiences' 'orientalizing' expectations and provided the approval that Japanese jazzmen had so long craved" (Atkins 2001: 226).

This latter, more positive dimension of *Sakura Sakura* ought not be neglected, however. The Shiraki Quintet's tour to Germany was seen as a momentous event at home and the international acclaim which it and other similar tours garnered created a great deal of highly productive self-confidence in the Japanese jazz scene (Atkins 2001: 238).

Beyond *Sakura Sakura*

In many respects, Japanese jazz musicians found themselves in a very similar material and mental state as their West German counterparts during the 1960s. By mid-decade there was a growing awareness that Japanese musicians should seek some form of independence from American jazz, which had been consumed all too eagerly in the postwar era. In this respect it should not surprise us that there was a close interest among German commentators like Berendt in the Japanese jazz scene, even if they did not yet expressly draw the parallel between it and the situation they found at home.

For all their similarities, *Nihonteki jazu* and the dawning idea of the European "emancipation" also had different inflections. Whereas the West German discourse tended to avoid "Germanness" as a discursive quality, there was not the same degree of anxiety in relation to the notion of "Japaneseness." In fact, the idea of "Japanese jazz" was imbricated with neo-nationalism (Atkins 2001: 37, 224–5). This undoubtedly reflected a divergent approach to past nationalism from that exhibited in West Germany and explains why recourse to domestic folklore was less problematic for a Hideo Shiraki than it was for an Albert Mangelsdorff.

It may be questioned whether *Sakura Sakura* represented a successful combination of jazz and Japanese music—however that success might be measured. Certainly, its kotos and kimonos tended to encourage an exoticist reception in West Germany. However, the 1965 invitation—which also included a straight jazz performance by the Shiraki Quintet at the Jazz Days' concluding party—was only the first in a string of opportunities for Japanese musicians to perform in Berlin and elsewhere. Berendt himself continued to take a keen interest in Japanese jazz, writing about it, acting as the director of the jazz festival at the 1970 Osaka World Expo, lobbying for the Goethe Institut to finance a German-Japanese Jazz Meeting in Tokyo in 1971, presenting Japanese jazz at the Jazz Days in 1971 and then, later, in other venues including Baden-Baden and Donaueschingen (Berendt 1966j; 1971c; 1971d; 1975c; 1980b). On these occasions, at least, the Japanese invitees were not subjected to orientalizing expectations that encouraged them to perform adaptations of Japanese folk music.[4] Furthermore, the laudable model, pioneered with Shiraki et al. in 1965, of presenting Other musicians live in Berlin was also continued in 1966, when Berendt included a performance by a *Folklore e Bossa Nova do Brasil* troupe in the Jazz Days.

---

4. This is confirmed, for example, by Terumasa Hino, who played with his quintet at the 1971 Jazz Days and also at another SWF event in Stuttgart in 1972 (Hino 2004).

CHAPTER 13

Doing the Bossa in Berlin

As we have already seen, on his first brief trip to South America in 1960 Berendt was exposed to bossa nova, an idiom developed in Brazil in the late 1950s which was soon to rocket to worldwide popularity when musicians like the North American saxophonist Stan Getz recorded their own versions of it. Although he was clearly taken by the music, the bossa nova was a deeply ambiguous affair for Berendt. In its "authentic" Brazilian form, it was "the most interesting encounter between jazz and folk music that has taken place outside the USA," which, together with his emerging love affair with Brazilian culture explored in chapter 10, goes some way toward explaining why he spearheaded the exposure of the music in Germany and also included two such productions in the *JMTW* series—the *Folklore e Bossa nova do Brasil* (*FeBNdB*) anthology recorded in conjunction with a Lippmann and Rau "authentic documentation" tour, and *Tristeza on Guitar,* an album featuring the Brazilian guitarist Baden Powell (Berendt 1966c; 1966l; 1967k; 1975a).[1] However, the blatant way in which the bossa nova had been exploited by the North American record industry and even its very popularity were matters of concern to him. It was in this field of tension that he considered the ethics of intercultural musical appropriation and re-

---

1. The *FeBNdB* package—which included both music and the dancing of Marly Tavares—covered twenty-four concerts from Stockholm to Rome, and also made a stop at the 1966 Berlin Jazz Days. In Berlin, the concert was intended to connect with the 1966 Jazz Days' overarching theme of the encounter between jazz and other art forms, in this case folklore and dance. Lippmann, Rau, and Berendt collaborated closely on this project: both Horst Lippmann and Berendt visited Brazil for several weeks in mid-1966 in order to engage Brazilian musicians for the tour (Berendt 1966c; 1966l: 20).

hearsed some of the arguments he would later raise in his defence of *Weltmusik*.

Brazilian Bossa Nova, 1958–66

The singer and guitarist João Gilberto's 1958 recordings of "Chega de Saudade" and "Desafinado" mark the beginning of what David Treece calls the "classic phase of bossa nova," which lasted until around 1962 (1997: 6 ff). The bossa nova was, as McGowan and Pessanha put it "a new type of samba, in which that genre's rhythmic complexity had been pared down to its bare essentials, transformed into a different kind of beat" (1998: 55). It had a new melodic and harmonic approach and a different mood, favoring, as one author notes, "touch" over "punch" (Perrone 1989: xx). However, the source of this innovation, and in particular the role that the cool jazz of the early to mid-1950s played, is hotly disputed.

On the one hand, some of the bossa's innovators, including Gilberto, openly confessed that cool jazz was a significant influence (Roberts 1999: 93, 119; Perrone and Dunn 2001: 17). On the other, the central figure of Antônio Carlos Jobim—who was apparently primarily influenced by the Brazilian samba-canção and by classical music—rejected the idea: "Many people said that bossa nova was an Americanized phenomenon. … Much to the contrary, I think what influenced American music was the bossa nova" (qtd. in McGowan and Pessanha 1998: 66). Jobim's almost offended tone is contextualized by later developments within the bossa nova world, both in Brazil and abroad.

By the early 1960s, the Brazilian bossa nova movement was, in Treece's words, "showing signs of strain" (1997: 12). Increasingly, left-leaning songwriters began to apply a more socio-critical approach than had previously been the case with Gilberto et al. (Schreiner 1993: 150 ff; Treece 1997: 12–19). Carlos Lyra's aptly titled 1962 song, "Influência do jazz," typifies the development. It is an "obituary" to the traditional samba and expresses dissatisfaction with the perceived cosmopolitanism and "urbane romanticism" of the bossa nova (Treece 1997: 16; Perrone and Dunn 2001: 18–19). The critic José Ramos Tinhorão was even more outspoken; he emphasized the links between jazz and the bossa nova to argue that the latter was a "culturally estranged product that contributed to the alienation of the Brazilian public by turning away from the samba" (Perrone 1989: xxv). In this context, Jobim's defensive comments make perfect sense, as does the strategy of singers and instrumentalists such as Edu Lobo and Baden Powell, who as part of the "second phase" of bossa nova, now turned to pre-urban African-Brazilian traditions for inspiration (Perrone 1989: xxvii; Treece 1997: 20–23).

Bossa Nova in North America, 1962–66

Discussions about the relationship between the Brazilian bossa nova and the culture of the United States are invariably also influenced by the way in which the United States took to the music. As John Storm Roberts has shown, there is a long tradition of jazz appropriating elements from Latin American music. However, the bossa nova particularly appealed to North American jazz musicians because of its harmonic complexity (1999: 115). And so, within a year of the first U.S. release of a Brazilian bossa record, North American musicians—including some erstwhile Jazz Ambassadors to South America—began to make their own bossa recordings. The first was *Jazz Samba*, a 1962 collaboration between the saxophonist Stan Getz and the guitarist Charlie Byrd, which included a version of "Desafinado" that reached number 15 on the singles charts that year (Gioia 1997: 286). Even greater commercial success came with *Getz/Gilberto*, a 1963 record made with João Gilberto that reached number 2 in the pop albums chart in 1964, and which featured Astrud Gilberto singing "The Girl from Ipanema," a number 1 hit the same year (Gioia 1997: 286; McGowan and Pessanha 1998: 69).

Many similar recordings followed as jazzmen and pop musicians alike caught the bossa bug (Roberts 1999: 116 ff). The motivations for this rash of activity were various. On the one hand, producers and musicians were presumably keen to replicate Getz's commercial success. On the other hand, many musicians must have felt an aesthetic affinity toward the music. Particularly in the context of the emergent free jazz, bossa nova offered jazzmen what the west coast saxophonist Paul Winter called a "possibility of a gentler way, in an increasingly noisy world" (qtd. in Van der Lee 1998: 52).

North American enthusiasm for the bossa nova occasionally had a downright exploitative dimension. An early low point was the (in)famous 1962 sell-out concert at Carnegie Hall. Organized by the president of a U.S. record company, it assembled some of the famous names in Brazilian bossa nova (Schreiner 1993: 145; Treece 1997: 13). According to Schreiner, the Brazilians were "were intentionally swindled. Conditions were set so that they had to play mainly new compositions that the United States manager could publish." Understandably, they were disillusioned—to say the least—by the experience (Schreiner 1993: 145).

Berendt on the Bossa: Ambivalence, Authenticity, Appropriation, and Artistic Alienation

Berendt's attitude to the bossa nova was thoroughly ambivalent, and also changed over time, as is every critic's prerogative. In mid-1963—at the height of the North American craze, which was now flowing to other parts of the world as well—he published in *Twen* his own guardedly enthusiastic account of the phenomenon, timed to coincide with the magazine's release of a proto-bossa album for its record series (1963c). Later, in the program notes for the 1966 Berlin Jazz Days—at which he presented both the Stan Getz Quartet with Astrud Gilberto and the *FeBNdB* "documentation"—he carved out acceptable forms of bossa, while distancing himself from the bulk of North American efforts (1966l: 18–20). Unsurprisingly, these acceptable forms coincided with the very music that he had programmed for the Jazz Days!

Berendt's ambivalence related partly to the bossa's aesthetic status. Writing in 1963, he took the view that Brazilian bossa—as typified by Gilberto and Jobim—was not at the same level as "true" jazz, but had a certain value as pop music: "As a jazz listener and critic, one might have reservations about the bossa; but as a musical listener who is interested in there being something on *Schlager* programs from which one doesn't have to immediately flee in horror, one can have no [such] reservations" (1963c: 40–41). Part of the attraction of the bossa nova and folkloric music which he and Horst Lippmann handpicked in Brazil for the *FeBNdB* documentation was that it was thought to have an emotional immediacy, much akin to the authenticity understood to inhere in "true" jazz: indeed it was this immediacy which was cited as justifying its inclusion in the Berlin Jazz Days, despite it not actually being *jazz* (Berendt 1966l: 18).

The fact that respected jazz musicians—including Stan Getz, and, in Germany, the saxophonists Hans Koller and Klaus Doldinger—were engaging with the bossa complicated the picture and called for additional fancy footwork on Berendt's part. Confessing that he was initially suspicious of jazzmen who recorded bossas, thinking that they did so for rank profit, Berendt now revised his opinion: these musicians were simply attracted by the idiom's charms, as he clearly had been himself (1963c: 41). Later, he also interpreted these activities as a natural reaction against the wild sounds of free jazz (1966l: 18). His underlying ambivalence here can surely be explained partly because this undeniably popular music blurred the divide between jazz and popular music, and potentially stood to jeopardize jazz's high art credentials.

Berendt was also quite ambivalent about the question of intercultural musical appropriation that lay at the heart of the bossa. He was openly critical of the "commercialization," "perversion," and "watering down" of the bossa nova in North America and of the fact that, in the past, the Brazilians had not received sufficient royalties for cover versions of their compositions (1963c: 40; 1966c; 1966l: 20). He also disapproved of the way in which North American studio musicians—who often had a very limited understanding of the bossa—were edging out Brazilian musicians from North American recording dates (1966c: 114). However, even while the *FeBNdB* "documentation" made a virtue out of its Brazilian authenticity, he did not give credence to those cultural nationalist voices who suggested that the North American bossa nova was per se a corruption of Brazilian music. This was because of his general aversion to cultural nationalism, and because he interpreted the bossa as a cross between Brazilian samba and jazz, whereby the U.S. component was at least as great as the South American (1963c: 39, 41). Cool jazz musicians like Stan Getz were therefore simply borrowing back what had been borrowed from them in the first place—an image of conviviality thoroughly in keeping with Berendt's attitudes about musical diplomacy (1966l: 20).

What counted most for Berendt was what a musician did with what he or she borrowed. Hence, legitimate jazz appropriations of the bossa—such as those of Getz or Sonny Rollins—artistically alienated and refined the raw material to fit within the musician's particular concept (1963c: 39; 1966l: 18). The problematic implication of this discourse was that it took a musician like Getz to render the relatively inferior bossa nova into high art again. Moreover, the approach of which Berendt was here approving again did not necessarily mandate a thorough knowledge of the Other idiom. Indeed, that would have been inconsistent with one of the themes he celebrated in the program notes for the 1966 Berlin Jazz Days; the ways in which artists had—in a creative and highly productive fashion—*mistaken* "jazz" (1966l: 2).

Fascinating Brazil

If Berendt had difficulty accommodating his contradictory feelings toward the bossa nova, how was the music that he and Lippmann and Rau presented received by German critics and the Berlin audience? Heinz Ohff summed up the audience's reaction for the *Berliner Tagesspiegel:* "The enthusiasm was great. Brazil exerted a fascination" (1966b). For his part, Berendt was thrilled by the way in which the audience in the normally sedate surrounds of the Berlin Philharmonic danced along to the *FeBNdB* concert—a new victory of the dionysian over the apollonian, perhaps, or perhaps simply a vindication after the lukewarm reception of *Sakura Sakura* the previous year (1967k). Manfred Miller and other critics praised the Brazilian component of the Jazz Days, even though they observed that *FeBNdB* had little to do with jazz per se (Miller 1966: 324, 328; Wilmer 1967: 23). Even *Sounds*, the strident organ of German free jazz, was positive about the concert, despite an obligatory grumble about folklore being out of place at a jazz festival, and a query about whether the *FeBNdB* percussion section was really as "authentic" as the organizers claimed (Blome 1966/67 10; Rahn 1966/67).

Given the exoticizing reception of the "Three Koto Girls" the previous year, it does not surprise that both the *FeBNdB* documentation and Astrud Gilberto—billed by Berendt at the time as the "most Brazilian of all Brazilian chanteuses"—were also esteemed for their exotic value (Berendt 1966l: 18; Schreiner 1997: 5). The Brazilian music and culture provided a fine opportunity for critics and pundits to reflect on what was missing not just from the festival but, by extension, from German culture itself. In his *Tagesspiegel* review, for example, Ohff wrote that Brazilian music possessed a "nest-warmth" that was absent in European jazz (1966b). Manfred Miller suggested that "it would scarcely have hurt many of the jazz musicians at the festival if they had had the rhythmic feel, the musical intelligence and above all, ... the vitality of the [Brazilian] musicians and the dancer Marly Tavares" (1966: 328). Rainer Blome of *Sounds* was also particularly glowing about the brown-skinned Tavares. According to his distinctly eroticized review, she was a "glowing ball of passion and fire ... [who] brought some of the South American sun into a cold and foggy Berlin. The skin, blood and heartbeat of a warm and lively continent, of which one [can] only dream, lay within reach" (1966/67). One suspects that the inclusion of Tavares' dancing—which was also featured on the cover of the *FeBNdB* recording—was calculated to increase the "authentic documentation's" exotic/erotic appeal. In much the same way, the illustration on the cover of Baden Powell's *Tristeza on Guitar* depicted a stylized nude woman partly obscured by a guitar.

Some years later, Brazilian music also provided Berendt with a rhetorical foil with which to excoriate Germany's popular music and, indeed, German society. Hence, he not only praised the way in which—unlike Germany—Brazilian society valued intellect and sensitivity in its popular culture; he also contrasted the harmless, joyful "intoxication"

Figure 16 | Brazilian dancer Marly Tavares gazes at the record buyer from the cover of *Folklore e Bossa Nova do Brasil*. Design: Marhold Eigen; courtesy of Universal Music. Used with permission.

that accompanied the Brazilian carnival's samba with the nationalist undertones of German *Karneval* music and the threatening "intoxication" of Germany's "martial" football fans (1977a: 241–4, 346). As with his broader image of Brazilian culture, this account of Brazil's music was clearly romanticized; in her study of samba, Barbara Browning has shown that Brazil's carnival is not without its threatening side, indeed for some commentators it is an "'unnerving dance' of social unrest" (Daniel Touro Linger qtd. in Browning 1995: 148). Even the assertion that there is nothing "martial" about the samba might be queried: Schreiner observes that Brazil's rigidly hierarchical samba groups "are nearly as well-organized as those of the military" (1993: 109).

However, it would be churlish just to dismiss Berendt's efforts in promoting Brazilian music in Germany on the basis that they were overly romanticized. As with the Japanese jazzmen whose work he fostered, he provided valuable opportunities to Brazilian musicians—in particular to Baden Powell, with whom he produced a total of four MPS albums during the 1960s and 1970s. This was surely not a completely selfless activity, yet Claus Schreiner has observed that Berendt promoted Powell's career in a climate where it would not have been easy for him to get a recording deal in Brazil (1993: 251). Berendt's and Lippmann and Rau's efforts in presenting contemporary Brazilian music did not involve a rip off either. By 1966, the international popularity of Brazilian music had faded distinctly. From a financial point of view the *FeBNdB* tour was a failure, and Lippmann and Rau were fortunate that the Brazilian airline company Varig discounted airfares for the visiting musicians otherwise they would have been out of pocket (Brigl and Schmidt-Joos 1985: 151; Perrone 1989: 204; Schreiner 1997: 2).

* * * * *

For Berendt, the bossa nova represented both the possibilities and the pitfalls of intercultural musical appropriation: at its highest, a creative and convivial borrowing of musical material was possible. However, the North American bossa fad also demonstrated how the process could degenerate into a "perversion" and "commercialization" in the hands of the recording industry. Just how and when the former shaded into the latter was never entirely clear though. Berendt obviously felt a strong affinity toward Brazilian music, particularly given its hybridity and the un-German qualities which he perceived in it, but felt compelled to carve out acceptable forms of bossa which allowed him to maintain the distinction of "true" jazz. This tended to both exculpate the very forms of bossa nova that he happened at any moment be presenting, and to obscure jazz's—and his own—relationship with commerce. The strategy no doubt proved so difficult partly because of the bossa's "[bridging of] 'mass' popular music and 'art' popular music" (McGowan and Pessanha 1998: 67). *FeBNdB* and Berendt's productions with Baden Powell also showed that even while he was interested in fostering the process of jazzmen creatively experimenting with Other musical material and musicians—a process that would reach its zenith in 1967—he remained committed to presenting the "original" material as well, even if it was dressed up (or undressed!) in such a way as to promote its exoticism.

CHAPTER 14

The 1967 World-Jazz Encounters
An East-West Jazz Divan?

The year 1967 represents the high-water mark of the *JMTW* series, which was officially launched in the May edition of *Jazz Podium*. The series was billed as including (retrospectively) *Sakura Sakura, Tristeza on Guitar,* and *Folklore e Bossa Nova do Brasil.* Forthcoming additions were also announced: *Noon in Tunisia, From Sticksland with Love, Flamenco Jazz, Djanger Bali,* and the never-to-eventuate *New Jazz from Russia* by the German Lukjanov trio ("Jazz Meets the World" 1967). In November 1967, the flagship concert at the Berlin Jazz Days was also titled *JMTW*, and it included two of these additions—*Flamenco Jazz* and *Djanger Bali*—together with *Jazz Meets India*. Following the model already pioneered with *Sakura Sakura*, each of these new projects boldly undertook an "encounter" between jazz musicians and musicians conversant in Other traditions. Just how these encounters were received at home and abroad will now be considered by turning our focus to three exemplary cases: *Noon in Tunisia, Jazz Meets India,* and *Djanger Bali*.

Noon in Tunisia

The Swiss pianist George Gruntz, who was introduced in chapter 6, was responsible for the concept behind *Noon in Tunisia*. He had been impressed by John Coltrane's 1960 modal classic "My Favorite Things"—which, with its soprano saxophone, sounded to Gruntz rather like North

African Bedouin music. His interest was then piqued when, during a 1964 artists' retreat in Hammamet, he encountered a band of itinerant Tunisian musicians who permitted him to record their music. Intrigued and inspired, he formulated the idea of a musical collaboration (in Tunisia) between modally oriented jazzmen and Tunisian musicians (Gruntz 2002: 63–4). This would involve selecting Tunisian rhythms and modes capable of being played on European instruments, then transcribing appropriate themes for the jazzmen and getting them to rehearse with their Tunisian colleagues for several days prior to recording (Gruntz 1983: 189).

For some years, Gruntz's proposal either fell on deaf ears or was ridiculed by European producers who were skeptical about the costs involved and whether the combination could even work (Gruntz 2002: 64). He found a far more receptive audience in Berendt, who sported his own musical curiosity and budding *JMTW* plans (Gruntz 2004). Berendt had referred to various jazzmen's "encounters with Arabic music" as early as 1962 (1962i: 18; 1962n: 92). Gruntz's idea offered a refreshing new approach compared with these previous activities, however, which he now considered rather "indirect and imitative." In supporting Gruntz's concept, he also raised ethical considerations a little at odds with his interpretation of experimental musical borrowing expounded in relation to the bossa nova: "The words of a Cairo jazz enthusiast have often been quoted in this respect: 'We are flattered [by the Western jazz musicians' engagement with our music]. But it would be better if they really knew our music'" (1967c). Here as elsewhere, Berendt seems to have been partly motivated by an ongoing bad conscience in relation to Germany's recent military past (and Europe's colonial history in North Africa). As he pointedly observed in his cover notes, *Noon in Tunisia* was a play on Dizzy Gillespie's "Night in Tunisia," a tune from the early 1940s: "[Then] it really was night in that country. Conquered by Rommel's Afrika-Korps, reconquered by the Allies, it was a country condemned to a colonial future, with its fighters for freedom throuwn [sic] into French prisons." In 1967, however, it was "noon," indicating that he regarded *Noon in Tunisia*—with its optimistic title and its collaborative approach—as a symbol for a new collegiality between Europe and its former colonies and even as a step toward making amends for past European chauvinism (Berendt 1967c).

Having enthusiastically greeted the proposal, Berendt now travelled to Tunisia in order to locate Tunisian musicians to participate in the project—and to enjoy a holiday. He went to the top, establishing contact with Dr. Salah El Mahdi (born 1925), a composer and musicologist who was head of the Rashidiyya Institute, director of Music and Popular Arts in the Tunisian government, and responsible for the Tunisian national anthem (Ben Redjeb 1996; R. Davis 1996). El Mahdi was attracted to the proposal because it was an opportunity to "put on stage our traditionnal tunisian music through the association with Jazz music [sic]" (El Mahdi 2004). In addition to securing El Mahdi's participation, three Tunisian folklore musicians were also selected (although this process was probably not as drawn out as Berendt later claimed).[1] For them, Berendt's offer must have had a special economic attraction. As Gruntz has observed, the fees paid had a significant value, once converted from European to Tunisian currency (Gruntz 2004).

On the home front, a group of European jazzmen was located, including the expatriate African American saxophonist Sahib Shihab. For Shihab, the project had a special cultural significance. Like many other African American jazzmen in the 1940s and 1950s, Shihab (formerly Edmund Gregory) had converted to Islam (Berendt 1967d: 347). Mike Hennessey points out that this step was generally motivated by a "composite of frustration at the racial injustice that existed in the so-called Christian world, a genuine search for spiritual enlightenment and fulfilment and a wish to identify politically with the Black Muslim movement" (1990: 56). Faith sometimes had musical consequences too: in the case of Yusef Lateef and Ahmed Abdul-Malik, it led to a specific interest in Arabic music and instrumentation (Pfleiderer 1998: 51–2). Likewise, *Noon in Tunisia* gave Shihab a welcome opportunity to engage with the music and culture of his brother Muslims, whom he was able to greet with suras from the Koran (Berendt 1967c).

Despite Berendt's success in securing Tunisian musicians, the recording session was relocated to West Germany, owing to the lack of stereo recording facilities in Tunisia (Gruntz 2002: 64). Gruntz thought this change of plan rather unfortunate because it removed the Tunisians from their home environment (Gruntz 2004). Indeed, the Tunisians now approached the session with some anxiety—not only was it cold in Germany, but they also felt unclear about the principles of jazz, and some of them were unfamiliar with the notated music in Gruntz's score. Their discomfort was only relieved when Gruntz announced a Tunisian musical term, after which the session quickly (and somewhat haphazardly) commenced, ending a mere four hours later (Gruntz 2002: 64). Events therefore conspired against Gruntz's original intention for the

---

1. Berendt observed that "in order to find the best Tunisian musicians, we listened for weeks to hundreds in all parts of the country," (1967c) whereas El Mahdi notes that after Berendt came to visit him "all the preparation part of the project was done in less than an hour," after which he told Berendt "now everything is done you can go with your fiancée to Djerba and take some hollydays [sic]" (2004).

session to occur in Tunisia and for the jazzmen to gradually get to know their Tunisian colleagues.

Gruntz's musical intentions for the two groups were—as with *From Sticksland With Love*—quite experimental: various permutations of "playing next-to, on-top-of, and against-one-another were structured in such a way as to allow a broad palette of combinations to be tried out" (Gruntz 1983: 191). Beyond that his ambitions were modest: he deliberately set out *not* to create an acculturation of jazz and Tunisian music, and considered that while *Noon in Tunisia* borrowed rhythmically from Tunisian music, it squarely remained jazz—itself a proto-*Weltmusik*, "in which musicians speak a common language without ... being able to understand each other verbally," and which was capable of assimilating other musics and musicians. Gruntz was nevertheless aware of limits to jazz's capability to assimilate, which will be explored below (Gruntz 1983).

Unlike most of the *JMTW* series, the *Noon in Tunisia* project was not immediately associated with a live concert. Despite this, it became the most popular record in the series, with the possible exception of *Tristeza on Guitar* (Berendt 1969c: 297; Gruntz 1983: 190). It was reviewed internationally, a recognition that did not befall all of the recordings in the rather poorly distributed series, and also received an award for the record of the year in 1969 from the French *Club de Disques* (Berendt 1969c: 297; El Mahdi 2004). It even resulted in 1969 in a film version directed in Tunisia by the New German Cinema director Peter Lilienthal.

However, *Noon in Tunisia* has split musicians, critics, and musicologists in relation to its success in combining the two idioms. In 1968, *Downbeat* praised the record, yet also considered that some of the characteristics of Tunisian music restricted the expressiveness of the jazz. Nevertheless, the magazine thought it a "pleasant and provocative beginning to what could become a fruitful meeting of musical cultures" (Kart 1968). The French reviewer Michel Savy was less restrained. For him this was no "mélange"; it was neither "jazzified folklore" nor "North-Africanized jazz." Gruntz had successfully "provoked a very interesting encounter," in which neither party lost its specificity (1971). The German musicologist Wolfgang Laade thought that *Noon in Tunisia* had "really fascinating moments" and was "without doubt the most interesting and lively result of an organized confrontation between such fundamentally different musics" (1970: 142–3). Pfleiderer similarly considers it a rather dense integration, but also observes that it occasionally takes on the appearance of a musical collage (1998: 77–8). However, this does not entirely surprise given Gruntz's experimental ethos—and his desire to occasionally contrast the two idioms.

From the jazzmen's point of view, reactions were also mixed, but even those most critical thought it a worthwhile experiment. Gruntz himself was clearly fond of the project, reviving it on several occasions over the next thirty years, in Europe and in Tunisia, both with and without Berendt's involvement—which, according to Gruntz, riled the producer, who considered himself to have some type of ownership in the project (Gruntz 2002: 90; 2004).[2]

The French violinist Jean-Luc Ponty was more critical of the project. In 1968, he took the view that *Noon in Tunisia* was "a little impure," an "impossible mélange," but an interesting experience nonetheless (qtd. in Serra 1968). He was also critical of the Tunisians for not being able to adapt their playing to the jazz idiom (qtd. in Endress 1969: 122). However, this was obviously an experiment he was interested in repeating, participating as he did in the revival of it at the Ossiach Music Festival in 1971. On the other hand, Sahib Shihab and the expatriate African American Don Cherry—who both participated in the 1969 revivals—were engaged at a much deeper level. Following the original 1967 recording session, Shihab was inspired to travel to Tunisia, in order to experience Tunisian culture on the ground (Berendt 1969c: 299). Returning two years later with Lilienthal's crew when it shot the film version, Shihab even participated in the symbolic gesture of what Nina Berman in another context, calls "cultural cross-dressing" (Berendt 1969c: 299; Berman 1998: 57).

Although not himself Muslim, Don Cherry evidently also underwent some form of spiritual rebirth during the 1969 trip, which romantically coloured his description of the country, and of the whole musical experience:

> If you look around you, here in Tunisia, you see the beautiful and creative in life, and this is what has given us strength in our music and has inspired us. ... We talk so much about love today. We, the jazz musicians and the Bedouins, have played together with love ... I come from Watts, the black ghetto of Los Angeles, but I felt here in Tunis: this is my music, a whole way of life, a conception we have lived, and not only learned. Our hearts, our music were in harmony, were vibrating together, for we all felt the common love. This is not Bedouin music on

---

2. The project was performed in Europe in September 1969 (at the Stuttgart Radio Exhibition), in July 1971 (at the Ossiach Music Festival in Austria), in 1974 (at the German Jazz Festival in Frankfurt) and most recently in September 1996 (at a special concert organized by the West German Radio broadcaster in Cologne). It was performed in Tunisia in May 1969 for a film version directed for the SWF by Peter Lilienthal and again in 1978, when Gruntz and a group of German jazzmen toured for the Goethe Institut.

Figure 17 | *Noon in Tunisia,* 1969. *From left to right:* Don Cherry, Hattab Jouini, Sahib Shihab, Jelloul Osman, Moktar Slama, unknown, Henri Texier. © Pete Ariel; courtesy of the Jazzinstitut Darmstadt. Used with permission.

one side, and jazz on the other. It is simply a unity of love ... (qtd. in Berendt 1978: 276; see also Berendt 1969c: 299)[3]

Salah El Mahdi was also very positive: "The collaboration with the jazz group and its leader was very friendly and rich of learnings. ... I think that both musics ... became close to each other to demonstrate that friendship and fraternity between people can be reached through music" (2004). In contrast to Gruntz, he did consider *Noon in Tunisia* a "marriage" of the two idioms (Berendt 1967c; Gruntz 1983: 191; El Mahdi 2004). It also involved a two-way learning process. While he had not initially been very interested in jazz, he now got to know much more about it and his interest blossomed. He also observes with satisfaction that the recordings and concerts—which often presented Tunisian music on its own as well—won a new audience in Europe for that Tunisian music (El Mahdi 2004). However, not all Tunisians took El Mahdi's view. When *Noon in Tunisia* was performed in Tunisia in 1969 and again in 1978, there was some interest in the project, but only among younger Tunisians; "the oldest generation didn't accepted [sic] this approchement [sic]" (El Mahdi 2004). Gruntz concurs and is convinced that *Noon in Tunisia* would not have appealed to the Bedouins, whose music had

---

3. We will return to Don Cherry's engagement with world musics in chapter 15.

originally inspired him; in any event, no Bedouins attended their concerts (1983: 192).

Jazz Meets India

The inclusion of *Jazz Meets India* in the *JMTW* series should come as no surprise given the widespread Western interest in Indian music during the 1960s.[4] Outside the subcontinent, modern jazzmen had already dabbled in Indian music for almost ten years.[5] In 1958, the pianist Dave Brubeck—a one-time Jazz Ambassador to India—recorded "Calcutta Blues," a tune that, in his words, used "Indian rhythms that were adaptable to the Blues" and employed piano "as a strictly melodic instrument such as the sitar or harmonium" (Brubeck 1958). Then, in 1961, Ravi Shankar recorded *Improvisations,* an album that featured several west coast jazzmen. As with Richard Bock's other productions in a similar vein—such as those with west coast saxophonist Paul Horn, made in India in 1965 and 1966—the jazzmen largely imitated the Indian idiom (Pfleiderer 1998: 72–4). As we have observed, Coltrane and other avant-gardists also developed an interest in Indian music in the early 1960s (Berendt 1980c: 5; Budds 1990: 51–3). Coltrane even began corresponding with Ravi Shankar in 1961, and paid tribute to his interest by recording "India" that same year, which rather than synthesizing or imitating the original is more an evocation of it (Budds 1990: 21, 52).

Berendt's own first-hand experience of Indian music came during his 1962 Asian trip, at which time he was already intrigued by its jazz potential (Berendt 1962c: 20). In particular, he was "sure that in the course of time it would be possible to develop a genuine musical fusion of jazz and tabla [hand] drumming" (1962i: 17). The 1964 Mangelsdorff Quintet tour offered an opportunity to revisit the matter. Not only did the Quintet adapt Shankar's composition "Pather Panchali," the drummer Ralf Hübner and the bassist Günter Lenz visited Shankar's Bombay music school and were inspired to compose the duet "Raknash"—the Indian musician's name in reverse (Berendt 1964a; 1964b: 140). As Lenz reflected at the time: "Much of what Charlie Mingus is playing today has been played by Indian sitar players for thousands of years. As a bass-

---

4. I use the term "Indian music" despite the fact that there is a great deal of variation within that category. As David N. Claman observes: "To discuss 'Indian music' as a single, undifferentiated genre is as problematic as grouping ... a Country-Western ballad, Beethoven, muzak and a recording by Cecil Taylor all under the rubric 'Western music'" (2002: 47).

5. On the reception of jazz in India itself, see Pinckney 1989/90.

ist it was therefore not hard for me to find new ideas and stimulation" (1964). When the group returned to Germany and performed at the 1964 German Jazz Festival in Frankfurt they also experimented with a raga, although *Jazz Podium* queried just how "Indian" this activity was: "by and large it sounded conventional. It was merely the declaration that was Indian" (Wachler 1964: 41).[6]

Activities combining Indian and Western musics—from pop through to concert music—began to take place with increasing frequency around 1965 or 1966. On the concert music front, Shankar and the violinist Yehudi Menuhin began performing a series of duets under the title "West Meets East" (Shankar 1969: 164–7). The Beatles famously used a sitar on *Rubber Soul* (1965), and many of their pop contemporaries followed suit over the next few years (Kneif 1984; G. Farrell 1987; Van der Lee 1998: 54–8). However, much of this "Sitar-Explosion," as Shankar dubbed it, engaged with Indian music on a highly superficial level—and for some listeners supplied no more than background music for the consumption of drugs (Shankar 1969: 179, 183–4; Kneif 1984: 108; G. Farrell 1987: 198; Pfleiderer 1998: 42–3). Like their pop contemporaries, jazz musicians remained active in this field in the second half of the 1960s (Tynan 1965: 14; Pfleiderer 1998: 42–3). While some of the results—such as the guitarist Gabor Szabo's 1966 recording *Jazz Raga*—were superficial in the extreme, various collaborative efforts seemed to promise more fruitful results. These included, in the United States, the Californian trumpeter Don Ellis's and the Indian instrumentalist Hari Har Rao's short-lived 1965 Hindustani Jazz Sextet, and, in the United Kingdom, the John Mayer–Joe Harriott Double Quintet, which was active between 1965 and 1968 (Hardy 1965; Pfleiderer 1998: 65, 149). It was this latter group that furnished not only two of the Indian musicians who participated in *Jazz Meets India*, but also an anti-model for the German production.

The "Indo-Jazz" concept essentially belonged to the expatriate Indian composer John Mayer.[7] He composed a piece for the Indian musi-

---

6. Mangelsdorff, who had picked up an infection on the tour and was too ill to participate in the Frankfurt concert, himself remained skeptical about attempts to fuse jazz with Indian music, to whose basic principles he had been introduced by a musicologist in Dakar (Mangelsdorff 1964a; 1964b; Paulot 1993: 144).

7. Born in Calcutta in 1930, John Mayer studied composition in the U.K. under Mátyás Seiber, the director of the Frankfurt's Hoch'sche Conservatorium jazz course during the early 1930s, and Adorno's erstwhile advisor on jazz (Berendt 1980c 71; Steinert 1992: 35, 77, 93–4; Pfleiderer 1998: 149). In 1958 Mayer wrote "Three Dances of India," a composition for Indian instruments and a symphony orchestra, which in turn encouraged him to consider other such fusions (Cotterrell and Tepperman 1974: 13). The English producer Denis Preston finally commissioned him to create an Indo-Jazz piece in 1964, which

cians and then instructed Harriott's jazzmen on the particular raga on which it was based (Robertson 2003: 159–61, 166). The musical empathy between the disparate members of the Double Quintet—which recorded several albums and also performed numerous live concerts—evolved over time (Robertson 2003: 168). However, the group's early music has been described by one musicologist as a "mixture ... in which the Indian elements are substantially dissolved from their musical context" (Pfleiderer 1998: 145, 149–55).

By 1967 at the latest, Berendt was well aware of the Mayer–Harriott Double Quintet (Berendt 1967n: 34). However, it disappointed him: Harriott had fallen victim to an Indian music fad, and Mayer understood nothing of jazz. "The music ... sounds as if it were from the MGM filming of an Indian 'Love Story' that has been made in a Hollywood studio" (Berendt 1967g: 3–4). Elsewhere, he complained that it was a "meeting in an intermediate no-man's land ... in which the Indian music retained too little of the 'Indian' and in which there was too little 'jazz' left [in the] jazz" (1967n: 34). He clearly thought that he could do better, and now had little difficulty persuading European jazz musicians to participate. One important factor contributed to this: a strong belief that free jazz was especially open to world musics.

In early 1966, for example, Alexander von Schlippenbach and Manfred Schoof both spoke of the new jazz as involving a global dimension, which rendered it capable of assimilating Other musical material, particularly from foreign folklore. In doing so, they also cited their colleague, the vibraphonist Karl Berger's own views ("'Own Thing'" 1966: 68). In fact, Berger went even further in explaining just what Westerners could gain from these Other musics. During 1967 and 1968, he published a series of reviews of ethnomusicological recordings for *Jazz Podium* and *Sounds*, in which he suggested that through listening closely to world musics, Western listeners could rediscover the *experience* of music—something that had been buried for too long under academic approaches (Berger 1967: 30). Like Berendt five years earlier, he advocated a universal concept—"the unity of music throughout the world"—but he also retained the idea that this unity manifested itself in countless dif-

---

then so resonated with the U.S. producer Ahmet Ertegun, that he suggested a whole album (Robertson 2003: 157–8). Preston duly introduced Mayer to the Jamaican expatriate saxophonist Joe Harriott, a highly talented free jazz pioneer on the British scene (Cotterrell and Tepperman 1974: 13; Robertson 2003: 162). On the reception side, the three Indo-Jazz records and the group's various concerts met a certain amount of fame, including beyond the confines of the jazz scene (Cotterrell and Tepperman 1974: 13, 18; Robertson 2003: 163–5). While reviled by some critics as "curried jazz," it also clearly appealed to some U.K.-Indian audiences (Robertson 2003: 163, 168–9).

ferent ways (1968c; see also 1967: 31). For Berger, opening up to world musics was a natural process for a jazz musician given that "from its very beginnings, jazz has been *Weltmusik*" (Berger 2004).

Free jazz's practical engagement with world musics took many different forms. In some instances, an exotic instrument was adopted as a new source of sound. The Swiss percussionist Mani Neumeier (born 1940)—who was a lynchpin of *Jazz Meets India*—typifies this approach. Like many of his free jazz contemporaries, he was interested in using the widest palette of sounds ("Gespräch mit dem Irene Schweizer Trio" 1967: 134). By the mid-1960s, Neumeier had become particularly interested in the capabilities of Indian tabla drums—which in his view were "the most perfected percussion instrument that mankind has discovered" (qtd. in Berendt 1967g: 3). Inspired by the way in which tabla players were capable of changing the pitch of their drums while playing, he not only took up tabla drumming, but also developed the so-called "Mani-Tom" drum, whose pitch he was able to alter by blowing air into the body of the drum. A meeting in London with Keshav Sathe, a U.K.-Indian percussionist and member of the Mayer–Harriott Double Quintet, was a watershed in Neumeier's process of musical discovery. He promptly purchased a set of tabla and sought some rudimentary instruction from Sathe. This might have formed the basis of Neumeier's own "free" tabla technique, however, as he noted at the time "I didn't want to do it in an Indian way—you just cannot master that—but instead what I was interested in doing was playing completely freely and openly." Or, as his colleague Uli Trepte added: "We don't want to take over the other music; we have to find our [own] way toward our own forms of expression" ("Gespräch mit dem Irene Schweizer Trio" 1967: 133). This attitude—which Peter Niklas Wilson later called "calculated inauthenticity"—reflected the fact that, in order to attain proficiency on such instruments, a significant degree of practice was required, yet it was also consistent with the discourse of emancipation (Wilson 2001: 113).

Like Neumeier, Keshav Sathe was another lynchpin of the *Jazz Meets India* project (Berendt 1967n: 34). Born near Bombay, he moved to Britain in 1956. Although initially uninterested in performing with South Indian musicians, let alone Westerners, Sathe nevertheless possessed a strong musical curiosity. Before long he had begun to frequent jazz clubs and opened himself up to Western music (Robertson 2003: 160; Sathe 2004). When Neumeier suggested that they perform together at some stage in the future, Sathe readily agreed ("17 Fragen an Mani Neumeier" 167; Sathe 2004).

Berendt's plans for *Jazz Meets India* were also gelling around this time. In late 1966, he attended a concert in Cologne, at which Neumeier's free tabla drumming impressed him (Berendt 1966f). Then, at that year's inaugural Baden-Baden Free Jazz Meeting, he encouraged Barney Wilen to perform an electro-acoustic improvisation over a Ravi Shankar recording (Zimmerle 1967a). This proved controversial, not only because it took longer than anticipated and prevented other invitees from realizing their own projects, but also because, as one musician rightly complained, Shankar's recordings were so accomplished that one could add nothing to them (Berendt 1967g: 4; Zimmerle 1967a). Berendt somewhat disingenuously acknowledged the point, but then tried to justify Wilen's activity on the basis that it was only an experiment and had been handled with care, respect and empathy (Berendt 1967g: 4). Despite this controversy, Berendt had no difficulty finding participants for *Jazz Meets India*, which was to move Wilen's experiment into the live domain. Wilen himself needed no encouragement; nor did Neumeier, who brought his own band, the Irène Schweizer trio, with him, and who also acted as conduit to Sathe and the sitar player Dewan Motihar, Sathe's colleague from the Mayer-Harriott Double Quintet. Manfred Schoof, who thus far had had little exposure to Indian music but who had witnessed Wilen's activity at the Free Jazz Meeting, came to *Jazz Meets India* at the behest of Berendt (Zimmerle 1967a; Schoof 2004). In fact, although the contrary was asserted at the time, none of the Europeans had had a long exposure to Indian music—certainly nothing like the years of study that Ravi Shankar had advocated in 1965 as a prerequisite for these types of activities (Tynan 1965: 15–16, 43; Berendt 1967b; "17 Fragen an Mani Neumaier" 1967).

Neumeier—who was nominated as "mediator" between the Europeans and the Indians—was, like Berendt, critical of other Indo-Jazz activities for being too highly arranged and "corny." By contrast, his own graphic arrangements, which only suggested the idea of the piece, were intended to avoid constricting the Indian music—or the jazz, for that matter.[8] Apart from this basic sketch, and several rehearsals during which the Indian musicians explained rhythmic figures, everything else was improvised ("17 Fragen an Mani Neumaier" 1967; Schweizer 2004). The idea of freedom was, of course, philosophically very important within Neumeier's free jazz conception. It had an effect on the musical dynamic too, skewing it from the "meditative character of Indian music" toward the "impulsive character of the western [music]," as Manfred Schoof later put it, and as Berendt also conceded at the time (Berendt

---

8. It should be pointed out that although Neumeier was the "arranger," he did not claim sole copyright to the resulting recordings. Of the three titles recorded, one was credited to both Motihar and Neumeier. Another was credited to Motihar alone and the third to Schoof.

1967n 34; Schoof 2004). Just as Gruntz rejected the idea of seeking to create a fusion of two idioms, Berendt also eschewed that notion here. He expressly disavowed those "tempted to prove what certainly can't be proved: a unit of jazz and Indian music." Nevertheless, he remained convinced of the possibility of communication across the difference: "it is so revealing to hear how musicians of two widely separated cultures are able to communicate intelligently, how they can play together with superb sensitiveness" (1967b).

Despite Berendt's sanguine belief, the extent of the musical communication and, more broadly, the success of the *Jazz Meets India* project was—even more so than with *Noon in Tunisia* and, before that, *Sakura Sakura*—the subject of some debate. Indeed, of all the *JMTW* records, *Jazz Meets India* was perhaps the most controversial. Berendt may have thought it "the most artistically important record in the series"—reflecting the fact that *Jazz Meets India* was also performed at the prestigious Donaueschingen Music Days—but critics just could not agree about its combination of energetic free jazz and the more meditative Indian music (Berendt 1968f: 54). In a review of the Berlin performance, Dieter Zimmerle observed that there had been neither a "duel" nor a "duet" between the two groups, and that while the Indians followed the jazz soloists with interest, they did not "allow ... themselves to be drawn out of the musical ductus." (1968a). He was marginally more positive in his review of the Donaueschingen concert, suggesting that notwithstanding the intention not to create a fusion, there had been a noticeable mutual influence (1967b). Ulrich Olshausen was one for whom the frictions between the two groups were a positive: "the common ground ... provided a broad enough basis so as to avoid the impression of a stylistic disjuncture; that which separated the musics provided the fascinating frictions and contrasts, without which no work of art can survive" (1968). Heinz Ohff also cited the often "compellingly beautiful points of interaction" between the two groups (1967a). The classical music critic K. H. Ruppel even spoke of "an interchange of sensibilities, of differentiated rhythmic impulses, of improvisational inspiration ... a chamber symposium of ancient eastern and modern western music" (qtd. in Berendt 1967b).

However, *Jazz Meets India* has had its critics too. In a *Melos* review of the Donaueschingen concert, H. H. Stuckenschmidt observed that in its very conception, *Jazz Meets India* was questionable: "the meditative nature of Indian music rules out the extroverted technique of Occidental musical arts, just as the Indian tuning excludes our tempered intervals." These fundamental differences rendered jazz and Indian music as unable to mix as oil and quicksilver (1967: 459). While musicologists have not been quite as categorical in their thinking, they too have been disappointed by the relatively low level of interaction between the groups. In 1970, Wolfgang Laade identified moments where the two idioms came together, but also observed that they promptly fell apart afterward (1970: 142). Pfleiderer has also observed that the musics tend to exist side by side and that this record, too, occasionally gives the impression of a collage (1998: 145). Part of the problem lies with the free jazz approach. Having eschewed tonal centers and scales as well as a basic rhythm, the only possible point of contact is individual melodic motifs which "bounce like ping-pong balls" between Motihar and the jazz soloists (1998: 77).[9] Among jazz musicians, Albert Mangelsdorff was critical of attempts to combine free jazz and Indian music. He took the view that the jazz musicians ought to be courteous and accommodate themselves to the rules of Indian music, rather than playing free (Paulot 1993: 144). George Gruntz—whom Berendt engaged to assemble a three-hour SWF radio special on Indian music during the early 1970s—is even more scathing of unreflective and superficial attempts by jazz musicians to engage with Indian music. He takes the view that they should keep well away from it, unless they learn all about it first (Gruntz 1983: 194–7; 2002: 143–4).

But how did the musicians who took part in *Jazz Meets India* view the experience? Schweizer takes the view that the encounter worked well and that the Indians were flexible improvisers, but notes that it has had no subsequent consequences for her own music making (Schweizer 2004).[10] Neumeier—a convert from free jazz to psychedelic "Krautrock"—was proud of the encounter and has creatively engaged with Indian music since (Neumeier 2004). Schoof is the most explicit about what he gained: "It made me wonder 'what am I playing here?' The [Indians] gave me time. I learned to understand the [musical] dimension of time in a different way" (2004). He too engaged with Indian music on subsequent occasions, particularly during his Goethe Institut tours of Asia in 1971 and in 1975 (Berendt 1975e; Zimmerle-Betzing 1975). For his part, Keshav Sathe enjoyed the *Jazz Meets India* experience, but like Schweizer, did not think that it had really influenced his playing style. Much like Salah El Mahdi's comments about *Noon in Tunisia*, he explicitly disagreed with the notion advanced by Neumeier and Berendt that the Indian players had been left to perform their own "authentic" music:

---

9. Pfleiderer nevertheless maintains that there are significant possibilities for a more fulsome combination of the two idioms. Indeed, this is realised on "Yaad," a short (and somewhat anomalous) piece on *Jazz Meets India*, in which the jazz musicians accommodate themselves more to the Indian idiom (1998: 77).

10. In an earlier interview, she was more critical, indicating that she was not at all happy with the results (Noglik 1981: 304).

for him it was definitely, as he put it to me, a "meeting of the minds." He was not aware of the reception of the *Jazz Meets India* record among Indian audiences, but did note that the Mayer–Harriott Double Quintet's music was occasionally criticized from the Indian side for being "too European." He put this attitude down to ignorance and insularity on the part of those critics, anticipating that, had they been exposed to Western music as he had, they would have loved to engage in similar activities (Sathe 2004).[11]

Djanger Bali

Djanger Bali was another production that had its genesis in Berendt's Asian trip of 1962. During that trip, he had introduced himself to various members of the Indonesian jazz scene, including the pianist Bubi Chen and the guitarist Jack Lesmana, both of whom he later profiled in articles and whose recordings he also broadcast on the *SWF* (Berendt 1962i; 1963a; 1967a). Berendt had been tipped off about these musicians by the clarinettist Tony Scott (1921–2007), who was at that time living in Southeast Asia (Berendt 1967a).

Motivated by a combination of despair at the way in which the clarinet was being neglected in modern jazz, disgust with the American music business, and inner restlessness, Scott had left the United States for Japan in 1959 (Berendt 1963a: 23; 1967n: 33; "Tony Scott Reflections" 1965; Endress 1980: 162; Scott n.d.). Then, having received a grant from the USIS to perform and lecture about jazz in Indonesia, he traveled there in September 1960 and remained for many weeks (Scott n.d.). During his time there, Scott—"a lover of jam sessions," as one critic put it—performed with various local jazzmen, including many of those later appointed Indonesian All-Stars (Morgenstern 1965: 19). He also immersed himself in Indonesian musical traditions, even performing at one time with a Balinese gamelan orchestra (Berendt 1963a: 23; Scott n.d.).

The impulse for *Djanger Bali* itself came from an unexpected quarter. In late 1966, Berendt was approached out of the blue by an associate of Lesmana's, who proposed that he travel to Indonesia early the next year, assist in selecting a group of "All-Star" musicians and then help them tour Europe (Berendt 1967a; 1967p: 73). In the context of President Sukarno's and the PKI's fall—and an ensuing thaw in official attitudes to

---

11. For criticism of jazz in India, see Pinckney 1989/1990: 56, and of the Mayer-Harriott group, see Robertson 2003: 163, 168–9.

jazz—Indonesian jazzmen were now anxious to gain overseas playing experience (Berendt 1967a; Chen 2004). For them—like their Japanese counterparts—playing overseas was clearly a strategy to "authenticate" their music (cf. Atkins 2001: 12). We can assume that Berendt was instinctively attracted to the proposal, given the analogous situation of the Indonesian musicians compared with that of German jazz musicians after World War II and of Eastern Europeans after intermittent periods of jazz repression. However, he was also skeptical about the realization of their "utopian dream" (Berendt 1967a). He was uncertain that a tour would be financially viable, given the saturation of the European market with more famous American musicians (Berendt 1967j: 250). According to Chen, Berendt had also been relatively unimpressed by the overall standard of Indonesian jazzmen (Chen 2004). Various factors tipped the balance, however. Firstly, he was told that the Indonesians were prepared to perform for relatively low fees—their primary motivation not being a well-paid tour, but to gain playing experience (Berendt 1967j: 250). In addition, the Indonesians made a shrewd moral appeal to Berendt's conscience (and ego). As he wrote in *Jazz Podium*, "one of the [Indonesian] musicians let me know: 'You are the jazz critic who is most interested in Asian jazz. So you are the one to whom we can turn to and who can help us.' That sounded [to me] like an obligation" (1967j: 250).

A confluence of other factors also contributed to the realization of the Indonesians' proposal. Firstly, a relative of Lesmana's agreed to finance the musicians to rehearse comprehensively (Berendt 1967a; Chen 2004). They were able to secure free airfares to Europe from the Dutch carrier KLM, and the Marburg critic and promoter Claus Schreiner—the same Claus Schreiner who would become a historian of Brazilian popular music—agreed to organize their tour, despite the financial risk. In a canny move, Berendt also proposed that Tony Scott perform with the Indonesians (Berendt 1967a). This was doubtless calculated to increase the attractiveness of their concerts for a European jazz audience. Yet given that Scott had performed with many of the Indonesian All-Stars during his 1960 sojourn in Indonesia, the choice was a happy one. He responded to Berendt's proposal with relish (Berendt 1967a). Another crucial factor was that, at the very time that the Indonesian proposal reached him, Berendt was in the midst of planning the *JMTW* series. Having been impressed by Balinese gamelan music in 1962, he no doubt thought that the Indonesians' could be encouraged to engage with traditional Indonesian music, thereby furnishing another record for his series. In this respect, the choice of Scott was critical too. As Berendt knew, Scott had dabbled with gamelan music in the past.

The music that Scott and the All-Stars performed in Europe was a mixture of jazz adaptations of Indonesian folkloric themes, including "Burungkaka Tua," which Mangelsdorff had adapted in 1964, as well as Scott's compositions and jazz standards. In addition, the group "repaid the greeting" to Mangelsdorff et al. by adapting "Mahlke," a recent composition by Attila Zoller, an expatriate Hungarian guitarist and, until recently, a stalwart of the West German jazz scene (Berendt 1967a; Ohff 1967a; Feather 1968: 23; Chen 2004). Like the Hideo Shiraki Quintet before them, the Indonesians were encouraged to make their jazz more identifiably "Asian." This was achieved not only by adapting Indonesian folklore, but also by performing interludes on the *siter* (or *ketjapi*), an indigenous zither, and by employing indigenous Indonesian scales when improvising. The Indonesians had been accustomed to improvising modally à la Coltrane, but Scott now encouraged them to use an Indonesian rather than a Western scale (Berendt 1967a). This gave the music a unique feel, but nevertheless restricted the ability to improvise (Pfleiderer 1998: 141–3; Chen 2004).

The decision to Indonesianize their jazz was motivated by several factors, not least the need to compete in a saturated European jazz market. As Chen has indicated, it was thought that if the group performed only in a Western style, they would not be able to compete with other Western jazz bands in Europe (Chen 2004). The Indonesians' self-exotizing strategy was one in which Scott and Berendt played an active role. In addition to encouraging certain musical decisions, *Djanger Bali* was also marketed in an exotic fashion. The recording featured, for example, a photograph Berendt had taken of a relief from the Borobudur temple complex at Jogjakarta, and the shrewd reference to *Bali* made for good publicity too, even if it misrepresented the non-Balinese heritage of the band members. The decision to use the *ketjapi* and Indonesian scales certainly coincided with the musical curiosity of restless souls like Berendt and Scott. However, the decision to play on the Indonesian aspect was also congruent with "emancipation" and "jazz nationalist" discourses current not only in Europe and Japan respectively—but also now in Indonesia.

The Eurasian guitarist Jack Lesmana (born 1930) had been schooled in the European musical tradition. In postcolonial Indonesia, however, he had made the conscious decision to desist from playing European music, but with no experience playing traditional Javanese music, his choices were limited; so he took up jazz (Berendt 1967f). "Indonesian jazz" offered him a way of referencing and drawing on Javanese culture, while also distancing himself from American culture. As he noted, "we don't want to simply imitate the Americans. We are Indonesians, and we attempt to utilize our own musical tradition for modern jazz" (qtd. in Berendt 1967a).

Unlike Lesmana, the saxophonist Marjono (born 1938) was schooled in both European *and* Javanese music and was able to sketch out a traditional Indonesian motif on a bamboo flute and then change over to playing it on saxophone (Berendt 1967f). For him, modal jazz opened up new possibilities to incorporate Indonesian material, given that "the modal way of playing, as it came up only in the late 1950s through Miles Davis and John Coltrane, is an old hat to us. It already existed a thousand years ago in Javanese music" (qtd. in Berendt 1967n: 33). Modal jazz therefore offered Marjono a convenient way of drawing on and expressing his double orientation toward jazz and Indonesian traditional music. It allowed the demarcation of a style that self-consciously avoided being "merely a carbon copy of international jazz development[s]" (Berendt 1967n: 33).

The All-Stars' performance in Berlin was the culmination of a one-month European tour, playing in small clubs in West Germany, Switzerland, the Netherlands, and in the *Saba* recording studio in the Black Forest (Berendt 1967j: 250). While not a major financial success, the tour provided the playing experience the Indonesians craved (Sudibyo 2004a). Bubi Chen particularly relished performing with Philly Joe Jones, Manfred Schoof, and Benny Bailey, as well as with his old friend

Figure 18 | The Indonesian All-Stars perform in Germany, 1967. *From left to right:* Benny Mustafa, Yopi Chen, Jack Lesmana, Bubi Chen, Marjono. © Paul G. Deker. Used with permission.

Tony Scott. His playing and confidence improved markedly as a result of the tour and jam sessions associated with it (Chen 2004). On the European side, however, little attention appears to have been paid. Claus Schreiner recently indicated that "one did not really hang on to the memory of the concerts" (2004). Dieter Zimmerle simply observed that their Berlin performance was "clean and accurately rehearsed" and the veteran American critic Leonard Feather went no further than complimenting Chen's performance (Feather 1968: 23; Zimmerle 1968a). Heinz Ohff was alone in taking a more polemical stand. In his view, while the *Djanger Bali* performance started by sounding Indonesian, it quickly became decidedly American. Playing on the novelist Heinrich Böll's dictum that folklore is like naivity—when you are conscious that you have it, you no longer have it any more—Ohff concluded that "they obviously don't have naivity in Asia any more either" (1967a. Cf. Böll 1957: 137). In this respect, by playing (their version of) jazz, the Indonesian All-Stars may have actually upset some exoticizing expectations.

Unlike Ohff, however, musicologists have agreed that *Djanger Bali* is a remarkably successful hybrid. Wolfgang Laade thought that:

> [they] have created something of their own, something Indonesian, a genuine musical product of acculturation, which is extremely interesting for that reason. Simultaneously interesting and fascinating; sometimes we scarcely know whether we are listening to jazz or Indonesian music, which only goes to prove how thoroughly both have melded together here. (1970: 143. See also Pfleiderer 1998: 76, 136–44)

The Indonesian reception of *Djanger Bali* and the All-Stars' European tour was also characterized by enthusiasm. As P. R. Sudibyo observed:

> Their tour to Europe was well appreciated by the Indonesian jazz scene, because that was the first tour abroad ever done by Indonesian jazz musicians. Bubi Chen was selected by The Berlin Jazz Festival to be the pianist for the International All Stars group at the festival, and we were proud of him. His name was mentioned in *Down Beat Magazine* International Critics Poll that year as one of the world best jazz pianists [sic]. (2004a; cf. Feather 1968: 23; Chen 2004)

Unfortunately, the *Djanger Bali* record was only available in Indonesia as a private import and as a result was practically unheard in that country—as it was in most countries, given the limited production runs and distribution of Saba records (Sudibyo 2004a; Ticoalu 2004b). However, upon their return the All-Stars performed in the same style on several occasions and, according to Sudibyo, this "was well received by the public" (2004a). Although the style has been adopted by other Indonesian—

as well as Western— groups at various times, including by Marjono and others at the 1970 World Expo in Osaka, it was ultimately regarded as a worthwhile experiment, but nevertheless something of a novelty and it by no means became the rule with Indonesian musicians (Santamaria 1970; Chen 2004; Sudibyo 2004b). In this way, the Indonesian All-Stars recourse to "Indonesian Jazz" was very much akin to the strategy adopted by the Hideo Shiraki Quintet in 1965.

* * * * *

Nineteen sixty-seven's *JMTW* encounters were, on the whole, extremely novel and moved jazz into rather unknown territory. For this reason, they caused critics quite a deal of consternation. They were sometimes criticized for failing to achieve a full integration of the two idioms (see, e.g., Ohff 1967a; Feather 1968: 23; Laade 1970: 142–3). However, if this was not necessarily the intention, was that really a fair criticism? Other related queries were also thrown up. Were the frictions between the two idioms a negative aspect or rather, as a critic like Ulrich Olshausen thought, something praiseworthy? Was there not something inherently artificial, hodge-podge—and suspect—about experiments of this nature, as opposed to more organic acculturations? (Ohff 1967a; Kühn 1972a). Or were they interesting and indeed informative? (Laade 1970: 143–5). Sometimes, the criticisms were tied up in broader polemics; was not an ambitious project like *Jazz Meets India* concocted to spruce up the *E-Musik* credentials of jazz and, by inference, driving a further wedge between jazz and popular music? (Schmidt-Joos and Schmidt 1969: 120). The ethics of appropriation also started to be raised, just as they had been with earlier debates about the bossa nova. Was there not a problem when a musician like Barney Wilen improvised over the top of a Ravi Shankar recording? There was no consensus about these types of questions, which perhaps only goes to show how productive—in terms of creating meaning—the *Jazz Meets the World* encounters were.

In terms of the legacy for the participating musicians, the encounters were just as multivalent. It is true that some took relatively little from the experience. For others, the results were far more positive, and sometimes quite unexpected. Viewed as a whole, the encounters also tended to be quite symbiotic. For Gruntz, *Noon in Tunisia* was an opportunity to realize his long-standing musical curiosity; for El Mahdi, it began as a chance to promote Tunisian culture in Europe, and then generated his own interest in jazz. For Berendt, *Djanger Bali* was a welcome addition to the burgeoning *JMTW* series and another way of profiling himself as an expert on jazz in Asia; for Marjono, it was a chance to develop an empowering form of "Indonesian jazz," and a way of gaining valuable playing experience in Europe.

And yet despite their rich productivity, these intercultural encounters tailed off markedly after 1967. By 1968, Berendt considered that—but for a "Jazz Meets Africa" type of record—the *JMTW* series was now complete (1968f: 54). In retrospect, there were to be four more additions to the series—*Auto Jazz* (1968), *Eternal Rhythm* (1968), *Wild Goose* (1969), and *El Babaku* (1971)—although only *El Babaku* was billed at the time of its release as belonging to the series (Berendt 1971f). Apart from *Wild Goose*, these later recordings also eschewed the "encounter" model that was so dominant in 1967. Berendt did move on to other production activities; however, he did not completely turn his back on the idea of the intercultural musical encounter, as we shall see in the concluding chapter. By the 1980s, that concept had matured substantially, as had the criticisms.

CHAPTER 15

Finding the *Blut und Boden* in African Roots

Don Cherry's *Eternal Rhythm* (1968) and Billy Brooks' *El Babaku* (1971) were, as we have seen, two of the last recordings in the *JMTW* series. They squarely featured expatriate African American jazzmen and foregrounded two quite contrasting, ideologically driven approaches to world musics above and beyond Berendt's "encounter" model of 1967. Both recordings come from a phase when identity politics had taken a more militant turn, as many African Americans were becoming increasingly disillusioned about the possibility of a peaceful integration into American society, with some instead preferring a "separate but equal" doctrine for blacks and whites. That turn was making itself felt within jazz discourses as Black music ideology, and within the music as Afrocentric jazz (Jost 1982: 170–7; Budds 1990: 16, 116–21). These developments now came to be reflected upon in the West German jazz scene as Black music ideologists and Afrocentric jazzmen were invited to events such as the Donaueschingen Music Days and the Berlin Jazz Days. They were, as we shall see, developments about which German commentators like Berendt had extremely ambivalent feelings.

El Babaku: Imagining Africa

Billy Brooks (born 1943) is an African American drummer who, in 1964, moved to Europe and quickly became a stalwart of the German jazz scene. He and his four African American and Afro-Cuban colleagues in the *El Babaku* group engaged with (diasporic) West African music and culture in a way that was not atypical for the late 1960s and early 1970s. After a host of African states gained their independence in the late 1950s and early 1960s, a new positive image of Africa gained currency among African Americans (Jost 1973/74: 141–2; Budds 1990: 116 ff; Pfleiderer 1998: 45–7). This, together with the notion of an "African heritage," soon became motifs of the African American civil rights movement and manifested themselves in various ways, from the wearing of African clothes to the institution of Black Studies courses in U.S. universities (Pfleiderer 1998: 46). The reorientation toward Africa also bore fruit in the music of various jazzmen (Weinstein 1992; Gerard 1998: 60–70). From an ideological perspective, the close identification with Africa provided what Charley Gerard, in his discussion of *Kulu Sé Mama*, a 1965 John Coltrane record which engages with African music, calls "a psychic balm for 'all who have suffered the after-effects of slavery'" (1998: 69). The *specifics* of African musics were not altogether relevant in this process. Pfleiderer notes that jazz's engagement with Africa, which proliferated during the 1960s, did move beyond initially quite superficial references—in a title or cover art—to actually drawing on African musical principles (1998: 47, 95 ff). However, "the connection ... to Africa predominantly involved associative echoes of the instrumental/sound-based and rhythmic elements of African music. ... Fundamentally coming to grips with specific African music traditions was the exception" (Pfleiderer 1998: 96).

Billy Brooks' cover notes for *El Babaku* demonstrate this keen identification with Africa and its cultural traditions. Indeed, so strong was his attachment that he considered that he and the other members of *El Babaku* "are basically Africans." For Brooks, the discovery of his Africanness was highly empowering: "Knowing this—learning this—for me was the greatest discovery in my life" (Brooks 1971). In common with much early 1970s Afrocentric philosophy, the "Africa" with which Brooks identified was viewed holistically and was positively essentialized (cf. Gerard 1998: 41–2). It was also firmly underscored by disenchantment with the West:

> The harmonic progressions in European music are symbolising progress. Progress is the character of Europe—of the white man. ...
> Power is the African way. Power and subjection. In other words, the African submit to what they are doing.
> The European character is progress. To do a thing and outdo it next time. It became infectious. Like the atomic bomb. It progresses to its own end ... (Brooks 1971)

If Brooks was critical of the West, then he was also melancholic about the state of the African American community. Hence, *El Babaku*'s titles, lyrics and cover notes also reflected on the sense of isolation and loss that Brooks felt within African American musical practices—including jazz—and, more generally, in the African American community, particularly in the wake of the loss of leaders such as Malcolm X, the Black Muslim leader murdered in early 1965. One song, "Al Hajj Malik al Shabazz," was even a lament to Malcolm X's passing.[1] However, Brooks also universalized the black man's isolation:

> In North American [jazz] music the drummer is alone. He really is lonesome. ... We need group music. Because people today need group-feeling. The idea of having a drum solo and than [sic] a trombone solo and afterwards some tenor sax is a symbol of specialization in the Western world. ...
> Bird (Charlie Parker) was lonesome. As is [Charles] Mingus and Elvin [Jones] and Philly Joe Jones. *As is everybody in North America.* (1971; my emphasis)

For Brooks, the solution to this alienation lay in an ecstatic reconnection with African group drumming, which, in his view, was "more than musical—it's spiritual" (1971).

Brooks' critique of the alienation present in European/North American civilization and of the dangers associated with the all-too-ready pursuit of the "European character [of] progress" were certainly consonant with the cultural critique expressed by Berendt since the 1950s. His positive essentializing of the "African way" was also consistent with the *négritude*-like way in which Berendt had earlier spoken of Negro culture. In addition, Brooks' focus on the spiritual nature of music—as he put it "you have to have a religious outlook on music" (1971)—was consistent with the interpretation that Berendt had advanced in the 1950s and that, as we shall see, he advanced with renewed vigor during the 1970s and 1980s. However, there were clear limits to Berendt's readiness to accept views such as those of Brooks, which were also heavily tinged by Black music ideology—for, as the drummer stipulated, "jazz always has been *African*" (1971; my emphasis).

Roots = *Blut und Boden?*

Berendt by no means disregarded Black music ideology in his writings. Perhaps his outsider status from the U.S. jazz scene even gave him a special latitude to discuss it. So his 1953 *Jazzbook* gave vent to these ideas,

---
1. Like the saxophonist Sahib Shihab, who participated in *Noon in Tunisia*, Billy Brooks (a.k.a. Bilal Abdul Hakeem) was a convert to Islam.

before they began to be widely discussed within the (white) U.S. jazz scene. There, it will be recalled, he quoted a Californian jazzman who expounded upon the black ownership of jazz and the idea that the evolution of jazz was a result of black musicians wishing to keep one step ahead of the white copyists, who were constantly trying to steal their ideas (1953a: 93–5). In a 1962 article, he also referred to similar arguments that had been advanced by hard boppers (1962j). Nor did he overlook one of the most militant free jazzmen when programming the Jazz Days and other concerts: in 1967, he invited Archie Shepp to participate in both the Donaueschingen Music Days and the Berlin Jazz Days. He also referred—albeit tangentially—to Black music ideology in his treatment of free jazz in the 1968 edition of the *Jazz Book* (1968c: 41).

While giving air to these views, however, he also distanced himself from them. The Californian jazzman's views might have passed without comment in his 1953 *Jazzbook*, but, in 1962, he considered it tragic that militant African American hard boppers were excluding white jazzmen from their circle, even if their stance was psychologically understandable (1962j: 41). When introducing Shepp to German jazz fans, he tempered the saxophonist's strongest statements—"I am an American Negro. Of course I'm angry. I have every right to be angry"—with affirmations of the importance of love in his work. He also quoted Shepp in a more conciliatory tone: "But if the esthetic is Black, it need certainly not be exclusive. It simply asks to be taken on its own terms" (Berendt and Shepp 1967). In a contemporaneous review of Shepp's music, he also shrewdly suggested: "Shepp knows that the protest stance helps sell his music" (1967l). Elsewhere, he downplayed the significance of the Black music ideology by indicating that the emphasis on protest was but a minority perspective (1966i; 1966k: 149; 1967d: 349; 1968c: 41). Increasingly, Berendt also began to express alarm at the parallels he discerned between Black Nationalism and Nazi ideology, not unlike those that the (Jewish) American critic Leonard Feather began to identify in the mid-1960s (Gennari 2006: 56 ff).

In a 1970 essay in the *Frankfurter Hefte*, in which he examined a dispute between the African American writers Eldridge Cleaver and James Baldwin, he reflected, for example, on

> the secret—and often ... no longer secret—fascist tendencies of ... "Black Nationalism," which caused the black playwright Leroi Jones ... to observe in an interview in the *Spiegel*: "We conceive of ourselves in a certain sense as nationalists" and then as a complete afterthought, and for that reason all the more telling "and Germans know for sure what nationalism is ... " (1970b: 340)

He also openly questioned the Afrocentrism held by many African Americans: "the most dreadful exterminations since Hitler's attempt to destroy the Jews are now taking place on African soil. Do America's Blacks really want to create similar political conditions in the USA to those in Africa?" (1970b: 341). In this context, it is curious that Berendt gave Billy Brooks the opportunity the following year to wax lyrical in the cover notes for *El Babaku* about his own Afrocentrism (and the "power and subjection" in the "African way"). His desire to complete the *JMTW* series with a ready-made "Jazz Meets Africa" type of record perhaps caused him to overlook such matters in this instance.[2]

Berendt's identification of a fascist trait in Afrocentric rhetoric was also advanced in a particularly controversial essay written in late 1975.[3] This essay posed the question of fascist content in the music of the 1970s and, although clearly inspired by Susan Sontag's 1975 "Fascinating Fascism" essay on Leni Riefenstahl, and perhaps also by the opinions of Leonard Feather, it was certainly in keeping with the West German liberal "watchdog" disposition (Berendt 1976b: 9; Sontag 1980: 73–105; Gennari 2006: 56 ff). Berendt extended Sontag's reflections into his own area of expertise. Among other things—such as the inflated use of the term "beauty" by jazz critics—he was particularly critical of Afrocentric Black music ideology:

> They are doing exactly what the Nazis did with their forging of links to German art and German thinking. The Blacks—and in fact all the jazz people, including the whites, who are sitting in the same boat too—talk about "roots." ... The Nazis talked about *"Blut und Boden."* One can descend to specifics to show just how each corresponds with the other—"roots" and *"Blut und Boden."* (1976b: 10)

What's more, the well-traveled Berendt diagnosed that this "roots" discourse had become endemic throughout the "Third World" (1976a: 7).

---

2. *El Babaku* marked a belated conclusion of the *JMTW* series, which might have come four years earlier, had the *Jazz Meets Africa* segment of the 1967 Jazz Days—billed as being an encounter between the jazz drummer Philly Joe Jones and the Nigerian drummer Michael Olatunji—not been cancelled due to the inability of Olatunji to attend (Berendt 1967n: 35; 1968f: 54; Ohff 1967a; Feather 1968: 24). Unlike most earlier *JMTW* recordings, *El Babaku* was not commissioned by Berendt but instead represented the more or less opportunistic recording of a preexisting group.

3. The essay was first published in the Swiss weekly *Die Weltwoche* in November 1975 (1975f) and then republished in *Jazz Podium* in January 1976 (1976b) as well as in numerous other publications (in 1981, Berendt observed that the essay had been printed in twenty-one (!) separate locations [Holleufer 1981: 13]). The "definitive" version—which incorporated passages from Berendt's April 1976 rejoinder to his critics (1976a)—was then included in his 1977 compilation of essays *A Window out of Jazz* (1977a: 272–84).

A newly exotic flavor now lent neo-fascist discourse a dangerously seductive power *in Germany:* "it gets beamed back from distant, foreign worlds into our own and becomes all the more fascinating in the process. It doesn't have the opprobrium of the solely German and Aryan any more" (1976b: 10).

Although it was apparently quite well received when first published in Switzerland's *Weltwoche,* Berendt's essay was extremely controversial in the German jazz press; it was even reported to have caused as great a splash there as had free jazz fifteen years earlier (Berendt 1976a: 6; Lindenberger 1977). Some critics argued that he used the term *fascism* too loosely and that the African American minority's focus on roots as a tool for identity building was completely different from the way in which the Nazi state had used *Blut und Boden* ideology to justify its imperialist aims (see e.g. Spindler 1976). Others objected to Berendt's speculative reading of all sorts of ideological content into jazz, which was, truly seen, a nonpolitical music (see, e.g., Kille 1976). The older critic Karl Heinz Nass was perhaps the most evenhanded: he respected Berendt's moral warning and thanked him for giving his readers food for thought; yet by focusing on the ways in which the National Socialists had deployed art and aesthetics, he argued that Berendt had put the cart before the horse: it was not aesthetics that had given rise to National Socialism (Nass 1976). Berendt's article is certainly open to the criticism made by Lisa Gates in relation to Sontag's essay, that it involves a "watered-down version of fascism, devoid of ... historical specificity" (1998: 239). Yet it was also understandable within the context of a postwar West Germany only too aware of its past—as well as coming from a complex, highly sensitive man who wanted to provoke his readers (cf. Berendt 1976a: 8).

There was a lot at stake here for Berendt. Beyond its supposedly seductive, latent fascist traits, the stance of Black cultural nationalism interrupted his vision of peaceful intercultural dialogue. It undermined the liberal notion of jazz as an emblem of black-white hybridity and of the peaceful, creative overcoming of racism. Moreover, it also queried his role as a white critic explicating a black art form. By contrast, the divergent identity politics and ideology of Don Cherry, another African American jazzman who had a strong interest in the music of Africa were much easier for Berendt to assimilate.

Don Cherry's *Eternal Rhythm*

The trumpeter and multi-instrumentalist Don Cherry (1936–95) eschewed the Black music ideology and cultural separatism of some of his fellow African American free jazzmen in favor of a doctrine of tolerance. So while he may have expressed his sympathy "with all the movements that are going on to help suppressed people everywhere," he also distanced himself from hard-line political positions:

> I was always more interested in religion than politics ...
> But these days politics just slaps you in the face. As a Negro raised in a mixed neighborhood, white people put me down, and black people put the white people down. I soon discovered hate—and I soon learned that we have to fight hate. (qtd. in Hennessey 1966: 15).

In 1963, Cherry, a close musical associate of free jazz pioneer Ornette Coleman began touring and living in Europe for extended periods. Various factors persuaded him to do this, including better work opportunities in Europe, and a Swedish partner. Getting away from the United States also assisted Cherry in dealing with drug problems. In 1964, he established a polyglot quintet in Paris which consisted of the West German pianist and vibraphonist Karl Berger, the Argentinian saxophonist Gato Barbieri, the Italian drummer Aldo Romano, and the French bassist J. F. Jenny-Clarke (Hennessey 1966: 14). During the 1960s, Cherry also traveled and performed in North Africa, which he visited for the first time in 1965, during a two-month stint in Joujouka, Morocco (Hennessey 1966; Pfleiderer 1998: 168–71). As we have seen, he traveled to Tunisia in 1969, when he participated in the film version of *Noon in Tunisia*. Wrapped up in this will to travel were Cherry's very catholic musical tastes and a broad definition of "jazz." In the mid-1960s, for example, he expressed an interest in the music of Ravi Shankar, which he considered "as much jazz as any music I've heard" (qtd. in Hennessey 1966: 15).

Understandably, Berendt was quick to engage with a jazzman of Cherry's importance and wide-ranging musical interests. In particular, he was extremely impressed by the trumpeter's Parisian quintet when it performed in 1966 at the German Jazz Festival in Frankfurt. For him, the "well-integrated quintet ... [was] a symbol of the universality of the new jazz." Obviously inspired, he quoted Cherry's philosophy at length in his review: "It is like a miracle to me. ... We didn't know each other but made ourselves acquainted with the melodies and folk songs of our different homelands, and our ideas are completely compatible" (Berendt 1966m). Such a philosophy was, of course, of a piece with the concept that Berendt was formulating for *Jazz Meets the World*. Three members of Cherry's quintet—Berger, Romano, and Jenny-Clarke—were promptly invited to the first Baden-Baden Free Jazz Meeting in December 1966, and then Cherry himself was in attendance the following year, distinguishing himself in the process as the "humble star" of the Meeting ("Avantgarde-Treffen beim Südwestfunk" 1966; Olshausen 1967; Zimmerle 1967a). This Meeting provided Cherry with the opportunity to perform with a larger ensemble than usual and it was in this spirit of experimentation that he and Berendt then conceived of the *Eternal Rhythm* project for the Berlin Jazz Days the following year (Berendt 1968b; "Free Jazz in Baden-Baden" 1968).

Figure 19 | Don Cherry performing *Eternal Rhythm* in Berlin, 1968. © Paul G. Deker. Used with permission.

Musically, important decisions were also made at the 1967 Meeting. Just weeks after the Indonesian Allstars' performances at the Berlin Jazz Days, Berendt now discovered in Cherry a Western jazzman as interested as he was in the Indonesian idiom (Berendt 1968b; 1977a: 382; 1985a: 352). Accordingly, *Eternal Rhythm* was to be at least partly inspired by gamelan music, and also deploy some metallophone instruments to be borrowed from the Indonesian embassy in Bonn. Cherry's bandmate, Karl Berger, who was closely involved in the planning of *Eternal Rhythm* had his own idiosyncratic interest in gamelan music, too:

> [it] shows us how very slow movements over long cycles can swing, while the sound—from the heavy gongs to the high-pitched percussion melody instruments, the stringed instruments and voices—condenses into a cosmos, which appears to imitate the harmony of nature. ... At no time can I withdraw from the suggestive violence of this music; it shows me the power that sound is able to convey and in that way sets a benchmark. (1968c)

As we have seen, for Cherry, as for Berger, the interest did not stop with gamelan music. Hence, on the eclectic *Eternal Rhythm* Cherry may have used Indonesian instruments, but he also played a Bengali flute and a Haitian gourd, and named one piece "Turkish Prayer" (Berendt 1968b). The arsenal of exotic instruments was consistent with free jazz's expansive tendencies explored in the last chapter; however, in Cherry's case recourse to various world musics and instruments was also consistent with other, more spiritual, concerns.

Spirituality and the Music of the World

Cherry's spirituality was breathtakingly wide-ranging. At one stage he was a Jehovah's Witness; however, by the 1970s he was an adherent of Tibetan Buddhism (Hennessey 1966 15; Pfleiderer 1998: 200). Not that he was exclusive about it: in his performance at the 1972 Jazz Days, he dedicated his music to Buddha, Krishna, Jesus, and Mohammed, and his philosophical motto from the era was "to connect the overall oneness" (Echenoz 1971; "Jazz trifft Afrika und Indien" n.d.) It therefore does not surprise that Cherry's music from this time was also highly syncretic. In addition to Indonesian and Tunisian music, he also took to musics (and collaborators) from as far afield as Turkey, India, and South Africa (Pfleiderer 1998: 175–211). As Ekkehard Jost observes, Cherry was not interested in dealing with each of these musical cultures *separately*. Rather, he was "seeking to combine his experiences with these different musical cultures in a context which might have been very heterogeneous, but was, in the final analysis, interregional" (1973/74: 148). His efforts in doing so were considerably less superficial than many other attempts by jazz musicians at the time. On parts of *Eternal Rhythm*, for example, he and his colleagues used the gamelan and other instruments to create, from the jazz perspective, quite a different musical aesthetic and one that did connect up with certain Indonesian musical principles (Pfleiderer 1998: 201–02, 206).

Cherry's approach to world musics was also linked to a specific philosophy toward the notions of community and appropriation. In his view, music was fundamentally the joint property of all. As he observed in 1966 in a comment responding to Black music ideology: "As far as music is concerned—well I feel it belongs to everybody. ... We shouldn't fight over music" (qtd. in Hennessey 1966: 15). He also extended this attitude to his own innovative techniques. Hence, his technique of playing two flutes at once was actually an "eternal" pattern, which rendered it incapable of theft; instead it was free for all to use (Cherry qtd. in Berendt 1968b).

Finally, Cherry's music—intended, as it was, to "articulate and underscore his syncretic spiritual ideas by musical means" (Pfleiderer 1998: 213)—often sought to have a specific spiritual function. As Jost notes, his "endless melodies" were partly concerned with communicating emotional equilibrium and associated with meditative practices (1973/74 151-2. See also Pfleiderer 1998: 201). Indeed, it was not unusual for Cherry to perform seated in the lotus position, and to meditate prior to a performance (Jost 1973/74: 152; Berendt 1983: 352). Beyond this, he viewed music as nothing less than a healing power in a fragmented world (Berendt 1971b).

Landmark in Free Jazz or Redemption through Kitsch?

Eternal Rhythm divided the audience in Berlin. According to Leonard Feather, it caused "great anger on the part of some and immense joy for others" (1969: 29. Cf. Zimmerle 1968b: 375; Renaud 1969). However, jazz critics seem to have been unanimously impressed. Dieter Zimmerle thought it one of the standouts of the 1968 Berlin Jazz Days (1968b: 375). Another German reviewer praised Cherry's "attempt to create a musical cosmos" in which the diverse elements found a "new form of harmony" ("Nach allen Regeln dieser Kunst" n.d.). The studio recording also received wide critical acclaim. In 1969, Jacques Renaud considered it "one of the most important discs which free jazz has ever produced" (1969). Two years later, Gérard Noel thought the record "a landmark in the history of the new music" (1971). The following year, *Downbeat* hailed it as "one of the superior jazz albums of the last decade – and it's not even exclusively a *jazz* experience" (Smith 1972).

Berendt was particularly enamored of *Eternal Rhythm* (see, e.g., Berendt 1969b: 46). In his enthusiasm, he overplayed the link to a heavily romanticized view of Bali—"the Hindu jewel, the 'island of love'[:] one of the last pure, unspoiled places on earth"—and to Indonesian music— "Bali is swinging in every note" (Berendt 1968b. Cf. Laade 1970: 144). Karl Berger, for one, objected to this sort of talk. For him, this was a typical example of Berendt speaking for the musicians. From his perspective, the only link with Indonesian music were the gamelan instruments: the jazzmen did not play in an "Indonesian" or "Balinese" fashion (Berger 2004). Nor did Albert Mangelsdorff—who also participated—think that *Eternal Rhythm* was particularly infused with Balinese music or culture (Mangelsdorff 2004).

Regardless of such differences, Cherry's concept of *Eternal Rhythm*— and Berendt's interpretation of it—augured the spiritual direction that the German critic's notion of *Weltmusik* would take in the 1970s and 1980s. Indeed, Berendt would dub Cherry the musician who best represented the whole *Weltmusik*-movement (Berendt 1975a; 1981e: 54). And so he continued to lavish Cherry with prestigious invitations that invariably had a strong intercultural aspect. Cherry participated in both of the 1969 SWF-sponsored revivals of *Noon in Tunisia*, and then, in 1970, Berendt invited him back to the Free Jazz Meeting, where he performed "Universal," a piece based on a raga (Panke 1971a: 30). In October 1972, he performed "Humus"—which likewise engaged with Indian music—with the New Eternal Rhythm Orchestra at the Donaueschingen Music Days, an event that was distinguished by the Orchestra's performance of a companion piece by the noted Polish composer Krzysztof Penderecki. The following month he performed in a quartet with the South African pianist Dollar Brand at Berendt's last Jazz Days. Not that these performances were invariably well received by the critics. In a review of Cherry's Donaueschingen performance, for example, Werner Panke criticized his dilettantish raga as "[a bid for] redemption through kitsch" (1971b).[4] Jost has also observed that Cherry's music sometimes attracted the criticism that it was "an escape to exoticism" (1975b 128. See also Pfleiderer 1998: 213). Clearly, this spiritually-inflected music did not sit at all well with more critically-minded Germans.

---

4. Pfleiderer observes that in relation to Cherry's engagement with Indian music, the charge of dilettantism has some substance (1998: 212).

Although his experience as a white German was quite different from that of the African American expatriates Cherry and Brooks, Berendt clearly identified with the sense of alienation and disenchantment with Western civilization that Brooks expressed and—as will be seen in the Conclusion—also with the spiritual solace that Brooks and Cherry located in their music. In connecting jazz and African music, *El Babaku* offered Berendt a long-desired and ready-made opportunity to fill a lacuna in the *JMTW* series, as well as a chance to capitalize on what he himself identified in 1971 as an "Africa-Wave" (1971a). However, the Afrocentric strategy was one with which he was also uncomfortable. This was because it was not simply a way of expressing disenchantment with the overly rationalized West. It was also a rallying point for a politics of cultural separatism, which not only questioned his role as a white critic but, for Berendt, also had dangerous proto-fascist freight. It may not surprise then that Berendt's *A Window out of Jazz* (1977)—the book that most forcefully made his case—came to be seen by some Germans as a counterweight to the "overwrought" Black music ideology of an Amiri Baraka/LeRoi Jones or of Carles and Comolli (see, e.g., Bachmann 1977). As will be demonstrated in the concluding chapter, Berendt was ultimately most comfortable with a notion of *Weltmusik* that—building on the music of Don Cherry and others—engaged in a far more ecumenical way with world musics.

CONCLUSION

Berendt and the Utopia of *Weltmusik*

Although the *JMTW* series technically concluded in 1971, Berendt continued to produce various intercultural concerts and records, not just with Don Cherry, but notably also with an ensemble based around the African American saxophonist John Handy and the North Indian *sarod* player Ali Akbar Khan.[1] Along with Cherry and others, he engaged this group to perform at the 1972 Jazz Days and then again during a 1975 concert celebrating the SWF's five thousandth (!) jazz broadcast. During the mid- to late 1970s—when his heyday as a *jazz* producer was waning—he also produced two MPS albums with the ensemble. Then, in 1980, he was invited by his old friend, the Indian critic Niranjan Jhaveri, to contribute an extended essay on "Jazz and India" to the notes for Bombay's Jazz Yatra festival. It was around such "grandchildren" of *Jazz Meets India* that Berendt's notion of *Weltmusik*—with its ambition to integrate all sorts of music and with its strongly ideological dimensions—began to coalesce. By the mid-1980s—just as the broader popularity of world musics began to take off in the West—his *Weltmusik* theory and practices had reached maturity. An analysis of this concept—one of the last Berendt was to champion before essentially retiring from the jazz scene—and of the strong criticisms that it elicited, presents an excellent opportunity to reflect not just on Berendt's career but also on the German dimensions of intercultural musical appropriation.

---

1. The *sarod* is a North Indian lute with played and resonance strings.

Weltmusik and the Esoteric Turn

Just as there were others in the 1960s who were engaging in *JMTW*-like activities, Berendt's notion of *Weltmusik* did not exist in isolation. In Germany, *E-Musik* composers such as Karlheinz Stockhausen and Peter Michael Hamel were both active in related fields, as were "Krautrockers," including Can, with its "ethnological forgery series," and Eberhard Schoener, who recorded with a Balinese gamelan orchestra in the mid-1970s (Hamel 1976; Berendt 1977a: 382; Fritsch 1981: 16–19; Kneif 1984: 111; Schnebel 1984; Stroh 1994: 313–17). Berendt's *Weltmusik* was surely influenced by some of these contemporaneous activities—and by Stockhausen's and Hamel's theories—just as it was by his experiences with the *JMTW* series and by other developments in the international jazz scene.

In the jazz world, it continued to be men such as Don Cherry, John Handy, and Karl Berger who gave Berendt his cue. In 1973, the by now expatriate Berger founded a pathbreaking Creative Music Studio in Woodstock (NY) that offered courses to musicians from all sorts of backgrounds. Participants tested out their creative concepts collegially, and in many cases appropriated Other musical techniques (Panke 1983). Berendt followed these activities with interest and invited Berger and some of his Woodstock colleagues to perform at Donaueschingen in 1979, and at a concert he programmed in New York in 1982. Another important catalyst for his ideas was the English guitarist John McLaughlin (born 1942), who was an alumnus of Miles Davis's influential jazz-fusion groups before starting his own Mahavishnu Orchestra in 1971. McLaughlin incorporated Indian instrumentation in some of his early 1970s work, and also formed Shakti, an indo-jazz quartet comprising himself and three South Indian musicians in the mid-1970s. McLaughlin appealed to Berendt—who presented the Mahavishnu Orchestra at the 1972 Munich Olympics jazz festival—not only because of their joint interest in Indian music. Just like Don Cherry's efforts, it was McLaughlin's attempts to synthesize musical elements from *many* cultural sources that piqued his interest (see, e.g., Berendt 1973).

What began as musings on the significance of McLaughlin's eclectic music—"the 'great synthesis,' which integrates all of the different types of music of our time into a new overarching unity"—matured by the beginning of the 1980s into broader reflections on a new type of musician: the practitioner of *Weltmusik* (Berendt 1973: 22. See also 1974c; 1981e). These ideas were not created in a vacuum; they were increasingly associated with a wave of *Weltmusik* encounters that Berendt insitituted at a range of venues, including the Lincoln Center in New York (during Newport impresario George Wein's 1982 "Kool" Jazz Festival), the Baden-Baden New Jazz Meetings (in 1983 and 1984), and the Donaueschingen Music Days (1984 and 1985). These encounters became far more ambitious than the *JMTW* series had ever been; the 1985 Donaueschingen concert, for example, assembled on one stage musicians from the United States (jazz drummer Andrew Cyrille, the vibraphonist Tom van der Geld, and the bassist David Friesen), Eastern and Western Europe (the horn players Connie Bauer, Lennart Aberg, and Bernd Konrad), South America (the *bandoneon* player Luis di Matteo, and the Brazilian percussionist Dom Um Romao), the Caribbean (the steel drummer Rudy Smith), and the Subcontinent (Vikash and Pandit Prakash Maharaj on *sarod* and tabla respectively).

Before going on to analyze the detail of Berendt's *Weltmusik* theories, one additional and very important context must be mentioned, namely, his spiritual development in the 1970s and 1980s. As we have seen in chapter 2, Berendt had long had an interest in religious matters, and in

Figure 20 | Tabla player Pandit Prakash Maharaj performs as part of the *Weltmusik* Summit at the Donaueschingen Music Days, 1985. In the background, Luis di Matteo (*bandoneon*), Bernd Konrad, and Lennart Aberg (saxophones). © Hans Kumpf. Used with permission.

their interface with music. In 1971, however, the disaffected pastor's son had begun to meditate. This activity—which he shared with spiritual jazzmen like Cherry and McLaughlin—was, as he later observed, a major turning point in his life (1985a: 270). The awakening was, in turn, partly a consequence of his travels to India, Japan, and Bali and of his contacts with Coltrane and Cherry (Berendt 1985a: 275; Segler 1987; Broecking 1995: 76). One can also trace forward the consequences of this discovery.

At a personal level, he began—like many spiritually inclined young people, and jazz musicians such as Cherry and the saxophonist Clifford Jordan—to read and be influenced by the works of Hermann Hesse. This interest peaked in *Hesse Between Music* (1975)—another entry in his long-running series of jazz and poetry recordings—on which the actor Gert Westphal recited Berendt's selection of Hesse's texts to musical accompaniment by Peter Michael Hamel's group Between. *A Window out of Jazz* (1977) was dedicated, among others, to Hesse, and included an essay on jazz and spirituality. A selection of Berendt's favorite readings, which was published in 1981, also included various spiritual texts (Berendt 1981d). Above all, however, it was *Nada Brahma* (1983) that signified his arrival in the world of the so-called New Age movement. This movement began in the late 1970s and continues to exist today, even if its heyday was during the 1980s. It eclectically combines spiritual, esoteric, and popular philosophical elements, advances a "holistic" model of the world, and provides solace to those concerned about rationalized, (post)modern Western society, and searching for a heightened consciousness and a more meaningful existence (Stroh 1994: 9–11, 24–6).

Nada Brahma began life in 1982–3—just as New Age classics by Marilyn Ferguson and Fritjof Capra began appearing in German—as a series of Saturday-evening SWF radio programs that departed significantly from Berendt's usual jazz broadcasts. In these, he exhorted his listeners to engage in deep listening in order to identify the sounds and harmonic unity of the universe. Short musical interludes, including compositions inspired by the "harmony of the spheres," as well as recordings of things as diverse as whale song were also included to "prove" that unity. The overarching message was for Westerners to rediscover the sadly atrophied sense of hearing and to use it to conceive of the world holistically, as opposed to rationally and analytically (Berendt 1985a: 9, 274). The book version of *Nada Brahma* soon became a New Age cult-bestseller in West Germany and is still in print today (Stroh 1994: 11).[2]

---

2. By 1994 almost 100,000 copies had been printed.

The book's success may be explained by the way it spoke to the concerns of the New Age movement. In an apocalyptic yet readable tone, *Nada Brahma* diagnosed a looming crisis in the Western world. The only way to avert this was for individuals to adopt a new spiritual consciousness; or, as Berendt later summed it up, "we can only change the world if we change ourselves" (qtd. in Heidkamp 1996). For the more analytical reader, there is something faintly irritating about the book's highly speculative lay philosophy, its reliance on analogies, and its rather paradoxical critique of rationalism at the same time that it calls for a synthesis of Eastern spirituality *and Western science* (cf. Wilson 1990: 70–73; Stroh 1994: 11, 128–33). These reservations were clearly not shared by all readers, however. As the musicologist Wolfgang Martin Stroh observes, by using analogy, association, and plausibility in an "aesthetic" way, New Age books like *Nada Brahma* took on a persuasive quality that overcame their rejection of traditional standards of proof and argumentation (1994: 132). Relatively quickly, *Nada Brahma* launched Berendt into a fresh and comparatively lucrative niche of the book market, and numerous other New Age books and sound productions followed until his death in 2000.[3]

In many ways, *Nada Brahma* and its successors marked a turning away from jazz by a man who had, in any event, become increasingly marginal to the West German jazz scene. In 1978—the same year that his only child Christian died—he resigned as the artistic director of the annual "Jazz in the Garden" series financed by the Berlin Senate, thereby retiring from his last freelance post as jazz impresario ("Jazz News" 1978). A short while later, he also retired from advising the Goethe Institut about its jazz tours. He did continue to broadcast and to organize the annual Baden-Baden New Jazz Meetings and the Donaueschingen jazz concerts until his retirement from the SWF in 1987. He also updated the *Jazzbook* and wrote an occasional jazz review or essay. However, his jazz record productions tailed off noticeably during the 1970s and by the demise of MPS in the early 1980s these had mainly been reduced to spin-offs from the Baden-Baden Meetings or from Donaueschingen (cf. K-G Fischer 1999). Various factors contributed to Berendt's decline in importance in the jazz scene. On the one hand—as we saw in chapter 8—a new generation of critics and musicians were now outspoken in their criticism of the sometime "Jazz Pope." On the other hand, jazz was itself no longer providing him with the new experiences he craved, just as the progressivist "jazz development" scheme so dear

---

3. By way of comparison, the critic Hans Kumpf believes that Berendt's New Age activities would have brought him in more income than his jazz activities (Kumpf 2007).

to him broke down into post–free jazz fragmentation (Berendt 1977a: 411–25; Heidkamp 1996). Certainly, the increasingly dominant neo-traditionalism of a Wynton Marsalis—who first made his mark on the American jazz scene in the late 1970s—would not have appealed greatly to Berendt. *Nada Brahma* also drove a new wedge between Berendt and the German jazz scene. Werner Wunderlich, his colleague at the SWF at the time, thought that *Nada Brahma* and its successors led to an unfortunate "neglect" of jazz on Berendt's part (Wunderlich 2004). Berendt's esoteric turn likewise drew sharp criticism from many others in the jazz scene (see, e.g., Heidkamp 1996; Sidhu-Ingenhoff 2002: 9; Rüsenberg 2002: 6). However, in retrospect, and as Berendt himself stressed, *Nada Brahma* was not necessarily the radical break it appeared to be at the time (cf. Berendt 1996a: 24). The spiritual origins of this esoteric turn can be traced through his restless career right back to his first book, the *"Time-Critical Study,"* which reads as proto–New Age in places. *Nada Brahma* also continued to reserve special enthusiasm for jazz's engagement with Indian music and for intercultural musical activities in general (Berendt 1983: 326–39, 340–85). It was very much in the spirit of *Nada Brahma*, then, that Berendt's mature notion of *Weltmusik*—most forcefully put in a 1985 article for *Jazz Podium* (1985b)—was formed.

Berendt's *Weltmusik* Utopia

In a useful 1981 essay outlining the ways in which *Weltmusik* has been advanced in German-language music discourse, Ingrid Fritsch identifies several recurring tropes, both positive and negative. These include the idea of the *peaceful coexistence* of all music cultures; the notion of a *unification* of musics, either as western music enriched by "exotic" elements, or as a supranational music; the concept of a transcendental *musica mundana* corresponding with the ancient "harmony of the spheres," which may be accessed spiritually; and the idea of Western music as *musical environmental pollution* that kills off indigenous musics (Fritsch 1981).

As I will demonstrate below, Berendt's model of *Weltmusik* had a supranational and transcendental element, but it also espoused the continued coexistence of differentiated world musics.[4] By contrast, he downplayed the idea of "musical environmental pollution" by the West, by suggesting that, on the whole, musical diversity was actually pro-

---

4. Unless otherwise noted, this account of Berendt's model of *Weltmusik* is derived from his 1985 *Jazz Podium* article *"Über Weltmusik"* (1985b).

moted by the process of diffusion. Ever the champion of syncretism, he believed that contact between cultures was necessary and productive—"music would become boring, and in fact die of sterility, if processes of admixture did not take place constantly." Crucially, spiritually inclined practitioners of *Weltmusik*—like Cherry and McLaughlin—who took on musical idioms other than their own, acted as models for tolerant cosmopolitanism, and also hinted toward a way in which the fragmented, overly "specialized" (post)modern world might be reassembled into a new whole (1974c; 1981e: 53–5; 1983: 336–7, 350–55; 1985b: 13). Aware that he was peddling an ultimately unrealizable utopia, Berendt nevertheless maintained that symbols of hope such as *Weltmusik* were valuable and necessary for a society in crisis.

In this context, Berendt foregrounded the notion of the intercultural musical encounter, where disparate musicians came together on an equal footing and, without conceding any of their own territory, conducted a meaningful and transcendental dialogue. As before, the basis on which they were able to do so was the commonality of certain universals, or what he now called buried musical "archetypes" (in the Jungian sense), which were capable of being accessed by a musician searching within him or herself. One such universal was revealed to be the Western harmonic system. Berendt relied here on the hypothesis that the human ear is capable of "correctively hearing" musical tones which diverge marginally from the "cosmic"—but also European—harmonic system, so as to render divergent world musics in reality mere variants of the universal. After an intercultural encounter, an individual musician's identity—and consciousness—would be strengthened. This notion was supported by having recourse to biological, evolutionary, and anthropological theories about the "challenge," after which each of the partners in an encounter can grow more vigorously. It was also given sexual connotations by his pairing of "the god Eros and Lady Musica" as the two primary ways in which cultural difference had been transcended in the past, and by his renewed paean to the mixed-race woman.

In an attempt to out-moralize "purist" critics of *Weltmusik*, Berendt also considered that *Weltmusik* practitioners were helping to throw the porousness and fundamental impurity of cultures into focus, and thereby identifying and combating what he—yet again—perceived as latent fascist thought; this time in those who were interested in the notion of "authentic," pure cultures (a.k.a. races). He further sought to disarm these critics by hitting below the belt; that is by impugning their virility, suggesting that the encounter was a vitalizing moment, that pure cultures were sterile, and that purity fetishists were themselves weaklings.

Weltmusik Critiques

Those familiar with the course of world music debates in the English-speaking world will recognize some of Berendt's ideas, just as they will recognize some of the forceful critiques taken by his German opponents. As David Bennett has recently shown, the positions taken in English-language debates generally adhere to what Steven Feld has called either "celebratory" or "anxious" narratives. The celebratory narrative is a discourse of "fluidity, hybridity and collaborative exchange … underpinned by postmodern anti-essentialist theories of the performative, dialogical and porous nature of all cultural identities" (2005: 10). The anxious narrative takes a Neo-Marxist tack and focuses on the ways in which Western musicians and the large recording companies—protected by their position of relative economic power and by copyright law—are able to appropriate (or expropriate) musical material from the margins and turn a profit from it, a profit in which the musical creators from the margins do not equally share (Bennett 2005: 5–15). As will be shown, however, debates about *Weltmusik* also had specifically German dimensions that diverged in significant ways from the English-language debates.

Berendt's 1985 article precipitated a sharp reply from the critic Stephan Voswinkel, which gave voice to concerns that had clearly been brewing for some time (Voswinkel 1985). While criticisms of the *JMTW* series had been mostly limited to the musical success (or otherwise) of the concerts and recordings—things had begun to change in the 1970s. In a review of *Karuna Supreme*, Berendt's 1975 production of the Handy–Khan ensemble, for example, Helmut Artus called for a critical analysis of the music industrial fashions and musico-political ideologies operating behind recordings such as this (Artus 1976). Such an analysis only really began to be undertaken in earnest in the 1980s, however, as *Weltmusik* and—in the English-speaking world, "world beat" and "world music"—began to gather steam as a music industry marketing label.[5]

Critiques of Berendt's notion of an integrative *Weltmusik* and of the intercultural encounter were now not only musical, but also increasingly ideological, although judgments about the one inevitably bled into assessments of the other. On the musical front, opinions were divided about the success of individual *Weltmusik* "summits," just as they had been with the *JMTW* meetings. Some critics, whom one might otherwise have expected to be critical, actually expressed their praise. For in-

---

5. On the history of music industry classifications like "world music" and "world beat" (dating back to around 1983), see, e.g., Taylor 1997: 1–4; Klump n.d.: 2–8.

stance, Wilhelm Liefland observed in relation to the Handy–Khan's live performance in 1975 that "the most remarkable [thing] about [Handy's and Khan's] playing together ... was that both 'parties' remained within their idiom and did not fall into the temptation of mutually assimilating themselves to each other, but still mutually vitalized each other" (1975). However, others queried whether the musicians really managed a mutually fruitful dialogue, suggesting instead that they had simply traded in superficialities, and/or ceded their own territory (see, e.g., Artus 1976). The test-tube nature of the encounters was also criticized. In a review of the 1985 Donaueschingen summit, for example, Klaus Robert Bachmann observed that "the assemblage of diverse stylistic elements groans occasionally under the weight of force; where relationship-weaving has stiffened into a postulate, it is merely every-day babble that comes into being rather than *Weltmusik*" (1985).

Reviewers also queried the extent to which the different idioms had really integrated by drawing attention to the frictions and tensions evident. For example, in his review of the 1984 Baden-Baden World Music Meeting, Klaus Mümpfer asked:

> What is *Weltmusik*? [It is] certainly not a conglomerate of different musical cultures. But [it is] probably not an overarching integration either, in which the different musics yield up their character to [form] a community. The pieces [on this record] speak rather of a battle-like act of creation, of constant frictions, and of the equal rights of individual expressions that touch each other at points of commonality and then separate again. (1985)

On the ideological front, critics expressed horror at the dystopian prospect—inherent for them in the utopia of *Weltmusik*—of a unified world culture, in which difference was flattened out and culture centralized in the name of profits (cf., e.g., Berendt 1985b: 12). In a review of the Handy-Khan performance and of the other intercultural encounters at the 1972 Jazz Days, for example, Gerhard Kühn took on an Adornoesque tone when he asked:

> Who actually wants a unified *Weltmusik*, a unified world art? Is it not in the individual that the benefits of each conception of culture and art lies? Is there not already in other fields enough determining- and centralizing thinking aimed at taking part in the blessing of economic success? (1972a)

Other critics, including Voswinkel, rejected Berendt's sanguine belief that, on the whole, the diffusion of Western music caused a diversification of world musics, suggesting instead that there was a levelling tendency toward "unity-mush" (Voswinkel 1985: 10). Under such circumstances, a critic like Peter Niklas Wilson advanced the view that—among other things—cultural museums should be built to protect endangered world musics (1987: 8).

Ideological critiques of *Weltmusik* were often informed by the guilty memory of colonialism. Hence, Voswinkel challenged Berendt's simplistic historical account of the international, collegial spread of music, somehow independent of colonialism and divorced from questions of power (1985: 10). As with "anxious" interventions in the English-language world music debates, *Weltmusik* critiques now sought to reveal the "neocolonial" operation of the Western music industry. Critics homed in on Berendt's blind spot, namely, his failure to take proper account of the music industry, which was seen to be peddling Western popular music throughout the world, destroying indigenous cultures or, worse yet, superficially cannibalizing and exploiting parts of those cultures, simply in order to make a product more attractive to both domestic and "Third World" markets (Voswinkel 1985; Wilson 1987: 8; 1990: 76).[6] Some objected to the way in which musically inaccurate—yet ideologically soothing, and therefore remunerative—tags such as "fusion" or "synthesis" were capitalized upon in the process (see, e.g., Gruntz 1983: 194). In sharpening the charge of neocolonialism, critics pointed out that it was Westerners who were those driving these "syntheses" and who had ultimate control over them and the proceeds: "the Third World supplies the (cheap) raw materials; the production and distribution lie within Western control" (Wilson 1987: 8).

Weltmusik's "incense-stick" exoticism—which was stressed by identifying that music by the *Gastarbeiter* residing in Germany was conspicuously absent from the genre—was also attacked at various levels (Voswinkel 1985: 11). On the one hand there was its escapism. This perspective was succinctly summarized in Peter Brötzmann's laconic comment on "Humus," the title of Don Cherry's 1971 raga-esque composition for Donaueschingen: "What use to me is the smell of earth, and the sun peeking through pink clouds, when I myself am sitting so deeply in crap?" (qtd. in Panke 1971b: 424). On the other hand, critics considered that a musician's search for universal "archetypes" within him or herself

---

6. Berendt's discourse on this point was predictably contradictory and unresolved: in a variation of his earlier arguments about the bossa nova, pop jazz, and even "authentic" jazz itself—see chapters 1, 8 and 13—he observed that there was commercialized, Western-flavored popular music in places like Asia that did reduce cultural difference. However, he differentiated this pop music from *Weltmusik* (i.e., jazz), while still observing that Asian popular music was not all bad; there was also some Indian film music of a relatively high quality, for example (1985b: 8, 12).

was not only misguided; it also promoted the treatment of cultural difference in an arrogant, Eurocentric manner by failing to take the Other and his/her specific context seriously. In particular, Berendt's notion of the human ear's "correctively hearing" Other music was criticized for universalizing the Self (Voswinkel 1985; Wilson 1987: 7–8; 1990: 73–5). Instead, it was stressed that one was more capable of engaging in an encounter if one bore in mind the specificities of one's own (and the Other's) culture (Gruntz 1983: 197; Voswinkel 1985: 11).

Many critics attacked the spiritual basis of *Weltmusik*, smirking at "false Indians" like John McLaughlin and their meditation practices, or otherwise criticizing the wishy-washy spirituality of various indo-jazz activities (Panke 1971b: 424; Liefland 1975; Gruntz 1983: 190, 194–97). In a broadside on New Age music more generally, Wilson attacked the attempt to respiritualize music as befogging of critical faculties: "'Wherever musical values are subjected to a process of sacralization, it is difficult to penetrate attitudes of perception.' Very difficult" (1990: 70, quoting the musicologist Zofia Lissa). He and others particularly objected to the way in which ideologues such as Berendt foregrounded concepts of harmony and holism. This grand narrative was viewed as "a symptom of not being able to cope with complexity" and was thought to be both dogmatic and repressive of individual dissonances (Wilson 1990: 67). Unlike anxious English-language narratives of world music, this critique also cast one eye back to the National Socialist past. As the philosopher Peter Sloterdijk writes in his analysis of *Nada Brahma*: "The answer of the great harmony doctrine to my little dissonant questions must always, of course, be: it is you yourself who is the problem. And what it means to 'solve' this problem, well in history there are really only examples which make one shiver" (1987: 101).[7] In this way, commentators on both sides of the *Weltmusik* debate were influenced by and sought to invoke Germany's recent past in their argument.

Conclusion

As with so many of the other controversies that Berendt provoked over the course of his career, the *Weltmusik* debate was as much about cultural criticism, utopian imaginings, and reflecting on or moralizing about the National Socialist past and its causes—not to mention the matter of product placement—as it was about music per se. As with previous

---

7. Cf. Wilson's reference to the anti-Semitic remarks of the esoteric guru Rainer Holbe (1990: 68).

debates—with Liefland and Adorno, for example—it threw into sharp relief a conflict between quite different ways of talking about jazz, and beyond that further illustrates the difficulties inherent in attempting to fix meaning to music.

From a sociopsychological point of view, recourse by Berendt and others to world musics was, like the earlier passion for jazz, partly borne by curiosity in relation to new (musical) experiences. It was also a strategy to avoid issues arising from the ideological taint of some forms of German music, as the critic Günther Huesmann has observed:

> The idea of 'music of the world' [*Weltmusik*] emerged in German jazz in the 1960s, and this was no accident. The idea is to be seen as closely related to the dissatisfaction with German national culture. Ethnic music was not burdened by ideology, and the basic dialogue character of jazz continues in the meeting of musical cultures—thus the idea of music of the world was particularly appealing to German jazz musicians. (1986)

Over a decade later, the bassist Peter Kowald, a participant in the 1984 Baden-Baden World Music Meeting and someone who developed his own musical peripateticism, remarked in a similar fashion:

> What happens to someone who really has a broken relationship to his [own] tradition? My solution was to become a traveler, to travel a lot and very consciously, and to delight in playing with a great many people from different parts of the world and surely also to take on something from them. (qtd. in Wilson 2001: 112)

For Berendt himself, the concept of *JMTW* and *Weltmusik*, as well as of the Goethe Institut's jazz diplomacy, was also about seeking to overcome and make symbolic amends for past German nationalism, as well as providing a beacon for a tolerant, cosmopolitan future.

Because the West German interest in the musical Other was—like the interest in jazz before it—partly driven by a flight from Germanness, the presentation and reception of world musics was not infrequently romanticized. Vocal postcolonial populations did not exist in West Germany to interdict these discourses. However, that did not prevent some German critics from seeing through the trappings. Importantly, activities like *Jazz Meets the World* also opened up a space for Others like the Indonesian All-stars to make their own complicating representations of Self.

As Wolfgang Martin Stroh observes, there is a dilemma involved with the European recourse to world musics: on the one hand, it is legitimate to seek out new musical experiences; but on the other hand, there is the legacy of colonial history to contend with (1994: 311). I hold the view that the search for new experiences and an interest in the Other are positives—and understandable in a time of globalization, when exposure to Others is increasing, including as a result of postcolonial migration flows, but when wilful misunderstanding and a lack of empathy seem to be in no risk of declining. I also consider that the charge of neocolonialism is a little too undifferentiated, but equally I hold that Berendt's shrill and defensive account of *Weltmusik* is simplistic and misleading.

The difference in power and wealth between the "First" and the "Third Worlds," and the way in which the Western music industry banks on cultural difference, as well as on comforting—if perhaps inaccurate—images of intercultural "fusion" should not be erased from view. Nor should we fail to note how copyright laws can and do benefit Western musicians (cf. Seeger 1991). It is true that Berendt, in his project of advancing a utopian model of intercultural harmony (a.k.a. *Weltmusik*), tended to downplay or even disregard these types of questions. However, the charge of neocolonialism is also problematic. It implies bad faith on the part of the Western musicians and, as Stroh points out, it tends to operate on an assumption that "Third World" partners are "completely immature and, as soon as a European turns up, [just get] overridden" (1994: 342). These musicians are therefore denied the same level of maturity that is, for example, routinely ascribed to those European jazz musicians who have passed through a process of "emancipation" from American role models. The corollary is that they should inhabit some enclave (or, as Wilson puts it, "museum") of "authenticity."

I have attempted to show that, at least in the intercultural musical encounters presented in the *JMTW* series, these assumptions do not hold. While the Other musicians may not have always shared exactly the same intentions and motivations as the Westerners, they were not simply exploited. Bubi Chen and his Indonesian colleagues cannily manipulated Berendt into inviting them to Berlin; Salah El Mahdi used *Noon in Tunisia* as a platform from which to promote Tunisian music in Europe. Chen, El Mahdi and others remembered these activities with a good deal of fondness. Some of the European musicians, such as Manfred Schoof, also benefited in terms of their own musical development. However, it would be wrong to suggest—as Berendt did in his account of *Weltmusik*—that all of the participants did. One only needs to think of Jean-Luc Ponty's, Irène Schweizer's, and Terumasa Hino's experiences.

The *JMTW* series and its *Weltmusik* successors show that, even while a relatively integrated synthesis sometimes occurred, these intercultural musical encounters often threw up frictions and dissonances between the different musical idioms. Those dissonant aspects give the lie to the holistic and harmonious tropes Berendt advanced in the 1970s and 1980s.

However, frictions need not necessarily be a negative—which seems to be implicit in much of the criticism of the day. I consider instead that the moments of dissonance and friction are just as important and telling as the moments where dialogue did take place. In intercultural activities such as these, respect for the Other is obviously paramount. A musician ought to fully inform him- or herself about the Other musical culture (and, of course, respect any interdictions on the appropriation of music) before engaging with it. One can quite legitimately criticize universalist tropes, pointing out how they may crunch difference into a (Eurocentric) "universal" mold and thereby encourage exoticism. However, too much suspicion in relation to universals and too anxious an eye on fully mastering the intricacies of the Other's idiom may be asking too much, and would certainly have prevented some of the musically less "successful" yet highly revealing *JMTW* projects from coming into existence. We would be the poorer without them.

Many have been critical of Berendt's drive to experiment. However, in the 1960s—not least in Europe—jazz was a music in flux, with its traditions under question and its ability to take on foreign musical material expanding. In this context, Berendt's experimentation was both legitimate, and, for him, logical. As he observed in a 1966 interview: "Critics are always telling the people whom they should listen to. So why don't they bring them what should be heard?" (qtd. in Blume and De Beaumont 1966). That others disagreed with his interventions was hardly his fault. What was more problematic was that he—not infrequently—confused the roles of critic and producer, using his avenues as a powerful critic to promote his own productions as well as to ignore or attack those who had criticized him (cf. Gruntz 2002: 89–90). Despite this unfortunate trait, his absence from the German jazz scene is lamented by those who—in full consciousness of his egocentrism and foibles, and in the knowledge that he would not fit into the "polyphonic jazz goings-on of the new era" (i.e., the new, post-1968 structure of that part of the field of cultural production still referred to as the "jazz scene")—miss the impetus and energy that he imparted during his heyday (Huesmann qtd. in Rüsenberg 2002: 7. See also Pilz 2000). As the pianist and broadcaster Michael Naura put it, "the way he repeatedly got things off the ground that would not otherwise have been possible: I doff my cap, regardless of all the flaws" (2000b). Of course, not all in the German jazz scene share this view, and the reasons why not are also important. By pulling the "Jazz Pope" back into focus, we get a better sense of important dynamics running through the social history of jazz in postwar Germany—and of how broader changes in German society impacted the jazz scene—as well as of developments in the music itself.

The *JMTW* records and Berendt's *Weltmusik* summits are doubtless historical—and, for the most part, but a distant ancestor of what nowadays goes under the name "world music," particularly in the English-speaking world. However, with their various historical contexts unpacked, those records throw into relief the constructedness and dynamism of culture and identity in the second part of the twentieth century and beyond—not just in a Germany contending both with the National Socialist past and with its adoption of American culture, but also in other parts of the rapidly globalizing world. They also reflect some of the ways in which "race" and Otherness were discussed in post-Nazi Germany, despite the taboos. These records, and the discourses surrounding them, deliberately and provocatively put these and other matters up for debate and therefore continue to have significant value, even if the meaningful intercultural dialogues and utopian hopes craved by their producer did not fully eventuate. For that, we should thank him.

EPILOGUE

Joachim-Ernst Berendt
A Personal Reflection upon His Importance to Jazz in Germany

Like many other Germans, I grew up with Joachim-Ernst Berendt's *The Jazzbook* guiding me on my way through jazz history. He told me what swing and bebop were, who influenced Charlie Parker and who was, in turn, influenced by Parker. He shaped my idea of what jazz was and how it had evolved. When I became director of the Jazzinstitut Darmstadt in 1990 I finally met him in person. By then he had moved away from jazz, disenchanted with developments in the music that seemed to offer him nothing "new"—and he was always hunting for this experience of something new. I met him two or three times a year, usually at his house near Baden-Baden where I drove in order to get some more material for the archive of the Jazzinstitut. We usually had lunch or dinner together—either at a local restaurant or at his home. We talked about music, politics, his recent lectures, his current book projects and other things, besides. He reminisced about his experiences, about concerts and musicians who shaped his musical aesthetics. And he regularly asked me whether I had heard anything "new" recently, anything "really interesting." I told him about the concerts I had seen, and about musicians I had discovered for myself. He was always interested to learn more, but at some point he would usually put on a disappointed face and say, "But we already did that twenty years ago!" Of course, that was not true—he neither knew some of the projects I was talking about nor did he acknowledge the fact that "something new" means different things to different people. But it made me understand one part of his personality:

He was hungry for that kick of discovering a new experience. Jazz, in general, had moved in a direction where he didn't get that kick anymore. That was probably one of the reasons why he became disenchanted with jazz and moved to other realms. But he never forgot how important jazz was for his life. And he continued to listen to the great recordings of jazz history, to have them uplift him, to cheer himself up. They just no longer gave him that kick of discovering a new feeling.

Berendt's relationship to the German jazz scene grew tense in his last years. He was proud of many of the projects he had instigated—Albert Mangelsdorff's solo playing, for example, as well as some bands that had formed after they had first met at his Baden-Baden Jazz Meeting. He was sad because he felt that many of the musicians whom he had supported throughout his working life had forgotten about the help that he had given them earlier on. He sensed criticism everywhere. Sure, Berendt had been criticized a lot. That comes with being a power-conscious person in a powerful position. It seems to be a rule in the jazz business that the jazz promoters are often seen as an "enemy" by some musicians. Berendt was a radio producer, his *Jazzbook* was a standard reference work, he had started and organized important and influential festivals, he had acted as a record producer. He was seen as *the* German authority on jazz, and he made use of this reputation as well as of all the different positions he held. He made use of them to further jazz's interests; but he also had an ego, and sometimes his critics, by focusing on the fact that all of these activities had helped his ego and, possibly, his bank balance, forgot that he had actually supported jazz as well. He had made things possible, and without him German jazz history would have developed differently. He knew about his influence, and about his role in and for German jazz. And he felt that others—his critics as well as many musicians—denied him their gratitude for what he had done. As much as he needed to discover new experiences in music, he also needed the acknowledgement of the public as to how important he was, and how much he had influenced other peoples' lives—those of musicians just as much as those of fans who had discovered jazz through him.

Berendt had been at the center of many developments that shaped German jazz. His jazz department at Südwestfunk Radio became the model for jazz departments at public radio stations everywhere in Europe. The Berlin Jazz Days were one of the most "serious" jazz festivals anywhere: apart from having a good time there you also were supposed to learn something, because Berendt always had a musico-political agenda which he sought to realize through his concerts. In Berlin that agenda was nothing less than presenting the most diverse picture of what was going on in jazz at the moment: the most contemporary projects, as well as a look at what the big names from by-gone days were still doing. He liked to program events in such a way that apart from having heard the music itself, the audience came away having learned something about that music and its history, and perhaps having also broadened its knowledge and interest outside the rigid borders of jazz. Also, there was always at least one program idea that kept people talking and arguing, usually about the future or decline of jazz. Berlin became a "must" for jazz critics as well as aficionados, and the festival was not just a success because it was the only European festival held in November, as George Wein once commented, but also because of those programmatic elements which practically forced everybody who was seriously interested in the music to attend in order to be able to take part in next year's jazz discourse.

In the 1970s, Berendt set out on his path away from jazz. He published polemical articles about some of the most current developments, especially the music of some of the new acoustic virtuosos who had moved from the improvisational complexity of free jazz back to a newly re-discovered beauty of harmony. The evolutionary model of jazz had run its course. After all, in his view jazz history had been one of growing complexity: from New Orleans through Dixieland, swing, bebop, cool jazz and hard bop up to free jazz, the music had always added levels of complexity. Now that development seemed to have reached an end. The fusion of jazz and rock brought about by Miles Davis and some of his musicians seemed to be a counter-movement to what had evolved before. Berendt's model of a jazz history in which each decade could be accurately named and stylistically described, was now hard to maintain. What did one call this counter-movement, and how did it fit into his "evolutionary" concept of jazz? "New acoustical jazz" didn't really capture what Keith Jarrett, Chick Corea, John McLaughlin, Oregon and others were doing. And "eclectic jazz" might have been a fitting description of what John Zorn and other Downtown musicians did in the 1980s, but it didn't really catch on, or if it did, it was all too often misunderstood as "electric jazz" by the non-initiated.

Berendt's disenchantment with jazz had started in the early 1970s when he realized that the music of John Coltrane had opened new spiritual doors, but that few musicians or audience members were inclined to follow. He kept being interested in European free jazz, but his heart was not in a music he considered to be more destructive than genre-productive. He was probably more enthralled by European and especially German free jazz's political undertones than by the music per se, as the emancipation from American role-models also stood for a more general kind of liberation and thus mirrored his own concept of jazz as a liberator of thoughts, and an antidote for everything totalitarian. In his 1975 essay *"Die neue Faschistoidität in Jazz, Rock und überall,"* he compares the aesthetic beauty and quasi-religious atmosphere in Keith Jarrett's concerts to the dangerous beauty of Leni Riefenstahl's films and implicitly demands political responsibility both on the part of musicians and listeners. Later he became a follower of the Baghwan sect, even moving to Oregon for a while to be closer to the sect's leader, Baghwan Shree Rajneesh. Shortly after I first met Berendt, he invited me to a lecture he gave at Heidelberg's *Stadthalle*, a large auditorium filled to capacity with people who had now died their orange Baghwan clothes other colors, since their erstwhile spiritual leader had fallen out of favor after being publicly criticized for his luxurious demands (he supposedly owned 85 Rolls Royce automobiles), and his sect had been attacked for its authoritarian rules. Berendt's lecture on spirituality and the miracle of listening was framed by a performance by an overtone singer. At the end, Berendt invited his audience to participate in an extended meditation and a session of "Ommm" chanting. I felt so uncomfortable with the group emotion he tried to bring on, that I had to leave the hall, feeling that Berendt himself was doing the very thing that he had criticized in his essay from 1975.

Did Berendt fall victim to the power of success and the power of influence? He certainly enjoyed the fact that people hung on his every word and viewed him as the authority he knew he was. He thrived in the love and admiration he felt from others. He longed for peace and unity. Where he had once been fast to sue critics, he now tried to stay away from all such controversy. When we talked over lunch or dinner, at some point he usually mentioned his sadness that musicians and critics didn't acknowledge the role he had played supporting German jazz. I didn't quite understand, then. "Jochen, you yourself know how important you were for the music. Isn't it enough for you to know what you did? And don't you get enough positive reactions that you can just ignore those other voices?" I asked. He didn't see it that way. "Why do they hate me?" he asked. "I have done so much for them." It was the voice of an old man who had forgotten how to enjoy the fruits of his life because of his frustration with having critics—something that usually goes hand in hand with success. I used to console him. He had definitely been a power-conscious man, but that was exactly what jazz in Germany had needed at that time. When I first raised the importance of power and the consciousness of power to him, he vehemently objected. Then he conceded: "Yes," he said, "I guess I used the power structures that I was part of." And that he did. He used his position at the SWF, his different journalistic gigs, his role as the artistic director for the Berlin Jazz Days and later of the jazz festival held during the Olympic Games in Munich in 1972, his gigs as a radio as well as record producer and as author of *the* standard reference work on jazz. He used them to fight for the projects he wanted to come into being and to be heard. He bundled his many activities in ways that later were held against him (being a concert promoter, festival manager, radio- and record producer and critic all at the same time). His seriousness and his critical distance (or lack thereof) was questioned, and many saw his ego dictating his projects more than his aesthetic convictions.

In reality, though, German jazz needed someone like Berendt. It needed someone who knew the music but also knew the structure in which this music could thrive. It needed an advocate who knew how to deal with mayors and other politicians, with radio and TV executives, with potential sponsors and with other critics. It needed someone who was a professional in all of those things. Berendt was the right man in the right place at the right time. Without him, German (and European) jazz definitely would have sounded different.

—Wolfram Knauer

Chronology

1922 German foreign minister Walther Rathenau assassinated. Hyperinflation begins. Berendt born in Berlin (July).
1925 Berendt's mother Frieda separates from her husband, the Protestant pastor and director of the Bethabara-Beth-Elim-Trust for disadvantaged women (Berlin-Weissensee), Ernst Berendt Jr.
1926 Alfred Baresel publishes *Das Jazzbuch*.
1927 Ernst Krenek's jazz-opera *Jonny Strikes Up* premieres.
1928 Premiere of Bertolt Brecht's and Kurt Weill's jazz-influenced *Threepenny Opera*. Frankfurt's Hoch'sche Conservatorium introduces a jazz course (which quickly folds after Hitler's ascent to power).
1933 Hitler comes to power. First jazz bans introduced on German radio.
1936 Adorno publishes "On Jazz." Berendt hears jazz on the radio for the first time. Part of the Bethabara-Beth-Elim-Trust buildings requisitioned by the National Socialist Student Association.
1938 National Socialists put on *Degenerate Music* exhibition in Düsseldorf.
1939 World War II commences.
1940 Berendt undertakes his wartime higher school matriculation. Berendt's father leaves Berlin to work as a pastor in Baden-Baden.
1941 The United States enters the war. Berendt conscripted into the German Army and assigned to fight on the Eastern front.
1942 Berendt's father dies in Dachau after having been interned as a member of the Confessing Church.
1945 Germany defeated and divided into four zones. Berendt captured by the U.S. Army but soon released to travel south to Baden-Baden, where he is employed by the French, first as a

translator and then with the precursor of the SWF. "Midnight in Munich" jazz program broadcast on Radio Munich.

1946 SWF commences broadcasting. Berendt responsible for the music library and for *U-Musik* broadcasts.

1947 Berendt writes his first pieces of criticism. Adorno and Horkheimer publish their *Dialectic of Enlightenment*.

1948 Monetary reform in the Western zones. The Berlin Blockade commences (June). Trumpeter Rex Stewart performs and records in Berlin.

1949 FRG proclaimed (May); GDR established (Oct.). Berendt marries for the first time, is appointed as Jazz Editor at the SWF; institutes the long-running SWF concert series "Jazztime Baden Baden"; and writes *Jazz: A Time-Critical Study*. His (only) son, Christian is born (Dec.).

1950 German Jazz Federation formed, with Berendt as press officer. Berendt travels to the United States on the cultural exchange program (Sept.–Oct.).

1952 UNESCO launches an International Federation of Jazz. Louis Armstrong performs in Germany (Oct.). *Jazz Podium* established.

1953 Adenauer reelected as Chancellor. Worker demonstrations in GDR suppressed by force (June). First German Jazz Festival held in Frankfurt/Main (May). Adorno and Berendt clash over jazz in *Merkur*. Berendt makes the short film *Jazz - Yesterday and Today*. Berendt's *Jazzbook* published, quickly becoming a bestseller (Oct.).

1954 George Wein establishes the Newport Jazz Festival in the United States. The Kurt Edelhagen Big Band performs in Paris (May). Berendt and Leo Waldick clash over its success in the pages of *Jazz Podium*. First jazz performances at the Donaueschingen Music Days, including a proto Third Stream piece by Swiss composer Rolf Liebermann (Oct.).

1955 FRG rearms and joins NATO (May). Charlie Parker dies. First episode of Berendt's long-running TV series *Jazz - Heard and Seen* is screened (Jan.). Louis Armstrong performs in Hamburg, where members of the audience riot (Oct.).

1956 FRG signs Treaty of Rome. Lionel Hampton tours Spain and develops a "Flamenco sound." Dizzy Gillespie embarks on the first Jazz Ambassadors tour for the U.S. State Department. Berendt and Josef Tröller tour Germany with "Jazz and Old Music." The SWF celebrates its 1,000[th] jazz broadcast with a jubilee concert (including Miles Davis and the Modern Jazz Quartet).

1957 Adenauer reelected. Albert Mangelsdorff and colleagues perform at the Polish Jazz Festival (July). The Modern Jazz Quartet and Andre Hodeir perform at Donaueschingen (Oct.). Berendt separates from his first wife, Inge.

1958 Miles Davis records "Milestones," pioneering modal jazz. Cologne's Conservatorium of Music institutes a jazz course. Albert Mangelsdorff performs at Newport with the International Youth Band (Aug). The West German Defence Minister Franz-Josef Strauss launches a "military jazz band."

1959 Miles Davis and Gil Evans record *Sketches of Spain*. Saba makes its first jazz recordings. Berendt produces his first material for Saba.

1960 Newport Jazz Festival interrupted by rioting. Newport Rebel Festival mounted by Charles Mingus et al. Tony Scott travels to Indonesia. Kimio Eto and Bud Shank record together. John Coltrane records the modal *My Favorite Things*. Ornette Coleman records *Free Jazz*, launching a radical form of avant-garde jazz. Berendt tours Germany with "Jazz and New Music," before traveling extensively around the United States with the photographer William Claxton for their book *Jazz Life*.

1961 Adenauer reelected. Berlin Wall constructed (Aug). Coltrane records hommages to African, Spanish, and Indian music. He also tours Germany and performs for *Jazz – Heard and Seen*. Ravi Shankar's *Improvisations* recorded with jazzmen. Hideo Shiraki Quintet records with a koto player. Berendt's *Jazzbook* published in the United States.

1962 Lippmann and Rau put on the first American Folk Blues Festival. Berendt travels extensively through Asia for the first of many times (Feb.–June). Records *The Music From Bali*.

1963 FRG signs treaty of reconciliation with France. Stan Getz and João Gilberto record the top-selling bossa nova/jazz classic, *Getz/Gilberto* (including the hit, "Girl from Ipanema"). Don Cherry performs free jazz in Paris. Albert Mangelsdorff et al. perform for the Goethe Institut in Paris (Nov.). LeRoi Jones/Amiri Baraka publishes *Blues People*.

1964 The Mangelsdorff Quintet tours Asia—with Berendt—and adapts Asian musics for the purpose, subsequently recording them as *Now Jazz Ramwong* (Jan.–Mar). Tony Scott, Shinuchi Yuize, and Hozan Yamamoto record *Music for Zen Meditation and Other Joys* in Japan. The Joe Harriott Quintet (UK) performs free jazz at the German Jazz Festival. First Berlin Jazz Days (Sept.).

1965 Adenauer's successor, Ludwig Erhard dogged by budget deficit issues. Albert Mangelsdorff performs at Newport again. Lippmann and Rau launch their first *Flamenco Gitano* Festival. Berendt compiles Eastern European jazz for release in West Germany, *Jazz Greetings from the East*. The Mayer-Harriott group records their *Indo-Jazz Suite*. Hideo Shiraki Quintet and koto players perform at the Jazz Days (Oct.).

1966 Erhard resigns and a Great Coalition is formed, creating doubts about the adequacy of the parliamentary opposition. The Globe Unity Orchestra and *Folklore e Bossa Nova do Brasil* perform at the Jazz Days (Nov.). Berendt records Baden Powell's *Tristeza on Guitar* in Brazil (June) and institutes the annual Baden-Baden Free Jazz Meeting, at which Barney Wilen "duets" with a Ravi Shankar recording (Dec.). The Indonesian All-Stars lobby Berendt to help them tour Europe.

1967 West Germany's economy slows into recession for the first time. Tensions mount as student Benno Ohnesorg is shot by police at a demonstration in Berlin (June). *Jazz Meets the World* series launched (May). George Gruntz records *Noon in Tunisia* with Tunisian musicians and then *From Sticksland with Love* with Basel drum and fife corps (June). Jazz returns to Donaueschingen—with Archie Shepp, the Globe Unity Orchestra and *Jazz Meets India* (Oct.). Berlin Jazz Days themed around *Jazz Meets the World* and include Tony Scott and the Indonesian All-Stars, *Jazz Meets India* and Pedro Iturralde's *Flamenco Jazz* (Nov.).

1968 West German opposition to Vietnam War escalates. Attempted assassination of student leader Rudi Dutschke (April). West Germany passes emergency laws. Peter Brötzmann records the free jazz *Machine Gun* (May). Pop-jazz causes controversy among critics. Don Cherry's *Eternal Rhythm* and Barney Wilen's *Auto Jazz* performed at the Jazz Days. Free jazz musicians stage an "Anti-Festival" in Berlin.

1969 SPD's Willy Brandt elected as Chancellor. *Wild Goose* recorded (Feb.). *Noon in Tunisia* film shot in Tunisia (May). Independent German jazz labels FMP and ECM are founded.

1970 First phase of Baader-Meinhof (RAF) terrorism launched (May). Berendt curates the World Expo jazz festival in Osaka. Globe Unity Orchestra and Sun Ra perform in Donaueschingen. Berendt holds a public forum at the Jazz Days to discuss opposition to the festival. Don Cherry performs "Universal," a piece based on a raga, at the Baden-Baden Free Jazz Meeting.

1971 Billy Brooks records *El Babaku* in Berlin (May). Berendt resigns from the role of artistic director of the Jazz Days, but stays on as advisor. Siegfried Schmidt-Joos criticizes Berendt's artistic directorship of the Jazz Days in *Der Spiegel* (July). Cherry performs another piece engaging with Indian music at Donaueschingen (Oct.). "Now Music Night" attempts to bring the renegade Total Music Meeting on board with the Jazz Days, but fails (Nov.).

1972 RAF leaders arrested. Munich Olympics include a jazz festival curated by Berendt, but are marred by Israeli hostage crisis. Brandt signs a reconciliatory Basic Treaty with the GDR. Berendt's money-hungry and domineering practices are attacked by Schmidt-Joos in *Der Spiegel* (Oct.). John Handy—Ali Akbar Khan, Don Cherry—Dollar Brand/Abdullah Ibrahim and other ensembles perform in an "Encounters" session at the Jazz Days.

1975 SWF celebrates its 5,000th jazz broadcast (Oct.). Berendt produces the Handy-Khan ensemble's *Karuna Supreme* and a *Jazz Meets the World* compilation for MPS. He also writes articles on spirituality in jazz, and on proto-fascist aesthetics in music, the latter proving extremely controversial.

1977 The German Autumn commences when a second generation of RAF terrorists kidnap Hanns-Martin Schleyer, and climaxes with the execution of Schleyer and the suicide of the first generation terrorists imprisoned in Stammheim. Frankfurt freelance critic Wilhlem Liefland savages Berendt's most recent book, *A Window out of Jazz*, and then attacks his personal practices.

1978 George Gruntz tours Tunisia for the Goethe Institut. Berendt's son Christian dies. He relinquishes his artistic directorship of Berlin's Jazz in the Garden series, thereby reducing his regular commitments to the adjuncts to his SWF employment—namely Donaueschingen and the Baden-Baden New Jazz Meeting.

1980 Berendt writes articles on jazz and Indian music, stressing spiritual dimensions. Produces *Rainbow*, the Handy-Khan ensemble's second album (Sept.).

1981 Berendt begins to write articles about *Weltmusik*.

1982 Helmut Schmidt's SPD government unseated and Helmut Kohl becomes Chancellor. George Wein commissions Berendt to curate a "Jazz and World Music" concert at New York's Kool Jazz Festival (including Don Cherry's *Codona* group, a Handy-Khan ensemble and Karl Berger's "Music Universe Orchestra").

1983 Berendt becomes a follower of the Bhagwan, sells his jazz archive to the City of Darmstadt, receives an honorary professorship, and writes his New Age cult bestseller, *Nada Brahma*. Musi-

cians from various traditions perform a "Percussion Meeting" at Baden-Baden.
1984 Berendt receives the *Bundesverdienstkreuz* public honor. Donaueschingen features an intercultural "Percussion Summit," and Berendt stages a "*Weltmusik* Meeting" for the SWF (Nov.).
1985 Berendt writes an extended essay on *Weltmusik* (March) and Donaueschingen includes a *Weltmusik* summit (Oct.). His second New Age book, *The Third Ear*, is published.
1987 Berendt takes early retirement in the face of his criticism of SWF management for its CDU/CSU political bias. His involvement with the German jazz scene then reduces markedly, but he continues his schedule of writing and speaking about New Age topics. Peter Niklas Wilson and Peter Sloterdijk criticize Berendt's concept of *Weltmusik* and his New Age musico-philosophy.
1988 The City of Darmstadt mounts its encyclopedic exhibition *That's Jazz – The Sound of the 20th Century*. Berendt marries for the fourth time.
1989 The Berlin Wall falls.
1996 George Gruntz and his Western and Tunisian colleagues perform *Tunisian Journey* in Cologne (Sept.). Berendt publishes his memoir.
2000 Berendt dies in Hamburg after being hit by a car (Feb.).

Discography

NB. This discography contains only Berendt's *Jazz Meets the World*, *Weltmusik*, and related productions. Details of the Saba/MPS records have been reproduced from Klaus-Gotthard Fischer's discography, *Jazzin' the Black Forest* (1999), with kind permission from Monitorpop.

Instruments and Abbreviations

agogo	Brazilian cowbell
apito	Brazilian percussion instrument
arr	arranger
as	alto saxophone
atabaque	Brazilian percussion instrument
b	contrabass
bandoneon	South American accordion
bars	baritone saxophone
b-cl	bass clarinet
bendire	round frame drum from (Islamic) North Africa
berimbau	Brazilian musical bow
b-fl	bass flute
b-koto	bass koto (*see* koto)
b-s	bass saxophone
cavaquinho	Brazilian miniature guitar, not unlike a ukelele
cgas	conga (hand) drums
cl	clarinet
cond	conductor
cor	cornet

"cucumber"	friction percussion instrument
cuica	Brazilian friction drum
darbouka	hourglass-shaped hand drum from North Africa and the Middle East
dr	drum kit
dun-dun	African drum
el-p	electric piano
fl	flute
flexatone	percussion instrument
flh	fluegelhorn
g	guitar
gender	Indonesian metallophone with bamboo resonators
Haitian gourd	Haitian shaker
Koto	Japanese psaltery
lotus-fl	lotus flute
mani-tom	a drum whose pitch can be altered by blowing air into its body (devised by Mani Neumeier)
maracas	pair of Latin American hand-held shakers
marimba	African and Central American wooden xylophone-like instrument
mezoued	Tunisian bagpipe
nai	North African and Middle Eastern flute
org	organ
p	piano
pandeiro	Brazilian percussion instrument
pau	Brazilian percussion instrument
perc	percussion
prep-p	prepared piano (i.e., a piano where objects have been inserted into the strings so as to modify the timbre and tones produced when the piano is played)
reco-reco	Brazilian percussion instrument
sarod	North Indian lute with both played and resonance strings
saron	Indonesian metallophone as used in the gamelan
shakuhachi	Japanese bamboo flute
sitar	Indian lute with both played and resonance strings
siter (ketjapi)	Indonesian zither

sopranino-s	sopranino saxophone
ss	soprano saxophone
steel drum	Caribbean drum created from modifying a 44-gallon drum
surdo	Brazilian percussion instrument
tabla	pair of North Indian hand drums
tamb	tamborine
tambura	Indian lute used as a drone instrument
tom tom	a type of drum
tb	trombone
temple blocks	percussion instrument
tp	trumpet
trad	traditional (author unknown)
ts	tenor saxophone
vibes	vibraphone
viol	violin
voc	vocals/singing
zorna	Turkish shawm
zoukra	Tunisian bagpipe shawm

Pre-*Jazz Meets the World* Productions

1962

Various musicians. *The Music From Bali.* Dutch Philips 831 210 PY.

Recorded: March, April 1962, Bona, Bedulu, Sanur, Midjil & Iseh, Bali.

Personnel: Various.

Tracks:
a. The Ketjak of Bona;
b. Tabohr Tiga – Plajon (Gamelan Orchestra "Gong Gede of Bedulu");
c. Legong (Orchestra Pelegonggan of Abian-Kapas);
d. Margapati (Gamelan Orchestra "Gong Gede of Midjil");
e. Tluktak – Ginada (Geng Gong of Iseh);
f. Panji Semaran (parts 1 & 2) (Gamelan Orchestra "Gong Gede of Midjil").

Prod.: Berendt.

Cover notes: Berendt.

1964

Albert Mangelsdorff Quintet. *Now Jazz Ramwong.* German CBS 62 398.

Recorded: 6–7 June 1964, Walldorf bei Frankfurt am Main.

Personnel: Albert Mangelsdorff tb; Günter Kronberg as; Heinz Sauer ts, ss; Günter Lenz b; Ralf Hübner dr.

Tracks:
a. Now Jazz Ramwong (trad., arr. Mangelsdorff);
b. Sakura Waltz (trad., arr. Mangelsdorff);
c. Blue Fanfare (Mangelsdorff);
d. Three Jazz Moods (on a theme by Ravi Shankar, based on a Bengali folk song, arr. Mangelsdorff);
e. Burungkaka (trad., arr. Mangelsdorff);
f. Raknash (Lenz – Hübner);
g. Theme from Vietnam (Mangelsdorff);
h. Es sungen drei Engel (trad., arr. Mangelsdorff).

Prod.: Horst Lippmann.

Cover notes: Berendt, Lippmann, and Quintet members.

1965

Various musicians. *Jazz Greetings from the East.* German Fontana 885 416 TY.

Recorded: Various dates (in Eastern Europe).

Personnel: Various.

Tracks:
a. Roman II (Komeda Quintet, Poland);
b. Piontawka (Namyslowski Quartet, Poland);
c. Family Chronicle (S+H Jazz Group, Czechoslovakia);
d. The Man with the Top Hat (Janci Körössy and Jazz Studio Prague, Rumania and Czechoslovakia);
e. Mister Great Novgorod (Wadim Sakun Sextet, Russia);
f. Dalia (Aladar Pege Trio, Hungary);
g. Mit Schmerz Ward ich Geboren (Zagreb Jazz Quartet, Yugoslavia);
h. Concerto No. 2 for Big Band (Miljenko Prohaska and his Radio Zagreb Big Band, Yugoslavia).

Compiler: Berendt (supervision, Siegfried E. Loch).

Cover notes: Berendt.

The *Jazz Meets the World* series

* – indicates a track included on Berendt's 1975 *Jazz Meets the World* compilation (MPS 52023).

1965

Hideo Shiraki Quintet and Three Koto Girls. *Sakura Sakura.* **Saba SB 15064.**

Recorded: 1 November 1965, Berlin.

Personnel: Terumasa Hino tp (c-f); Takeru Muraoka ts, ss, fl (b-d, f); Yuzura Sera p; Hachiro Kurita b; Hideo Shiraki dr; Kinuko Shirane koto (a, c, d, f); Keiko Nosaka koto (a, c, d, f); Sachiko Miyamoto b-koto (a, d, f).

Tracks:
a. Sakura Sakura (trad., arr. Yashiro) (*);
b. Yosakoi-Bushi (trad., arr. Muraoka);
c. Yamanaka-Bushi (trad., arr. Muraoka);
d. Matsuri No Genzo (Yashiro) (*);
e. Alone, Alone and Alone (Takaka Hino, arr. Takaka Hino);
f. Suwa (Terumasa Hino).

Prod.: Berendt.

Cover notes: Shoichi Yui.

Sakura Sakura was also performed live in Berlin on 29 October 1965.

1966

Baden Powell. *Tristeza on Guitar.* **Saba SB 15090.**

Recorded: 1–2 June 1966, Rio de Janeiro.

Personnel: Copinha fl (a) agogo (i); Baden Powell g, agogo (b), surdo (i); Sergio b (a-c, f, j); Alfredo Bessa atabaque (b, e, i) cuica (d); Amauri Coelha Da Rosa atabaque (d), pandeiro (b, e, i); Milton Banana dr (a, b, d, i, j).

Tracks:
a. Tristeza (Lobo – Nitinho);
b. Canto de Xango (Powell – de Moraes);
c. Round About Midnight (Monk – Williams, arr. Powell) (*);
d. Sarava (Powell);
e. Canto de Ossanha (Powell – de Moraes);
f. Manha de Carnaval (Bonfa – Maria) 3:10;

g. Invençao em 7 (Powell);
h. Das Rosas (Caymmi);
i. Som do Carnaval (Powell – Copinha);
j. O Astronauta (Powell – de Moraes).

Prod.: Berendt; Wadi Gebara Netto.

Cover notes: Berendt.

Berendt also produced three additional records by Baden Powell for the Saba/MPS label (*Poema on Guitar* [1967] Saba SB 15150; *Canto on Guitar* [1970] MPS 15300; and *Images on Guitar* [1971] MPS 15328).

Various Musicians. *Folklore e Bossa Nova do Brasil.* Saba SB 15102.

Recorded: 14 November 1966, Villingen.

Personnel: J. T. Meirelles ts (d), fl (e, h, k, l), reco-reco (c), tamb (l); Salvador da Silva Filho p (d-h, k, l), agogo (d, l); Rosinha da Valença g (b, c, i, l) tamb (g), cavaquinho (l); Edu Lobo g (h, k), voc (h, k, l); Sérgio Portella Barroso (c- h, k, l), tamb (l), reco-reco (d); Rubens Bassini atabaque (a, h), pandeiro (c, d, g, l), pau (h); Jorge Arena apito (d), atabaque (a, c, d, h), berimbau (l); Chico Batera dr (d-h, k, l), agogo (a), tamb ((c), cuica (l); Sylvia Telles voc (g, i, l).

Tracks:
a. Macumba (trad.);
b. Uma Noite (trad.: Codo);
c. Tema Pro Luis (Pessoa);
d. O Orvalho Vem Caindo (Rosa –Pepe);
e. O Barquinho (Menescal – Boscoli);
f. Meu Fraco é Café Forte (da Silva Filho);
g. Discussão (Jobim – Mendonça);
h. Upa Neguinho (Lobo – Guarnieri);
i. Dindi (Jobim – de Oliveira) (*);
j. Pra Dizer Adeus (Lobo – Netto);
k. Finale: Berimbau (Powell – de Moraes)/ Cuica (Batera)/ Cavaquinho (de Valença)/ Tristeza (H. Lobo – Nitinho) (* - extract).

Prod.: Berendt.

Cover notes: Berendt.

Musicians assembled in Brazil by Berendt and Horst Lippmann for the Berlin Jazz Days and for a European tour organized by Lippmann and Rau.

The troupe performed live at the Berlin Jazz Days on 4 November 1966.

Alexander von Schlippenbach (and the Globe Unity Orchestra). *Globe Unity.* Saba SB 15109.

Recorded: 6–7 December 1966, Cologne.

Personnel: Claude Deron tp, lotus-fl (b); Manfred Schoof cor, flh, triangle (b); Willi Lietzmann tuba, maracas (b); Peter Brötzmann as, cucumber (b); Gerd Dudek ts, duck-call (b); Kris Wanders bars, zorna (b), as (b), lotus-fl (b); Willem Breuker bars, ss, ratchet (b); Gunter Hampel b-cl, fl, pandeira (b); Karlhanns Berger vibes (b); Buschi Niebergall b, siren (b); Peter Kowald b, bells (b); Jaki Liebezeit dr, kettledrums (b), temple blocks (b), darbouka (b); Mani Neumeier dr, tom tom (b), gongs (b), woodblocks (b), tabla (b), mani-tom (b); Alexander von Schlippenbach p, tubular bells, tom tom, gongs, knife (b), flexatone (b).

Tracks:
a. Globe Unity (Schlippenbach);
b. Sun (Schlippenbach);

Prod.: Berendt.

Liner notes: Berendt and von Schlippenbach.

"Globe Unity" was first performed on 3 November 1966 at the Berlin Jazz Days. It was also performed on 21 October 1967 at the Donaueschingen Music Days.

In 1967 and 1968, Berendt included the record in the *Jazz Meets the World* series, although he dropped it later on.

1967

The *Jazz Meets the World* series was launched in the May edition of *Jazz Podium*. It included *Sakura Sakura, Tristeza on Guitar* and *Folklore e Bossa Nova do Brasil*, and was forecast to include *Noon in Tunisia, From Sticksland with Love, Flamenco Jazz, Djanger Bali*, and the never-to-eventuate *New Jazz from Russia*.

George Gruntz et al. *Noon in Tunisia.* Saba SB 15132.

Recorded: 1–2 June 1967, Villingen.

Personnel: Sahib Shihab ss, fl, tamb; George Gruntz p, arr, cond; Jean-Luc Ponty viol; Eberhard Weber b; Daniel Humair dr; Salah El Mahdi nai, darbouka, bendire; Jelloul Osman mezoued; Moktar Slama zoukra; Hattab Jouini tabla, darbouka, bendire.

Tracks:
a. Salhé (arr. Gruntz) (*);

b. Maghreb Cantata (Gruntz);
   Is Tikhbar;
   Ghitta;
   Alaji;
   Djerbi;
   M'rabaa;
   Buanuara (*);
   Fazani (*);
c. Nemeit (Gruntz).

Prod.: Berendt.

Cover notes: Berendt.

Noon in Tunisia was also performed live in Tunisia in May 1969, when Gruntz, Shihab, Don Cherry (tp, fl), Henri Texier (b), and Daniel Humair performed with El Mahdi et al. for a 60-minute film version shot by Peter Lilienthal for SWF TV. The project was revived again on 15 September 1969 for a SWF concert at the Stuttgart Radio Exhibition, and then again—without Berendt's involvement—on 2 July 1971 at the Ossiach Music Festival in Austria. On this occasion, the jazzmen were Gruntz (el-p); John Surman (ss); Jean-Luc Ponty (viol); Barre Phillips (b); Stu Martin (dr). El Mahdi et al. also performed, as did a Tunisian liturgical choir, which gave a separate concert. Another revival took place at the 1974 German Jazz Festival in Frankfurt am Main. In 1978, Gruntz, Manfred Schoof (tp), Gerd Dudek (ss, ts), Eberhard Weber (b), and Fredy Studer (dr) traveled to North Africa on a Goethe Institut tour, again collaborating with a group of Tunisian musicians. *Noon in Tunisia* was most recently revisited on 13 September 1996 in Cologne.

George Gruntz *et al. From Sticksland with Love: Drums and Folklore.* Saba SB 15133.

Recorded: 22–3 June 1967, Basel (live).

Personnel: Franco Ambrosetti tp; Nathan Davis ts, ss; George Gruntz p, cond; Jimmy Woode b; Charly Antolini dr, Daniel Humair dr, kettledrums; Pierre Favre dr, Mani Neumeier dr, mani-tom, cgas; Alfred Sacher and the Tambouren Gruppe; George Mathys and the Pfeifer Gruppe.

Tracks:
a. D'Reemer (trad., arr. Gruntz);
b. From Sticksland with Love "s'Bysiwätter" (Gruntz);
c. Hightime Keepsakes "Glettere Foxtrott" (Gruntz);
d. Intercourse "Ein noon em andere wie z Barys" (Gruntz);
e. Change of Air "s'Nunnefirzli" (Gruntz) (*);

f. Sketches for percussion "Iber 8 git's Stämpeneye" (Gruntz);
g. Retraite Celeste (Gruntz) (*).

Prod.: Berendt.

Cover notes: Berendt.

The project was revived in Basel on 31 March 1974.

Dewan Motihar trio, Irène Schweizer Trio, Manfred Schoof, and Barney Wilen. *Jazz Meets India.* **Saba SB 15142.**

Recorded: 23 October 1967, Villingen.

Personnel: Manfred Schoof tp, cor; Barney Wilen ss, ts; Irène Schweizer p; Uli Trepte b; Mani Neumeier dr; Dewan Motihar sitar, voc; Keshav Sathe tabla; Kusum Thakur tambura.

Tracks:
a. Sun Love (Motihar – Neumeier);
b. Yaad (Motihar);
c. Brigach and Ganges (Schoof) (* - extract).

Prod.: Berendt.

Cover notes: Berendt.

The group performed on 21 October 1967 at the Donaueschingen Music Days and then in Berlin on 2 November 1967.

Tony Scott and the Indonesian All-Stars. *Djanger Bali.* **Saba SB 15145.**

Recorded: 27–8 October 1967, Villingen.

Personnel: Tony Scott cl; Marjono ts, fl, voc; Bubi Chen p, siter (ketjapi); Jack Lesmana g; Yopi Chen b; Benny Mustafa dr.

Tracks:
a. Djanger Bali (trad., arr. Scott, B. Chen) (*);
b. Mahlke from "Katz und Maus" (Zoller);
c. Gambang Suling (Sabdo);
d. Ilir, Ilir (trad., arr. Scott, Marjono);
e. Burungkaka Tua (trad., arr. B. Chen, Scott);
f. Summertime (Gershwin).

Prod.: Berendt.

Cover notes: Berendt.

The group performed in Berlin on 2 November 1967. It also performed various concerts in Germany, Switzerland, and the Netherlands during October.

Pedro Iturralde Quintet and Paco de Lucia. *Flamenco Jazz.* Saba SB 15143.

Recorded: 3 November 1967, Berlin.

Personnel: Dino Piana tb; Pedro Iturralde ts, arr.; Paul Grassl p; Paco de Lucia g; Eric Peter b; Peer Wyboris dr.

Tracks:
a. Valeta de tu Viento (Iturralde);
b. Cancion de las Penas de Amor (de Falla);
c. El Vito (Iturralde);
d. Cancion del Fuego Fatuo (de Falla).

Prod.: Berendt.

Cover notes: Olaf Hudtwalcker.

The group performed in Berlin on 2 November 1967.

1968

Barney Wilen. *Auto Jazz: Tragic Destiny of Lorenzo Bandini.* MPS 15164.

Recorded: 23 February 1968, Ludwigsburg.

Personnel: Barney Wilen ts; Francois Tusques p, prep-p, org; Beb Guerin b; Eddy Gaumont dr; soundtrack of 25th Grand Prix d'Automobile de Monaco (7 May 1967) Lorenzo Bandini Sefac Ferrari.

Tracks:
a. Tragic destiny of Lorenzo Bandini (Wilen)
   Expectancy "Bandini Bandini" – Announcements – National Anthem –In the Pits;
   Start;
   Tribune Princiere;
   Hair Pin (Virage des Gazometres);
   Canyon Sounds and Destiny (* – extract).

Prod.: Berendt.

Cover notes: Berendt.

Auto Jazz was also performed on 9 November 1968 in Berlin. The record was only retrospectively included in the *Jazz Meets the World* series.

Don Cherry. *Eternal Rhythm*. MPS 15204.

Recorded: 11–12 November 1968, Berlin.

Personnel: Don Cherry cor, fl, saron, Haitian gourd, bells, voice; Albert Mangelsdorff tb; Eje Thelin tb; Bernt Rosengren ts, oboe, cl, fl; Karl Berger p, vibes, gender; Joachim Kühn p, prep-p, Sonny Sharrock g; Arild Anderson b, Jacques Thollot dr, saron, gong, bells, voice.

Tracks:
a. Eternal Rhythm, Part One (Cherry):
   Baby's Breath – "Sonny Sharrock" – Turkish Prayer – Crystal Clear (Exposition) – Endless Beginnings – Baby's Breath (*);
b. Eternal Rhythm, Part Two (Cherry):
   Autumn Melody – Lanoo – Crystal Clear (Development) – Screaming J – Always Beginnings.

Prod.: Berendt.

Cover notes: Berendt.

Eternal Rhythm was also performed, with slightly different personnel, on 9 November 1968 in Berlin. The record was only retrospectively included in the *Jazz Meets the World* series.

1969

Colin Wilkie, Shirley Hart, Albert Mangelsdorff, Joki Freund et al. *Wild Goose*. MPS 15229.

Recorded: 2 February 1969, Walldorf bei Frankfurt am Main.

Personnel: Albert Mangelsdorff tb; Emil Mangelsdorff as, fl; Joki Freund ts, ss, arr.; Heinz Sauer ts, as; Günter Kronberg bars; Günter Lenz b; Ralf Hübner dr, darbouka, tamb; Colin Wilkie voc, g; Shirley Hart voc.

Tracks:
a. Icy Acres (Wilkie) (*);
b. Fourth Flight (trad., arr Freund – Wilkie);
c. Snowy Sunday (Wilkie);
d. Willow and Rue (Wilkie);
e. Lament (Wilkie);
f. Ich Armes Maidlein Klag Mich Sehr (trad., arr. Freund);
g. Sweet Primrose (trad., arr Freund).

Prod.: Ulrich Olshausen and Berendt.

Cover notes: Olshausen.

Wild Goose was only retrospectively included in the *Jazz Meets the World* series.

1971

El Babaku. *Live at the Jazz Galerie.* MPS 15314.

Recorded: 3 May 1971, Berlin (live).

Personnel: Billy Brooks (a.k.a. Bilal Abdul Hakeem) dr, bamboo fl, block b-fl, dun-dun; Carlos Santa Cruz cgas, voc, tamb, cowbell; Donald Coleman cgas, cowbell, voc; Charles Campbell cgas, voc; Burt Thompson b, voc.

Tracks:
a. El Babaku (Brooks);
b. Orisha (trad., arr. Brooks);
c. Aino Buca (trad. Cuban arr. Santa Cruz) (* – extract);
d. Al Hajj Malik Al Shabazz – For Malcolm X (Brooks);
e. Lament (trad. Nigerian – Warren, arr. Brooks);
f. El Lupe Chango (trad. Nigerian and Cuban, arr. Brooks).

Prod.: Berendt.

Cover notes: Berendt and Brooks.

Other Intercultural Concerts and *Weltmusik* Productions.

1970

Don Cherry attends the 1970 Baden-Baden Free Jazz Meeting, where he performs "Universal," a piece based on a raga.

1971

Cherry and the New Eternal Rhythm Orchestra perform his "Humus – the Life Exploring Force" (another piece engaging with Indian music) at the Donaueschingen Music Days on 17 October 1971.

1972

Berendt and Gruntz present an "Encounters" session at the Berlin Jazz Days on 3 November 1972. This includes performances by the Khan–Handy ensemble (Ali-Akbar Khan (sarod), John Handy (as), and Zakir Hussain (tabla)); the Terje Rypdal Trio (Rypdal (g), Barre Phillips (b) and Jon Christenson (dr); and the Don Cherry-Dollar Brand Quartet (Cherry (tr, fl), Brand (p), Marshall Hawkins (b), and Jimmy Hopps (dr)). The Khan–Handy group combine jazz and Indian music, Rypdal's

Trio combine elements of concert music and the Cherry–Brand Quartet draw on South-African music.

1975

John Handy and Ali Akbar Khan. *Karuna Supreme.* MPS 15455.

Recorded: 1–2 November 1975, Ludwigsburg.

Personnel: John Handy as; Ali Akbar Khan sarod; Zakir Hussain tabla; Yogish S. Sahota tambura.

Tracks:
a. Ganesha's Jubilee Dance (A. A. Khan – Handy);
b. Karuna Supreme (A. A. Khan);
c. The Soul And The Atma (A. A. Khan – U. A. Khan).

Prod.: Berendt.

Cover notes: Berendt.

The Handy–Khan ensemble also performed at an October 1975 concert celebrating the 5,000th jazz broadcast by the SWF.

1980

John Handy, Ali Akbar Khan, Dr L. Subramaniam. *Rainbow.* MPS 15576.

Recorded: 3–4 September 1980, Villingen.

Personnel: John Handy as; Ali Akbar Khan sarod; Dr L. Subramaniam viol; Shyam Kane tabla; Mary Johnson tambura.

Tracks:
a. Rajashik – The Magic of Wisdom (Khan);
b. Indian Boogie Shoes (Handy);
c. Rainbow Serenade (Subramaniam);
d. Garland of Flowers – Alap and Jod in Raga Mala (Khan – Handy – Subramaniam);
e. Kali Dance (Subramaniam).

Prod.: Berendt.

Cover notes: Berendt.

1982

Berendt presents a "Jazz and World Music" concert with Don Cherry's *Codona* group, a Handy–Khan ensemble and a "Music Universe Orchestra" under the leadership of Karl Berger and consisting of musicians from the United States, Europe, India, Brazil, Turkey, Japan, and Senegal at the 1982 Kool Jazz Festival in New York.

1983

Berendt invites percussionists from different traditions (India, Turkey, Cuba, Africa, Europe, and the United States) to the Baden-Baden New Jazz Meeting in November for a "Percussion Meeting."

1984

Berendt presents an intercultural "Percussion Summit" at the Donaueschingen Music Days in October.

Various Musicians. *World Music Meeting.* Eigelstein ES 2024

Recorded: 23 November 1984, Mainz (live).

Personnel: Hozan Yamamoto shakuhachi; Krzesmir Debski viol; Charlie Mariano as, ss; Alfred 23 Harth ss, ts, b-cl, tp; Juan Jose Mosalini bandoneon; Karl Berger, vibes, p, marimba; Peter Kowald b; Ken Johnson steel drum, cgas, perc; Ponda O'Bryan African drums, cgas, perc; Trilok Gurtu tabla, d, perc; Barry Altshul d.

Tracks:
a. Again and again, again (C. Wallcott, arr Berger);
b. Naomi (Mosalini);
c. Kaze (Yamamoto);
d. Pascha Love (Gurtu);
e. Eujapica (Yamamoto – Mosalini – Debski).

Prod.: Berendt (assisted by Werner Wunderlich).

This was a live recording of the 1984 Baden-Baden New Jazz Meeting, which assembled musicians from the United States, Europe, South America, the Caribbean, Africa, India, and Japan.

1985

Various Musicians. *To Hear The World in a Grain of Sand.* Soul Note SN 1128.

Recorded: 19 October 1985, Donaueschingen (live).

Personnel: Connie Bauer tb; Lennart Aberg sopranino-s, ss, ts, fl; Bernd Konrad ss, ts, bars, b-s; Luis di Matteo bandoneon; Vikash Maharaj sarod;

Tom van der Geld vibes, marimba; Rudy Smith steel drum, cgas; David Friesen b; Pandit Prakash Maharaj tabla; Dom Um Romao perc; Andrew Cyrille d.

Tracks:
a. Hinglaj (P. Maharaj);
b. Six Rivers (Bauer);
c. To Hear the World in a Grain of Sand (Konrad);
d. Firefly (Um Romao).

Prod.: Berendt (assisted by Werner Wunderlich; executive producer Giovanni Bonandrini.

Cover notes: Berendt.

Recorded live at the Donaueschingen Music Days. The summit assembled musicians from Europe, South America, India, the Caribbean, the United States, and Brazil.

Works Cited

"10 Jahre MPS-Records." 1974. *Jazz Podium* (April): 20–21.
"17 Fragen an Mani Neumeier." 1967. *Sounds* 4: 11.
Adorno, Theodor W. 1936. "On Jazz." In *Essays on Music*, ed. Richard Leppert. trans. Susan H. Gillespie. Berkeley, Los Angeles and London: University of California Press, 2002, 470–95 [1936].
———. 1937. "Oxforder Nachträge." In *Moments musicaux*. Frankfurt am Main: Suhrkamp, 1964, 115–24 [1937].
———. 1953a. "Für und wider den Jazz." *Merkur* 7: 890–3.
———. 1953b. "Perennial fashion—jazz." In *Prisms*. trans. Samuel and Shierry Weber. Cambridge, Mass.: MIT Press, 1981, 121–32 [1953].
———. 1962. *Introduction to the Sociology of Music*. trans. E.B. Ashton. New York: Seabury Press, 1976 [1962].
———, and Max Horkheimer. 1947. *Dialektik der Aufklärung*. Frankfurt am Main: Fischer Taschenbuchverlag, 1969 [1947].
Altgelt, Erika. 1958. "Jazz am kleinen Wannsee." *Berliner Berichte* newspaper clipping. Berendt Papers. Jazzinstitut, Darmstadt.
Anders, Johannes. 1972. "Für Toleranz und contra Vorurteile. Gespräch mit George Gruntz." *Jazz Podium* (November): 15–17.
———. 1975. "Attraktive Ausweitung des SWF-Jazzprogramm-Angebots." *Jazz Podium* (January): 17.
Ansell, Gwen. 2004. *Soweto Blues*. New York and London: Continuum Books.
"Anti-Festival Berlin." 1968. *Sounds* 9: 4.
Artus, Helmut M. 1976. "John Handy/Ali Akbar Khan." *Jazz Podium* (September): 34–6.
Atkins, E. Taylor. 2001. *Blue Nippon: Authenticating Jazz in Japan*. Durham, N.C.: Duke University Press.
Ausländer, Peter, and Johannes Fritsch, eds. 1981. *Weltmusik*. Cologne: Feedback Studio.
"Avantgarde-Treffen beim Südwestfunk." 1966. *Jazz Podium* (December): 316.
Bachmann, Klaus Robert. 1975a. "Das Freiburger Jubiläumskonzert zur 5000. Jazz-Sendung des SWF." *Jazz Podium* (December): 22.
———. 1975b. "Jazz als pädagogische Leidenschaft." *Jazz Podium* (December): 23.
———. 1975c. "New Jazz Meeting Baden Baden." *Jazz Podium* (January): 15.
———. 1977. "Fensterstoß mit Zivilcourage." *Badische Zeitung*, 15 & 16 October.

———. 1985. "'Weltmusik' – mal Stil und mal nur Stilisierung." *Jazz Podium* (December): 24.
Back, Jack. 1948. *Triumph des Jazz*. trans. Hardo Nüring. Vienna: Alfa.
Baraka, Amiri/Leroi Jones. 1963. *Blues People: Negro Music in White America*. New York: W. Morrow.
Baresel, Alfred. 1926. *Das Jazzbuch*. Leipzig: Zimmermann.
Baumann, Max Peter, ed. 1991. *Music in the Dialogue of Cultures: Traditional Music and Cultural Policy*. Wilhelmshaven: Florian Noetzel Verlag.
Baumann, Peter. 1968. "Untitled Article." *Berliner Tagesspiegel* article. In *Berliner Jazztage Documentation*, ed. Rein.
Baur, Elke, dir. 2006. *Jazzin' the Black Forest*. Monitorpop Entertainment.
Bayles, Martha. 1994. *Hole in Our Soul: The Loss of Beauty and Meaning in American Popular Music*. New York: The Free Press.
Beatles, The. 1965. *Rubber Soul*. Parlophone, 1A 062-04115.
Ben Redjeb, Nouri. 1996. "Salah El Mahdi." *WDR Tunisreise* program notes: 15–16.
Bennett, David. 2005. "Postmodern Eclecticism and the World Music Debate: The Politics of the Kronos Quartet." *Context* 29 & 30: 5–15.
Berendt, Joachim-Ernst. 1950a. *Der Jazz: Eine zeitkritische Studie*. Stuttgart: Deutsche Verlagsanstalt.
———. 1950b. "Die Unterhaltungsmusik und der Rundfunk." *Melos* 17: 213–18.
———. 1951. "Americana." *Melos* 18: 78–82.
———. 1952a. *Bei Vollmond tanzt ganz Afrika*. SWF radio transcript. Berendt Papers. Jazzinstitut, Darmstadt.
———. 1952b. "Lena Horne. Die Story von Jim Crow." *Der Spiegel*, 9 July.
———. 1952c. "Salon du Jazz." *Melos* 19: 195–6.
———. 1952d. "Über den modernen Jazz." *Melos* 19: 100–103.
———. 1952e. "Vom 'schwarzen' Amerika." *Merkur* 6: 197–200.
———. 1952f. "Vom 'schwarzen' Amerika." Typescript. Berendt Papers. Jazzinstitut, Darmstadt.
———. 1952g. "Vom Stilkrieg im Jazz." *Bunte*, January.
———. 1952h. "War auch in Sosa dabei." *Der Spiegel*, 23 April.
———. 1953a. *Das Jazzbuch*. Frankfurt am Main and Hamburg: Fischer.
———. 1953b. "Für und wider den Jazz." *Merkur* 7: 887–90.
———. 1953c. "Zur Problematik der Unterhaltungsmusik." *Das Orchester* 1.2: 43–4.
———. 1954a. "Form und Rhythmus im modernen Jazz." *Melos* 21: 135–8.
———. 1954b. *Jazz-Optisch*. Munich: Nymphenburger Verlagshandlung.
———. 1954c. Letter to Herbert Weiß. 24 July. Berendt Papers. Jazzinstitut, Darmstadt.
———. 1954d. Letter to Stefan Buchholtz. 2 November. Berendt Papers. Jazzinstitut, Darmstadt.
———. 1954e. Letter to Stefan Buchholtz. 6 November. Berendt Papers. Jazzinstitut, Darmstadt.
———. 1954f. "3. Salon international du Jazz." *Jazz Podium* (August): 10.
———. 1955a. "Benny Goodman und die Begeisterung." *Die Schallplatte* (August): 11.
———. 1955b. "Jazz in Deutschland." *Colloquium* (April): 10–11.
———. 1955c. "Jazz in Europa." *Magnum* (July): 67–8.
———. 1955d. "John Lewis – König des Cool Jazz." *Melos* 22: 348–50.
———. 1955e. "Schwarz und Weiss in USA." *Frankfurter Hefte* 10: 787–98.

———. 1955f. "Schwarz unter Weiss. Zur Situation des Negers in den USA." *Gehört – Gelesen* (August): 732–49.
———. 1955g. "Schwarz unter Weiss. Zur Situation des Negers in den USA." Typescript. Berendt Papers. Jazzinstitut, Darmstadt.
———. 1956a. "Jazz in Germany." *Second Line* (June): 17–18.
———. 1956b. "Schwarz und Weiß in der Jazzmusik." *Frankfurter Allgemeine Zeitung*, 5 May.
———. 1956c. "Schwarz und Weiß in der Jazzmusik." Typescript. Berendt Papers. Jazzinstitut, Darmstadt.
———. 1956d. "Tanz als Ausbruch." *Deutsche Woche*, 21 November.
———. 1956e. *Variationen über Jazz: Aufsätze*. Munich: Nymphenburger Verlagshandlung.
———. 1957a. "5. Deutsches Jazz Festival." *Jazz Echo* (August): 40–44.
———, ed. 1957b. *Blues: Ein Essay*. Munich: Nymphenburger Verlagshandlung.
———. 1957c. "Der arrivierte Jazz." *Jazz Echo* (December): 40–41.
———. 1957d. "Der Einbruch des Technischen in die Musik." *Die Zeitwende* 28.1: 18–29.
———. 1957e. "Der Jazz schlug Brücken." *Musikalische Jugend* (August).
———. 1957f. "Jazz in West Germany." *Saturday Review*, 16 November.
———. 1957g. "Polnisches Jazz Festival 1957." *Jazz Echo* (September): 40–42.
———. 1958a. Review of *Knaurs Jazzlexikon*, ed. S. Longstreet and A.M. Dauer. *Jazz Echo* (March): 43–4.
———. 1958b. "Tanz als Ausbruch." In *Der Tanz in der modernen Gesellschaft*, ed. Heyer. Hamburg: Furche Verlag, 125–38.
———. 1958c. "Was halten Sie vom Jazz Herr Verteidigungsminister?" *Iserlohner Kreisanzeiger*, 22 August.
———. 1959a. *Das neue Jazzbuch*. Frankfurt am Main: Fischer.
———. 1959b. "Deutsche Jazz Szene 59." *Twen* (December): 35–7.
———. 1959c. "Die Situation des Jazz in Deutschland 1959." *Der Musikmarkt* (March): 14.
———. 1959d. "Ist der Jazz müde geworden?" *Stuttgarter Zeitung*, 1 April.
———. 1959e. *Jazz-Optisch: Fan-Edition*. Munich: Nymphenburger Verlagshandlung.
———. 1959f. "Jazz und Neue Musik." In *Prisma*, eds. Berendt and Uhde, 183–201.
———. 1959g. "Keine Angst vor Maschinen." *Das Schlagzeug* (August): 22–3.
———. 1959h. "Künstlerische Wahrheit." *Das Schlagzeug* (March): 6–7.
———. 1959i. "Neutralisierter Protest." *Das Schlagzeug* (July): 22–3.
———. 1960a. "Cool + Bop." *Twen* (June): 45.
———. 1960b. "1959/60 Deutscher Jazz Poll." *Jazz Echo* (March): 40–41.
———. 1960c. "Rassenschranken in der Jazzwelt." *Jazz Echo* (November): 42.
———. 1960d. Review of *Change of the Century* by Ornette Coleman. *Jazz Echo* (November): 44.
———. 1960e. "Wider die Diktatur des harmonischen Gerüsts." *Jazz Echo* (January): 40–41.
———. 1961a. "2 Mal Geschimpft und 1 Mal Geweint." *Twen* (June & July): 57, 97.
———. 1961b. "Dixieland ist zur Epidemie geworden." *Die Welt*, 1 April.
———. 1961c. "Festivalitis." *Twen* (December): 97.
———. 1961d. "Jazz-Notizen." *Twen* (August & September): 15.
———. 1962a. "Amateure verdienen zu viel." *Twen* (April): 12–13.

———. 1962b. " 'Auch' ein Zeitalter der Angst." *Jazz Echo* (October): 40–42; (November): 40–42.

———. 1962c. "Berendt's Asienreise. I" *Twen* (September): 17, 20–23.

———. 1962d. Cover notes for *The Music from Bali*, by various musicians.

———. 1962e. "Deutsche ohne Plattenchance." *Twen* (December): 12–13.

———. 1962f. "Heute Kimono, morgen Swing." *Die Welt*, 8 September.

———. 1962g. "Jazz in Germany." *Downbeat*, 11 October: 22–3.

———. 1962h. "Jazz in Japan." *Downbeat*, 6 December: 15–16.

———. 1962i. "Jazz in Southeast Asia." *Downbeat*, 22 November: 17–18, 47.

———. 1962j. "Schwarz contra weiß." *Jazz Echo* (May): 40–41.

———, ed. 1962k. *Schwarzer Gesang II*. Munich: Nymphenburger Verlagshandlung.

———. 1962l. "Seine Majestät spielen Jazz." Newspaper clipping. Berendt Papers. Jazzinstitut, Darmstadt.

———. 1962m. "Twen präsentiert American Folk Blues Festival." *Twen* (October): 54 ff.

———. 1962n. "John Coltrane." *Twen* (November): 73 ff.

———. 1963a. "Berendt's Asienreise. II." *Twen* (January): 22–7.

———. 1963b. "Berendt's Asienreise. III." *Twen* (March): 16–20.

———. 1963c. "Die Bossa Nova Story." *Twen* (May): 36–41.

———. 1963d. "Jazz Notizen." *Twen* (June): 13.

———. 1963e. "Oh Jesus, my Jesus …" *Die Zeitwende* 24: 439–54.

———. 1964a. Cover notes for *Now Jazz Ramwong*, by the Albert Mangelsdorff Quintet.

———. 1964b. "Jazz für den fernen Osten. JEB berichtet über die Asien Tournee des Albert Mangelsdorff Quintets." *Jazz Podium* (June): 138–40.

———. 1964c. Berlin Jazz Days program notes.

———. 1964d. "Teutonic Tour." *Downbeat*, 10 September: 13–15.

———. 1965a. "Berendt's Mai Jazz." *Twen* (May): 110–11.

———. 1965b. "Berendt's Oktober Jazz." *Twen* (October): 119.

———. 1965c. "Freier Jazz und Serielle Musik." *Jazz Podium* (May): 116–17.

———. 1965d. "Jazz in Deutschland." *Stern*, 24 October.

———. 1965e. Berlin Jazz Days program notes.

———. 1965f. Cover notes for *Jazz Greetings from the East*, by various musicians.

———. 1966a. "Berendt's Juli Jazz." *Twen* (July): 20–21.

———. 1966b. "Berendt's August Jazz. Das gibt es: Free Jazz – made in Germany." *Twen* (August): 8–9.

———. 1966c. "Berendt's September Jazz." *Twen* (August): 114–15.

———. 1966d. "Europas Jazz formt sein Gesicht." *Twen* (March): 106–8.

———. 1966e. "Januar Jazz Notizen." *Twen* (January): 82–3.

———. 1966f. "Jazz auf türkischer Trommel." *Die Welt*, 4 November.

———. 1966g. "Jazzkritik in der Krise." *Die Welt*, 13 April.

———. 1966h. "Jazz Panorama." *Deutsches Panorama* (October).

———. 1966i. Review of *A Love Supreme*, by the John Coltrane Quartet. *Deutsches Panorama* (October).

———. 1966j. "J.E. Berendt's Dezember Jazz Notizen." *Twen* (December): 108–9.

———. 1966k. "J.E. Berendt's November Jazz-Notizien." *Twen* (November): 148–9.

———. 1966l. Berlin Jazz Days program notes.

———. 1966m. Review of the German Jazz Festival. *Downbeat*, 30 June: 38.

———. 1966n. "Zwischen zwei Stadien der Jazzkritik." *Jazz Podium* (May): 136–7.
———. 1966o. Cover notes for *Globe Unity*, by Alexander von Schlippenbach and the Globe Unity Orchestra.
———. 1966p. "Die Avantgarde und das Chaos." *Der Tagesspiegel*, 16 October.
———. 1967a. Cover notes for *Djanger Bali*, by Tony Scott and the Indonesian All-Stars.
———. 1967b. Cover notes for *Jazz Meets India*, by various musicians.
———. 1967c. Cover notes for *Noon in Tunisia*, by various musicians.
———. 1967d. "Free Jazz – der neue Jazz der sechziger Jahre." *Melos* 34: 343–52.
———. 1967e. "Free Jazz in Donaueschingen." Typescript. Berendt Papers. Jazzinstitut, Darmstadt.
———. 1967f. "'Ich muß zu meinem Gott beten.'" *Die Welt*, 17 August.
———. 1967g. "Indien – die uralte indische Musik." Typescript. Berendt Papers. Jazzinstitut, Darmstadt.
———. 1967h. "Jazz auf Saba." *Der Musikmarkt* newspaper clipping. Berendt Papers. Jazzinstitut, Darmstadt.
———. 1967i. "Jazz in Djakarta (Indonesien)." Typescript. Berendt Papers. Jazzinstitut, Darmstadt.
———. 1967j. "Jazz in Südostasien." *Jazz Podium* (September): 248–50.
———. 1967k. "Jazz Panorama." *Deutsches Panorama* (April): 47.
———. 1967l. Review of *On this Night*, by Archie Shepp. *Deutsches Panorama* (February): 61.
———. 1967m. "J.E. Berendt's Jazz Notizen." *Twen* (December): 132.
———. 1967n. Berlin Jazz Days program notes.
———. 1967o. Cover notes for *From Sticksland with Love*, by various musicians.
———. 1967p. "Jazzarbeit im Wandel der Zeit." *Jazz Podium* (March): 72–3.
———. 1968a. Cover notes for *Auto Jazz*, by Barney Wilen.
———. 1968b. Cover notes for *Eternal Rhythm*, by Don Cherry.
———. 1968c. *Das Jazzbuch. Von New Orleans bis Free Jazz*. Frankfurt am Main and Hamburg: Fischer.
———. 1968d. "Duo für Ferrari und Tenor-Saxophon." *Twen* (December): 56–7.
———. 1968e. "Gegen Festival?" *Jazz Podium* (November): 337.
———. 1968f. "Jazz Meets the World" *Der Musikmarkt*, 15 October: 54–6.
———. 1968g. Berlin Jazz Days program notes.
———. 1969a. "Apropos Berliner Jazztage." *Jazz Podium* (November): 397–9.
———. 1969b. "Berlin. Eine kritische Nachlese." *Twen* (January): 46–7.
———. 1969c. "Noon in Tunesia." *Jazz Podium* (September): 297–9.
———. 1969d. Berlin Jazz Days program notes.
———. 1970a. *Blues*. Cologne: Edition Gerig.
———. 1970b. "Den Schwarzen der USA fehlen die Politiker." *Frankfurter Hefte*: 339–42.
———. 1970c. "Old, old New Jazz." *Twen* (April): 150.
———. 1970d. Berlin Jazz Days program notes.
———. 1971a. "Chris McGregor's Brotherhood of Breath." Berlin Jazz Days program notes: 10.
———. 1971b. "Don Cherry." Typescript. Berendt Papers. Jazzinstitut, Darmstadt.
———. 1971c. "Impressions on Jazz in Japan." *Jazz Forum* 3 & 4: 81–3.
———. 1971d. "Observations on a Far East Tour." *Jazz Forum* 1: 66–7.
———. 1971e. Berlin Jazz Days program notes.

———. 1971f. Cover notes for *El Babaku*, by Billy Brooks and *El Babaku*.

———. 1972a. "In der Schußlinie." *Evangelischer Pressedienst Kirche und Rundfunk (Sonderdienst)*, 18 October.

———. 1972b. "Jazz und Manipulationen 'mit Unterstützung der ARD'? Zu den Vorwürfen des 'Spiegel.' " *Evangelischer Pressedienst Kirche und Rundfunk*, 18 October.

———. 1972c. Berlin Jazz Days program notes.

———. 1973. "John McLaughlin: Maestro der Synthese." *Stereo* (April): 22–6.

———. 1973/4. *The Jazz Book*, trans. Dan Morgenstern. Frogmore: Paladin, 1976 [1973/74] (original: *Das Jazzbuch. Von Rag bis Rock*. Frankfurt am Main: Fischer, 1973/74).

———. 1974a. "Deutscher Jazz '74" *Stereo* 16: 16–18.

———. 1974b. "John McLaughlin. Apocalypse: Symbol für den Untergang und Neubeginn?" *Stereo* (December): 18–19.

———. 1974c. "Seid umschlungen, Kontinente." *Deutsche Zeitung*, 8 March.

———. 1975a. Cover notes for *Jazz Meets the World*, by various musicians.

———, ed. 1975b. *The Story of Jazz*, trans. E.L.S. Consultant Linguists. London: Barrie and Jenkins, 1978 [1975] (original: *Die Story des Jazz*. Stuttgart: Deutsche Verlagsanstalt, 1975).

———. 1975c. "Japaner schreiben Jazzgeschichte." *Stereo* 26: 12–14.

———. 1975d. "Mit Jazz für Goethe durch Asien." *Deutsche Zeitung*, 2 May.

———. 1975e. "Mit Jazz für Goethe in Asien." *Badisches Tageblatt*, 27 May.

———. 1975f. "Schönheit, die ich meine. Der neue Faschismus in Jazz und Rock." *Die Weltwoche*, 12 November.

———. 1976a. "Nochmals: Schönheit, die ich meine." *Jazz Podium* (April): 6–8.

———. 1976b. "Schönheit, die ich meine. Der neue Faschismus in Jazz und Rock." *Jazz Podium* (January): 9–12.

———. 1977a. *Ein Fenster aus Jazz: Essays, Portraits, Reflexionen*. Frankfurt am Main: Fischer Taschenbuch Verlag, 1978 [1977].

———. 1977b. "Grenze der Kritik." In *W. Dauner's Urschrei ohne Echo?* eds. Bodenstein et al, 1979 [1977], 14.

———. 1977c. Letter to Wilhelm Liefland. 17 August. In *rundy*, 13 September.

———. 1978. *Jazz: A Photo History*, trans. William Odom. New York: Schirmer Books, 1979 [1978] (original: *Photo-Story des Jazz*. Frankfurt am Main: Wolfgang Krüger Verlag, 1978).

———. 1980a. Cover notes for *Now Jazz Ramwong*, by the Albert Mangelsdorff Quintet (reissue).

———. 1980b. "Jazz in Japan." *Jazz Podium* (August): 9–13.

———. 1980c. "Jazz und Indien." *Jazz Podium* (May): 4–8.

———. 1980d. "Jazz und Indien." *Jazz Podium* (June): 10–14.

———. 1981a. *Das große Jazzbuch. Von New Orleans bis Jazz-Rock*. Frankfurt am Main: Wolfgang Krüger Verlag.

———. 1981b. "Jazz mit Goethe und Fragezeichen." *Stereo* (March): 10–11.

———. 1981c. "I'll remember Sopot." *Jazz Forum* (May): 20–24.

———. 1981d. *Mein Lesebuch*. Frankfurt am Main: Fischer Taschenbuchverlag.

———. 1981e. "Über einen neuen Musikertyp." *Jazz Forum* (February): 53–6.

———. 1983. *Nada Brahma. Die Welt ist Klang*. Frankfurt am Main: Insel Verlag.

———. 1985a. *Nada Brahma. Die Welt ist Klang*. 2nd ed. Reinbek bei Hamburg: Rororo.

———. 1985b. "Über Weltmusik." *Jazz Podium* (March): 8–13.
———. 1985c. *Das Dritte Ohr.* Reinbek bei Hamburg: Rowohlt.
———. 1985d. "Das philharmonische Auge." *Mein heimliches Auge: Das Jahrbuch der Erotik.* 2: 48–49.
———. 1996a. *Das Leben: Ein Klang.* Munich: Droemersche Verlagsanstalt, 1998 [1996].
———. 1996b. "Jazz in Donaueschingen 1954–1994." In *Spiegel der Neuen Musik*, ed. Häusler, 408–16.
———. 1999. Interview. In *Jazzin' the Black Forest*, ed. K-G Fischer, 67–73.
———. n.d.a.. "Black and White." Typescript. Berendt Papers. Jazzinstitut, Darmstadt.
———. n.d.b.. "Curriculum vitae." Typescript. Berendt Papers. Jazzinstitut, Darmstadt.
———. n.d.c.. "Der 'Hate-' folgt die 'Love-Generation.' " Typescript. Berendt Papers. Jazzinstitut, Darmstadt.
———. n.d.d.. "Jazz in Germany." Typescript. Berendt Papers. Jazzinstitut, Darmstadt.
———. n.d.e.. "Man hat in den letzten Jahren …" Typescript. Berendt Papers. Jazzinstitut, Darmstadt.
———. n.d.f.. Review of "Israel", by the Miles Davis Nonet. Typescript. Berendt Papers. Jazzinstitut, Darmstadt.
———. n.d.g.. "Rock 'n' Roll." Typescript. Berendt Papers. Jazzinstitut, Darmstadt.
———. n.d.h.. "Musik ohne Grenzen." *Rheinischer Merkur* newspaper clipping. Berendt Papers. Jazzinstitut, Darmstadt.
———, and William Claxton. 1961. *Jazz-Life.* Offenburg (Baden): Burda Druck und Verlag.
———, and William Claxton. 2005. *Jazz-Life: A Journey for Jazz across America in 1960.* 2nd ed. Cologne: TASCHEN.
———, and Günther Huesmann. 1989. *Das Jazzbuch. Von New Orleans bis in die achtziger Jahre.* Frankfurt am Main: Wolfgang Krüger Verlag.
———, and Günther Huesmann. 2005. *Das Jazzbuch. Von New Orleans bis ins 20. Jahrhundert.* Frankfurt am Main: Fischer.
———, and Ralf Schulte-Bahrenberg. 1972. Letter to *Der Spiegel*, 16 October: 14.
———, and Archie Shepp. 1967. "Archie Shepp." Berlin Jazz Days program notes: 47.
———, and Josef Tröller. 1959. "Jazz und Alte Musik." In *Prisma*, eds. Berendt and Uhde, 162–82.
———, and Jürgen Uhde, eds. 1959. *Prisma der gegenwärtigen Musik.* Hamburg: Furche Verlag.
———, and Paridam von dem Knesebeck, eds. (1955). *Spirituals.* Munich: Nymphenburger Verlagshandlung, 1955.
"Berendt dreht Jazzfilm in den USA." *Jazz Podium* (August): 100.
Berger, Karl. 1967. "Musik der Weltvölker." *Sounds* 4: 30–31.
———. 1968a. "Blues und Swing sind überall." *Jazz Podium* (May): 152.
———. 1968b. "Blues und Swing sind überall." *Jazz Podium* (July): 211.
———. 1968c. "Blues und Swing sind überall. II" *Jazz Podium* (August): 236.
———. 1968d. "Blues und Swing sind überall. III" *Jazz Podium* (October): 303.
———. 1968e. "Musik der Weltvölker" *Sounds* 7: 21.
———. 2004. Email to the author. 18 November.

Bergmeier, Horst and Rainer Lotz. 1996. "Charlie and His Orchestra. Ein obskures Kapitel der deutschen Jazzgeschichte." In *Jazz in Deutschland*, ed. Knauer, 13–48.

———. 1997. *Hitler's Airwaves. The Inside Story of Nazi Radio Broadcasting and Propaganda Swing*. New Haven & London: Yale University Press.

"Berliner Jazztage 1965." 1965 *Jazz Podium* (November): 288–92.

"Berliner Jazztage 71." 1971 *Jazz Podium* (August): 270.

Berman, Nina. 1998. "Orientalism, Imperialism and Nationalism: Karl May's Orientzyklus." In *The Imperialist Imagination*, eds. Friedrichsmayer, Lennox and Zantop, 51–68.

Bernhard, Paul. 1927. *Jazz: Eine musikalische Zeitfrage*. Munich: Delphin.

Blome, Rainer. 1966. "Ein neues Gesicht im Jazz: Peter Brötzmann." *Jazz Podium* (August): 216.

———. 1966/67. "Berliner Jazztage." *Sounds* (Winter): 9–10.

———. 1967. "Globe Unity." *Sounds* (Autumn): 37.

Blume, Friedrich. 1979. *Classic and Romantic music: A comprehensive survey*. 2nd ed. trans. M.D. Herter. Norton. London: Faber.

Blume, Mary and Paul de Beaumont. 1966. "Sous les toits de Paris." *Realities* (March).

Boas, Günter. 1969. Review of the Berlin Jazz Days. *Jazz Podium* (December): 390–96.

Bockhoff, Baldur. 1963. "Nekrolog auf die Jazz-Literatur." *Merkur* 17: 914–20.

Bodenstein, G. 1977. Letter. *Frankfurter Rundschau*, 17 September.

——— et al. 1979. *W. Dauner's Urschrei ohne Echo?* Göttingen: Galerie APEX, 1979.

Böll, Heinrich. 1957. *Irisches Tagebuch*. Munich: Deutscher Taschenbuch Verlag, 1961 [1957].

Bourdieu, Pierre. 1993. *The Field of Cultural Production: Essays on Art and Literature*, ed. R. Johnson. New York: Columbia University Press.

Brigl, Kathrin. 2001. *"Alles wieder auf Anfang": Siegfried Schmidt-Joos zum 65. Geburtstag*. Stockstadt: rundy media.

———, and Siegfried Schmidt-Joos. 1985. *Fritz Rau: Buchhalter der Träume*. Berlin: Quadriga.

Broecking, Christian. 1995. "Diese Injektion an Schwärze." Berlin JazzFest program notes: 74–6.

———. 2002. "Adorno versus Berendt revisited." In *Jazz und Gesellschaft*, ed. Knauer, 41–53.

Brooks, Billy. 1971. Cover notes for *El Babaku*, by Billy Brooks and *El Babaku*.

———, and *El Babaku*. 1971. *Live at the Jazz Galerie*. MPS, 15314.

Brötzmann, Peter. 2004. Personal interview. 25 September.

——— Octet. 1968. *Machine Gun*. BRÖ, 002.

———, and Han Bennink. 1977. *Schwarzwaldfahrt*. FMP, 0440.

"Brown, Joe" (a.k.a. J-E Berendt). 1952a. "Gondel Jazz Poll." *Die Gondel* (August): 62–3.

———. 1952b. "Jazz contra Jazz." *Die Gondel* (March): 64–5.

———. 1952c. "Gondel Jazz Poll." *Die Gondel* (December): 59–61.

———. 1953a. "Erstes Deutsches Jazz Festival." *Die Gondel* (June): 62–3.

———. 1953b. "Jazz Gäste aus Übersee." *Die Gondel* (July): 60–61.

———. 1953c. "Jazz in der Süddeutschen Zeitung." *Jazz Echo* (July): 63.

———. 1954a. "Deutscher Jazz Poll 1954/55." *Jazz Echo* (September): 38–9.

———. 1954b. "Wo bleibt Jazz-gestern und heute?" *Jazz Echo* (September): 42.
———. 1954c. "Zeitgenössische Musiktage Donaueschingen." *Jazz Echo* (November): 47.
———. 1955a. "Jazz in der Ostzone." *Jazz Echo* (July): 43.
———. 1955b. "Kirche und Jazz." *Jazz Echo* (March): 43.
———. 1958. "Wer will nach Newport?" *Jazz Echo* (March): 49.
Browning, Barbara. 1995. *Samba: Resistance in Motion*. Bloomington and Indianapolis: Indiana University Press.
Brubeck, Dave. 1958. Cover notes for *Jazz Impressions of Eurasia*, by the Dave Brubeck Quartet.
——— Quartet. 1958. *Jazz Impressions of Eurasia*. Columbia, CL 1251.
Buchholtz, Stefan. 1954. Letter to J-E Berendt. 29 October. Berendt Papers. Jazzinstitut, Darmstadt.
Budds, Michael. 1990. *Jazz in the Sixties: The Expansion of Musical Resources and Techniques*. 2nd ed. Iowa City: University of Iowa Press.
———, ed. 2002. *Jazz and the Germans*. Hillsdale, New York: Pendragon Press, 2002.
Bullivant, Keith and C. Jane Rice. 1995. "Reconstruction and Integration: The Culture of West German Stabilization 1945 to 1968." In *German Cultural Studies*, ed. Burns, 209–55
Burde, Wolfgang. 1978. "A Discussion of European Free Jazz." In *For Example*, ed. Gebers, 46–52.
Burns, Rob, ed. 1995a. *German Cultural Studies: An Introduction*. Oxford: Oxford University Press.
———. 1995b. "Introduction." In *German Cultural Studies*, ed. Burns, 1–8.
———, and Wilfried van der Will. 1995. "The Federal Republic 1968 to 1990. From the Industrial Society to the Culture Society." In *German Cultural Studies*, ed. Burns, 257–323.
Campt, Tina, Pascal Grosse and Yara-Colette Lemke-Muniz de Faria. 1998. "Blacks, German and the Politics of Imperial Imagination." In *The Imperialist Imagination*, eds. Friedrichsmayer, Lennox and Zantop, 205–32.
Carles, Philippe and Jean-Louis Comolli. 1971. *Free Jazz/Black Power*. Frankfurt am Main: Fischer.
Carvalho, John. 1998. "Improvisations on Nietzsche, on jazz." In *Nietzsche, Philosophy and the Arts*, eds. Salim Kemal, Ivan Gaskell and Daniel W. Conway. Cambridge and New York: Cambridge University Press, 187–211.
Chand, Richard. 1961. "Deceived." *Downbeat*, 8 June: 8.
Chen, Bubi. 2004. Telephone interview. 5 November.
Cherry, Don. 1968. *Eternal Rhythm*. MPS, 15204.
Chervel, Thierry. n.d.. "Untitled Article." *Süddeutsche Zeitung* article. In *Berliner Festwochen Chronik*, ed. Krüger, 253.
Claman, David Neumann. 2002. "Western Composers and India's Music: Concepts, History and Recent Music." (PhD diss., Princeton University, 2002).
Clarke–Boland Big Band. 1960. *Jazz is Universal*. Atlantic, 1401.
———. 1963. *Big Band*. Atlantic, 1404.
Claxton, William. 2005. "Foreword." In Berendt and Claxton, *Jazz Life*. 2nd Ed, 27–33.
Clifford, James. 1988. *The Predicament of Culture: Twentieth-century Ethnography, Literature and Art*. Cambridge, Mass.: Harvard University Press.
Coleman, Ornette. 1960. *Free Jazz (A Collective Improvisation)*. Atlantic, 1364.
Coltrane, John. 1960. *My Favorite Things*. Atlantic, 1361.

———. 1961. *Olé*. Atlantic, 1373.
———. 1965. *Kulu Sé Mama*. Impulse, 9106.
Conover, Willis. 1961. "The Ubiquity of Jazz." *Down Beat Music Handbook:* 32–8.
Cooley, Timothy J. 1997. "Casting Shadows in the Field. An Introduction." In *Shadows in the Field. New Perspectives for Fieldwork in Ethnomusicology*, eds. Gregory F. Barz and Timothy J. Cooley. New York, Oxford: Oxford University Press.
Corbett, John. 1994. *Extended Play: Sounding Off from John Cage to Dr Funkenstein*. Durham, N.C. & London: Duke University Press.
Cotterrell, Roger, and Barry Tepperman. 1974. *Joe Harriott Memorial*. Gant's Hill: R. Cotterell.
Cover notes for *Big Band*, by the Clarke–Boland Big Band. 1963.
Curjel, Hans. 1957. "Donaueschingen feiert Strawinsky." *Melos* 24: 326–8.
"Das Forum." 1954. *Jazz Podium* (November): 8.
"Das Free Jazz Treffen des SWF." 1970. *Jazz Podium* (February): 56.
"Das Klaus Doldinger Quartet in Südamerika." 1965. *Jazz Podium* (May): 112.
Dauer, Alfons M. 1958. *Der Jazz: Seine Ursprünge und Entwicklungen*. Kassel: Röth.
———. 1961a. "Herkunft des Jazz." *Jazz Podium* (July): 172–5.
———. 1961b. *Jazz: Die magische Musik*. Bremen: Schünemann.
———, and Stephen Longstreet, eds. 1957. *Knaurs Jazz-Lexikon*. Munich: Knaur.
Davis, Miles. 1958. *Milestones*. Columbia, CK 85203.
———. 1959. *Kind of Blue*. Columbia, 1355.
———. 1959/60. *Sketches of Spain*. Columbia, 8271.
Davis, Ruth. 1996. "The art/popular music paradigm and the Tunisian Ma'luf." *Popular Music* 15: 313–23.
"Debatten um 'Jazz und alte Musik.'" 1956. *Jazz Podium* (January): 11–12.
DeMichael, Don. 1964. "Jazz From Germany." *Downbeat*, 13 February: 29.
"Deutscher Jazz. Verstimmt und verstummt." 1965. *Der Spiegel*, 18 August: 75–6.
DeVeaux, Scott. 1997. *The Birth of Bebop: A Social and Musical History*. Berkeley and Los Angeles: University of California Press.
"Die Stephanus-Stiftung: Aus der Geschichte." 2003. Stephanus-Stiftung. 14 Jan. 2008. <http://www.stephanus-stiftung.de/organisation/publikationen_hintergruende/geschichte/index.html>
Dillmann, Raymund. 1992. "Foreword." In Liefland, *Jazz Musik Kritik*, 7–11.
Dilloo, Rüdiger. 1969. "The German Allstars." *Twen* (April): 37.
"DJF: Bollwerk gegen die Diffamierung." 1953. *Jazz Podium* (August): 5.
"Doldinger füllt Titelseiten – überwältigender Erfolg einer Südamerika-Tournee." 1965. *Jazz Podium* (July): 175–6.
Dollase, Rainer, Michael Rüsenberg and Hans J. Stollenwerk. 1978. *Das Jazzpublikum*. Mainz: B. Schott's Söhne.
Dümling, Albrecht. 1994. "Reine und Unreine Musik. Jazz und Jazzverwandtes in der NS-Ausstellung 'Entartete Musik.'" In *Jazz und Sozialgeschichte*, ed. Mäusli, 47–68.
——— and Peter Girth, eds. 1988. *Entartete Musik: Dokumentation und Kommentar zur Düsseldorfer Ausstellung von 1938*. Düsseldorf: City of Düsseldorf.
Echenoz, Jean. 1971. "Don Cherry" *Jazz Hot* (June).
Eckhardt, Ulrich. 1975. Extract from the 25th Berliner Festwochen magazine. In *Berliner Festwochen Chronik*, ed. Krüger, 3.
———. 1979. Extract from the 1979 Berliner Festwochen magazine. In *Berliner Festwochen Chronik*, ed. Krüger, 4–7.

---. 2000a. "Berliner Festwochen im 5. Jahrzehnt. Eine subjective Chronik." In *Berliner Festwochen Chronik*, ed. Krüger, 8–142.
---. 2000b. "Veränderung als Konstante." In *Berliner Festwochen Chronik*, ed. Krüger, 148–53.
Egg, Bernhard. 1927. *Jazz-Fremdwörterbuch*. Leipzig: Ehrler.
El Mahdi, Salah. 2004. Letter to the author. 7 December.
Endress, Gudrun. 1969. "Free Fiddle: Jean-Luc Ponty." *Jazz Podium* (April): 120–23.
---, ed. 1980. *Jazz Podium: Musiker über sich selbst*. Stuttgart: Deutsche Verlagsanstalt.
Ermarth, Michael, ed. 1993. *America and the Shaping of German Society, 1945–1955*. Oxford, Providence: Berg.
Erskine, Gilbert. 1964a. Review of *Animal Dance*, by John Lewis, Albert Mangelsdorff and the Zagreb Jazz Quintet. *Downbeat*, 7 May: 28-9.
---. 1964b. Review of *Die Deutschen Allstars*. *Downbeat*, 10 September: 29.
Eto, Kimio. 1960. *The Japanese Koto Music of Kimio Eto: Koto & Flute Featuring the Flute of Bud Shank*. World Pacific, WP 1229.
Evans, Nicholas. 2000. *Writing Jazz: Race, Nationalism and Modern Culture in the 1920s*. New York and London: Garland.
Fackler, Guido. 1994. "Zwischen (musikalischem) Widerstand und Propaganda-Jazz im 'Dritten Reich.' " In *Musikalische Volkskultur und die politische Macht*, ed. Günther Noll. Essen: Blaue Eule Verlag, 437–84.
---. 1996. "Jazz im KZ. Ein Forschungsbericht." In *Jazz in Deutschland*, ed. Knauer, 49–91.
Fark, Reinhard. 1971. *Die mißachtete Botschaft: Publizistische Aspekte des Jazz im soziokulturellen Wandel*. Berlin: Volker Spiess Verlag.
Farrell, Christa. 1977. Letter. *Frankfurter Rundschau*, 17 September.
Farrell, Gerry. 1987. "Reflecting surfaces: The use of elements from Indian music in popular music and jazz." *Popular Music* 7: 189–205.
Feather, Leonard. 1968. "Berlin Jazz Days." *Downbeat*, 11 January: 23–4, 42.
---. 1969. "Jazz Journey." *Downbeat*, 9 January: 18–19, 29.
Finkelstein, Sidney 1947. *Jazz: A people's music*. New York: Citadel Press.
---. 1951. *Jazz*. trans. Elke Kaspar. Stuttgart: Hatje.
Fischer, Klaus. 1965. "Der Marco Polo des Jazz." *Badisches Tagblatt*, 26 October.
Fischer, Klaus-Gotthard. 1999. *Jazzin' The Black Forest*. Berlin: Crippled Library.
"Free Jazz in Baden-Baden." 1968. *Jazz Podium* (January): 6–7.
Friedrichsmeyer, Sara, Sara Lennox, and Susanne Zantop, eds. 1998. *The Imperialist Imagination: German Colonialism and its Legacy*. Ann Arbor: University of Michigan Press.
Fritsch, Ingrid. 1981. "Zur Idee der Weltmusik." In *Weltmusik*, eds. Ausländer and Fritsch, 3–27.
Fruth, Willi. 2004. Telephone interview. 17 September.
Fuchs, Ralf-Peter. 2002. "Neue Menschen und Kultur der Moderne: Der Jazz und sein Publikum in der deutschen Nachkriegspresse 1945–1953." In *Jazz und Gesellschaft*, ed. Knauer, 17–40.
Ganns, Harald. 1956. Letter. *Jazz Echo* (March): 44.
Gates, Lisa. 1998."Of seeing and Otherness: Leni Riefenstahl's African Photographs." In *The Imperialist Imagination*, eds. Friedrichsmeyer, Lennox and Zantop, 233–48.
Gebers, Jost. 1972. Letter. *Jazz Podium* (November): 6–7.
---, ed. 1978. *For Example*. Berlin: Akademie der Künste and FMP.

Gendron, Bernard. 1995. "'Moldy Figs' and Modernists: Jazz at war (1942–1946)." In *Jazz among the discourses*, ed. Krin Gabbard. Durham, N.C.: Duke University Press, 31–56.

Gennari, John. 2006. *Blowin' Hot and Cool: Jazz and its Critics*. Chicago and London: University of Chicago Press.

Gerard, Charley. 1998. *Jazz in Black and White: Race, Culture, and Identity in the Jazz Community*. Westport, Conn.: Greenwood Press.

"Gespräch mit dem Irene Schweizer Trio." 1967. *Jazz Podium* (May): 132–4.

"Gespräch mit Joachim-Ernst Berendt." 1988. In *That's Jazz*, eds. Wolbert et al., 677–9.

Getz, Stan and Charlie Byrd. 1962. *Jazz Samba*. Verve, V6 8432.

———— and João Gilberto. 1963. *Getz/Gilberto*. Verve, V6 8545.

Gioia, Ted. 1988. *The Imperfect Art: Reflections on Jazz and Modern Culture*. New York: Oxford University Press.

————. 1997. *The History of Jazz*. New York: Oxford University Press.

Glaser, Hermann. 1997. *Deutsche Kultur 1945–2000*. Munich and Vienna: Carl Hanser Verlag.

Gemünden, Gerd. 1998. *Framed Visions: Popular Culture, Americanization and the Contemporary German and Austrian Imagination*. Ann Arbor: University of Michigan Press.

Goethe Institut. 1965. Yearbook. Munich: Goethe Institut.

————. 1966. Yearbook. Munich: Goethe Institut.

————. 1967. Yearbook. Munich: Goethe Institut.

————. 1968. Yearbook. Munich: Goethe Institut.

————. 1969. Yearbook. Munich: Goethe Institut.

————. 1970. Yearbook. Munich: Goethe Institut.

————. n.d.. "Zur Geschichte des Goethe-Instituts." Goethe Institut. 17 March 2004. <http://www.goethe.de/uun/ges/deindex.htm>.

Goodbody, Axel, Dennis Tate and Ian Wallace. 1995. "The Failed Socialist Experiment: Culture in the GDR." In *German Cultural Studies*, ed. Burns, 147–207.

Graves, Barry. 1972. "Gerät das Festival ins Rutschen?" *Die Welt*, 7 November.

Gruntz, George. 1972a. "Berliner Jazztage 1972." *Jazz Podium* (September): 18–23.

————. 1972b. "Gescheite Organisation." *Jazz Podium* (October): 14–16.

————. 1983. "Jazz ist Weltmusik." In *Jazzrock: Tendenzen einer modernen Musik*, ed. Burghard König. Reinbek bei Hamburg: Rororo, 188–97.

————. 2002. *Als weißer Neger geboren: Ein Leben für den Jazz*. Berneck: Corvus Verlag.

————. 2004. Personal interview. 9 September.

————. 2006. Email to the author. 7 January.

Hamel, Peter Michael. 1976. *Durch Musik zum Selbst*. Berne, Munich and Vienna: Scherz Verlag.

———— and Between. 1975. *Hesse Between Music*. Wergo, SM 1015-50.

Handy, John and Ali Akbar Khan. 1975. *Karuna Supreme*. MPS, 15455.

————. 1980. *Rainbow*. MPS, 15576.

Hardy, John William. 1965. Review of a performance by the Hindustani Jazz Sextet. *Downbeat*, 18 November: 34–5

Harth, Walther. 1954. "Ein Kompendium der Jazzmusik." *Melos* 21: 45.

Häusler, Josef, ed. 1996. *Spiegel der Neuen Musik: Donaueschingen*. Kassel: Bärenreiter Verlag.

Heffley, Mike. 2000a. "Northern Sun, Southern Moon: Identity, Improvisation and Idiom in Freie Musik Produktion." (PhD diss., Wesleyan University). 7 November 2003. <http://mheffley.web.wesleyan.edu/almatexts/almamusicosophy.htm>
———. 2000b. "Peter Kowald and the New York Unity Village." *The Squid's Ear*. 7 November 2003. <http://www.squidsear.com/cgi-bin/news/newsView.cgi>.
———. 2005. *Northern Sun, Southern Moon: Europe's Reinvention of Jazz*. New Haven: Yale University Press.
Heidkamp, Konrad. 1996. "Bloß kein Jazz!" *Die Zeit*, 27 December.
Hellhund, Herbert. 1986. "Third Stream. Zum Verhältnis eines strittigen Begriffes und einer mißverständlichen Sache." In *Die heimliche Liebe des Jazz zur europäischen Moderne*, ed. Ingrid Karl. Vienna: Wiener Musik Galerie, 37–61.
Hennessey, Mike. 1966. "Cherry's Catholicity." *Downbeat*, 28 July: 14–15.
———. 1990. *Klook: The Story of Kenny Clarke*. London and New York: Quartet Books.
Hindemith, Paul. 1941. *The Craft of Musical Composition*, trans. Otto Ortmann. 3 Vols. London: Schott.
Hino, Susan. 2004. Email to the author. 18 March.
Hobsbawm, Eric (a.k.a Francis Newton). 1959. *The Jazz Scene*. London: MacGibbon and Kee.
Hodeir, André. 1954. *Hommes et problèmes du jazz*. Paris: Flammarion.
Hoehl, Egbert. 1968. "Neues von Saba" *Jazz Podium* (May): 160.
Höhn, Maria. 2002. *GIs and Fräuleins: The German-American Encounter in 1950s West Germany*. Chapel Hill: University of North Carolina Press.
Hömberg, Johannes. 1965. "Musikreferat: Größere Ensembles, Bildungshilfe und Ostkontakte." *Goethe Institut* Yearbook: 49–51.
Hoffmann, Bernd. 1994. "Der un-heimliche Widerstand. Jugendkultur im Rezeptionsschatten einer kollektiven Entlastungsstrategie." In *Jazz und Sozialgeschichte*, ed. *Mäusli*, 83–95.
———. 1996. "'Die Mitteilungen' Anmerkungen zu einer verbotenen Fanpostille." In *Jazz in Deutschland*, ed. Knauer, 93–136.
———. 1999. "Zur westdeutschen Hot-Club Bewegung der Nachkriegszeit." In *Jazz in Nordrhein-Westfalen seit 1946*, ed. von Zahn, 64–98. (refs to typescript version).
———. 2000. "Von der Liebe der deutschen Musikpädagogik zum Jazz-Kunstwerk. Zur Rezeption afro-amerikanischer Musik in der schulischen Situation der 50er Jahre." In *Populäre Musik im kulturwissenschaftlichen Diskurs*, eds. Helmut Rösing and Thomas Phleps. Karben: CODA, 279–93. (refs to typescript version).
———. 2003a. "Aspekte zur Jazz-Rezeption in Deutschland, Afro-Amerikanische Musik im Spiegel der Musikpresse 1900–45." *Jazzforschung/Jazz Research* 35.
———. 2003b. "…als 'wertvoll' anerkannt – Jazz in NRW." In *Jazz in Nordrhein-Westfalen seit 1946*, ed. von Zahn, 17–53. (refs to typescript version).
Holleufer, Astrid. 1981. "Gespräch mit Joachim Ernst Berendt." *Jazz Podium* (August): 10–14.
Horn, David. 1991. Review of *The Imperfect Art*, by Ted Gioia. *Popular Music* 10.1: 103–7.
Hudtwalcker, Olaf. 1957. "Reise zum polnischen Jazzfestival." *Jazz Podium* (September): 5–6.
———. 1966. "Festival Flamenco Gitano." *Twen* (January): 8, 10.
———. 1967. Cover notes for *Flamenco Jazz*, by the Pedro Iturralde Quintet.

Hüdepohl, Karl-Ernst. 1968. "Das Kulturprogramm – Stand und Entwicklung." *Goethe Institut* Yearbook: 19–23.
Huesmann, Gunther. 1986. "Jazz in West Germany since 1945." *Music Today* (November): 8.
Hultin, Randi. 1972. "Caught in the act." *Downbeat*, 20 January: 32–5.
Hund, Dr. 1958. Letter to J-E Berendt. 2 October. Berendt Papers. Jazzinstitut, Darmstadt.
Hunkemöller, Jürgen. 1977. Review of *Ein Fenster aus Jazz*, by J-E Berendt. *Jazzforschung/Jazzresearch* 9: 186–8.
Huyssen, Andreas. 1992. "The Inevitability of Nation: German Intellectuals after Unification." *October* 61 (Summer): 63–73.
"Im Jazz ist das Gefühl unserer Zeit." 1957. *Iserlohner Kreisanzeiger*, 13 December.
Iturralde, Pedro. 1967a. *Flamenco Jazz*. Saba, 15143.
———. 1967b. *Jazz Flamenco*, Hispavox, HH (S) 11-128.
Jänichen, Lothar. 1979. "10 Jahre Free Music Production in Berlin: Ein Gespräch mit Jost Gebers." *Jazz Podium* (October): 15–17.
"Jazz auf den Donaueschinger Musiktagen." 1954. *Jazz Podium* (November): 11.
"Jazz aus Deutschland für Südamerika." 1968. *Jazz Podium* (September): 277.
"Jazz News." 1954a. *Die Gondel* (January): 64.
———. 1954b. *Jazz Echo* (July): 40–5.
———. 1954c. *Jazz Echo* (September): 46.
———. 1955a. *Jazz Echo* (March): 43.
———. 1955b. *Jazz Echo* (April): 44.
———. 1955c. *Jazz Echo* (May): 42.
———. 1955d. *Jazz Echo* (August): 44.
———. 1955e. *Jazz Echo* (October): 41.
———. 1955f. *Jazz Echo* (December): 44.
———. 1956a. *Jazz Echo* (January): 46.
———. 1956b. *Jazz Echo* (March): 44.
———. 1956c. *Jazz Echo* (April): 43.
———. 1956d. *Jazz Echo* (September): 49.
———. 1956e. *Jazz Echo* (November): 47.
———. 1956f. *Jazz Echo* (December): 44.
———. 1957a. *Jazz Echo* (May): 47.
———. 1957b. *Jazz Echo* (June): 47.
———. 1957c. *Jazz Echo* (October): 43.
———. 1957d. *Jazz Echo* (December): 46.
———. 1958a. *Jazz Echo* (February): 46–8.
———. 1958b. *Jazz Echo* (July): 43.
———. 1958c. *Jazz Echo* (September): 45.
———. 1958d. *Jazz Echo* (December): 42.
———. 1960a. *Jazz Echo* (February): 45.
———. 1960b. *Jazz Echo* (April): 46.
———. 1960c. *Jazz Echo* (May): 42.
———. 1960d. *Jazz Echo* (August): 43–4.
———. 1961a. *Jazz Echo* (January): 46.
———. 1961b. *Jazz Echo* (March): 44.
———. 1962a. *Jazz Echo* (January): 46.
———. 1962b. *Jazz Echo* (October): 46.

———. 1962c. *Jazz Echo* (November): 46.
———. 1978. *Jazz Podium* (April): 25.
"'Jazzpapst' Joachim-Ernst Berendt ist tot." 2000. *dpa-Meldung.* 5 February.
"Jazz-Tage einer Evangelischen Akademie." 1954. *Die Schallplatte* (March): 3.
"Jazz trifft Afrika und Indien." n.d. *Berliner Tagesspiegel* article. In *Berliner Jazztage Documentation*, ed. Rein.
"Jazz und Dichtung." 1958. *Jazz Echo* (June): 42.
"Jazz und Pop. Ein Offener Brief." 1969. *Jazz Podium* (February): 4.
"Jazz und theoretische Physik: Joachim-Ernst Berendt." 1953. *Jazz Podium* (February): 7.
"Jazz zwischen Icking und Indonesien." 1969. *Jazz Podium* (May): 164–7.
Jeske, Lee. 1983. Review of *The Jazz Book*, by J-E Berendt. *Downbeat*, January: 58, 64.
"Joachim Berendt's American Journey." 1960. *Downbeat*, 21 July: 20–21.
Johanns, Willi. 1966. "Notizen von einer heißen Reise." *Jazz Podium* (April): 94–5.
Johnson, Randal. 1993. "Pierre Bourdieu on Art, Literature and Culture." In *The Field of Cultural Production: Essays on Art and Literature*, by Pierre Bourdieu. ed. Randal Johnson. New York: Columbia University Press, 1–25.
Jost, Ekkehard. 1973. "Zum Problem des politischen Engagements im Jazz." *Jazzforschung/Jazz Research* 5: 33–43.
———. 1973/74. "Free Jazz und die Musik der Dritten Welt." *Jazzforschung/Jazz Research* 3 & 4: 141–54.
———. 1975a. *Free Jazz: Stilkritische Untersuchungen zum Jazz der 60er Jahre*. Mainz: B. Schott's Söhne.
———. 1975b. "Free Jazz." In *The Story of Jazz*, ed. Berendt, 117–33.
———. 1978. "European Jazz Avantgarde – Where Will Emancipation Lead." In *For Example*, ed. Gebers, 54–64.
———. 1982. *Sozialgeschichte des Jazz in den USA*. Frankfurt am Main: Fischer Taschenbuchverlag.
———. 1987. *Europas Jazz, 1960–80*. Frankfurt am Main: Fischer Taschenbuchverlag.
———. 1988a. "Jazz in Deutschland von der Weimarer Republik zur Adenauer-Ära." In *That's Jazz*, eds. Wolbert et al, 357–78.
———. 1988b. "Die europäische Jazz-Emanzipation." In *That's Jazz*, eds. Wolbert et al, 501–12.
———. 1994. "Über das Europäische im europäischen Jazz." In *Jazz in Europa*, ed. Knauer, 233–49.
———. 2004. Personal interview. 30 October.
Jungheinrich, Hans-Klaus. 1992. "Mit freundlicher Unerbittlichkeit." In Liefland, *Jazz Musik Kritik*, 12–17.
Kahl, Wolfgang. 1954. "Jazzklänge ertönen bei Pfarrer Sommer." *Die neue Zeitung*, 27 January.
Kart, Larry. 1968. Review of *Noon in Tunisia*, by George Gruntz. *Downbeat*, 31 October: 21.
Kaestner, Heinz. 1951. "Der Jazz und die abendländische Kultur." *Junge Musik Zeitschrift für Musikpflege in der Jugend* 2: 42–4.
Kater, Michael H. 1992. *Different Drummers: Jazz in the Culture of Nazi Germany*. New York: Oxford University Press.
———. 1994. "Jazz as Dissidence in The 'Third Reich.'" In *Jazz und Sozialgeschichte*, ed. Mäusli, 69–81.

———. 1997. *The Twisted Muse: Musicians and their Music in the Third Reich*. New York: Oxford University Press.

———. 2006. "New Democracy and Alternative Culture: Jazz in West Germany after the Second World War." *Australian Journal of Politics and History* 52.2: 173–87.

Kennedy, Michael. 1988. *The Concise Oxford Dictionary of Music*. Oxford and New York: Oxford University Press.

Kirk, Roland and Benny Golson. 1963. *The Roland Kirk Quartet Meets the Benny Golson Orchestra*. Mercury, 20844.

Kille, Helmut. 1976. Letter. *Jazz Podium* (February): 3–4.

———. 1977. Unpublished letter to *Frankfurter Rundschau*. 26 August. In *rundy*, 13 September.

Kjellberg, Erik. 1994. "Old Folklore in Swedish Modern. Zum Thema Volksmusik und Jazz in Schweden." In *Jazz in Europa*, ed. Knauer, 221–31.

Kleber, Karl-Heinz. 1953. "Gibt es eine deutsche Jazzliteratur?" *Die Gondel* (December): 61–3.

Kleinschmidt, Gabriele. 1977. Letter. *Frankfurter Rundschau* 6 September.

Klump, Bradley. n.d. "Origins and Distinctions of the World Music and World Beat Classifications." Typescript. Jazzinstitut, Darmstadt.

Knauer, Wolfram, ed. 1994a. *Jazz in Europa*. Hofheim: Wolke Verlag.

———. 1994b. "'Musicianers' oder: Der Jazzmusiker als Musikant. Anmerkungen zum Verhältnis von Jazz und Folklore." In *Jazz in Europa*, ed. Knauer, 185–200.

———. 1996a. "Emanzipation wovon? Zum Verhältnis des amerikanischen und deutschen Jazz in den 50er und 60er Jahren." In *Jazz in Deutschland*, ed. Knauer, 141–57.

———, ed. 1996b. *Jazz in Deutschland*. Hofheim: Wolke Verlag.

———, ed. 1998. *Jazz und Sprache. Sprache und Jazz*. Hofheim: Wolke Verlag.

———. 1999. "Der Analytiker-Blues. Anmerkungen zu Entwicklung und Dilemma der Jazzanalyse von den 30er Jahren bis heute." *Jazzforschung/Jazzresearch* 31: 27–42.

———, ed. 2002. *Jazz und Gesellschaft*. Hofheim: Wolke Verlag.

———. 2005. Biographical note on J-E Berendt. In Berendt and Claxton, *Jazz Life*. 2nd Ed.

Kneif, Tibor. 1984. "Exotik im musikalischen Underground." In *Europäische Musik zwischen Nationalismus und Exotik*, eds. Oesch, Arlt and Haas, 99–114.

Koch, Gerhard R. 2000. "Lust am ödipalen Vatermord." *Frankfurter Allgemeine Zeitung*, 5 February.

Koch, Thomas. 1985. "Das Portrait: J. E. Berendt." *SWF Journal* (October).

Kofsky, Frank. 1998. *John Coltrane and the Jazz Revolution of the 1960s*. New York, London, Montreal and Sydney: Pathfinder.

"Korrespondenten berichten über Kirche und Jazz." 1958. *Das Schlagzeug* (April): 6.

Kotschenreuther, Helmut. 1956. "Glanz und Elend des Jazz." In *Musikstadt Berlin zwischen Krieg und Frieden. Musikalische Bilanz einer Viermächtestadt*. Berlin and Wiesbaden: Bote and Bock.

Krauth, Günther. 1977. Letter. *Frankfurter Rundschau*, 6 September.

Kriegel, Volker. 1998. *Manchmal ist es besser, man sagt gar nix*. Zurich: Haffmanns Verlag.

Krüger, Bernd, ed. 2000. *50 Jahre Berliner Festwochen: Eine kommentierte Chronik*. Berlin: Berliner Festspiele.

Kühn, Gerhard. 1972a. "Eubie Blake zeigte es den Jungen." *Stuttgarter Nachrichten*, 6 November.
———. 1972b. "Zum Zerreißen gespannt." *Stuttgarter Nachrichten*, 8 November.
Kultermann, Udo. 1971. *Art and Life*. trans. John W. Gabriel. New York, Washington: Praeger.
Kumpf, Hans. 1974. "Donaueschinger Musiktage 1973." *Jazz Podium* (January): 25–6.
———. 1975a. "John Cage und der Jazz" *Jazz Podium* (October): 6–9.
———. 1975b. *Postserielle Musik und Free Jazz*. 2nd ed. Rohrdorf: Rohrdorfer Musikverlag, 1981 [1975].
———. 1979. "Stellenweise unterbelichtet." *Stuttgarter Nachrichten*, 15 January.
———. 2007. Telephone interview. 27 October.
Laade, Wolfgang. 1970. "Globe Unity – Jazz Meets the World." *Jazzforschung/Jazz Research* 2: 138-46.
Lange, Horst H. 1960. "Die Herkunft des Jazz." *Jazz Podium* (May): 110.
———. 1988. " 'Artfremde Kunst und Musik unerwünscht' Jazz im Dritten Reich." In *That's Jazz*, eds. Wolbert et al, 391–403.
———. 1996. *Jazz in Deutschland. Die Deutsche Jazz-Chronik bis 1960*. 2nd ed. Hildesheim, Zurich and New York: Olms Presse.
Lauth, Wolfgang. n.d. *These Foolish Things: Jazztime in Deutschland. Ein Swingender Rückblick*. Mannheim: Verlag der Quadrate Buchhandlung.
Le Bris, Michel. 1968. "Barney Wilen. Ma direction c'est le rock." *Jazz Hot* (December): 28–9.
Lenz, Günter. 1964. Cover notes for *Now Jazz Ramwong*, by the Albert Mangelsdorff Quintet.
Lewis, George E. 2002. "Gittin' to know y'all." Von improvisierter Musik, vom Treffen der Kulturen und von der "racial imagination." In *Jazz und Gesellschaft*, ed. Knauer, 213–47.
Liefland, Wilhelm E. 1975. "Jazzgeschichte und mehr." *Frankfurter Rundschau*, 5 November.
———. 1976. "Free Jazz – Nur eine Geschichtsdelle?" *Jazz Podium* (June): 10–12.
———. 1977a. "Am Jazzkeller nagen die Jazz-Killer." *Neue Musikzeitung* (August & September): 11.
———. 1977b. "Herr Berendt öffnet seinen Plattenschrank." *Frankfurter Rundschau*, 26 August.
———. 1977c. Letter to J-E Berendt. 21 August. In *rundy*, 13 September.
———. 1977d. Letter to Werner Holzer. 4 September. In *rundy*, 13 September.
———. 1977e. Letter to Gabriele Kleinschmidt. 4 September. In *rundy*, 13 September.
———. 1977f. "Lieflands Letzte." In *W. Dauner's Urschrei ohne Echo?* eds. Bodenstein et al, 15.
———. 1992. *Jazz Musik Kritik*, ed. Raymund Dillmann. Hofheim: Verlag der Buchhandlung Raymund Dillmann, 1992.
Lindenberger, Herbert. 1977. "Ein kleines bißchen Anthologie." *Stuttgarter Zeitung*, 11 October.
Linke, Uli. 1991. *German Bodies: Race and Representation after Hitler*. New York and London: Routledge.
Lippmann, Horst. 1954. "Jazz als zeitgenössische Musik." *Jazz Podium* (December): 16.

———. 1962. "Die Solisten des American Folk Blues Festivals 62." *Jazz Podium* (August): 181.
Litweiler, John. 1984. *The Freedom Principle: Jazz after 1958*. New York: W. Morrow.
Longyear, Rey M. 1988. *Nineteenth-Century Romanticism in Music*. Englewood Cliffs: Prentice Hall.
Maase, Kaspar. 1992. *BRAVO-Amerika. Erkundungen zur Jugendkultur der Bundesrepublik in den fünfziger Jahren*. Hamburg: Junius Verlag.
McCormick, Richard. 1991. *Politics of the Self: Feminism and the Postmodern in West German Literature and Film*. Princeton: Princeton University Press.
McGowan, Chris and Ricardo Pessanha. 1998. *The Brazilian Sound: Samba, Bossa nova, and the Popular Music of Brazil*. Philadelphia: Temple University Press.
McLeod, John. 2000. *Beginning Postcolonialism*. Manchester and New York: Manchester University Press.
Mais, Heidelore. 1977. Letter. *Frankfurter Rundschau*, 6 September.
Malm, William P. 1959. *Japanese Music and Musical Instruments*. Tokyo and Rutland, Vermont: Charles E. Tuttle Co.
Mangelsdorff, Albert. 1964a. "Jazz für den fernen Osten." *Jazz Podium* (July): 158–9.
———. 1964b. Cover notes for *Now Jazz Ramwong*, by the Albert Mangelsdorff Quintet.
———. 2004. Personal interview. 13 September.
——— Quintet. 1963. *Tension*. German CBS, 62 336.
——— Quintet. 1964. *Now Jazz Ramwong*. German CBS, 62 398.
———, the HR Jazzensemble, Colin Wilkie and Shirley Hart. 1969. *Wild Goose*. MPS, 15229.
Margull, Geges F. 1971. "Gespräch über die Ziele der Free Music Production in Berlin." *Jazz Podium* (June): 209–13.
Mausbach, Wilfried. 2006. " 'Burn, ware-house, burn!' Modernity, Counterculture, and the Vietnam War in West Germany." In *Between Marx and Coca-Cola*, eds. Schildt and Siegfried, 175–202.
Mäusli, Theo, ed. 1994. *Jazz und Sozialgeschichte*. Zurich: CHRONOS Verlag.
Mayer, John, and Joe Harriott Double Quintet. 1965. *Indo-Jazz Suite*. EMI, SCXO 6025.
Mecklenburg, Herzog zu. 1968. "Swing in Jazz & Pop." *Jazz Podium* (November): 348–50.
Meifert, Franziska. 1999. "Doch Hunde, Schakale, die haben auch ihr Lied." *Testcard* 7: 160–177.
Miller, Manfred. 1966. "Berliner Jazztage 1966." *Jazz Podium* (December): 324–8.
———. 1968. "Musiker und Gesellschaft." In *Jazz Aktuell*, ed. Schreiner, 85–104.
———. 1969. "Kulturindustrie und Emanzipation." Berlin Jazz Days program notes: 25.
Minor, William. 2004. *Jazz Journeys to Japan: The Heart Within*. Ann Arbor: University of Michigan Press.
Montes, Paco, and Juan Claudio Cifuentes. 1967. Cover notes for *Jazz Flamenco*, by the Pedro Iturralde Quintet.
Morgenstern, Dan. 1965. "The Long-Awaited Return of Tony Scott." *Downbeat*, 2 December: 19–20.
———. 1968. "European Impressions." *Downbeat*, 11 January: 20-22.
Mortimer, Rex. 1974. *Indonesian Communism under Sukarno: Ideology and Politics*. Ithaca and London: Cornell University Press.

Mosse, George L. 1975. *The Nationalization of the Masses: Political Symbolism and Mass Movements in Germany from the Napoleonic Wars through the Third Reich.* New York: H. Fertig.

Müller-Wirth, Moritz. 2000. "Nichts wird, wie es war. Gedanken über die Zukunft der Berliner Festspiele." In *Berliner Festwochen Chronik*, ed. Krüger, 242–52.

Mümpfer, Klaus. 1974. "Kammermusikalischer Jazz und Exoten-Trip." *Jazz Podium* (January): 23–4.

———. 1985. Review of *World Music Meeting*, by various musicians. *Jazz Podium* (October): 57.

Münz, H. 1953. Letter. *Konstanz Südkurier* newspaper clipping. Berendt Papers. Jazzinstitut, Darmstadt.

"Nach allen Regeln dieser Kunst." *Berliner Tagesspiegel* article. In *Berliner Jazztage Documentation*, ed. Rein.

Nass, Karl Heinz. 1956. "Zum 1000. Mal Jazz." *Jazz Podium* (December): 8, 10.

———. 1976. Letter. *Jazz Podium* (March): 27–8.

Naura, Michael. 1988. "Im Untertagebau der Jazzkeller." In *That's Jazz*, eds. Wolbert et al, 405–9.

———. 2000a. "Hey Joe!" *Jazzthing* (April & May): 28.

———. 2000b. "Zum Tod von Joachim-Ernst Berendt. Trommler in der Wüste – Erinnerungen an den Jazz Mentor." *Der Tagesspiegel*, 5 February.

Nelson, Oliver. 1970a. *Berlin Dialogues for Orchestra*. Flying Dutchman, FD 10134.

———. 1970b. Cover notes for *Berlin Dialogues for Orchestra*, by Oliver Nelson.

Neumeier, Mani. 2004. Telephone interview. 16 August.

Noel, Gérard. 1971. Review of *Eternal Rhythm*, by Don Cherry. *Jazz Hot* (February): 34.

Noglik, Bert. 1981. *Jazz-Werkstatt International*. Berlin: Verlag Neue Musik.

———. 1988a. "Jazzmusik und Euro-Folk." In *That's Jazz*, eds. Wolbert et al, 513–22

———. 1988b. "Vom Linden Blues zum Zentral-Quartett. Fragmentarisches zur Entwicklung des Jazz in der DDR." In *That's Jazz*, eds. Wolbert et al, 421–32.

———. 1990. *Klangspuren: Wege improvisierter Musik*. Berlin: Verlag Neue Musik.

———. 1994. "Osteuropäischer Jazz im Umbruch der Verhältnisse. Vom Wandel der Sinne im Prozeß gesellschaftlicher Veränderungen." In *Jazz in Europa*, ed Knauer, 147–62.

———. 1996: "Hürdenlauf zum freien Spiel. Ein Rückblick auf den Jazz der DDR." In *Jazz in Deutschland*, ed Knauer, 205–21.

———. 1997. Cover notes for *Jazz Meets Asia*, by various musicians.

"Now Jazz Ramwong – Asiatische Themen aber Jazz a la Mangelsdorff." 1964. *Jazz Podium* (August): 192.

O'Brien, Peter. 1996. *Beyond the Swastika*. London and New York: Routledge.

Oesch, Hans, Wulf Arlt and Max Haas, eds. 1984. *Europäische Musik zwischen Nationalismus und Exotik*, eds., eds. Winterthur: Amadeus.

Ohff, Heinz. 1965. "Ein schwarzer Freitag für den Jazz." *Berliner Tagesspiegel* article. In *Berliner Jazztage Documentation*, ed. Rein.

———. 1966a. "Die Problematik vorweg." *Berliner Tagesspiegel* article. In *Berliner Jazztage Documentation*, ed. Rein.

———. 1966b. "Faszinierendes Brasilien." *Berliner Tagesspiegel* article. In *Berliner Jazztage Documentation*, ed. Rein.

———. 1966c. "Vorbild für die Festwochen." *Berliner Tagesspiegel* article. In *Berliner Jazztage Documentation*, ed. Rein.

———. 1967a. "Glanz und Elend des Eintopfes." *Berliner Tagesspiegel* article. In *Berliner Jazztage Documentation*, ed. Rein.

———. 1967b. "In den Schoß gefallen." *Berliner Tagesspiegel* article. In *Berliner Jazztage Documentation*, ed. Rein.

———. 1971a. "Der ganze Jazz." *Berliner Tagesspiegel* article. In *Berliner Jazztage Documentation*, ed. Rein.

———. 1971b. "J.E. Berendts (vorläufig) letzte Jazztage." *Berliner Tagesspiegel* article. In *Berliner Jazztage Documentation*, ed. Rein.

Olshausen, Ulrich. 1967. "Free Jazz in Klausur." *Frankfurter Allgemeine Zeitung*, 21 December.

———. 1968. Review of *Jazz Meets India*, by various musicians. *Jazz Podium* (September): 290.

———. 1969. Cov. notes for *Wild Goose*, by Albert Mangelsdorff et al.

"Ost-Jazz Meister der Fröhlichkeit." 1964. *Der Spiegel*, 9 September: 86.

"'Own Thing' Drei vom Manfred Schoof Quintett in einem JP Gespräch." 1966. *Jazz Podium* (March): 66–9.

Panke, Werner. 1971a. "Baden-Baden Free Jazz Meeting." *Jazz Podium* (January): 30–31.

———. 1971b. "Jazz bei den Donaueschinger Musiktagen." *Jazz Podium* (December): 424–5.

———. 1983. "Zentrum der Weltmusik." *Jazz Podium* (September): 4–5.

Partsch, Cornelius. 2000. *Schräge Töne: Jazz und Unterhaltungsmusik in der Kultur der Weimarer Republik*. Stuttgart and Weimar: J.B. Metzler.

Pasquier, Samuel. 2000. "Free Jazz in Deutschland, 1960-70: Zeichen einer Gesellschaft im Umbruch." (MA diss., Université Catholique de l'Ouest, Angers).

Paulot, Bruno. 1993. *Albert Mangelsdorff: Gespräche*. Waakirchen: Oreo.

Perrone, Charles A. 1989. *Masters of Contemporary Brazilian Song: MPB, 1965–1985*. Austin: University of Texas Press.

———, and Christopher Dunn, eds. 2001. *Brazilian Popular Music and Globalization*. Gainesville: University of Florida Press.

Pfankuch, Gert. 1988. "Amateurjazz in den fünfziger Jahren." In *That's Jazz*, eds. Wolbert et al, 411–20.

Pfleiderer, Martin. 1998. *Zwischen Weltmusik und Exotismus. Zur Rezeption asiatischer und afrikanischer Musik im Jazz der 60er und 70er Jahre*. Karben: CODA.

Pfeiffer, Peter H. 1965. Preface. *Goethe Institut* Yearbook.

———. 1966. Preface. *Goethe Institut* Yearbook.

———. 1968. Preface. *Goethe Institut* Yearbook.

Pike, Dave Set and Grupo Baiafro. 1972. *Salomão*. MPS, 15370.

Pilz, Michael. 2000. "Wer swingt, der marschiert nicht. Der Jazz-Missionar Joachim-Ernst Berendt ist tot." *Die Welt*, 5 February.

Pinckney, Warren R. Jr. 1989/1990. "Jazz in India. Perspectives on Historical Development and Musical Acculturation." *Asian Music* 21.1 (Autumn & Winter): 35–77.

Poiger, Uta. 2000. *Jazz, Rock, and Rebels: Cold War Politics and American Culture in a Divided Germany*. Berkeley: University of California Press.

"Polish Writer Calls for More Jazz Diplomacy." 1966. *Downbeat*, 16 June: 14.

Pollack, Heinz. 1922. *Die Revolution des Gesellschaftstanzes*. Dresden: Sibyllen.

Porter, Lewis. 1998. *John Coltrane: His Life and Music*. Ann Arbor: University of Michigan Press.

"Positives Resultat der Hechinger Gespräche." 1969. *Jazz Podium* (January): 20.
Powell, Baden. 1966. *Tristeza on Guitar.* Saba, 15090.
———. 1967. *Poema on Guitar.* Saba, SB 15150.
———. 1970. *Canto on Guitar.* MPS, 15300.
———. 1971. *Images on Guitar.* MPS, 15328.
Prieberg, Fred K. 1963. "Der lebendige Jazz ist universaler als jedes Volkslied." *Melos* 30: 294–5.
Rahn, Eckhart. 1966/67. "Berlins Festival muß geändert werden." *Sounds* 1: 52.
Ramstedt, Martin. 1991. "Revitalization of Balinese Classical Dance and Music." In *Music in the Dialogue of Cultures*, ed. M.P. Baumann, 108–20.
Rein, Dieter, ed. n.d. *Berliner Jazztage Documentation.* Berlin: Hochschule der Künste.
Reiniger, Franz 1983. "Die deutsche Jazzszene. Der Kreis um Albert Mangelsdorff." Typescript. Jazzinstitut, Darmstadt.
Reinle, Jean-Pierre, ed. 2001. *"Your own Thing." Ein Kaleidoscop von improvisierter Musik und die Musiken der Welt.* Zurich: Chronos Verlag, 2001.
Renaud, Jacques. 1968. Review of *Auto Jazz*, by Barney Wilen. *Jazz Hot* (November): 40.
———. 1969. Review of *Eternal Rhythm*, by Don Cherry. *Jazz Hot* (July & August): 40.
Review of *Jazz und Alte Musik*, by J-E Berendt et al. 1958. *Jazz Podium* (April): 88.
Review of *Sakura Sakura*, by the Hideo Shiraki Quintet and Three Koto Girls. 1966. *Jazz Podium* (July): 192.
Richter, Stephan. 1998 "Magic books and a jam session. Das Spannungsfeld von Literatur, Literaturtheorie und Jazz." In *Jazz und Sprache. Sprache und Jazz*, ed. Knauer, 21–36.
Roach, Max. 1960. *We Insist: Freedom Now Suite.* Candid, CCD79002.
Roberts, John Storm. 1999. *Latin Jazz: The First of the Fusions, 1880s to Today.* New York: Schirmer Books.
Robertson, Alan. 2003. *Joe Harriott: Fire in his Soul.* London: Northway Publications.
Robinson, J. Bradford. 1994. "The Jazz Essays of Theodor Adorno: Some Thoughts on Jazz Reception in Weimar Germany." *Popular Music* 13.1: 1–25.
Rollins, Sonny. 1958. *Freedom Suite.* Riverside, 258.
Rosenberg, Alfred. 1959. "Der Jazz ist ein Mischling." *Das Schlagzeug* (August): 30.
———. 1961. "Die Wiener Klassik war – eurasisch …" *Jazz Podium* (August): 217.
Ross, Werner. 1965. "Das Goethe-Institut gestern, heute, morgen." *Goethe Institut* Yearbook: 7–15.
Roth, Richard. 1961. "Der Blues vom deutschen Jazz." *Die Kultur,* February.
Rudorf, Reginald. 1964. *Jazz in der Zone.* Cologne and Berlin: Kiepenheuer and Witsch.
Ruppel, K. H. 1954. "Drehscheibe der internationalen Musik." *Melos* 21: 319–20.
Rüsenberg, Michael. 2002. *Der Sohn des Pfarrers, der Papst wurde. Joachim Ernst Berendt zum 80. Geburtstag.* HR radio transcript. 19 July.
———. 2004. Personal interview. 22 October.
Russell, George. 1969. *Electronic Sonata for Souls Loved by Nature.* Flying Dutchman, 10124.
"Saba bringt Jazz-Plattenserie." 1965. *Jazz Podium* (May): 112.
Sandner, Wolfgang. 1971. "Berliner Jazztage '71." *Jazz Podium* (November): 430–33.
———. 2004. "Vom Vermischten ins Feuilleton. – Der Jazz und seine Kritiker." In *Der Frankfurt Sound*, ed. Schwab, 280–85.

Santamaria, Freddy. 1970. "Osaka-en-jazz." *Jazz Magazine* (October): 8–9.
SarDesai, D.R. 1989. *Southeast Asia: Past and Present*. Houndmills and London: MacMillan.
Sathe, Keshav. 2004. Telephone interview. 16 September.
Savy, Michel. 1971. Review of *Noon in Tunisia*, by George Gruntz. *Jazz Hot* (May): 32.
Schaal, Hans-Jürgen. 1981. "Der Wiedergeborene Dionysos." *Jazz Podium* (February): 6–13.
———. 1983. "Theodor W. Adorno und der Jazz." *Jazz Podium* (November): 17–19.
Schade, Horst. 1971. "Leo Wright griff zur Trompete." *Jazz Podium* (January): 26–8.
Schatt, Peter W. 1995. *"Jazz" in der Konzertmusik*. Kassel: Gustav Bosse.
Schildt, Axel. 2006. "Across the Border: West German Youth Travel to Western Europe." In *Between Marx and Coca-Cola*, eds. Schildt and Siegfried, 149–60
———, and Siegfried, Detlef, eds. 2006a. *Between Marx and Coca-Cola: Youth Cultures in Changing European Societies, 1960-1980*. New York: Berghahn Books, 2006.
———. 2006b. "Youth, Consumption, and Politics in the Age of Radical Change." In *Between Marx and Coca-Cola*, eds. Schildt and Siegfried, 1–35.
Schmidt-Garre, Helmut. 1954. "Jazz in der evangelischen Akademie." *Melos* 21: 82.
Schmidt-Joos, Siegfried. 1959a. Review of *Das neue Jazzbuch*, by J-E Berendt. *Das Schlagzeug* (February): 24.
———. 1959b. Review of *Prisma der gegenwärtigen Musik*, ed. by J-E Berendt and Jürgen Uhde. *Das Schlagzeug* (November): 27.
——— (a.k.a. "George Joos"). 1959c. Review of *Prisma der gegenwärtigen Musik*, ed. by J-E Berendt and Jürgen Uhde. *Jazz Echo* (September): 42.
———. 1960. "Amateur Jazz ist wenn man nach Amerika fährt." *Jazz Echo* (November): 40–41.
———. 1965a. "Ein Votum für Populärer Jazz." *Jazz Podium* (December): 320–21.
———. 1965b. Review of *Jazz Greetings from the East*, by various musicians. *Jazz Echo* (July): 42–3.
———. 1966. "Jazz-Festival des Pianos." *Jazz Echo* (January): 40-42.
———. 1967a. "Musikalische Koexistenz oder Integration?" *Jazz Podium* (January): 17.
———. 1967b. "Musikalische Koexistenz oder Integration?" *Jazz Podium* (May): 140.
———. 1967c. "Musikalische Koexistenz oder Integration?" *Jazz Podium* (August): 220–1.
———. 1967d. "Musikalische Koexistenz oder Integration?" *Jazz Podium* (September): 260–62.
———. 1968. "Weil viele Dinge geändert werden müssen." *Jazz Podium* (April): 128–9.
———. 1970. "Sun Ra. Kosmisches Chaos." *Der Spiegel*, 16 November: 226, 228.
———. 1971. "Dieses Trauerspiel." *Der Spiegel*, 12 July: 110.
———. 1972. "Etwas Abgezapft." *Der Spiegel*, 2 October: 198–201.
———. 2005. Telephone interview. 13 September.
———, and Felix Schmidt. 1969. "Reisst die Barrieren nieder." *Der Spiegel*, 27 January: 118–20.
Schnebel, Dieter. 1984. "Neue Weltmusik." In *Europäische Musik zwischen Nationalismus und Exotik*, eds. Oesch, Arlt and Haas, 115–28.
Schoener, Eberhard. 1975. *Bali Agung*. Electrola, 1 C 062-29 647.

Schönherr, Ulle. n.d. "Adorno und Jazz. Reflexionen zur Geschichte einer Begegnung." Typescript. Jazzinstitut, Darmstadt.
Schoof, Manfred. 2004. Personal interview. 22 September.
Schreiber, Hermann. 1958. "Jazz goes to Church." *Stuttgarter Zeitung*, 29 January.
Schreiner, Claus, ed. 1968. *Jazz Aktuell*. Mainz: B. Schott's Söhne.
———. 1969. "Besucher von Jazzkonzerten proben den Aufstand." Berlin Jazz Days program notes: 16.
———. 1972. Cover notes for *Salomão*, by the Dave Pike Set and Grupo Baiafro.
———. 1993. *Música Brasileira: A History of Popular Music and the People of Brazil*. trans. Mark Weinstein. London, New York: Marion Boyars.
———. 1997. Cover notes for *Jazz Meets Brazil*, by various musicians.
———. 2004. Email to the author. 14 October.
Schrimpf, Helmut. 1954. Letter to J-E Berendt. 25 October. Berendt Papers. Jazzinstitut, Darmstadt.
Schuller, Gunther. 1961. "Jazz und zeitgenössische Musik." *Jazz Podium* (January): 10–12.
Schulte-Bahrenberg, Ralf. 2004. Telephone interview. 17 August.
Schulz-Köhn, Dietrich. 1951. *Wesen und Gestalten der Jazzmusik*. Kevelaer: Butzon and Bercker.
Schwab, Jürgen, ed. 2004. *Der Frankfurt Sound: Eine Stadt und ihre Jazzgeschichte*. Frankfurt: Societätsverlag.
Schweizer, Irène. 2004. Telephone interview. 12 August.
Scott, Tony. n.d. "The Way of the Orient." 10 March 2004. <http://www.tonyscott.it/way_of_orient.htm>.
———, Shinuchi Yuize and Hozan Yamamoto. 1964. *Music for Zen Meditation and Other Joys*. Verve, 2332 052.
——— and The Indonesian All-Stars. 1967. *Djanger Bali*. Saba, 15145.
Segler, Daland. 1987. "Das Ohr ist der Weg." *Deutsches Allgemeines Sonntagsblatt*, 9 August.
Seeger, Anthony. 1991. "Creating and Confronting Cultures. Issues of Taping and Selection in Records and Videotapes of Musical Performances." In *Music in the Dialogue of Cultures*, ed. M.P. Baumann, 290–301.
Serra, Philippe. 1968. "Ponty par lui-meme." *Jazz Hot* (May, June & July): 25–6.
Shakespeare, Nicholas. 1999. *Bruce Chatwin*. London, Vintage.
Shankar, Ravi. 1961. *Improvisations*. World Pacific, ST 1416.
———. 1969. *Meine Musik, mein Leben*. Munich: Nymphenburger Verlagshandlung.
Shapiro, Peter, ed. 2000. *Modulations: A History of Electronic Music*. New York, Caipirinha Productions Inc.
Shepp, Archie. 1965. "An Artist Speaks Bluntly." *Downbeat*, 16 December: 11, 42.
Shiraki, Hideo. 1961. *In Festival*. Teichiku, NL-3008.
———, Quintet and Three Koto Girls. 1965. *Sakura Sakura*. Saba, 15064.
Sidhu-Ingenhoff, Anette. 2002. *Zur Person Joachim Ernst Berendt zum 80. Geburtstag*. Radio transcript. Berendt Papers. Jazzinstitut, Darmstadt.
Sieg, Katrin. 1998. "Ethnic Drag and National Identity: Multicultural Crises, Crossings and Interventions." In *The Imperialist Imagination*, eds. Friedrichsmayer, Lennox, and Zantop, 295–319.
———. 2002. *Ethnic Drag: Performing Race, Nation, Sexuality in West Germany*. Ann Arbor: University of Michigan Press.

Silvert, Conrad. 1979. "A Critic With an International Reputation." *San Francisco Chronicle*, 25 December.
Slawe, Jan. 1948. *Einführung in die Jazzmusik*. Basel: National-Zeitung.
Sloterdijk, Peter. 1987. *Kopernikanische Mobilmachung und ptolemäische Abrüstung*. Frankfurt am Main: Suhrkamp.
Smith, Will. 1972. Review of *Eternal Rhythm*, by Don Cherry. *Downbeat*, 23 November: 18.
Smith Bowers, Kathryn. 2002. "East Meets West: Contributions of Matyas Seiber." In *Jazz and the Germans*, ed. Budds, 119–40.
Solothurnmann, Jürg. 1994. "Die Alpine Jazz Herd. Zeitgenössischer Jazz und nationale Folklore, paßt das zusammen?" In *Jazz in Europa*, ed. Knauer, 201–20.
Sontag, Susan. 1980. *Under the Sign of Saturn*. New York: Farrar, Straus & Giroux.
Soufflot, Armand. 1952. "Der Pariser Salon International du Jazz." *Die Gondel* (May): 62–3, 84.
Spindler, Mathias. 1976. Letter. *Jazz Podium* (February): 3.
Starr, S. Frederick. 1994. *Red and Hot: The Fate of Jazz in the Soviet Union 1917–1991*. New York: Limelight Editions.
Steinbiß, Florian. 1984. *Deutsch-Folk: Auf der Suche nach der verlorenen Tradition*. Frankfurt am Main: Fischer Taschenbuchverlag.
Steinert, Heinz. 1992. *Die Entdeckung der Kulturindustrie: Oder Warum Professor Adorno Jazz-Musik nicht ausstehen konnte*. Vienna: Verlag für Gesellschaftskritik.
Stern, Frank. 1992. *Whitewashing the Yellow Badge: Anti-Semitism and Philosemitism in Postwar Germany*. trans. William Templer. Oxford and New York: Pergamon Press.
Storb, Ilse. 1978. "Fragen an Alexander von Schlippenbach." *Jazz Podium* (October): 4–7.
Stroh, Wolfgang Martin. 1994. *Handbuch New Age Musik*. Regensburg: ConBrio Verlagsgesellschaft.
Stuckenschmidt, H.H. 1967. "Nachwuchssorgen auch in Donaueschingen." *Melos* 34: 456–62.
Sudhalter, Richard M. 2001. *Lost Chords: White Musicians and their Contribution to Jazz, 1915–1945*. New York and Oxford: Oxford University Press.
Sudibyo, P.R. 2004a. Letter to the author. 4 May.
2004b. Telephone interview. 15 March.
Sur, Tahir Hakki. 1963. Cover notes for *Now hear our meanin'*, by the Clarke–Boland Big Band.
Taylor, Timothy D. 1997. *Global pop: World music, World markets*. New York: Routledge.
Teraoka, Arlene A. 1996. *East, West and Others: The Third World in Postwar German Literature*. Lincoln and London: University of Nebraska Press.
Theobald, Adolf. 1956. "Der schwarze und der weiße Jazz. Volksmusik wurde exportiert und verfälscht." *Rheinischer Merkur*, 13 April.
Ticoalu, Alfred D. 2004a. Email to the author. 30 March.
———. 2004b. Telephone interview. 15 March.
"Tony Scott – Reflections, Views and Prognosis." 1965. *Downbeat* 26 August: 15.
Tormann, Uwe. n.d. "Ein Blues für Hans-Georg." Typescript. Jazzinstitut, Darmstadt.
Traber, Habakuk. 2000. "Eine Epoche. Die Berliner Festwochen – Ein Musikfest." In *50 Jahre Berliner Festwochen*, ed. Krüger, 168–79.

Treece, David. 1997. "Guns and roses: bossa nova and Brazil's music of popular protest, 1958-68." *Popular Music* 16.1: 1–29.
Twittenhoff, Wilhelm. 1953. *Jugend und Jazz*. Mainz: Schott's Söhne.
Tynan, John A. 1965. "Ravi Shankar – India's Master Musician." *Downbeat*, 6 May: 14–16, 43.
"Überraschend abgesagt: Filmreise 'Auf den Spuren des Jazz.'" 1959. *Schlagzeug* (October): 4.
Ulanov, Barry. 1952. *A History of Jazz in America*. New York: Viking Press.
Usinger, Fritz. 1953. *Kleine Biographie des Jazz*. Offenbach: Kumm.
Van der Lee, Pedro. 1998. "Sitars and Bossas: World Music Influences." *Popular Music* 17.1: 45–69.
Van der Will, Wilfried. 1995. "Culture and the Organization of National Socialist Ideology 1933-1945." In *German Cultural Studies*, ed. Burns, 101–45.
Various musicians. 1957. *Jazz und Alte Musik*. Telefunken, LA 6193.
———. 1963. *Brasilien, Jazz und Poesie*. Philips Twen Serie, 17.
———. 1965. *Jazz Greetings from the East*. Fontana, 885 416 TY.
———. 1966. *Folklore e Bossa Nova do Brasil*. Saba, 15102.
———. 1967a. *From Sticksland with Love – Drums and Folklore*. Saba, 15133.
———. 1967b. *Jazz Meets India*. Saba, 15142.
———. 1967c. *Noon in Tunisia*. Saba, 15132.
———. 1968. *Modern Jazz VII Anthology 68*. Qualiton, LPX 17392.
———. 1969. *Gittin to know y'all*. MPS, 15269.
———. 1971. *Ossiach*. BASF, 49 21119-3/1-3.
———. 1985. *World Music Meeting*. Eigelstein, ES 2024.
———. 1986. *To Hear the World in a Grain of Sand*. Soul Note, SN 1128.
———. 1997. *Jazz Meets the World*. Vols. 1–4. Universal, 533-133-2, 533-132-2, 531-847-2, 531-720-2.
"Visiting Jazzman." 1962. *Newsweek*, 27 August.
Von Eschen, Penny. 2004. *Satchmo Blows up the World: Jazz Ambassadors Play the Cold War*. Cambridge, Mass. and London: Harvard University Press.
Von Herwarth, Hans. 1970. Preface. *Goethe Institut* Yearbook.
Von Schlippenbach, Alexander. 1966. Cover notes for *Globe Unity*, by Alexander von Schlippenbach and the Globe Unity Orchestra.
———. 1975. "Potenzierung musikalischer Energien: Das Globe Unity Orchester." *Jazz Podium* (March): 11–13.
———. 1981. "Jazz mit Berendt – reaktionär." *Jazz Podium* (March): 32.
———. 2004. Letter to the author. 26 September.
———, and the Globe Unity Orchestra. 1966. *Globe Unity*. Saba, 15109.
Von Zahn, Robert. 2003. *Jazz in Nordrhein-Westfalen seit 1946*. Cologne: Musikland NRW.
Voswinkel, Stephan. 1985. "Über die Vielfalt der Musik." *Jazz Podium* (May): 10–11.
Wachler, Ingolf. 1964. "Festival Marginalien." *Jazz Echo* (July): 40–41.
———. 1966. "Jazz aus Japan." *Jazz Echo* (August): 44–5.
Waldick, Leo. 1954a. "Aphorismen zum '3. Salon international du Jazz.'" *Jazz Podium* (July): 7–9.
———. 1954b. "3. Salon international du Jazz" *Jazz Podium* (October): 10.
———. 1954c. Letter to Helmut Schrimpf. 3 November. Berendt Papers. Jazzinstitut, Darmstadt.

———. 1954d. Letter. *Jazz Podium* (December): 8.
Washabaugh, William. 1996. *Flamenco: Passion, Politics and Popular Culture*. Oxford and Washington: Berg.
Weber, Eberhard. 1977. Unpublished letter to *Frankfurter Rundschau*. 8 September. In *rundy*, 13 September.
Weidemann, Siegfried. 1972a. "Ein Wiederaufblühen des langen totgesagten Swing." *Bild und Funk* newspaper clipping. Berendt Papers. Jazzinstitut, Darmstadt.
———. 1972b. "Ich dulde keine Kompromisse." *Bild und Funk* newspaper clipping. Berendt Papers. Jazzinstitut, Darmstadt.
Wein, George (with Nate Chinen). 2003. *Myself Among Others: A Life in Music*. Cambridge, Mass.: Da Capo.
Weinstein, Norman. 1992. *A Night in Tunisia: Imaginings of Africa in Jazz*. Metuchen, N.J. and London: Scarecrow Press.
Welding, Pete. 1965. Review of *Now Jazz Ramwong*, by the Albert Mangelsdorff Quintet. *Downbeat*, 11 February: 29–30.
Wertheim, W.F. 1959. *Indonesian Society in Transition. A Study of Social Change*. The Hague and Bandung: W. van Hoeve.
Widmaier, Wolfgang. 1966. "Jazz – ein wilder Sturm über Europa." *Melos* 33: 12–17.
Wilen, Barney. 1968. *Auto Jazz*. MPS, 15164.
Wilkie, Colin and Shirley Hart. 2004. Personal interview. 11 September.
Willett, Ralph. 1989. *The Americanization of Germany, 1945–1949*. London and New York: Routledge.
Wilmer, Valerie. 1967. "Berlin Jazz Festival." *Downbeat*, 12 January: 23–4.
———. 1970. "Caught in the Act." *Downbeat*, 22 January: 26–7.
Wilson, Peter Niklas. 1987. "Zwischen 'Ethno-Pop' und 'Weltmusik.'" *Neue Zeitschrift für Musik* 148.5: 5–8.
———. 1990. "Die Ratio des Irrationalismus." In *Die Musik der achtziger Jahre*, ed. Ekkehard Jost. Mainz: B. Schott's Söhne, 62–77.
———. 2001. "Fluchthelfer, Projektionsfläche, Sample." In *"Your own Thing,"* ed. Reinle, 107–117.
Wolbert, Klaus, et al, eds. 1988. *That's Jazz. Der Sound des 20. Jahrhunderts*. Darmstadt: City of Darmstadt.
Wunderlich, Werner. 1968. "Die Deutsche Jazz-Föderation e.V." In *Jazz Aktuell*, ed. Schreiner, 250–52.
———. 1987. Letter to J-E Berendt. 10 July. (in the possession of the author)
———. 1998. Letter to J-E Berendt. 16 October. (in the possession of the author)
———. 2004. Personal Interview. 24 September.
Yui, Shoichi. 1965. Cover notes for *Sakura Sakura*, by the Hideo Shiraki Quintet and Three Koto Girls.
Zenetti, Lothar. 1953a. "Der Jazz und die Religion." *Jazz Podium* (May): 5.
———. 1953b. "Der Jazz und die Religion." *Jazz Podium* (June): 7.
Ziegler, Dr. 1954. Letter to J-E Berendt. 25 October. Berendt Papers. Jazzinstitut, Darmstadt.
Zimmerle, Dieter. 1957. "Jazz im Kreuzfeuer der Meinungen." *Jazz Podium* (April): 5–7.
———. 1960. "Die braune Walze." *Jazz Podium* (March): 52.
———. 1964. "Berliner Jazz-Tage und Nächte." *Jazz Podium* (November): 266–70.
———. 1967a. "SWF Avantgarde Session." *Jazz Podium* (January): 21.

———. 1967b. "Wieder Jazz in Donaueschingen." *Jazz Podium* (November & December): 317.
———. 1968a. "Berliner Jazztage 1967." *Jazz Podium* (January): 15.
———. 1968b. "Berliner Jazztage." *Jazz Podium* (December): 374–9.
———. 1969a. "20 Free-Jazzer beim SWF." *Jazz Podium* (January): 19.
———. 1969b. "Berliner Jazztage '69" *Jazz Podium* (December): 390–96.
Zimmerle-Betzing, Gudrun. 1975. "SWF Jazz Session in Konstanz." *Jazz Podium* (August): 16.
Zimmermann, Heinz Werner. 2002. "The influence of American music on a German composer." In *Jazz and the Germans*, ed. Budds, 179–93.
"Zum Armstrong-Skandal in Hamburg." 1955. *Jazz Echo* (December): 41.

Index

1968 Generation, 2, 6, 116–17, 120, 141

Abdul-Malik, Ahmed, 188
Aberg, Lennart, 220, 220 (fig. 20)
Abendroth, Walter, 37
Adorno, Theodor, 26–27, 30–31, 43, 49, 130, 132, 193n7, 226
   "Culture Industry" theory (with Max Horkheimer), 6, 31–33, 37–38, 76
   debate with Berendt, 27, 32–34, 49, 53, 169, 229
   Introduction to the Sociology of Music (1962), 32
   jazz and fascism, 37–39
   opposition to jazz, 31–35, 41
   See also Horkheimer, Max
Adenauer, Konrad, 39; Adenauer "restoration," 116, 120
Africa, 5, 10, 68, 74, 80, 205–17. *See also* North Africa
African Americans, 9–10, 39, 42, 44, 61, 64–69, 75, 83, 91–92, 102, 142, 149, 155, 188, 190, 206–17
   civil rights movement, 60–63, 65, 75, 83, 207
   "roots" discourse, 10, 91, 206–11; parallels to *Blut und Boden* discourse, 139, 210–11
   See also negrophilia; Berendt, Joachim-Ernst on African American "roots" discourse, the Negro, racial discrimination

Afrocentric jazz, 91, 206–10, 217. *See also* "Black music ideology"
Afrocentrism, 207, 210, 217. *See also* negrophilia
Akiyoshi, Toshiko, 173
Altgelt, Erika, 43
American Folk Blues Festivals, 95–97, 96 (fig. 7). *See also* Lippmann, Horst; Rau, Fritz
Anders, Günther, 36, 41, 113
Anglo-American folk music, 91, 95, 97–98
Ansermet, Ernest, 24
anti-Americanism, 89, 138, 141, 163–66
Anti-Festival/Total Music Meeting (TMM), 121–25
anti-Semitism, 18–19, 28, 64–65, 67, 228n. *See also* Philosemitism
Arabic music, 187–88
ARD, 80n4, 123, 125, 134
Armstrong, Louis: and the *Halbstarken* riots 35–36; on race, 67
Artus, Helmut, 225
Association for the Advancement of Creative Musicians (AACM), 142
Association P.C., 128n
Auger, Brian, 116
Auto Jazz. *See Jazz Meets the World* series (*JMTW*)
Ayler, Albert, 106n3

Bach, J. S., 27–28, 33, 138
Bachmann, Klaus-Robert, 107, 226

Baden-Baden Free Jazz Meeting. *See* Free Jazz Meeting
Baden-Baden World Music Meeting, 226, 229
Bailey, Benny, 202
Baldwin, James, 209
Bali, 150–51, 153–55, 170, 199–204, 216, 219, 221
Balliet, Whitney, 1
Baraka, Amiri (LeRoi Jones), 75, 110, 209, 217
Barbieri, Gato, 212
Baresel, Alfred, 18, 30, 47
baroque music, 27–28, 80n5, 99
Bauer, Connie, 220
Beatles, The, 127, 193
bebop, 22, 30, 114, 233, 235
Bennink, Han, 123 (**fig. 10**), 134n14, 143 (**fig. 11**)
Berendt, Joachim-Ernst
   on African American "roots" discourse, 10, 208–11
   on Bali and the Balinese, 150–51, 153–54, 216
   on Brazil, the Caribbean and the Creole, 151–53, 177, 182–84
   "Dance as Escape" (essay, 1956), 40
   Das Leben: Ein Klang (1996), 8
   family, 20, 22, 25, 63, 76, 222
   on free jazz, 76, 83, 106–110, 114–15, 122, 139–40, 142, 180, 194, 209, 235
   Hesse Between Music (1975), 221
   "Jazz and India" (essay, 1980), 218
   Jazz: A Time-Critical Study (*Jazz: eine zeitkritische Studie*, 1950), 21–22, 36, 40–41, 43n, 46, 109, 223
   Jazzbook, The (*Das Jazzbuch*, 1953), xi, xiii, 2, 2n3, 8, 17, 21–24, 32, 60–61, 77, 80, 109, 114, 126, 131–33, 209, 222, 233–34
   Jazz Greetings from the East (1965), 56, 111
   Jazz – Heard and Seen (television series), 17, 170
   Jazz Life (1961), xiii, 76, 147. *See also* Claxton, William
   as "jazz pope," xiii, 1–11, 17, 47, 115–16, 128, 130, 135, 147, 158, 222, 231
   as "Joe Brown," 17, 57 (*Jazz Echo* pseudonym)
   Music from Bali, The (1962), 155
   Nada Brahma (1983), xiii, 221–23, 228
   on the Negro, 61, 65–69, 150, 152–53, 208–9
   New Age movement, 8, 10, 221–223
   Nietzschean interpretation of jazz, 40–41, 65
   on racial discrimination, interracial "mixing," and interracial sexual relationships, 39, 60–63, 65, 67–69, 152–53
   religion/spirituality, 9, 25, 40, 42–45, 82, 86, 125, 132, 168, 217, 220–23, 235–36
   travels to the United States, 22–23, 42, 53, 60, 63, 76, 89, 147–49
   travel writings, 76, 147, 149–57
   on *Weltmusik*, 4n7, 6, 10, 178, 216–24, 229–30; critiques of his views 225–28
   Window out of Jazz, A (1977), 130–31, 135n, 210n3, 217, 221
   See also Jazz Meets the World series (*JMTW*)
Berendt Jr, Ernst, 3; death in Dachau 3, 20, 63, 131
Berger, Karl, 8, 194–95, 212, 214, 216, 219. *See also Jazz Meets the Word: Eternal Rhythm*
Berlin, 5, 10, 16, 51–52, 54, 78–84, 86, 94, 110, 112–13, 115–17, 122, 125–26, 128–30, 157, 167, 171–73, 176–77, 181–82, 197, 202–3, 215, 222, 230, 234–35. *See also* Berlin Wall
Berlin Jazz Days/Berlin JazzFest, xiii, 2, 9, 78–85, 105–7, 116, 121–22, 125–26, 128–30, 133–34, 206, 234, 236
   (1964), 56, 79, 82, 85
   (1965), 10, 79, 82, 106–7, 171–74, 176

(1966), 82, 106n3, 110, 116–17,
   133n, 176–177, 180–82
(1967), 82, 106n3, 116, 128n, 186,
   209–10, 214
(1968), 81 (**fig. 5**), 106n3, 112, 117,
   121–22, 128n, 213, 215
(1969), 116–17, 128n, 133n
(1970), 113, 122, 133n
(1971), 117, 122–23, 128n, 133n,
   135, 176
(1972), 81, 123, 129, 133n, 214,
   216, 218, 226
   See also Anti-Festival/Total Music
   Meeting
Berlin JazzFest. *See* Berlin Jazz Days
Berlin Jazz Salon, 56n, 79, 113
Berliner Festwochen (Berlin Festival
   Weeks), 73, 78–80, 83, 130, 173
Berlin Wall, 52, 78
Bhumipol, King of Thailand, 154,
   156–57, 160; Royal Jazz Sextet
   154, 160
Bizet, Georges, 41
Blacher, Boris, 110
"Black music ideology," 75–76, 107,
   110, 206, 208–11, 215, 217. *See
   also* Afrocentric jazz
Black Nationalism, 75, 209
Blome, Rainer, 111, 182
blues, 75, 95–97, 149, 192
Bock, Richard, 171, 192
Bockhoff, Baldur, 29
Boland, Francy. *See* Clarke-Boland Big
   Band
Böll, Heinrich, 203
bossa nova, 10, 97, 149, 177–85, 187,
   204, 227n
Bourdieu, Pierre, 6
Brand, Dollar, 216
Brandt, Willy, 51
Brazil, xiv, 10, 129, 150–53, 162, 177–
   85. *See also Jazz Meets the World:
   Folklore e Bossa Nova do Brasil*
Brecht, Bertolt, 18
Brooks, Billy, 206–10, 217. *See also Jazz
   Meets the World: El Babaku*
Brötzmann, Peter, 8, 109, 114, 118–24,
   120 (**fig. 9**), 133–34, 139–44,
   143 (**fig. 11**), 227

Brown, Marshall, International Youth
   Band (Newport Jazz Festival),
   79n, 89
Brubeck, Dave, 192
Brunner-Schwer, Hans-Georg, 84–86,
   106, 106n2. *See also* Saba/MPS
   labels
Burde, Wolfgang, 111, 120
Burnin' Red Ivanhoe, 116, 128n
Burg Waldeck folk festival, 95
Burton, Gary, Quartet, 128n
Byrd, Charlie: *Jazz Samba* (1962), 179

Cage, John, 112n6, 118
Can, 219
Capra, Fritjof, 221
Carles, Philippe, 76, 131, 217
Caribbean, 10, 147, 151–52, 157,
   220
CBS label, 84, 89, 137
CDU/CSU, 51, 117n
Césaire, Aimé, 67
Chand, Richard, 166
Chen, Bubi, 8, 157, 160, 164, 199–
   203, 202 (**fig. 18**), 230. *See also*
   Indonesian All-Stars
Chen, Yopi, 202 (**fig. 18**). *See also*
   Indonesian All-Stars
Cherry, Don, 106–107, 120–21, 190,
   191 (**fig. 17**), 206, 211–19, 213
   (**fig. 19**), 221, 224, 227
   "Humus," 216, 227
   and spirituality, 214–15
   *See also Jazz Meets the World:
   Eternal Rhythm*
civil rights movement. *See* African
   Americans: civil rights
   movement
Clarke, Kenny. *See* Clarke-Boland Big
   Band
Clarke-Boland Big Band, 57–58
Claxton, William, xiii, 23, 63, 76, 96,
   147, 149
   Jazz Life (1961), xiii, 76, 147
Cleaver, Eldridge, 209
Cold War, 2, 9, 39, 45, 51–54, 58,
   78–79, 82–84, 120, 136, 164
Coleman, Ornette, 74, 76–77, 106,
   106n3, 118, 212

colonialism, 153, 163, 165–66, 187, 227, 229–30
Coltrane, John, 74, 76–77, 148 (fig. 12), 149, 174, 186, 201–2, 207, 221, 235
  "India," 192
  Kulu Sé Mama (1965), 207
  and Other musical traditions, 74, 91, 93–94, 192
Comolli, Jean-Louis, 76, 131, 217
Conover, Willis, 51–53, 58. *See also* "Voice of America"
cool jazz, 76, 178, 181, 235
Corea, Chick, 4 (fig.1), 235
Creative Music Studio (Woodstock, NY), 219
"Culture Industry." *See* Adorno, Theodor
Cyrille, Andrew, 220

Darmstadt Jazz Institute. *See* Jazzinstitut Darmstadt
Dauer, Alfons M., 68, 127n
Davis, Miles 112, 116, 219, 235
  and modal jazz, 73–74, 202
  and philosemitism, 65
  and Spanish music, 91, 93–94
Delaunay, Charles, 21, 66, 137
de Ménil, François Conrad, 112
DeMichael, Don, 138
Deutsche Jazz Föderation (DJF). *See* German Jazz Federation
di Matteo, Luis, 220, 220 (fig. 20)
Dixieland revival, 77, 91, 95, 235
Djanger Bali. *See Jazz Meets the World* series
Döblin, Alfred, 46, 46n
Doldinger, Kurt, 161, 162 (fig. 14), 180
Dollase, Rainer, 6
Donaueschingen Music Days, 25–26, 76, 92, 105–7, 110–11, 114, 129–30, 141, 176, 197, 206, 209, 216, 219–20, 222, 226–27
Dortmund Jazz Salon, 36
Downbeat (magazine), 53, 138, 189, 216
Driscoll, Julie, 128n
Dylag, Roman, 55n

East Germany. *See* GDR
Eastern European jazz, 9, 53–56, 82–83, 86, 104, 115n, 200
ECM label, 134, 134n15
Edelhagen, Kurt, 17; Edelhagen Big Band 43; Kurt Edelhagen Orchestra 47, 57, 137–38, 159, 163
Eicher, Manfred, 134n15
El Babaku. *See Jazz Meets the World* series
Eldridge, Roy, 68n
electro-acoustics, 112–13, 196
Ellington, Duke, 16, 80n3; Duke Ellington Orchestra 125
Ellis, Don, 193
El Mahdi, Salah, 9; and *Noon in Tunisia* 187–89, 191, 198, 204, 230
E-Musik, 24–27, 29–31, 33–34, 36, 111, 204, 219
England, 2, 138
Erhard, Ludwig, 39
Erskine, Gilbert, 138
Essen Jazz Days, 79n
Eternal Rhythm. *See Jazz Meets the World* series
ethnomusicology, 155–56, 194
Eto, Kimio, 171
"European jazz," 9–10, 84, 87–94, 110–11, 136–44, 182, 200–201, 237. *See also* Eastern European jazz

Fanon, Frantz, 153n
Feather, Leonard, xi–xii, 22, 68, 68n, 86, 203, 209–10, 215
Ferguson, Marilyn, 221
Festival Folklore e Bossa Nova do Brasil, 97. *See also* Lippmann, Horst; Rau, Fritz
Festival Musica Folklorica Argentina, 97. *See also* Lippmann, Horst; Rau, Fritz
Finkelstein, Sidney, 24
Fischer, Klaus, 78
flamenco, 91–94, 97
Flamenco Gitano Festivals, 97. *See also* Lippmann, Horst; Rau, Fritz
Flamenco Jazz. *See Jazz Meets the World* series

Folklore e Bossa Nova do Brasil. See Jazz Meets the World series
France, 142
Frankfurter Rundschau debate, 130, 132
Free Jazz Meeting, 106–7, 108 (**fig. 8**), 112, 114, 130, 142, 196, 212, 216. *See also* New Jazz Meeting
free jazz, 6, 10, 73–76, 83, 86, 89, 91, 103, 105–18, 120–22, 124, 127, 130–32, 139–40, 142, 179–80, 182, 194–98, 209, 211–16, 223, 235
Free Music Production (FMP) label, 124, 131, 134
Freund, Joki, 55, 103; Joki Freund Quintet 54
Friesen, David, 220
From Sticksland with Love. See Jazz Meets the World series
Fruth, Willi, 85

gamelan music, 1, 154, 199–200, 214–16, 219
GDR/East Germany, 51–53, 58, 79, 83, 103, 126
Gebers, Jost, 122, 124
Geipel, Willi, 131
Gennari, John, 3, 6
German Jazz Federation (DJF), 16–17, 26, 51, 54–55, 96
German Jazz Festival, 16, 54, 56n, 91, 106n3, 190n, 193, 212
Gershwin, George, 29
Getz, Stan, 91, 177, 179–81
 Jazz Samba (1962), 179
 Stan Getz Quartet, 180
 See also Getz/Gilberto
Getz/Gilberto (1963), 179
Gilberto, Astrud, 180, 182
Gilberto, João, 178–79. *See also Getz/Gilberto*
Gillespie, Dizzy, 67, 187
Giuffre, Jimmy, 91
"global folklore," 95–98
Globe Unity. See Jazz Meets the World series
Globe Unity Orchestra (GUO), 106, 110–11, 115–18, 140–42, 144, 162n3

Globke, Hans, 120
Gmelin, Otto, 117
Goebbels, Joseph, 50
Goethe Institut, 8, 98–101, 103, 157–67, 176, 229; jazz tours, 8, 10, 98–101, 138, 157–67, 190n, 198, 222
Goffin, Robert, 21, 66
Golson, Benny, 102–3
Gondel, Die (magazine, later *Jazz Echo*), 16, 154
 Berendt's contributions as editor, 17, 54, 57n5, 76, 126
 German "All-Stars," 46–47
 readers' poll, 30, 46–47
gospel music, 44, 97
Granz, Norman, 16
Gruenewald, Matthias, 102
Gruntz, George, 8, 80n5, 92–94, 112n8, 125–26, 130, 130n, 186–91, 197–98, 204. *See also Jazz Meets the World: Noon in Tunisia*
Grupo Baiafro, 162
Gullin, Lars, 91
Gumpert, Ulrich, 103–4

Halbstarke, 35–37, 39. *See also Swingheinis*
Hamel, Peter Michael, 219, 221; Between 221
Hammond, John, 60, 86
Hampel, Gunter, 123 (**fig. 10**); Gunter Hampel Quintet 106; *Heartplants* 106, 139
Hampton, Lionel, 91
Handy, John, 218–19. *See also* Handy-Khan ensemble
Handy-Khan ensemble, 218, 225–26; *Karuna Supreme* (1975) 225
Harriott, Joe, 106, 193–94. *See also* Mayer, John and Joe Harriott Double Quintet
Hart, Shirley, 97
Heffley, Mike, 4
Hessischer Rundfunk (HR), 95, 97
Heider, Werner, 91
Heidland, Dr. (evangelical theologian), 42

Hentoff, Nat, 22–23, 61n1
Herder, Johann Gottfried, 94
Hesse, Hermann, 221
Hindemith, Paul, 19, 25–27, 33, 102, 138; *Mathis der Maler,* 102
Hino, Terumasa, 8, 160, 171, 173n3, 175–76, 230. *See also* Shiraki, Hideo, Quintet
Hitler, Adolf, 4, 18, 28, 95, 210. *See also* National Socialism
Hitler Youth, 50
Hobsbawm, Eric, 2n4
Hoch'sche Conservatorium, Frankfurt am Main, 18, 193n7
Hodeir, André, 24
Hoffmann, Bernd, 31n, 49
Hoffmann, Ingfried, 139
Holbe, Rainer, 228n
Horkheimer, Max, 32. *See also* Adorno, Theodor
Horn, Paul, 91, 192
Horne, Lena, 30n, 63, 63 **(fig. 4)**
Hot Clubs, 16–17, 39, 47
Hove, Fred van, 106n3, 143 **(fig. 11)**
Hör Zu (radio magazine), 19
Hübner, Ralf, 101, 192. *See also* Mangelsdorff, Albert, Quintet
Hudtwalcker, Olaf, 55, 93–94, 97
Huesmann, Günther, 8, 95, 229. *See also* Berendt, Joachim-Ernst: *Jazzbook*
Hüdepohl, Karl-Ernst, 99. *See also* Goethe Institut

India, 74, 147, 157, 192–99, 214, 218, 221
    Indian music, 10, 74, 154–55, 159, 161, 192–99, 216, 218–19, 223, 227n
    See also Jazz Meets the World: Jazz Meets India
Indonesia, xiv, 10, 151, 154, 163–65, 199–204, 214
    Indonesian Jazz, 1, 10, 157, 159–61, 163, 165n8, 199–204, 214–16
    Indonesian All-Stars, 1, 199–205, 202, 214, 229 **(fig. 18)**. *See also* Scott, Tony; *Jazz Meets the World: Djanger Bali*

Indonesian Communist Party (PKI), 163–65, 199
International Federation of Jazz (UNESCO), 56
Iturralde, Pedro, 93–94

Japan, xiv, 80n5, 147, 157–58, 168–76, 199–201, 221
    Japanese jazz/*Nihonteki jazu*, 10, 168–71, 173–76, 184
    Japanese traditional music, 154, 160, 167, 170–76
    See also Jazz Meets the World: Sakura Sakura
Jarrett, Keith, 235–36
jazz
    as democratic art form, 45–47, 49–51, 58
    as musical diplomacy, 101, 160–63, 166, 172, 181, 229
    as resistance, 38–41, 49–53, 58, 102, 164, 236
"Jazz Ambassadors." *See* U.S. State Department; Goethe Institut
"Jazz and Old Music" lecture tour, 27–28, 51
Jazz: A Time-Critical Study (*Jazz: eine zeitkritische Studie,* 1950). *See* Berendt, Joachim-Ernst
Jazzbook, The (*Das Jazzbuch,* 1953). *See* Berendt, Joachim-Ernst
Jazz Composers Orchestra Association (JCOA), 142, 144
Jazz Echo (magazine). *See Gondel, Die*
JazzFest. *See* Berlin Jazz Days
Jazzinstitut Darmstadt, xii, 2n2, 3n5, 7, 233
"Jazz in the Garden" series (Berlin), 222
Jazz Meets India. See Jazz Meets the World series
Jazz Meets the World series (*JMTW*)
    Auto Jazz (1968), 2, 111–115, 118, 121, 205
    Djanger Bali (1967), 1, 157, 186, 199–205
    El Babaku (1971), 1, 205–8, 210, 210n2, 217
    Eternal Rhythm (1968), 2, 107, 205–6, 211–17

Folklore e Bossa Nova do Brasil (1966), 1, 177–86
Flamenco Jazz (1967), 1, 92–94, 111, 186
From Sticksland with Love (1967), 92–93, 97, 111, 186, 189
Globe Unity (1966), 105–106, 110–18, 140–44, 162n3
Jazz Meets India (1967), 1, 106–7, 186, 192–99, 204, 218
Noon in Tunisia (1967), 1, 92, 186–92, 197–98, 204, 208n, 212, 216, 230
Sakura Sakura (1965), 1, 80n5, 157, 171–76, 182, 186, 197.
Tristeza on Guitar (1966), 1, 177, 182, 186, 189
Wild Goose (1969), 2, 97–98, 103, 205
Jazz Podium (magazine), 16, 27, 107, 127, 160, 172, 193–94
   Berendt's contributions, 17, 200, 223
   JMTW, 186
   Waldick-Berendt debate, 48
Jazz Samba (1962), 179. *See also* Byrd, Charlie; Getz, Stan
Jazz Yatra festival (Bombay), 157, 218
Jenny-Clarke, J. F., 212
Jhaveri, Niranjan, 157, 218
Jobim, Antônio Carlos, 178, 180
Johanns, Willi, 159, 163
Jones, LeRoi. *See* Baraka, Amiri
Jones, Philly Joe, 202, 208, 210n2
Jordan, Clifford, 221
Jost, Ekkehard, 2n4, 4–5, 76, 88–89, 106, 111, 118, 134, 140–41, 214–16; *Europas Jazz* 4
Jouini, Hattab, 191 (fig. 17)

Kaestner, Heinz, 36, 41
Kaputtspiel-style jazz, 118, 139
Kassner, Rudolf, 46
Kater, Michael, 15, 19, 50
Kenton, Stan, 116
Khan, Ali Akbar, 218. *See also* Handy-Khan ensemble
Kieser, Günther, 80 (fig. 5), 96 (fig. 7)
Kirk, Roland, 102–3

Knauer, Wolfram, 7n8, 89, 89n, 91, 94; epilogue 233–37
Kofsky, Frank, 52, 76, 130, 136, 142
Koller, Hans, 26, 85, 180
Koller, Hans, Quartet (with Oscar Pettiford), 85
Komeda, Kryzsztof, 55n
Konrad, Bernd, 220, 220 (fig. 20)
Kool Jazz Festival (New York), 80n3, 220
Kotschenreuther, Helmut, 37
Kowald, Peter, 95, 118, 229
Krautrock, 198, 219
Krenek, Ernst, 18, 25
Kriegel, Volker, 1, 130, 134
Krupa, Gene, 93
Kühn, Gerhard, 226
Kurylewicz, Andrzej, 55n

L+R. *See* Lippmann, Horst; Rau, Fritz
Laade, Wolfgang, 156n5, 172, 189, 198, 203
Lange, Horst H., 24, 68
Lateef, Yusef, 188
Lauth, Wolfgang, 27
Lenz, Günter, 192
Lesmana, Jack, 157, 160, 164, 199–202, 202 (fig. 18). *See also* Indonesian All-Stars
Lewis, John, 23 (fig. 3), 138
Liebermann, Rolf, 25, 92
Liefland, Wilhelm, 130–35, 226, 229
Lilienthal, Peter, 189–190
Lippmann, Horst, 84, 89, 95, 97–98, 103, 152, 177, 180–1, 184. *See also* Rau, Fritz
Litterscheid, Richard, 19
Lobo, Edu, 178
Lucia, Paco de, 93
Lukjanov, German, Trio, 186
Lyra, Carlos, 178

Maharaj, Pandit Prakash, 220, 220 (fig. 20)
Maharaj, Vikash, 220
Mahavishnu Orchestra, 219
Malle, Louis, 112
Malm, William P., 169–70
Mangelsdorff, Albert, 8, 55, 89, 89n,

90 (fig. 6), 98, 101–3, 108 (fig. 8), 133, 136–38, 143 (fig. 11), 159–60, 162–63, 165–66, 176, 193n6, 198, 201, 216, 234
Mangelsdorff, Albert, Quartet, 137–38
Mangelsdorff, Albert, Quintet, 98, 100–3, 157–60, 162–63, 166, 171, 192
  "*Drei Engel,*" 98, 101–3
  Now Jazz Ramwong (1964), 98, 102, 138, 159–62, 166
  Tension (1963), 89, 138
  See also Goethe Institut: jazz tours
Marjono, 202, 202 (fig. 18), 204. *See also* Indonesian All-Stars
Marsalis, Wynton, 223
Mathys, George: fife corps, 93
Mayer, John, 193–94
Mayer, John and Joe Harriott Double Quintet, 193–96, 199
McLaughlin, John, 219, 221, 224, 228, 235; Shakti 219. *See also* Mahavishnu Orchestra
Mecklenburg, Duke of, 127
Melos (magazine), 25–26, 109
Menuhin, Yehudi, 193
Merkur (magazine): Adorno's criticisms of Berendt 27, 32–33
Meyer, Ernst H., 52
Miller, Manfred, 117, 122, 133, 182
Mingus, Charles, 75–76, 118, 138, 192, 208
Metronome (magazine), xi, 68n
Milhaud, Darius, 24–25
modal jazz, 1, 73–74, 76, 91, 186–87, 201–2
Modern Jazz Quartet (MJQ), 26–27, 138
Montgomery, British Field Marshall, 51
Motihar, Dewan, 196, 196n, 198
Mümpfer, Klaus, 226
Munich Olympics Jazz Festival/Jazz Now Festival, 114n, 129, 219, 237
Murray, Sunny, 106n3
Musik Produktion Schwarzwald (MPS). *See* Saba/MPS labels
Mustafa, Benny, 202 (fig. 18). *See also* Indonesian All-Stars

Nabokov, Nicolas, 79
Nada Brahma (1983). *See* Berendt, Joachim-Ernst
Namyslowski, Zbygniew, 55n
Nass, Karl Heinz, 211
National Socialist opposition to jazz, xi, xiii, 2, 15, 18–20, 25, 36–39, 49–50, 58, 64–65, 67, 105, 128, 166. *See also* anti-Semitism; Hitler, Adolf; Third Reich
Naura, Michael, 17, 88, 132n, 231
Nazis. *See* National Socialism
NDR, 106
negrophilia, 65–67. *See also* Afrocentrism
Nelson, Oliver: *Berlin Dialogues for Orchestra* (1970), 83
Neumeier, Mani, 195–96, 198. *See also Jazz Meets the World: Jazz Meets India*; Schweizer, Irène, Trio
New Jazz Meeting, 86, 110, 114, 220, 222. *See also* Free Jazz Meeting
New Music, 2, 24–28, 103, 105, 110–15, 141
Newport Jazz Festival, 57, 76, 79–80, 89
Newport Rebels Festival, 76, 121
Newton, Francis. *See* Hobsbawm, Eric
Niebergall, Buschi, 108 (fig. 8)
Nietzsche, Friedrich, 41. *See also* Berendt, Joachim-Ernst: Nietzschean interpretation of jazz
Noel, Gérard, 216
Noon in Tunisia. See Jazz Meets the World series
North Africa, 147, 159, 163, 187, 212
Norvo, Red, 116
Now! Music Night (Berlin Jazz Days 1971), 122–23, 133n

Ohff, Heinz, 80, 94, 181–82, 197, 203
Olatunji, Michael, 210n2
Oléary, Etienne, 112
Olshausen, Ulrich, 97, 107, 109, 197, 204
Oregon, 235
Osman, Jelloul, 191 (fig. 17)
Ossiach Music Festival (Austria), 190, 190n

Paeschke, Hans, 32
Paik, Nam June, 118
Panassié, Hugues, 21, 66
Panke, Werner, 216
Parker, Charlie, 208, 233
Parker, Evan, 123 (fig. 10)
Penderecki. Krzysztof, 216
Peterson, Oscar, 85
Pfeiffer, Peter H., 99. *See also* Goethe Institut
Pfleiderer, Martin, 5
Philosemitism, 64–65, 67, 69. *See also* anti-Semitism
Pike, Dave, Set, 162
PKI. *See* Indonesian Communist Party
Poiger, Uta, 3, 18–19
Poland, 54–56, 134n13, 163
Polish Jazz Festival, 54, 134n13
Ponty, Jean-Luc, 190, 230
popular (pop) music, 29–33, 38, 97, 100, 127–28, 149, 152, 164, 166, 179–80, 182, 185, 193, 200, 204, 227, 227n, 229. *See also Schlager; U-Musik*
postcolonialism, 6, 120, 153–54, 159, 166, 201, 229–30
Powell, Baden, 177–78, 182, 184–85. *See also Jazz Meets the World: Tristeza on Guitar*
Preston, Denis, 193n7

Ra, Sun, 129
Radio Bremen, 106, 126
raga, 74, 193–94, 216, 227
Rajneesh, Baghwan Shree, 236; Baghwan sect 236
Rao, Hari Har, 193; Hindustani Jazz Sextet 193
Rau, Fritz, 1, 95, 97–98, 103, 152, 177, 177n, 181, 184. *See also* Lippmann, Horst
Rauschenberg, Robert, 112
Reinhardt, Django, 91n
Renaud, Jacques, 215
RIAS, 110
Richmond Jazz Festival, 137
Riefenstahl, Leni, 210, 236
Roach, Max, 75

rock 'n' roll, xii, 35–36, 38, 40, 77, 169; jazz and rock 116, 128, 235–36
Rollins, Sonny, 75, 181
Romano, Aldo, 212
Romanticism, 28–29, 57–58, 137–39, 155
Romao, Dom Um, 220
Rose, Barbara, 172
Rosenberg, Alfred, 65, 127n
Ross, Werner, 99. *See also* Goethe Institut
Rudorf, Reginald, 52–53, 126
Ruppell, K. H., 197
Rüsenberg, Michael, 6
Russell, George, 113

Saba/MPS labels, 1, 8–9, 73, 78, 80, 83–87, 92, 106, 110, 115n, 121, 124, 128–29, 134, 172, 184, 202–3, 218, 222
Sacher, Alfred: drum clique, 93
Sakura Sakura. *See Jazz Meets the World* series
Salon International du Jazz (Paris), 48, 137
Sanders, Pharoah, 121, 123 (fig. 10)
Sathe, Keshav, 8, 195–96, 198–99. *See also Jazz Meets the World: Jazz Meets India*
Sauer, Wolfgang, 30n
Savy, Michel, 189
Schaeffer, Pierre, 113
Schelsky, Helmut, 39
Schlager, 29–31, 33, 180
Schmidt, Felix, 128
Schmidt-Joos, Siegfried, 8, 84n, 86n, 125–30, 172–73; criticism of Berendt 128–30, 132–34
Schoenberg, Arnold, 19, 110
Schoener, Eberhard, 162n4, 219
Schoof, Manfred, 8, 106, 107n, 108 (fig. 8), 132–33, 136, 144, 161, 194, 196, 196n, 198, 202, 230
Schoof, Manfred, Sextet, 161, 165
Schreiner, Claus, 133, 200, 203
Schuller, Gunther, 25, 25n8
Schulte-Bahrenberg, Ralf, 8, 79, 79n, 121, 124, 129

Schweizer, Irène, 9, 198, 230. *See also* *Jazz Meets the World: Jazz Meets India*
Schweizer, Irène, Trio, 196. *See also* Neumeier, Mani
Scott, Tony, 164, 164n, 171, 174, 199–201, 203. *See also* Indonesian All-Stars
SED, 52
Segawa, Masahisa, 174
Seiber, Mátyás, 18, 193n7
Senghor, Léopold, 67
SFB, 80n4
Shank, Bud, 171, 174
Shankar, Ravi, 160, 192–93, 196, 204, 212
　Improvisations (1961), 192
　"Pather Panchali," 160, 192
"Sharps and Flats, The," 170
Sharrock, Sonny, 121, 123 (fig. 10)
Shepp, Archie, 76, 106n3, 110, 141, 209
Shihab, Sahib, 188, 190, 191 (fig. 17), 208n
Shiraki, Hideo, 171, 175–76
Shiraki, Hideo, Quintet, 10, 167, 170–76, 201, 204. *See also Jazz Meets the World: Sakura Sakura*
Slama, Moktar, 191 (fig. 17)
Sloterdijk, Peter, 228
Smith, Willie "The Lion," 117
Smith, Rudy, 220
Soft Machine, 128n
Sontag, Susan, 28, 210–11
Sounds (magazine), 111, 121, 182, 194
South America, 10, 147, 152, 157–58, 161, 177, 179, 181–82, 220
Spain, 74, 91–95, 97–98
SPD, 51, 117n
Spiegel, Der, 8, 61–62, 84n; Schmidt-Joos' criticisms of Berendt 125–30
Spiritual and Gospel Festivals, 97. *See also* Lippmann, Horst; Rau, Fritz
Spree City Stompers, 54
Stearns, Marshall, 24, 47, 56, 68
Stein, Werner (Berlin Senator for Science and the Arts), 79, 84

Stewart, Rex, 16
Stockhausen, Karlheinz, 112n6, 219
Stollenwerk, Hans, 6
Strauß, Franz Josef, 50n, 51, 58
Stravinsky, Igor, 25, 27, 33
Strobel, Heinrich, 25, 28, 92, 102n, 105, 105n
Stuckenschmidt, H. H., 18, 111, 197
Stuttgart Radio Exhibition, 190
Sudibyo, P. R., 164, 164n, 203
Südwestfunk (SWF), 3, 8, 16–17, 20, 22, 25–26, 29, 46n, 48, 53, 55, 56n, 80n4, 102n, 106–7, 114n, 126, 129, 134n13, 149, 154, 176n, 190n, 198–99, 216, 218, 221–23, 234, 236
Sukarno, President (Indonesia), 10, 151n, 154, 163–66, 199
Swingheinis, 35–40. *See also Halbstarke*
Swing music, 17, 21, 30, 35, 50–51, 76, 91, 93, 118, 137, 169, 172, 233, 235
"Swing Youth," 50
Swiss folk music, 92–93
"symphonic jazz," 25, 29
Szabo, Gabor, 193

Tavares, Marly, 177n, 182, 183 (fig. 16)
Taylor, Cecil, 192n
Taylor, Cecil, Quartet, 117
Texier, Henri, 191 (fig. 17)
Thai music, 154–56, 160–61. *See also* Bhumipol, King of Thailand
Theobald, Adolf, 36–37
Third Reich, xiv, 7, 9, 19, 49–51, 54, 103, 154, 164. *See also* National Socialism
"Third Stream," 25, 105, 110–11
Ticoalu, Alfred, 164n, 165nn7–8
Tinhorão, José Ramos, 178
Total Music Meeting. *See* Anti-Festival
Trepte, Uli, 195
Tristeza on Guitar. See Jazz Meets the World series
Tröller, Josef, 27
Tunisia, xiv, 10, 92, 186–91, 197–98, 204, 212, 214, 230
Twen (magazine), 149, 155, 180

Twittenhoff, Wilhelm, 36
Tyrmand, Leopold, 55–56

Uhde, Jürgen, 27
Ulanov, Barry, 24
U-Musik, 24–25, 29–34
UNESCO: International Federation of Jazz, 56
USIS, 51, 53, 158, 158n, 199
U.S. State Department, 51–53, 56, 58, 136, 158n; "Jazz Ambassadors" 52, 159, 165, 179

Valente, Caterina, 30n
van der Geld, Tom, 220
Vaughan, Sarah, 116
"Voice of America" (VOA), 51, 53, 55, 58
Volksmusik, 94, 97, 101, 103, 128
Von Schlippenbach, Alexander, 8, 108 (fig. 8), 109–11, 114, 118n, 137, 144, 162, 162n4, 194
Voswinkel, Stephan, 225–27

Wachler, Ingolf, 172–73
Wagner, Richard, 28, 159; Wagner Festival (Bayreuth) 80
Waldick, Leo: dispute with Berendt in *Jazz Podium* 47–48, 121
Wandervögel movement, 40, 40n3, 97
Warhol, Andy, 112
WDR, 57, 80n4
Weber, Eberhard, 132, 134, 161
Weill, Kurt, 18, 25
Weimar Republic, 17–18, 21, 25
Wein, George, 57, 79–80, 121, 125, 220, 235
Welding, Pete, 138

Weltmusik, 4–6, 10, 69, 178, 189, 195, 216–32. *See also* world musics
Westphal, Gert, 221
Wild Goose. *See Jazz Meets the World* series
Wilen, Barney, 112–14, 118, 121, 128n, 196, 204. *See also Jazz Meets the World: Auto Jazz; Jazz Meets India*
Wilkie, Colin, 95, 97–98
Williams, Tony, 116, 128n
Wilson, Peter Niklas, 226, 228, 228n, 230
Windelboth, Horst, 172
Winter, Paul, 179
World Expo Jazz Festival (Osaka), 176, 204
world jazz, 2, 187
world musics, xiv, 2, 5n, 10, 74, 80n3, 103, 109, 147, 149, 154–57, 162n4, 166–67, 194–95, 206, 214–15, 217–18, 224–29, 232. *See also Jazz Meets the World; Weltmusik*
World War II, 3, 54–55, 159, 200
Wunderlich, H. Werner, 8, 54–55, 134n13, 223

X, Malcolm, 208

Yui, Shoichi, 174
Yuize, Shinuchi, 171

ZDF, 80n4
Zimmerle, Dieter, 48, 127n, 197, 203, 215
Zimmermann, Heinz Werner, 43
Zoller, Attila, 201
Zorn, John, 235